Dreams of Authority

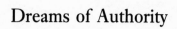

Dreams of Authority

FREUD AND THE FICTIONS
OF THE UNCONSCIOUS

Ronald R. Thomas

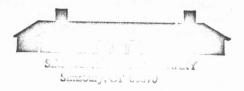

Cornell University Press

Ithaca and London

First published 1990 by Cornell University Press.

International Standard Book Number 0-8014-2424-0 (cloth)
Library of Congress Catalog Card Number 90-33550
Printed in the United States of America
Librarians: Library of Congress cataloging information
appears on the last page of the book.

Contents

Acknowledgments

There are a number of people who have helped to transform the dream of this book into a reality. John Kucich and Rosemarie Bodenheimer provided thoughtful readings of the manuscript and offered valuable contributions to it. I am especially indebted to them. I am also grateful to many of my colleagues at the University of Chicago for their commentary on portions of the book as it took shape, particularly Beth Ash, James Chandler, Robert Ferguson, Bruce Redford, Lisa Ruddick, and Stuart Tave. Philip Fisher and Mark Halliday provided inspiration at the earliest stages and have helped to keep the dream alive along the way.

Parts of Chapter 1 appeared under the title "*Traumdeutung* as *Bildungsroman*: Freud's Dream Interpretation and the Novel of His Life" in *Michigan Germanic Studies* 132 (1986): 157–73. The same parts of Chapter 1 and a portion of the introduction for Chapter 5 were the basis of an article called "The Narrative of Theory: The Novel in *The Interpretation of Dreams*," which appeared in *Psychohistory Review 18* (Fall 1989): 1–31. Another part of Chapter 1 was published as "Profitable Dreams in the Marketplace of Desire: *Alice in Wonderland, A Christmas Carol*, and *The Interpretation of Dreams*," in *Nineteenth-Century Contexts* 12 (Spring 1988): 285–97. I thank the editors of these journals for permission to reprint this material here.

Bernhard Kendler, Helene Maddux, and Judith Bailey are excellent editors, and I have appreciated their care and skill in helping to bring the book into focus and into print. Paul Ryan and Marianne Eismann provided very helpful editorial assistance in the preparation of the final manuscript. I am grateful to these and to all my friends and colleagues who have shared their dreams with mine.

R. R. T.

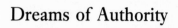

Dreams of Authority

Theoretical Fictions

I do hope it's my dream and not the Red King's! I don't like belonging to another person's dream.
—Lewis Carroll, *Through the Looking-Glass*

We deduce these laws through an analysis of fiction, just as we discover them from cases of real illness.
—Sigmund Freud, *Delusion and Dream*

Every dream is a possession. If Alice didn't recognize her dream on the other side of the looking glass and acknowledge it as her own, she would be subject to the authority of the kings and queens who threatened to dismember and diminish her. In that case, her dream would be a more frightening kind of possession, a force that lived its own life and told its own story through her. Like the literary dreams in other novels of the nineteenth century, Alice's is a dream of authority. She must recover it, resist those who would take it from her, and diagnose its significance by confronting the challenge presented to every dreamer: how is the dream to be controlled and expressed in language? *Dreams of Authority* considers responses to that challenge in three major forms of the novel in nineteenth-century England: gothic, autobiographical, and detective fiction. Each of them adopts some discourse of mastery—from medicine, economics, or politics—to describe the operation of the mind at the moment of its deepest indecipherability, the moment of the dream.

The same discourses employed by the nineteenth-century novel to describe dream experience were also adopted later on by Freud in his "scientific" theory of dream interpretation. Freud would regard dreams as "symptoms" of some mental pathology, for example, as unconscious "capital" in a psychic economy of desire, and as scenes in which the political agencies of "repression" and "censorship" operate within the individual psyche. Freud's dream theory was based upon the realization that all we can know about our dreams is rooted in the language in which we express them. Ultimately, our

1

concepts of dreaming derive not from dreams themselves but from the familiar phenomenon we call "telling a dream." In our dreams, we find ourselves, like Scheherazade, telling stories every night, stories in which we are not only the tellers and the audience but the story itself. Accordingly, Freud described our dream recollections as "texts" and treated them as models for all the disguised, substitutive, and fictive expressions of human wishing. His work demonstrated that the dreams we dream, like the novels we read and write, are scenes of psychological creation and investigation. Both articulate another, uncertain world—the unspoken world of our desire. Both express our need to master through language what is hidden, unexplained, and uncontrolled within us. And both are engaged in inventing our ideas of who we are. The dialectical relationship between the nineteenth-century novel and psychoanalysis in developing strategies to control our dreams through language, through telling, is my subject.

The debt Freudian theory owes to Victorian novels is widely recognized, and the correspondences between certain formal features of nineteenth-century narrative and psychoanalytic technique are often acknowledged. But the claim of this book is that the paradigmatic plot in both domains, as mediated by the dream, revolves around questions of authority. Nineteenth-century literary dreams are *always* dreams of authority. They consistently demonstrate a fundamental ambivalence about the nature and constitution of subjectivity by representing both controlled moments of private expression and instances of invasion of the self by patterns of discourse with nonsubjective origins. The treatment of dreams by their nineteenth-century writers symptomatizes over and over again an inability to resolve this double valence of the dream. These dreamers wish, on the one hand, to affirm individual control of psychic materials and, on the other, to appeal to larger fictional patterns in order to justify a discourse of subjectivity. The result is a characteristic nineteenth-century compromise: an appeal to plots of wider authority than the particular self—plots such as the "family romance"—balanced with a narrative struggle to appropriate that authority as a bolster to private self-fashioning.

This book is largely devoted to the literary strategies by which dreamers sought to represent themselves in and beyond their dream accounts. My intent is to investigate the literary roots of psychoanalysis without drawing any reductive, deterministic connection between literary texts and psychoanalytic theory. I am interested, rather, in presenting the dialogic relationship between the two and in tracing an interdependence between psychoanalysis and literature, in which each is altered by the other and in which each retains an equal authority. *Dreams of Authority* takes part in the contemporary revision of traditional assumptions about the Victorian self by demonstrating how central the discourse of psychoanalysis is to any properly historicized understanding of the social processes implicated in subjectivity.[1] I begin, therefore, not with the implicit theory of dreams contained in the nineteenth-century novel but with the implied novel contained in Freud's theory of dreams. The remainder of the book goes on to demonstrate how Freud's appropriation of certain discursive models to describe human consciousness was facilitated and informed by their prior appropriation in the novel, how psychoanalysis and the novel have collaborated in composing the fictions of the unconscious that have formed our understanding of who we are and of how our minds work.

The great work in which Freud articulated the principles of dream interpretation at the very end of the nineteenth century is as much a part of literary tradition as it is of scientific history. Not only does Freud make use of a confessional and novelistic style in *The Interpretation of Dreams* (1900), but he derives many of his dream examples from the novels that influenced him deeply. *The Interpretation of Dreams* may even justifiably be read as Freud's own autobiographical novel in which he recovers the unconscious material of his own childhood, refashions it into an account of the operations of the mind, and establishes his authority as a scientist of the psyche.[2] Freud's reputation as a literary man is well recognized and justly earned, and the most persistent influence on his writing was narrative fiction. His library contained many novels from the period, and he alluded to them consistently in his scientific writing. When he began to publish the case histories in which his dream interpretations figured so prominently, he repeatedly acknowledged how much his accounts of those cases resembled fictional narratives. Freud would even recommend the reading of novels as part of his treatment, and he frequently represented the recovery of his patients in terms of their recovery of the ability to tell their own life stories in a coherent way.[3]

If Freud's writing career effectively began with the writing of one novelis-

---

[1]John Kucich, *Repression in Victorian Fiction: Charlotte Brontë, George Eliot, and Charles Dickens* (1987), and Nancy Armstrong, *Desire and Domestic Fiction: A Political History of the Novel* (1987), have recently helped to frame this debate.

[2]Marthe Robert says that in *Moses and Monotheism* Freud "resumed the novelistic confession begun forty years before between the lines of the *Traumdeutung*" (*From Oedipus to Moses: Freud's Jewish Identity* [1976], p. 154). Edward W. Said has described the "protocol" of *The Interpretation of Dreams* as "not at all that of a conventional scientific text, but rather that of a narrative account of multifaceted experiences" (*Beginnings: Intention and Method* [1975], p. 163). Michel de Certeau's essay "The Freudian Novel: History and Literature" identifies literature as the "theoretical discourse that allowed the 'science' of psychoanalysis to be thought" (*Heterologies: Discourse on the Other*, trans. Brian Massumi [1986], pp. 17–34). My task here is to demonstrate the importance and power of this frequently noted underlying relationship.

[3]Philip Rieff's introduction to the Collier edition of the Dora case (1963) suggests that Freud's case histories "may yet alter the way in which both the novel and history will be written" (*Dora: An Analysis of a Case of Hysteria*, p. 9). Freud urged both the Wolf-Man and the Rat-Man to read novels in the course of their treatment.

tic version of his own life, it ended with his writing of another. He gave the last book published in his own lifetime the title *Moses and Monotheism: A Historical Novel* (1939), one more work that consciously mixed scientific and fictional accounts and was directly linked to the story of the author's own life as well. Freud also combined literature and science in the literary criticism he wrote. In one of the most elaborate of those efforts, he referred to a novella as "an entirely correct study in psychiatry, by which we may measure our understanding of psychic life, a story of illness and cure which seems designed for the inculcation of certain fundamental teachings of medical psychology."[4] Literature, that is, served Freud as a source of knowledge and a standard by which to measure the truth of science just as much as science did for literature. "The creative writer cannot evade the psychiatrist," Freud would say in *Delusion and Dream* (1907), "nor the psychiatrist the creative writer" (65). The founder of psychoanalysis certainly attempted no such evasions himself, and he may have been speaking of novelists as well as psychological theorists when, at the end of *The Interpretation of Dreams*, he hailed the comprehensiveness of his own theory as a synthesis of all that had gone before him: "We have thus been able to find a place in our structure for the most various and contradictory findings of earlier writers, thanks to the novelty of our theory of dreams, which combines them, as it were, into a higher unity."[5]

Novelists recognized the connection between novel and dream long before Freud. From *Don Quixote, The Pilgrim's Progress*, and *The Castle of Otranto* to *David Copperfield, Crime and Punishment*, and *Ulysses*, dreams have permeated the history of the novel. As these and many other texts demonstrate, dreams can serve many different purposes in a novel. A dream may act simply as a convenient fictive frame device. Or it may serve as an embedded narrative that reveals psychic complexities and conflicts unknown to the character. A dream often provides an opportunity for the novelist to relay an indirect commentary on a character or a veiled meditation on some social or philosophical issue. Dreams have also foreshadowed plot development, provided sources of mystery, contributed to an atmosphere of doom or confusion, and suggested the existence of some other reality. These affinities between dream and novel were immeasurably heightened in the nineteenth century when the superstitions and mystifications of romance encountered the harder facts of science and realism in both literary and scientific realms. The evolution of the novel during this period reflected its increasing investment

---

[4]Sigmund Freud, *Delusion and Dream in Jensen's "Gradiva,"* trans. Harry Zohn (New York: Beacon Press, 1956), p. 65.

[5]Freud, *The Interpretation of Dreams*, vols. 4 and 5 of *The Standard Edition of the Complete Psychological Works of Sigmund Freud*, ed. and trans. James Strachey (London: Hogarth Press and the Institute for Psychoanalysis, 1953–72), p. 592; hereafter cited in the text. Volume 4 contains pages i–338, and volume 5 begins with page 339.

in problems of psychological motivation and desire, and the use of dreams became more complex and sophisticated as the novel turned its interests inward.

Paradoxically, the domain of the novel—especially the realistic social novel in England—was normally considered to be confined to the empirical and thus explainable regions of human experience. So-called serious British fiction has conventionally been inclined to dwell with more care on the events of daylight than on those of darkness. When the novel does venture into the more mysterious realms of sleep, it tends to give dreams only perfunctory attention, using them (as E. M. Forster has said) in strictly "purposive" ways rather than attempting to recreate the strange, uncanny character of the dream world itself.[6] George Eliot, whose novels best represent this commitment to the value of the real and the everyday, articulated an aesthetic preference as well as a psychological opinion when she refused the suggestion of her friend and publisher John Blackwood that she include a dream account in one of her stories because, she claimed, "Dreams usually play an important part in fiction, but rarely, I think, in real life."[7]

Even during her own century, this view came under attack not only by psychological theorists but by writers of serious fiction as well. With the dreamy atmosphere of *Daniel Deronda* (1874–1876) and the dark, dreamlike character of *A Lifted Veil* (1878), Eliot's later fiction began to show the effects of this attack. The Victorian period brought dreams down from the stars to the very different psychological universe of the human mind. In literary terms this shift was expressed in the development of a separate novelistic tradition alongside that of the realistic novel. The role of dreams in the novel became paramount in the new, more psychologically sophisticated genre of gothic fiction. Dream accounts, linked as they were to psychological realities, could also dominate the assessment of a character's developing self-consciousness in autobiographical fiction. The detective novel, which fully emerged during this period, made consistent use of dream events as well; at stake were the hidden motives for murder, theft, and other intrigues that had their origins in the compulsions and repressions of a whole society. In each of these forms, a dark and unarticulated underworld dominates the events of the everyday, and dreams offer an avenue of access to this otherwise unreachable territory of force and meaning. Gothic, autobiographical, and detective fiction also differed from most realistic novels of the period by stressing the importance of first-person narration. Foregrounding the language of personal experience, these novels acknowledged that words in themselves can manufacture an implicit theory of the self. These works were not stories

[6]E. M. Forster, *Aspects of the Novel* (1975), pp. 49–53.

[7]Letter of 11 March 1857. See George Levine, *The Realistic Imagination: English Fiction from Frankenstein to Lady Chatterley* (1983), for a study of the complications and elusiveness of the nineteenth-century idea of "the realistic."

that happened to contain dream interpretations. They were specifically intended to contain and understand the force of dreams within the structure of a story.

Even the plots of gothic, autobiographical, and detective novels correspond suggestively to certain aspects of the dream process. By confronting the irrational and expressing the need to reduce it to a rational form, gothic fiction parallels our impulse to confront and explain the disturbing images of a nightmare. The autobiographical novel, on the other hand, in its effort to recover and reconstruct the material of the past and to make it into a life story, echoes our attempts to appropriate the images of our dreams, to identify them as aspects of our waking lives, and to understand ourselves from them. And just as the detective novel tracks down the mysterious origins of an inexplicable event and associates random clues into a coherent account of a crime, so our desire to interpret the fragmented, cryptic images of our dreams aims at assigning meaning to them. When Pip dreams in *Great Expectations* (1860–1861) of finding himself on stage, assigned to play the role of Hamlet before a large audience but without any idea of what words he is supposed to speak, the dream manifests not only Pip's anxiety about his own authority but also a desire common to all these texts—a desire to find the words in which to articulate the dream.

The new prominence of these fictional forms during the nineteenth century has a social subtext as well as a formal and psychological one. Psychiatry developed as an influential profession throughout Europe even as these new forms of the novel took shape. At the outset of the Victorian age, dreams belonged as much to the supernatural world as to science. Dream theorists were sharply divided about both the origins and the significance of these nightly psychic events. Spiritualists maintained that dreams permitted communication with a supernatural world, while more scientifically oriented thinkers sought to reduce dreams to mere manifestations of physiological processes. As a result of the dramatic movements in intellectual history which have come to be called "natural supernaturalism," "religious humanism," or "secularization," the nineteenth century reassigned more and more phenomena hitherto considered supernatural to a new but as yet undefined place in the human psyche. Meanwhile, moralists of various kinds took a different course and attempted to demonstrate the didactic and ethical lessons that dreams might contain.[8] These and other manifestations of a more

---

[8]See Catherine A. Bernard, "Dickens and Victorian Dream Theory," in *Victorian Science and Victorian Values: Literary Perspectives*, ed. James Paradis and Thomas Postlewait (1981); and L. S. Hearnshaw, *A Short History of British Psychology, 1840–1940* (1964), for elaborations of these points of view.

repressive Victorian mentality exerted countervailing pressures against the expression of controversial social, personal, and political issues in the individual unconscious.[9] When, against a background of widespread revolution in Europe, Marx was theorizing about the pressure being exerted upon the existing centers of political power by an emerging working class, the scientific community was theorizing about a model of human consciousness which was also at war with itself, struggling to control forces emerging from a dark, subconsicous underworld within. Among the ensuing "compromise formations" that the culture produced in response to these tensions between the private and the public worlds were a profusion of literary dreams and the popular fictional forms that contained them. The great popularity of the more sensational narratives in the gothic, autobiographical, and detective modes enabled them directly to absorb the professional discourses that were beginning to dominate the culture and to adapt those discourses in representing private, psychological experience. Medical science, economics, and politics would dictate the dominant terms to explain human behavior in the culture for some time. Their use and popularization in these novels contributed as much to the evolving conception of what it meant to be a person in the nineteenth century as did the theories generated by the increasingly reputable human sciences of psychiatry and sociology.

My special interest is the literary status of dreams in this process. *Dreams of Authority* seeks to map out the transformation of dream events into literature in nineteenth-century fiction. I am concerned with how dreamers express their dreams in language, how they make use of literary operations to confront the dream material, how they appropriate that material as their own and then convert it into the story of their lives. Other interpretations of Victorian fiction have analyzed the individual dreams of characters, but none has attempted to identify the underlying literary strategies by which dreamers sought to represent themselves in and beyond their dream accounts.[10] Critics as diverse as Peter Brooks, Fredric Jameson, Barbara Johnson, Dianne Sadoff, and Malcolm Bowie have helped to develop methodologies that

---

[9]According to Michel Foucault (*The History of Sexuality*, vol.1: *An Introduction* [1980], p. 23), "the repressive hypothesis" did not eliminate talk about sexuality but succeeded in producing "an ever greater quantity of discourse about sex, capable of functioning and taking effect in its very economy." Kucich, *Repression in Victorian Fiction*, shows how this "discursive explosion" operated in the nineteenth-century novel in Britain.

[10]See, for example, Taylor Stoehr, *Dickens: The Dreamer's Stance* (1965); Margaret Homans, *Bearing the Word: Language and Female Experience in Nineteenth-Century Women's Writing* (1986); Kucich, *Repression in Victorian Fiction*; and (for the Russian novel) Michael R. Katz, *Dreams and the Unconscious in Nineteenth-Century Russian Fiction* (1984).

make use of psychoanalytic theory to understand how narrative works.[11] My concern, however, is to make use of a whole set of nineteenth-century narratives to understand the literary roots of psychoanalytic theory. Because my emphasis is on the languages in which dreams came to be expressed, I have limited my investigation to first-person novels or novels in which first-person narration plays an important role. Such texts approximate the psychoanalytic situation most closely, and they also dramatize the importance of the dream account in understanding the significance of a dream. I interpret these novels as, at once, manifestations of a desire to manage dreams and partial fulfillments of that desire as well. The novels in question imply a fragmented theory of dream interpretation, much as Freud's *Interpretation of Dreams* implies an incipient autobiographical novel. Taken together, they demonstrate how deeply the use of dreams has informed the history and interpretation of the English novel.

My subject is not dreams themselves but the language and plots the novel uses to explain and make use of its dreams. Freud's own emphasis on the conversion of dream images into language demands that his theoretical work on dream interpretation provide a constant frame of reference, though not the only one. Freud managed to generate sweeping and compelling claims about an entire culture from his analysis of the unconscious, and he has had more influence than any other dream theorist on the art of the novel as well as on the history of psychology. His prominence in my account of dreams and the novel results as much from the role the novel plays in his theory as from the role his theory plays in our understanding of the novel. In the final chapter of *The Interpretation of Dreams*, Freud suggests his debt to fiction when he isolates certain principles for which he can provide no absolute evidence and calls them "theoretical fictions" (603). The same term could be used to describe the novels I examine since they, too, strive to provide a language for what is felt to be true but for which there is no empirical evidence.

The dialogical relationship between psychoanalysis and literature is crucial here. Just as psychoanalysis points to the unconscious of literature, so literature represents the unconscious of psychoanalysis.[12] The authority of

---

[11]Peter Brooks, *Reading for the Plot: Design and Intention in Narrative* (1984), has shown how psychoanalytic ideas of desire help produce and shape our ideas of narrative plot, for example. Dianne F. Sadoff, *Monsters of Affection: Dickens, Eliot, and Brontë on Fatherhood* (1982), combines psychoanalytic and feminist perspectives to interpret three Victorian novelists' work in terms of one of Freud's "primal fantasies." Malcolm Bowie, *Freud, Proust, and Lacan: Theory as Fiction* (1987), explores the interconnections between scientific theorizing and fiction writing. Joseph H. Smith, Robert Con Davis, Shoshana Felman, and Françoise Meltzer have edited collections that explore the rich relationship between psychoanalysis and literary discourse.

[12]See Shoshana Felman, ed., *Literature and Psychoanalysis* (1977), pp. 5–10.

psychoanalysis in my book matches but does not exceed the authority of the novels with which I am concerned. Their interdependence is the issue. Of course, to work with psychoanalytic interpretation is not necessarily to exemplify it. The critic who would truly demonstrate the dialogue between psychoanalysis and literature is best situated above rather than within. Moreover, the natural power of the connection enables a more meaningful mediation in which it may be demonstrated how certain literary fictions made certain scientific theories imaginable. Psychoanalysis is a peculiarly insistent and demanding intertext for literary analysis. Both disciplines complicate our understanding of how the mind presents reality to us even as they explain that process. And both expose to us our illusions about ourselves while they construct the new, "necessary fictions" by which we dream, desire, interpret, and constitute ourselves as human subjects.[13] My goal is to carry this case into the "necessary fictions" that compose the cultural realities of both psychoanalysis and the novel in nineteenth-century Britain.

Dreams of Authority reaches beyond the fact that "poets" anticipated Freud.[14] My concern is first to find out what we can learn from the specific metaphors of mind present in the novelists' language about dreams. How do those linguistic models relate to Freud's eventual theories and to the common historical realities out of which they both emerged? At the same time, the relationship between fiction and the psychoanalytic process has much to tell us about the nature of the novel in nineteenth-century Britain. For all its affiliations with the cult of secular individualism, the novel—especially the first-person novel—repeatedly expresses the desire for an authority outside the individual self. And it expresses that desire by weaving together and appealing to the power of certain kinds of authoritative language within the culture. In this interpretive project, the novel—like psychoanalysis— mystifies as it demystifies. While drawing from historical discourses to define the self, the novel often uses them in ways that suppress the importance of the historical in the formation of character. Peter Stallybrass and Allon White have shown how culture is always made up of a set of "discursive domains," each of which can be reconstucted within the terms of the other domains in order to constitute that culture's conception of the person.[15] The

---

[13]See Brooks's persuasive argument, "The Idea of a Psychoanalytic Literary Criticism," in *The Trial(s) of Psychoanalysis*, ed. Françoise Meltzer (1988), p. 159. Brooks's own *Reading for the Plot* is one of the best demonstrations of the kind of interdependence of psychoanalysis and literature he advocates.

[14]See *The Literary Use of the Psychoanalytic Process* (1981), in which Meredith Anne Skura demonstrates how different kinds of psychoanalytic literary criticism derive from aspects of the psychoanalytic process.

[15]Peter Stallybrass and Allon White, *The Politics and Poetics of Transgression* (1986), pp. 192–94.

novel and psychoanalysis are two of the most productive discursive domains of the nineteenth century directly concerned with the construction of personality. Even though the conceptions of self which the novel and psychoanalysis help to generate may be progressive, however, they are neither fixed nor absolutely authoritative. They prove instead to be the inventions of a particular historical moment and a specific ensemble of social discourses that contain within them the seeds of their own revision.[16]

My own interpretations demonstrate how novelists of the nineteenth century collaborated in producing the terms and, in many cases, the interpretive strategies Freud would combine into a scientific theory of how we conceive of ourselves as human subjects. The first problem Freud encountered in *The Interpretation of Dreams* springs from this seemingly universal and inescapable creative activity we share, and it is a problem particularly relevant to the literary critic exploring the significance of dreams. Freud was troubled by the inaccessibility of dreams in any unmediated form. He knew that as soon as we remember a dream, we have already begun to revise it. Since our recollection of dreams is necessarily partial and even faulty and since we have no "objective confirmation" in distinguishing what was already in a dream from what we have filled in with falsified "additions and embellishments," Freud asks, "what value can we still attach to our memory of dreams?" (46–47).

Freud's great work is, in a sense, a response to this question. After he demonstrates that the natural impulse of the human imagination is to interpret a dream even as it is remembered and to transform what seems a random collection of images into a well-crafted story, Freud converts that difficulty into an advantage. He reads all dreams as disguised literary "texts." His solution to the problem of deciphering those texts is not to penetrate the editorial distortions of the dream but to regard the language of distortion itself as the most significant clue to meaning. A dream, Freud would claim, is a repressed wish. But its repression comes about because it is also a symptom, an investment of psychic capital, and a piece of subversive information that requires censoring. He concludes that "the modifications to which dreams are submitted under the editorship of waking life" are not arbitrary; on the contrary, they are "associatively linked to the material which they replace, and serve to show us the way to that material, which may in its turn be a substitute for something else" (515).

Bearing in mind this claim for the textuality of our dreams and the interpretive value of the "revision" and "editing" of them by consciousness, I have focused on novels in which a first-person narrator seeks to recover (or

---

[16]For an analysis of the metaphorical dimensions of Freudian theory, see Donald P. Spence, *The Freudian Metaphor: Toward Paradigm Change in Psychoanalysis* (1987).

modify) a set of dreams in language and thereby tries to preserve what Marlow refers to in *Heart of Darkness* (1902) as "the terrific suggestiveness of words heard in dreams."[17] Because single dream events cannot have the impact of a sequence, I have not treated the isolated dreams that frequently appear in nineteenth-century novels, including *Hard Times*, *Martin Chuzzlewit*, *The Mill on the Floss*, *The Return of the Native*, and *New Grub Street*, to name just a few. Instead, I have selected novels in the gothic, autobiographical, and detective modes which either are centered on a single dream event or contain several dreams, each of which can be related to the unfolding character of the dreamer and to problems of narrative self-representation within the text. More specifically, I have looked to those novels that strikingly convey three distinct kinds of language in talking about dreams, each of which was later adopted in psychoanalytic dream theory. I have also included two exceptional cases. In the chapter on gothic, I examine what is technically not a novel—DeQuincey's *Confessions of an English Opium-Eater* (1822)—because of its elaborate use of both gothic and novelistic conventions, because of its profound influence on the development of the English autobiographical novel, and because of its place in the history of dream theory. The detective chapter includes Dickens's unfinished novel *The Mystery of Edwin Drood* (1870). My interest here is in the diary entries written into the novel, and in the first-person narrative that does *not* appear in the text. Dickens had planned to conclude the book with a long confessional section that would be spoken by the chief suspect, a confession that would finally explain the disturbing dreams that remain indecipherable throughout the story. As in Wordsworth's Arab Dream (1850), *A Christmas Carol* (1843), and *Alice in Wonderland* (1865)—all of which I treat briefly in my first chapter as emblematic Victorian dream texts—the dreamers in these books struggle with the problem of how best to write their dreams into their life stories. All of them dream of authority.

The moments in a novel when the words and phrases of a dream are told to someone are revealing moments for the dreamer, especially when that dreamer carries the burdens and opportunities of narration. In making a dream account, the dreamer converts the material of the unconscious into the language of consciousness and "shows us the way" he or she has defined an otherwise inaccessible self. In my analysis of these moments, I have identified a set of rhetorical strategies through which dreamers in nineteenth-century fiction began to describe their dreams and the unconscious that produced them. Whereas medical, economic, and political terms may figure to some degree in all these novelistic representations of the mind,

---

[17]Joseph Conrad, *Heart of Darkness* (Harmondsworth, Eng.: Penguin, 1973), p. 95.

I have emphasized how one of these psychological metaphors is employed in each genre.

It is commonly accepted among critics of gothic fiction, for example, that the genre combines supernatural effect and an atmosphere of dream and illness with as-yet-untheorized psychological concerns. But my reading of gothic texts shows that at the heart of this genre is a desire to reformulate the understanding of the human mind in medical terms, to demonstrate how the mind in its operation resembles a body subject to disease more than it does a soul subject to supernatural possession. The predominant setting for nineteenth-century gothic moves, therefore, from the castle or the convent to the laboratory and the sickbed. Mary Shelley's *Frankenstein* (1818) is a case in point. There, a promising young scientist is urged by his teachers to "give new names" to the ideas previously articulated by occultists and alchemists.[18] But Frankenstein's tragedy is that he remains fascinated by the occult. When in a fevered and conflicted state, he dreams of the monstrous human body he has made, he calls it a "spectre" and a "demon" instead of recognizing and naming it as a symptom of inner conflict that bears both scientific and psychological significance. Gothic texts commonly demand that their dreamers make this kind of interpretive choice if they are to take authority over the unconscious forces at work in their own minds. Catherine Earnshaw provides a dramatic contrast to Frankenstein in this regard, claiming that her own fevered dreams in *Wuthering Heights* (1847) are both symptomatic of her distressed state of mind and effective in her recovery as well. "I've dreamt in my life dreams that have stayed with me ever after, and changed my ideas," she says, dreams that have "altered the colour of my mind."[19]

A similar imperative appears to the dreamers in autobiographical novels such as *Jane Eyre* (1847) or in detective novels such as *The Moonstone* (1868). But in these texts an economic or a political dynamic functions more powerfully as the organizing metaphor for the psyche. Jane Eyre integrates her dreams into a story of financial independence and psychological self making, and she gives them a prominent place in the management of her own psychic economy. The dreams of Franklin Blake in *The Moonstone*, however, become the keys that not only unlock a mystery of imperial conquest but reveal an even more deeply repressed and exotic empire within his own mind as well. The extensive production and popularity of each of these related genres and

---

[18]Mary Shelley, *Frankenstein, or the Modern Prometheus*, the 1818 text, ed. James Rieger (Chicago: University of Chicago Press, 1982), p. 43.

[19]Emily Brontë, *Wuthering Heights*, ed. Hilda Marsden and Ian Jack (Oxford: Oxford University Press, 1981), p. 79.

the specific discourses they utilize in explaining their dreams play an important role in the cultural redefinition of how the mind works. Indeed, fictive redefinitions of the psyche in novels like these eventuated in the "higher unity" of Freud's more systematic science of the self at the end of the century.

My sequential analysis of gothic, autobiographical, and detective fiction does not imply a corresponding sequential history of literary genres or discourses for the self. Nor do I wish to claim an exclusive prerogative for any novelistic subgenre over a particular discourse. To be sure, the boundaries separating literary genres were never less stable than in the nineteenth century, and each of the subgenres with which I am concerned borrowed from the others throughout the period. *Jane Eyre*, for example, is often regarded as a gothic novel as well as a fictional autobiography. *Dr. Jekyll and Mr. Hyde* (1886) has been read both as a gothic tale and a work of science fiction, though I have treated it as a detective story here. Similarly, the medical, economic, and political representations of subjectivity cannot be isolated in any absolute way. They appear in fiction throughout the period and (as I will show) often interact with one another in these subgenres. The psychological discourses of *Wuthering Heights* and *The Moonstone* both draw from politics as well as medicine, for instance, even though I have given priority to only one of these disciplines in each case. Novels with more serious ambitions—such as *Bleak House* or *Middlemarch*—combine elements from all these narrative forms and employ all these discursive strategies to produce perhaps the most elaborate literary expressions of nineteenth-century psychological theory. But in the first-person narrative forms I have focused on here, the formation of the self is not merely described; it is performed. And those performances consistently foreground specific psychological assumptions that correspond to specific generic intentions. Through the spoken words of its narrator, each dramatizes how certain cultural discourses of mastery and particular kinds of stories were integrated with private patterns of expression in the nineteenth century through the articulation of dream material.

In taking up such issues, we are confronted by an inevitable question about the degree to which the novelists were consciously aware of their manipulation of social discourses in representing literary dreams. Posed in this way, the question engages the vexed issue of authorial intention. But posed in a slightly different way, it restates the central problem with which this book is concerned: What are the origin and authority for the terms in which we speak of ourselves, try to understand ourselves, make ourselves up? In fact, as these novelists search for a language to represent unconscious processes, they struggle with the same question their fictional dreamers confront. This book will show that the ways they give voice to dreams most often are symptomatic of a discursive gap, a cultural sense of strain between opposing models of interpretation and different conceptions of the self. That strain manifests the very cultural problem or blindness that Freud would later bring to light and seek to manage in his more systematic deployment of those same discursive models in *The Interpretation of Dreams*.

Of course, dreams figure prominently in literary forms other than the novel during this period as well, especially in its poetry. Coleridge, Keats, and Shelley used dreams extensively in their work. Tennyson alluded to the world of dreams and the dark underworld of the unconscious in elaborate ways throughout his career. The visions and reveries of Pre-Raphaelite and symbolist poets were often set into dream events as well. But as important as dreams may be in poetry, they play a very different role there from what they play in the novel. To suggest that difference, I treat Wordsworth's Arab dream from *The Prelude* in the first chapter as a representative poetic text. There, appropriately, the dreamer poses the problem of interpretation as a choice between the language of poetry and the language of prose. When Freud spoke of poetry in *The Interpretation of Dreams*, he spoke of it as analogous to the dream work rather than to the activities of interpretation. The ambiguous, concentrated imagery of poetic language, he reasoned, resembles the condensed and overdetermined images produced in our dreams. Dream analysis, however, demands that such imagery be translated into the prosaic language of the everyday, into narratives that link the dream thoughts with waking life. Since my concern is with the emerging language of dream interpretation, I have limited my analysis to the world of the novel, where just this kind of translation was taking place throughout the period. The use of dreams in nineteenth-century poetry is a subject for another book.

While *Dreams of Authority* identifies the ways in which Freud's "theoretical fictions" about dreams inherit certain novelistic traditions, my final chapter points to a distinct shift in this relationship. In the novel after Freud, he is no longer the recipient of novelistic traditions, he has become a direct influence upon them. The curious part of this development is that we find the high-modern and postmodern novelist trying to recover from Freud's attempt to control the dream process through analysis and rational examination. In effect, these novelists seek to reclaim the dream as art by subverting Freud's distinction between the dream work and dream interpretation. The post-Freudian novel insists that the dream will always remain the interest of the creative writer as much as it is the prerogative of the scientist. If the nineteenth-century novel was the fiction that allowed psychoanalysis to be thought, the twentieth-century novel is the fiction that allows it to be re-thought and revised. Indeed, in its increasingly self-reflexive character, the modern novel makes the same claim for the importance of language in shaping consciousness that will be made by Jacques Lacan and others in the field of psychoanalysis. The course taken by the modern novel turns Freud's observation about writers of fiction into a prophecy of literary history. "Creative writers are valuable allies and their evidence is to be prized highly," he reminds us, "for they are apt to know a whole host of things between heaven and earth of which our philosophy has not yet let us dream."[20]

[20]Freud, *Delusion and Dream*, p. 27.

Moritz von Schwind, *Traum des Gefangenen* (1836)

Freud reproduced *The Prisoner's Dream* as an illustration for one of his essays on dreams in the *General Introduction to Psychoanalysis*. As his commentary indicated, the dream's content is at once a form of escape from enforced confinement, a psychic substitution for a desire unfulfilled in waking life, and a release from the darkness of the dreamer's own unconsciousness—all expressed in images from German folk literature. The details of the painting—a figure of authority (the crowned king at the base of the ladder of fantastic gnomelike figures) obscured in the dreamer's vision by a more realistic, human authority (the female figure dispensing a potion)—perhaps suggest the dream's curative power as well as its liberating effect. (Reproduced with the permission of the Schack Gallery, Munich.)

CHAPTER ONE

Dreams of Authority and
the Authority of Dreams

> Life and dream are leaves of one and the same book.
> —Arthur Schopenhauer

Freud begins his book *On the History of the Psycho-Analytic Movement* by explaining its "subjective character." No one "need wonder what part I play in it," he says, "for psycho-analysis is my creation." The history of psychoanalysis, that is, is also the history of Sigmund Freud, and it is his invention as well. When he recounts the events in that history which surround the writing of his greatest work, *The Interpretation of Dreams*, he compares himself to Robinson Crusoe, the narrator and hero of one of the first great fictional autobiographies in English.[1] In doing so Freud connects his own personal and professional history to a literary tradition as well as a scientific one. Freud was a great admirer of the novel, and allusions to many works of fiction riddle his own writings. *David Copperfield* (1849–1850) was his favorite Dickens novel, and as part of his courtship ritual, Freud presented Martha with a copy of this novelized version of Dickens's life. Later, when Freud revised his theory of the origin of hysterical symptoms from a physiological to a psychological explanation, he pointed to his reading of works of fiction as the source for the explanatory models that led to the shift. He even cautioned readers of the Dora case history not to read it as a *roman à clef*, presumably because its resemblances to a novel were so great.[2] The history of psychoanalysis—and of Sigmund Freud as well—not only has a "subjective character," then, it also has a novelistic character, which informs Freud's theory of dream interpretation as deeply as it does his case histories and his theory of hysteria. We should read Freud's great book on dream

[1]Sigmund Freud, *On the History of the Psycho-Analytic Movement, SE* 14:7.
[2]Freud, "Fragment of an Analysis of a Case of Hysteria," *SE* 7:23.

interpretation not only as his contribution to the "science" of psychoanalysis but as a contribution with a distinctively literary interest, since it is—like *Robinson Crusoe*—also the novel of its narrator's own "life and adventures."

No one need wonder, therefore, at the part the novel plays in *The Interpretation of Dreams*. Early in the book, Freud tells a dream of his own—the dream of the Three Fates—to illustrate one of the central claims of his theory. Within a dream, he says, "we find the child and the child's impulses still living on" (191). As Freud begins to analyze the material in that dream, he thinks "quite unexpectedly of the first novel I ever read" (204). "I have never known the name of the novel or of its author; but I have a vivid memory of its ending. The hero went mad." It is striking that the first novel read by the founder of psychoanalysis should be a novel ending in madness, that "the child and the child's impulses" should live on in Freud in his memory of this childhood novel that shaped his dream and perhaps his entire career. Equally striking are Freud's admission that his reading of this novel was incomplete (since he never read its first volume) and his decision to allow the name of the book and its author to remain unknown. Later, in order to make another important point about the significance of this same dream, he refers to the novel again. As he was transcribing the dream, he says, he found himself writing down the word *plagiarizing*. Freud associated that word with one of the characters in the unnamed novel (a character named Pelagie) and with a scene in the dream in which he is being accused of stealing an overcoat. "The idea of plagiarizing," Freud says, "of appropriating whatever one can, even though it belongs to someone else," was the crucial link between the parts of this dream (205).

The linkage of the "idea" of plagiarism with Freud's memory of the first novel he had ever read and his suppression of the author and title of the novel resonate with several of Freud's other dreams in *The Interpretation of Dreams*. A number of them are elaborately concerned with the significance of writing books and with properly recognizing or failing to recognize their authors. The dreams and their interpretations often deal specifically with novels, including works by Zola, Eliot, Kingsley, Meredith, Haggard, Goethe, Dumas, Rabelais, and others. Since Freud sees dreams as concealed forms of writing, it is significant that he should unexpectedly discover the key to one dream in a novel with an unnamed author and should find himself writing down a word that means "writing down" or "appropriating" someone else's words as one's own. Freud often describes dreams as plagiarists of the material of waking life, particularly infantile life; and he portrays himself as the scholar tracking down the borrowed sources of the dreams. In this, his conception of the dream work resembles the "work" of the novel as well.

The novel was described by Henry James in the same year in which Freud completed writing *The Interpretation of Dreams* (1899) as "the most com-

prehensive and the most elastic" representation of human experience because it "will stretch anywhere—it will take in absolutely anything." According to James, the novel is the best expression of man's "eternal desire for
more experience" and his "infinite cunning as to getting his experience as
cheaply as possible." As the novel demonstrates, "he will steal it whenever he
can."[3] Mikhail Bakhtin, who would mount a critique of "Freudianism" in the
1920s, also characterized the novel as a plagiarizing form: he regarded it not
as a genre itself, in fact, but as a "force" that "novelizes" other genres. The
novel borrows, distorts, ironizes, permeates, and appropriates their features,
he says, and "inserts into these other genres an indeterminacy, a certain
semantic openendedness."[4] In much the same way, Freud claims that the
"work" of the dream condenses, distorts, displaces, revises, and even "steals"
the material of waking life and presents it in another form.

In Freud's analysis of the dream of the Three Fates, he says that his
writing down of the word *plagiarism* formed a "bridge" that united the
dream's disparate parts, opened up the dream's "semantics," and led him to
think of his life in terms of the "old novel" of his childhood (206). One of the
meanings of this dream may be that Freud's writing of his own book—like
his writing down of the dream that contains it—appropriates and rewrites
that "first novel" he read as a child with himself in the role of the hero as
author. In *The Interpretation of Dreams*, he writes the original volume that for
him never existed; he provides a history of the hero's madness and perhaps a
cure for it as well. Freud steals the cloak of authorship in this book by
appropriating the untitled and anonymous novel of his childhood and giving
it a new name and author: himself.

My consideration of *The Interpretation of Dreams* as Freud's autobiographical novel claims that this text is vitally affiliated with the novel as a literary
form. This reading of *The Interpretation* has two complementary objectives.
First, it is organized around an examination of several of Freud's own
dreams, which he presumably includes in the text as examples of his theory
of dreams. But rather than regard these dreams simply as aspects of a theory,
I consider them parts of a "hidden plot" within *The Interpretation of Dreams*.
That plot is the account of Freud's becoming the author of his own novelistic
life story as well as the author of this book. Second, I examine how books,
specifically novels, figure in Freud's dream thoughts and his dream syn-
theses in order to demonstrate the increasing importance of the novel in
Freud's conception of his own book on dreams and the theory it contained.
The Interpretation of Dreams is, of course, many other things in addition to

[3] Henry James, "The Future of the Novel," *Theory of Fiction: Henry James*, ed. James E. Miller,
Jr. (1981), p. 338.
[4] Mikhail Bakhtin, "Discourse in the Novel," *The Dialogic Imagination*, ed. Michael Holquist,
trans. Caryl Emerson and Michael Holquist (1981), p. 338.

Bildungsroman: it is epic, polemic, philosophical speculation, scientific theory. But my reading of Freud's masterpiece emphasizes its novelistic character. Freud not only alluded to recurring themes from certain novels of the nineteenth century to illustrate and substantiate his theory of dream interpretation; he also derived formal and substantive features from these novels as well, features that influenced the structure of his book and the shape of his argument. The novelist, Freud said, "has always been the precursor of science and of scientific psychology."[5] This is never more clearly the case than in the science of dream interpretation as he defined it in *The Interpretation of Dreams*, the text in which Freud formulated a language for the unconscious and launched his most ambitious quest for both scientific and literary authority.

Georg Lukács's *Theory of the Novel*, which he was writing as Freud was revising *The Interpretation of Dreams*, refers to the novel as "the epic of a world that has been abandoned by God."[6] The same claim could be made for *The Interpretation of Dreams*. For Freud, the dream is not only a "text," it is a replacement for a sacred text. "We have treated as Holy Writ," Freud says of his treatment of dream material, "what others have regarded as arbitrary improvisation, hurriedly patched together in the embarrassment of the moment" (514). This claim reveals a fundamental similarity between Freud's objectives for *The Interpretation of Dreams* and the objectives of the novel throughout the nineteenth century. Both replace religious authority with forms of treatment. Both seek to recuperate the fragmentary experience of human life by imposing a "plot" upon the seemingly random and insignificant. Just as the novel "seeks, by giving form, to uncover and construct the concealed totality of life," in Luckács's words (60), Freud's method of dream interpretation uncovers the disguised meanings written into the chaotic dream images, translates them into "the language of the dream thoughts," and "assigns" them a place in the dreamer's emerging life story (277). With the attention and care of a novelist, the author of *The Interpretation of Dreams* reconstructs the impressions of his predecessors and restores them to their proper place in the "chain of events" that compose the waking life of the dreamer. Like the writing of a novel, the writing of Freud's book itself is an act of replacement, in which he substitutes a text of human construction for the master text of Holy Writ. This new text appropriates the strategies and privileges of the novelist in order to make the operations of the unconscious

---

[5]Freud, *Delusion and Dream*, p. 65. For more on Freud's debt to novelistic discourse, see Michel de Certeau, "The Freudian Novel," *Heterologies*. Certeau argues that Freud's interest in literary discourse enables his theoretical discourse. "Indeed," he goes on to say, "the Freudian discourse is the fiction which comes back to the realm of scientificity, not only insofar as it is the object of analysis, but insofar as it is the form" (p. 20).

[6]Georg Lukács, *The Theory of the Novel: An Historico-Philosophical Essay on the Forms of Great Epic Literature*, trans. Anna Bostock (1982), p. 88.

narratable. To do so, it deploys the same controlling discourses that were deployed by the dominant forms of the novel in the nineteenth century.

The act of writing is so central to *The Interpretation of Dreams* that many of the dreams Freud recounts in the book are about his writing it, about the process of becoming the author of the book we are reading.[7] Where the subject of creating the book does not appear in the manifest content of the dream, it often emerges in the course of interpretation. Finally, authorship as a means to power and self-possession consistently turns out to be at the heart of Freud's dream thoughts. "The underlying meaning" was this, he says of a dream in which Goethe critiques a book written by a friend of Freud's: "if you don't understand the book it's you [the critic] that are feeble-minded and not the author" (327). Freud's own warning that the ego is everywhere present in the dream suggests that we should read the "underlying meaning" of this dream as referring to his own book and to himself as "the author" at least as much as it refers to his friend. And the "underlying meaning" of many of Freud's dreams is directed toward combining just this sort of defense of his authorial power with an articulation of the costs and privileges that power entails. *The Interpretation of Dreams* is both theory and autobiography, then. It is Freud's "sacred story" of himself as author and critic as well as prophet and scientist.

Dreams and authorship had already become intricately linked in nineteenth-century culture before Freud. There was a widespread tendency in the period to conceive of the dream as an unfinished book, as a fragmented experience that required conversion not simply into language, but into a book—into an object that was complete, that told a story. When Schopenhauer said that "life and dream are leaves of one and the same book," he expressed one of the deepest anxieties of the culture and one of its most profound wishes: the anxiety that life was as chaotic as a dream and the wish that both might have the form and design of a book.[8] The period witnessed the publication of unprecedented numbers of autobiographical texts in many forms: autobiographies and autobiographical novels, letters, memoirs, travel accounts, apologias, criminal confessions, religious conversion narratives, medical case studies, diaries—all of which reflected obsessive concern with the act of self-expression in narrative terms. It was common for these narratives to contain accounts of dreams, visions, trance states, somnambulism, automatic writing, or similar inexplicable psychic events.

---

[7]"Starting with the *Traumdeutung*," Derrida claims, "the metaphor of writing *will appropriate simultaneously the problems of the psychic apparatus in its structure and that of the psychic text in its fabric*" ("Freud and the Scene of Writing," in his *Writing and Difference* [1978]). Derrida maintains that there is no "originary text" in Freud's description of the unconscious, since the conscious mind can only transcribe what is already a "weave of pure traces," which compose the unconscious (p. 206).

[8]Arthur Schopenhauer, *The World as Will and Representation*, trans. E. F. J. Pogue (1969), 1:18.

The challenge of the narrative was to seek an explanation, to fit these events into the speaker's life story, to control the uncontrollable by making it part of a coherent story about a particular self.

The Interpretation of Dreams is one of the most important of those first-person narratives. Freud makes himself the subject of the book as well as its author when he includes his own dreams as crucial data for his study. He begins the text with words that call attention to his voice speaking through the book: "In the pages that follow I shall bring forward proof that there is a psychological technique that makes it possible to interpret dreams" (1). The "I" that speaks is contained "in the pages that follow" as an essential part of the "proof" of a technique. That "I" is encoded within the dreams Freud will tell and interpret, some forty-six of which are his own. My analysis of a set of these dreams and the novels in them attends to the ways in which Freud blends three forms of discourse—medical, political, and economic—to unite his dreams into the constituents of a book: this book that both forms a general theory of dream interpretation and makes up the very specific story of Freud's life as an author.

Freud defined dream interpretation as a therapeutic rewriting of the dream itself. He regarded the dream thoughts and the dream content as two versions of the same subject matter presented in two different languages. The act of interpreting dreams was essentially an act of translation, which "transposed" the dream's "pictographic script" back into "the language of the dream thoughts" (53, 277). But Freud's entire project in *The Interpretation of Dreams* may be seen as a translation of another kind: the replacement of the religious language for describing dreams with a medical and scientific one, a "proof" that the dream is not a divinely given message but the symptom of a psychic infirmity. In the case history of Dora, Freud indicates that his first therapeutic procedure was always to have the patient "give me the whole story of his life and illness," a story that was (like a dream) invariably incomplete and inadequate, "leaving gaps unfilled and riddles unanswered" (30). The goal of Freud's treatment is the cure of this narrative illness through the recuperation of the patient's "whole story." In Dora's case, he based his entire analysis and treatment on the precise wording of two dreams as she recounted them to him: "The wording of these dreams was recorded immediately after the session, and they thus afforded a secure point of attachment for the chain of interpretations and recollections which proceeded from them" (10). The cure of the patient was to be achieved in the repair of her story and the words in which she expressed her dream. When Freud warned his readers not to read this case history as a novel, he must have recognized how much his presentation of it resembled an act of literary creation. Freud would draw the analogy himself between the recuperation of the subject in his theory of dream interpretation and the construction of a character in any novel when he claimed that "His Majesty the Ego" is "the hero of all daydreams and every story." The "special nature" of the "psychological novel," he said, is based in "the inclination" of the novelist "to split up his ego by self-observation, into many part-egos, and, in consequence, to personify the conflicting currents in his own mental life."⁹ This description is almost an exact echo of Freud's claim in *The Interpretation of Dreams* that the ego of the dreamer is everywhere present in the dream, identified in concealed ways with all the "persons" that appear in it (322–23).¹⁰

In addition to his use of medical discourse to describe the origin and operation of dreams, Freud appropriated political and economic language for them as well. For him, the dream is a "battlefield" in which the power and "authority" of the individual are at stake, and the "governing" and "mastering" of psychic material is played out amid a drama of "repression," "censorship," and "resistance." The conflict could be dealt with when the dreamer recognized the economic character of his or her relationship to the dream. The dreamer must "own" the dream as his or her "production," as something the dreamer has manufactured to fulfill his or her own desire, rather than a "possession" that has been imposed from the outside. "A daytime thought may very well play the part of *entrepreneur* for a dream," Freud would even say, "and the capitalist who provides the psychical outlay for the dream" is a "wish from the unconscious" (561). In each of these definitions of dream processes, Freud was also defining the nature of the dreamer. The unconscious mind was being theorized as a participant in a marketplace, as a state divided against itself, and as a diseased body in need of cure. The individual was not an immortal soul but a patient, an entrepreneur, a political agent. These were the very metaphors the novel borrowed from the culture in the nineteenth century to tell the story of the self in the modern world.¹¹ Like *Robinson Crusoe* or *David Copperfield*, *The Interpretation of Dreams* interprets the dreams of a culture while it writes the story of a particular self in the very terms that culture offered.

⁹Freud, "Creative Writers and Day-Dreaming," *SE* 9:150.

¹⁰This description also accords with Freud's admiration of Dickens's work in general and of *David Copperfield* in particular. For a consideration of the significance of Dickens's "style" of memory and forgetfulness for Freud, see Ned Lukacher, *Primal Scenes: Literature, Philosophy, Psychoanalysis* (1986), pp. 330–36. See also Stoehr, *Dickens*. Stoehr points out how closely Dickens's use of split narratives, character doublings, displacements of emotion and animation from the characters into their surroundings, and simultaneous concealment and revelation of meaning resembles the devices of dream work.

¹¹See Roger Caillois, "Logical and Philosophical Problems," in *The Dream and Human Societies*, ed. G. E. von Grunebaum and Roger Caillois (1966), p. 51: "The dream remains the common property of the sleeper who has dreamed it and the waking person who remembers it; in an analogous sense the novel fulfills itself with a mediation between the writer who has created it and the reader who is introduced for a brief instant, for an interlude, as a supernumerary character into a fictional world."

The Novel in *The Interpretation of Dreams*

The novelist has always preceded the scientist.

—Sigmund Freud

The basic stages of the dream plot in *The Interpretation of Dreams* may be deciphered in the series of dreams that Freud explicitly interprets as being about his writing of the book: the Botanical Monograph dream, the Autodidasker dream, and the Self-dissection dream. The analysis of the Botanical Monograph dream appears early in the presentation of the theory, in the chapter "The Material and Sources of Dreams." The Autodidasker and the Self-dissection dream interpretations are respectively placed toward the beginning and end of the main chapter on the theory, "The Dream Work." Each of the three dreams is, in turn, associated with one of the fundamental features of Freud's theory about dreams, and each is represented as a narrative strategy: censorship, condensation, and secondary revision. Together, these dreams and Freud's analysis of them form the outline of a novelistic story of self-authorship, and they gradually expose the plot of his family romance as well. In the first, Freud's interpretation is primarily concerned with a conflict among a series of books which he unearths in his dream thoughts. In the second, he identifies himself as the author of *The Interpretation of Dreams* with the writer of novels. In the last of these dreams that center on Freud's production of "my book upon dreams," the form and meaning of the dream are decidedly "derived" from his reading of a particular novel.

There are certain additional thematic features that not only tie these dreams together but relate them to many of the other dreams in *The Interpretation* as well. Each involves a struggle for authority between Freud and his father or some father figure within a scene of writing that involves the acquisition of property or power. These are also the essential elements of the plot of the classic nineteenth-century European novel. Edward Said has described the "generic plot situation of the novel" as an intention "to repeat through variation the family scene by which human beings engender human duration in their action."[12] Since to be "novel" is also to be original and therefore to challenge repetition, the novel has a paradoxical project. The "plot" of Freud's *Interpretation of Dreams* contains just this paradox, and the plots of the novels he draws from reinforce the resemblance between "this present book about dreams" and what Said calls the "special procreative yet celibate enterprise" of self-authorship in the novel.[13] Each of the dreams

[12]Said, "On Repetition," in Said, *The World, the Text, and the Critic* (1983), p. 117.
[13]Said, *Beginnings*, pp. 477 and 145.

also has to do with Freud's professional "authority" as a physician, and in each the act of healing becomes implicitly connected with the act of writing. Freud's "speaking cure" is presented in these dreams more accurately as a "writing cure," and specifically as the writing of one's own life story. That story represents the repossession and mastery of the dreamer's psychic territory by a narrative action.[14]

His dream of the Botanical Monograph is one of the first Freud analyzes in detail in *The Interpretation of Dreams*. The dream and the interpretation dramatize Freud's own playing out of a double part, a part that moves between his desire to present the dream as data for his theory, on the one hand, and his desire to be the author of the book that contains and explains the dream, on the other. The single object seen in this dream is a book, and even on the manifest level the dream is about the dreamer as author: "I had written a monograph on a certain plant. The book lay before me and I was at the moment turning over a folded coloured plate. Bound up in each copy there was a dried specimen of the plant, as though it had been taken from a herbarium" (169). The book Freud sees before him in the dream is a monograph for which he claims complete authorship: "I had written" it, he says. Yet in his analysis of the dream, the book immediately becomes associated with two other books—one he had not written (a "new book" he had seen in the window of a bookshop that morning) and one he had written (his dissertation on the coca plant). This split of the book into two other books expresses the central issue of the dream: Freud's disappointment and anger over not being acknowledged as the author of the theory that established cocaine as an anaesthetic. He had written a book, but he was not recognized as an author.

The sequence of "free" associations which Freud then develops in his interpretation of the dream continues to be organized around the issue of his authority over a series of books. Freud first admits to seeing the book in the shop window but not to buying it. This book was for sale; it had a price, a public value, and it required an investment to be owned. It did not belong to him. And while the work he had written on the coca plant did belong to him, it commanded no price in the intellectual marketplace since Freud was never recognized as the "author" of the theory of the plant's medical value. As his analysis of the dream proceeds, Freud then recalls a fantasy the dream had

[14]In Freud, Certeau says, "the literary work will appear rather as a setting of historical alterations within a formal framework. Moreover, there is a continuity between Freud's manner of listening to a patient, his manner of interpreting a document (literary or other), and his manner of writing. There is no essential break between these three operations. The 'novel' in this sense can characterize at once the utterances of a patient, a literary work, and the psychoanalytic discourse itself" (p. 21). This continuity is even more direct—and more complex—when Freud is (as he is in *The Interpretation*) both doctor and patient, author and interpreter, writer and reader of the text.

triggered, in which he apparently intended not to be recognized for the cocaine discovery. He imagines himself going to a surgeon "incognito" and having an operation on his eyes in which he benefits from the plant's anaesthetic powers. The eye surgeon "would have no idea of my identity," Freud says, but would boast about how valuable the introduction of cocaine had been for the performance of the operation (170). Freud describes the secret pleasure he would derive from his anonymity. Because of it, he says, he would "be able to pay his fees like anyone else."

This daydream is rich in implications, especially since Freud explicitly connects it with his father's eye operation, thereby expressing a desire effectively to *replace* his father in the fantasy. That these operations are performed to correct faulty vision and involve a failure to recognize the identity of the patient exposes Freud's ambivalence about identifying with and replacing his father here. This material will become increasingly important later in this analysis and in the other dreams Freud tells. But of special significance at this point is Freud's recurrent interest in the financial value of the cocaine discovery, even if the discovery was not seen as Freud's by this surgeon whose job it is to restore sight to those who cannot see. I read Freud's desire to pay the fee as his desire to buy back his own book, to affirm its value, to secure it for himself. This is the essential work that the dream does for him. It is a repossession of his own book, a recognition of himself as the book's author. To reinforce this reading, it would seem, Freud immediately introduces another problematic book into the dream analysis here. It is a *Festschrift* celebrating the man who had been credited with the discovery of the anaesthetic properties of cocaine. This book combines the ambivalence of the previous two in that it should have been a book about Freud, but it was not; he should have been "one of the authors" included in it, but he was not permitted to be. Freud's work was in the book, but he could not be seen in it (171). The publication of *The Interpretation of Dreams* would correct that oversight, prominently figuring Freud as the author of a new theory of the unconscious.

The next book Freud introduces into the interpretation is the crucial one in the analysis of the dream. Its appearance is evoked by Freud's return to the wording of the dream as he reported it at the outset: "I saw the monograph which I had written *lying before me*" (172). He now associates the book he saw in the dream with the very book he is writing—*The Interpretation of Dreams*—the book that we see lying before us. It is as if the restoration of sight by the operation has corrected the distorted vision of the dream by replacing the monograph with the true text of the dream, *The Interpretation of Dreams*. The memory that releases this association for Freud is his recollection of a letter he received from Wilhelm Fliess the day before, which included the following passage: "I am very much occupied by your dreambook. *I see it lying finished before me and I see myself turning over its pages*" (172).

Freud's only comment on this association is brief but quite obviously deeply felt: "How much I envied him his gift as a seer! If only *I* could have seen it lying finished before me!" This is quite clearly the most explicitly expressed wish uncovered by the interpretation: to be the author of the book we are reading, to "see" it and have it be seen, to let it "occupy" a reader who recognizes it and identifies it to Freud as his dream book. The connection with Freud's fantasized eye surgery and his desire to replace his father in the dream is important here ("How much I envied him his gift as a seer!"). The dream expresses Freud's desire to have second sight, to see himself as a seer, to be the one to whom "the Secret of Dreams was Revealed" (121). This dream is an operation upon the dreamer in which he performs the role of author as well as physician and patient.

But this is not the end of the significance of the dream for Freud, though it does form a center. He introduces—and then tries to erase—one more book in his interpretation. The "coloured plates" in the dream monograph recall to Freud the drawings he had made as illustrations when he began to publish scholarly papers. In the wake of this memory, "there followed, I could not quite make out how, a recollection from very early youth" of a book Freud's father had given to him and his sister "to destroy" (172). Freud has already noted in the analysis of this dream that "forgetting is very often determined by an unconscious purpose and that it always enables one to deduce the secret intentions of the person who forgets" (170). So we should take his failure to make out this recollection quite seriously and be alert to the secret intentions that may lurk behind the forgetting of the connection between this book and the others in the dream.

Freud claims that virtually his only memory of this period of his life was this scene of himself and his sister "blissfully pulling the book to pieces" (172). Then as quickly as he introduces it, he explains the scene away as a " 'screen memory' for my later bibliophile propensities"(173). Certainly this "propensity" to possess books is important to the meaning of the dream and is deeply consistent with Freud's repeatedly expressed desire in the dream to have a book of his own. But the "screen memory" itself is more than just a screen. Freud's wish to write his own book and to see it finished is directly juxtaposed to this "scene" of the destruction of another book, which he had not written, a book his father had handed over to him with the express intention that it be destroyed. The book Freud pulls apart here comes to stand for the elimination of all the other books from the dream content—the ones he had not written but should have. This dream is concerned in a fundamental way with the book Freud wishes to put together, but it is also concerned with other books he would like to pull to pieces—"leaf by leaf" (172). In the dream, the two processes are inherently related. Notably, the book that must be destroyed here was given to him by his father. This memory, like the fantasy of the eye surgery, is a desire to replace the father

and to cooperate with him as well. In this, it repeats in miniature many of the
complexities of the entire dream. The destruction of the book represents an
act of obedience to the father while it figures a dismembering of the object
that represents him. The productive action proves to be inseparable from the
destructive one, and an act of piety exists in the dream alongside an act of
impiety.

That this scene of destroying a book is more important to the dream than
Freud admits is implied by his own interpretation. He has already focused
attention on the overdetermined significance of books in the dream, evoked
an atmosphere of violence in the surgical scenes, and plainly admitted his
resentment over not receiving credit for the theory, at least as "co-author."
Freud reinforces the importance of the violence in the scene when he returns to the dream later in *The Interpretation* to illustrate how a seemingly
"indifferent affect" often hides a "struggle" between "intense psychical impulses." "This reminds one of the peace that has descended upon a battlefield strewn with corpses," Freud says of the dream of the Botanical
Monograph; "no trace is left of the struggle which raged over it" (467). What
is true of the dream work is also true of the work that was written about this
dream. The writing of a book with the ambitions of *The Interpretation of
Dreams* represents a political as well as a medical intervention. It must resist
the claims of other writers and struggle with—"rage over"—their competing
explanations of dreams. "Having now repelled the objections that have been
raised against us," Freud says in the beginning of his final chapter, "or
having at least indicated where our defensive weapons lie, we must no longer
postpone the task of setting about the psychological investigations for which
we have so long been arming ourselves" (533). Like war, and like surgery,
writing this book involves both risk and destruction. The dreams within it—
at least as they are interpreted by Freud—leave traces of the struggle that
produced the book; and they also leave traces of the other books its author
took some pleasure in destroying. Freud's writing of one book involves an
arming against and a tearing apart of others.[15]

Immediately prior to his analysis of the dream of the Botanical Monograph, Freud introduces the role of "censorship" in dreams and argues for
an essential similarity among dreams, politics, and writing. Freud claims that
"the political writer who has difficult truths to tell those in authority" must
sometimes distort his text. As dream interpreter Freud confronts a "similar
difficulty: "When I interpret my dreams for my readers I am obliged to adopt
similar distortions" (142). Here Freud explicitly identifies himself (the phy-

---

[15]"Dreams provide access to a basic phenomenon . . . the phenomenon of *regression*. . . . In
regression, we are led from concepts of meaning to concepts of force. . . . Thus dreams,
inasmuch as they are the expression of wishes, lie at the intersection of meaning and force"
(Paul Ricoeur, *Freud and Philosophy: An Essay on Interpretation*, trans. Denis Savage [1970], p.
91).

sician interpreting the symptoms of dreams) with the political writer. Like the political writer, Freud informs his readers of "difficult truths" and he "adopts distortions" to counteract the "authorities that will suppress his words." He writes to "his readers" in order to take control of a situation where others possess "a certain degree of power" over him (142–43). He must tell them fictions in order for them to understand the truth. Writing is in this sense always "censored" before the fact because the writer's relationship to his or her readers is a relationship of control in which words sometimes carry hidden force and meaning.

This political language is clearly echoed in Freud's description of the dream thoughts composing the dream of the Botanical Monograph: they consisted, he says, of "a passionately agitated plea on behalf of my liberty to act as I chose to act and to govern my life as seemed right to me and me alone" (467). The secret intentions and screens of this dream analysis distort but do not erase the nature of Freud's dream and his book about dreams as, among other things, personal political acts, attempts to wrest from other writers the power to "govern" his own life as well as to interpret dreams. In his analogy of himself with the political writer, Freud enacts the complicated relationship of his own dreams to his book about them. He writes about the activity of censorship, he admits to practicing censorship himself as he writes this book, and then he claims that he does so in order to avoid the censorship of others. In an analogous way, his dreams function in the book not only as illustrations of a theory but also as covert expressions of his desire and attempts to assert his own authority in opposition to others in medical, economic, and political terms.[16]

The act of dream interpretation as it is performed here is paradigmatic of the whole of Freud's theory: the book destroyed is a book of colored plates that is replaced first by Freud's narrative of the dream thoughts behind that action, and then by the book of his own authorship which contains that narrative. The puzzling "pictographic" images of the dream work are replaced and mastered by the interpretive language of dream synthesis and then placed into the larger narrative of the "life story" of the dreamer. And as it is described here, the act of dream interpretation also strikingly resembles the paradoxical project of the novel as it had been described by Freud's contemporaries in literary theory—James, Lukács, and Bakhtin—each of whom saw the genre as an essentially biographical form involving a simulta-

[16]Carl E. Schorske finds that by "reducing his own political past and present to an epiphenomenal status in relation to the primal conflict between father and son, Freud gave his fellow liberals an a-historical theory of man and society that could make bearable a political world spun out of orbit and beyond control" (*Fin de Siècle Vienna: Politics and Culture* [1981], p. 203). This important objection to Freud must be balanced by an acknowledgment that his identification and systemization of the political as it exists within generational conflict may also be seen as an extension of the power of the political.

neous imitation of something prior and origination of something new. In an analogous way, Freud sees his book *The Interpretation of Dreams* as absorbing and surpassing the theories of his predecessors on the same subject, as it tells the story of his own life.

The original book that Freud saw in the dream had "bound up" in it a specimen of the very plant about which the book was written. The book was not just a representation of something, in other words, but was bound up with—contained—the thing itself. *The Interpretation of Dreams* also has the mind of its author bound up in it, as does any representation of dream experience. When Freud summarizes its significance at the end of his analysis, he cogently states how important it is that the dream portrays him as an author. "What it meant was: 'After all, I'm the man who wrote the valuable and memorable paper (on cocaine)'" (173). The phrase "on cocaine" is appropriately contained within parentheses, since the essential wish expressed here is Freud's identification of himself as "the man who wrote" something valuable and memorable—the very book we see lying finished before us. What the dream of the Botanical Monograph meant for Freud was: "After all, I'm the man who wrote."

The dream of the Botanical Monograph appears in the chapter called "Material and Sources of Dreams," but the dream is quite evidently concerned with revealing the "material and sources" of Freud's book about dreams as well. This dream identifies the act of interpreting dreams with the act of authorship, with the production of a book about the self. In the beginning of the following chapter, "The Dream-Work," Freud analyzes the Autodidasker dream to illustrate the "work" of condensation. But like the Botanical Monograph dream, this dream is also about the connection between authorship and power, and it develops the "plot" of Freud's writing of his book as well as providing an example of a particular dream process. Here he identifies himself not simply with the author, but specifically with the novelist.

Again, books are crucial to the interpretation, but in this case, the dream analysis specifically reveals Freud's interest in the novel as a literary form that provides a model for what the work of interpretation should do and for the kind of book he is producing. In particular, Freud relates the dream to Zola's novel *L'Oeuvre* (The work or The masterpiece, 1886). Unlike the dream of the Botanical Monograph, the Autodidasker dream contains no books in its manifest content, but once again Freud discovers several books in the dream thoughts as sources for the dream. His memory of the dream "consisted of two separate pieces" that are unified in the course of analysis by their common concern with the dreamer's "authority": "The first piece was the word '*Autodidasker*', which I recalled vividly. The second piece was an exact reproduction of a short and harmless phantasy which I had produced some days before. This phantasy was to the effect that when I next saw Professor N. I must say to him: 'The patient about whose condition I consulted you recently is in fact only suffering from a neurosis, just as you suspected'" (298–99). The major portion of Freud's analysis of the dream concerns its first part: the one word *Autodidasker*. The first association he makes is Autor, the German word for "author." His other associations are *Autodidakt*, "self-taught," and the proper names "Lasker" and "Lassalle."

In this set of associations, Freud has again brought together the ideas of authorship and self-mastery and associated them with issues of power— here, explicitly political issues. Ferdinand Lasalle founded the German Social Democratic movement, and Eduard Lasker the National Liberal party in Germany. Both were revolutionaries, Lasker having fought against the imperial forces in Vienna in 1848. He resigned from the party he had helped to found when Bismarck became its leader. But in Freud's interpretation of the dream, these national political issues are made secondary to personal politics. In this regard, it is worth noting that both Lasker and Lassalle led scandalous romantic lives, Lassalle's ending in a duel over a lover. But in addition, both were also writers, and Lasker had even published an autobiographical novel in 1873 before a form of progressive brain disease took his life. This novel must have been important for Freud since he sees the strategic center of his associations with the neologism in the "first of these words"—*author*. The word *author*, Freud says, "led to the precipitating cause of the dream—this time a significant one" (299).[17]

In this slide from the political to the psychological, Freud implies how much the private world of his own unconscious was dictated in the terms of the public world, how deeply political circumstances shape the individual's psychological condition. But Freud's analogy between the dream work of censorship and the tactics of the political writer also typifies certain tendencies within Freud's theory of the unconscious which are in conflict with this implication. Early on, Bakhtin critiqued Freud's tendency to neutralize political realities by abstracting them and transforming them into mere background for a more important private drama of the psyche, and Carl Schorske, Fredric Jameson, Terry Eagleton, and others have repeated the critique. This tension is clearly present throughout Freud's work, and it is characteristic of the course taken by many of his Victorian predecessors, who often responded to the nineteenth-century crisis of authority by displacing social conflict, internalizing and domesticating it as a conflict within an individual psyche. Nancy Armstrong has maintained that this sealing off of the private world from the public, formalized by both psychoanalysis and the novel in the nineteenth century, was itself a political act that effectively

[17]For many of the allusions in these dreams, I depend on Alexander Grinstein, *On Sigmund Freud's Dreams* (1968).

rendered the bourgeois subject politically unconscious.[18] The traces of that suppression, however, remain evident in the very language with which Freud described the psyche.

Characteristically, then, Freud recognizes the word *author* in its literary terms as the *significant* cause of this dream. The sequence of Freud's associations with this crucial word again begins to suggest a pattern organized around the writing of a book. He first associates the word with the well-known Austrian writer J. J. David, with whom he immediately identifies by adding that David "was a native of my own birth-place" (299). Freud then explains that he had once given his wife several volumes of David's work as a gift. She had recently related to Freud a tragic story from one of these books about "a man of talent" who "went to the bad," and she was concerned that their own talented children might follow the same tragic path (299). Freud's commentary on this issue is limited to a mention that he consoled his wife and eased her concern. He then pursues the path of his dream thoughts by once again focusing on the figure of the author, recalling some remarks the writer had made about "the danger of coming to grief over a woman." Freud does not tell us anything further about the story his wife read—the narrative of grief *this* woman had brought to *him*. In fact, the story concerns an "author" who finally commits suicide because of his failure to make a living as a writer. Freud must have identified with such a figure since he was at this time struggling to establish himself as an "author," and as we have already seen, he was deeply concerned about the consequences of failing to do so.

Freud reinforces this identification of himself with the figure of the author when he alludes to another book: "In Zola's novel of an artist's life, *L'Oeuvre*, the subject of which must have been close to my dream-thoughts," Freud says, "its author, as is well known, introduced himself and his own domestic happiness as an episode" (300). Freud goes on to describe how Zola disguises his own name in the novel ("Sandoz") "in much the same fashion" as he himself had created the word *Autodidasker* in the dream. But the larger point here is that Freud resembles Zola in a more fundamental way: he is doing in this work, *The Interpretation of Dreams*, precisely what Zola did in *L'Oeuvre*—introducing himself and the episodes of his own domestic life as an essential part of the content. Further, he is doing so with the intention of making a story out of that life material, making his dream into a "structure which has a meaning" (1). Finally, just as Zola had done, Freud is writing himself into this book in the role of "its author." In the previous chapter of his book, Freud had compared himself as physician to a "political writer" (142). In this chapter he explicitly compares himself to a novelist who condenses and converts the details of his own life into a work of art.

Freud's discovery of Zola as a disguised author in his dream thoughts here

[18]See Armstrong, *Desire and Domestic Fiction.*

may be related to the other writer, already alluded to but not explicitly mentioned—the threatening figure of the failed author, actually a poet, in David's book *Ein Dichter?* (A poet?). Later in this chapter on the dream work, Freud compares the "pictorial language" of dream formation to the writing of poetry and likens the act of interpretation to the conversion of poetry into prose. The author in Zola's novel is distinguished from David's not only because he is successful but also because he writes in prose. Moreover, the objectives of the prose the novelist Sandoz writes bear a striking resemblance to those of *The Interpretation*. "This is the idea," Sandoz says of his projected series of novels: "to study man as he really is. Not this metaphysical marionnette they've made us believe he is, but the physiological human being, determined by his surroundings, motivated by the functioning of his organs."[19] The complex relationship between the disciplines of psychology and physiology must be examined in order to understand the functioning of the "human mechanism," Sandoz claims, anticipating the very issues at stake in *The Interpretation* in general and in the problematic "diagnosis" in this dream in particular. Psychology and physiology have "overflowed into each other to such an extent that they've become one," Sandoz says, "and human mechanism has come to be the sum total of human functions" (163).

It can also be said of *The Interpretation of Dreams* that the disciplines of science and literature have "overflowed into each other to such an extent that they have become one," that Freud's science of the mind is deeply indebted to his reading of the novel. Both the subject and the language of Zola's novel do indeed seem to be "close" to Freud's "dream-thoughts" in this particular dream, and the similarity will become even more apparent in the "psychical apparatus" language of chapter 7 of *The Interpretation*, where Freud explains his theory of the interpenetration of psychic and organic systems in the production of dreams. That the novelist survives and the poet dies in the narrative of this dream is in perfect accord with the unfolding of the argument and the hidden plot of narrative authority in *The Interpretation*. The demystified "masterpiece" of interpretation and exposition replaces the allusive, poetic ambiguity and compression of the dream. It is not just language that must replace the dream images but a particular kind of language—a language like that employed by the novelist who wrote *L'Oeuvre*.

But Freud's lingering anxiety over the risks of authorship is not entirely counteracted by the author figure in *L'Oeuvre*, since this novel also contains the story of another artist, the painter Lantier, who kills himself because he fails to paint his masterpiece. Freud does not mention Lantier in his analysis of the dream, just as he does not mention the failed author who killed himself in David's book. The omission is significant, for Lantier and his

[19]Emile Zola, *L'Oeuvre* (*The Masterpiece*) (Ann Arbor: University of Michigan Press, 1968), p. 162, hereafter cited in the text.

painting are consistently associated with dream experience in the novel to the point that the painter's entire life becomes the "dream" of his painting: "He preferred the illusion he found in his art, the everlasting pursuit of unattainable beauty, the mad desire which could never be satisfied. He wanted all women, but he wanted them created according to his dreams" (246). The novel directly contrasts the mad, dreamlike quality of Lantier's painting to the saner realism of the novelist's prose; in *L'Oeuvre*, Sandoz the novelist buries Lantier the painter. The significance for Freud in the interpretation of this dream recalls his already expressed desire to be "the man who wrote." In *The Interpretation of Dreams*, Freud wants to be the successful author of the book rather than the character who dies within it. He represses even from his analysis, therefore, the specter of the failed artist and the costs of that failure.

There may be another reason for Freud's omission of this artist from his interpretation. The two artist figures in *L'Oeuvre*, the novelist and the painter, correspond to the two essential forms in which, according to Freud, the dream works: in verbal language and in visual imagery. The project of dream interpretation as Freud defined it is to master the dream by converting its hallucinations into words. These two forms of dream experience are, in fact, suggested in the form of this dream. The dream occurs in "two pieces," one of which consists entirely of a word and the other of the "exact reproduction" of a fantasy, presumably visual as well as verbal in content. In addition, the dream includes in its analysis another book that contains two artists who enact the features of the theory as well. Freud's exclusion of the painter from his interpretation of the dream may be read as his desire to replace him with the writer, to control the unmastered and possibly threatening images of the dream by turning them into words. But it is a particular kind of writer that replaces the painter—the novelist who turns his life into a book. The failed artist in *L'Oeuvre* is the one who does not work in words, the one who does not write the book, the one who does not escape the images of the dream by putting them into the story of his life.

When Freud goes about establishing the "solid relation" between the key word in this dream and its fantasy, he bases the connection on the dramatization of an error in diagnosis: "This phantasy was to the effect that when I next saw Professor N. I must say to him: 'The patient about whose condition I consulted you recently is in fact only suffering from a neurosis, just as you suspected.'" Freud first interprets this scene as an expression of his "desire to be wrong" for worrying over his children's future (which he associated with the first half of the dream). "More precisely, " he then adds, "I wanted my wife, whose fears I had adopted in the dream-thoughts, to be wrong" (301). First, Freud explicitly contradicts himself when he says that *he* doesn't wish to be wrong at all; rather, he wishes his wife to be wrong. Second, the concern over his children seems to have occupied Freud only minimally compared to his consideration of the attractions and dangers of authorship as a profession. This second piece of the dream seems to be more solidly related to the first in its representation of a challenge to Freud's professional authority than in any concern for his children or in a desire to be wrong. But the "link" Freud does offer here, his wish for his children's success, once again joins the subjects of father and author. As the analysis continues, the motive for the dream becomes more explicitly tied to Freud's desire to be a successful author and a successful diagnostician. This connection becomes quite clear when Freud's interpretation of the dream fantasy transforms a concession to his father figure Professor N. into a vindication of his own theory of neurosis. Freud's apology to Professor N. becomes an apologia for his own book.

The fantasy shows Freud admitting that he made a wrong diagnosis to "a man . . . before whose authority I am readiest to bow" (300). On the manifest level, Freud seems to be confirming the diagnosis of Professor N., but the case history of the patient as Freud recounts it here indicates, on the contrary, that he is actually confirming his own. Freud's original diagnosis had depended upon the occurrence of a certain sexual history without which, according to Freud's theory, the patient's illness could not have been considered a neurosis. After he vehemently "repudiated" this sexual history for some time, the patient finally admitted to having lied about this behavior and provided "precisely the pieces of sexual aetiology which I had been expecting" (300–1). Now, Freud's more daring and precise diagnosis is confirmed and his theory of the etiology of neuroses is given compelling support. This development establishes the content of the fantasy as a professional accomplishment by Freud, not a mistake; and the fantasy must be joined to the other piece of the dream interpretation in which Freud clearly expresses his wish to be an "author" who writes about himself. In the two pieces of this dream, Freud first replaces Zola and David as successful authors, and then he replaces Professor N. as a medical "authority" to whom he no longer had to bow. He is the successful novelist and the successful doctor, and in this dream the two roles become "solidly related" to each other.

Freud's analysis of this dream demonstrates how much his admiration for the novel may have affected the structure of psychoanalysis as he designed it. Edward Said has explicitly related Freud's work to the late nineteenth-century novel, pointing out the common task of "accurately describing man as fundamentally connected" with "the problem of biography as embodied in genealogical sequence" and with the "utilitarian" value of human "fiction-making capabilities."[20] It is appropriate, therefore, that in his own crucial chapter "The Dream-Work" Freud should make such extensive use of a novel whose author has reconfigured his life and titled it, "The masterpiece." And it is equally appropriate that the novelist with whom he identifies

[20]Said, *Beginnings*, p. 158.

himself is Zola, who, by his own account, had adapted his own theory of the novel from a scientific work on medicine. "Usually it will be sufficient for me," Zola claimed, "to replace the word 'doctor' by the word 'novelist' in order to make my thought clear and to bring to it the rigor of scientific truth."[21] Freud turned the analogy around. He essentially defined psychoanalysis as surgery on our ability to work out our own life stories, a healing of our capacity to integrate ourselves and our desires into the realities of the world and to govern the impulses that drive us. As part of his treatment of the Rat-Man, Freud appropriately gave his patient a copy of Zola's novel *Joie de vivre*. To make our lives "work" in a productive and healthy way, psychoanalysis prescribes a narrative therapy, and *The Interpretation of Dreams* is its paradigmatic narrative.[22]

The next analysis in *The Interpretation of Dreams* concerning authorship carries out Freud's own prescription upon himself. Freud ostensibly presented the account of the Autodidasker dream to illustrate a form of narrative distortion that takes place in the dream work: condensation. Here, through a "manipulative process," the dream becomes a composite of elements that can represent in concentrated form a "whole mass of dream thoughts" (284). Freud presents the work of condensation as a form of poetic writing, much as he has presented censorship as a form of political writing in the previous chapter. There, rather than concentration or overdetermination of the dream thoughts in words and images, omissions in the text of the dream disguise its latent content. But in both censorship and condensation, the narrative coherence of the dream thoughts is "distorted," the material of waking life is "stripped to a large extent of its relations" (339) and presented in the dream in the form of "fragments" (449).

If the dream is a poem, however, it is a poem that contains the desire for its own translation into prose. Just prior to Freud's telling of the final dream that he explicitly interprets as being about his writing of *The Interpretation of Dreams*—the dream of his own dissection—he introduces the "force" he claims is "at work in dreams," which leads to this act of translation. That force is secondary revision. Like censorship and condensation, "secondary

[21]Emile Zola, "The Experimental Novel," in *Documents in Modern Literary Realism*, ed. George J. Becker (Princeton: Princeton University Press, 1968), p. 162.

[22]On the relation of narrative to Freud's theories, see Steven Marcus, "Freud and Dora: Story, History, Case History," in Marcus, *Representations: Essays on Literature and Society* (1974); and Brooks, *Reading for the Plot*. For Lacan's development of the relation, see Jacques Lacan, *Speech and Language in Psychoanalysis*, trans. Anthony G. Wilden (1982); and the collection of essays edited by Robert Con Davis, *Lacan and Narration: The Psychoanalytic Difference in Narrative Theory* (1983). Said argues that *The Interpretation* challenges certain novelistic conventions (such as sequentiality, "adequacy" of the text, finality of parts to whole) while it imitates others (see *Beginnings*, pp. 162–63). I believe that these challenges are already built into the novel and become conventional themselves in the late nineteenth- and early twentieth-century novel.

revision" is also a form of writing. But rather than distort and break down narrative connectedness as they do, it "creates" an "apparent connectedness" between elements of the dream. When secondary revision has been at work, Freud argues, the act of interpretation has already begun within the dream itself: "They are dreams which might be said to have been already interpreted once, before being submitted to waking interpretation" (490). Here the dream anticipates its own interpretation, lending to itself a deceptive "coherence," providing "links" where previous forms of the dream work inserted gaps. Freud explains this process as a revising or rewriting of the other psychic forces at work in dreams. And in the final dream concerned with the writing of *The Interpretation of Dreams*, Freud effectively rewrites and revises much of the material from the first two dreams that dealt with the same subject. Once again, the novel figures prominently in that process.

Freud's dream of his own dissection and his analysis of it strongly resemble the Botanical Monograph and the Autodidasker dreams in that they are all fundamentally concerned with the desires and dangers involved in authorship. Like the second of these dreams, the Self-dissection dream contains no books in its manifest content, but its dream thoughts and analysis are dominated by the plots of two novels. It is essentially linked to the earlier dreams, even on the manifest level, in that it shows Freud in the role of both surgeon and patient. Moreover, it is linked to them latently in the use Freud makes of the two novels he discovers in the dream thoughts, which form the basis of his interpretation of the dream. Freud moves within these three dreams from the simple expression of a desire to be a writer, to an identification of himself specifically with a novelist, to the appropriation of the plots of two novels as the basis for the interpretation and as the predecessor to his own book on dreams.

The Self-dissection dream is distinguished from the others by the lengthy, detailed account Freud gives of it. He recounts the first half of the dream as follows:

Old Brücke must have set me some task; STRANGELY ENOUGH, it related to a dissection of the lower part of my own body, my pelvis and legs, which I saw before me as though in the dissecting room, but without noticing their absence in myself and also without a trace of any gruesome feeling. Louise N. was standing beside me and doing the work with me. The pelvis had been eviscerated, and it was visible now in its superior, now in its inferior, aspect, the two being mixed together. Thick flesh-coloured protuberances (which, in the dream itself, made me think of haemorrhoids) could be seen. Something which lay over it and was like crumpled silver-paper had also to be carefully fished out. I was then once more in possession of my legs and was making my way through the town. But (being tired) I took a cab. To my astonishment the cab drove in through the door of a house, which opened and allowed it to pass along a passage which turned a corner at its end and finally led into the open air again. (452)

Freud goes on to describe in some detail a precarious journey through a changing landscape peopled by an Alpine guide, some exotic gypsylike figures, a girl, two reclining adults, and two sleeping children. It ends with Freud poised at an open window overlooking a chasm that he had to cross. He awakens, he says, "in a mental fright"(453).

Despite the length of this account, the analysis of the dream is uncharacteristically short, because, Freud explains, "in the present context I need only take up one point in it, which provides an example of astonishment in dreams, as exhibited in the interpolation *'strangely enough'*" (453). Despite all the very suggestive erotic material in the manifest content of the dream, Freud finds the strangeness of the experience of dreaming primary here. He cuts directly to a phrase he had used just prior to the dream in a conversation with Louise N., whom he identifies as "the lady who was assisting me in my job in the dream." She had asked to borrow a book from Freud, and he offered her Rider Haggard's romance novel *She*: "'A *strange* book, but full of hidden meaning', I began to explain to her; 'the eternal feminine, the immortality of our emotions'" (453).

This strange dream, then, has its direct source in Freud's description of a strange book. But the book does not seem strange at all as he describes it. Its resemblance to his own book is striking: *The Interpretation of Dreams* is designed to expose the "hidden meaning" that dreams are full of; it demonstrates the persistence of our wishes and emotions in our dreams—even those from infancy and especially those directed to the mother. What is astonishing about Freud's summary of the book is the familiarity of its contents, not their strangeness. The novel stands in as a substitute for the book that he is writing at the time of the dream. Whereas Freud does not explicitly acknowledge this substitution here, the conversation with Louise N. about the novel leads him directly to reflecting on his writing of *The Interpretation of Dreams*:

> Here she interrupted me: "I know it [*She*] already. Have you nothing of your own?"—"No, my own immortal works have not yet been written."—"Well, when are we to expect these so-called ultimate explanations of yours which you've promised even *we* shall find readable?" she asked, with a touch of sarcasm. At that point I saw that someone else was admonishing me through her mouth, and I was silent. I reflected on the amount of self-discipline it was costing me to offer the public even my book upon dreams—I should have to give away so much of my own private character in it. (453)

The conversation reveals important points about the dream and about Freud's view of the significance of *The Interpretation of Dreams* in it. First, the "work" of dissection which Louise N. was assisting in the dream is quite plainly Freud's writing of his "immortal work." As he describes it, the dissection scene resembles both a self-castration and a childbearing in which

Freud becomes a "She" and gives birth to this book that is "fished out" of his pelvis one sheet at a time. The journey through the narrow passage culminating with the images of the sleeping children in the next part of the dream repeats this birth fantasy. In writing this book, Freud gives birth to—conceives—himself. Second, he sees the writing of *The Interpretation of Dreams* as a response to the problem of "having nothing of your own"; it becomes a way of possessing (by giving birth to) himself. Third, writing this book represents an expense, a costly "giving away" of his "own private character." These features of *The Interpretation of Dreams* move it beyond a work of scientific analysis for Freud. As a conversion of the author's life into precious sheets of silver paper, it represents the exposure and the loss of his own character.

Since Freud is both destroying and remaking himself in *The Interpretation of Dreams*, he suffers in a state of strained ambivalence about completing it, as he reveals at this point in the analysis: "The dissection meant the self-analysis which I was carrying out, as it were, in the publication of this present book about dreams—a process which had been so distressing to me in reality that I had postponed the printing of the finished manuscript for more than a year" (477). Freud's presentation of these dreams suggests with increasing force that his book conceals a plot about its own genesis, a plot that is revealed by his analysis of the dreams he includes in it. The first dream I looked at clearly portrayed Freud's desire to be "the man who wrote" this "present book about dreams." The second dramatized his authorship as dangerous but invested with power and prestige if successfully managed with the appropriate balance of self-presentation and disguise. Now an element of suspense is introduced into the story of the creation of this book. The entire project seems at risk. The author's commitment to bringing the book into print has been undermined by his own anxieties over self-exposure; its costs seem too great, and the completion of the project must be postponed.

But this is not the end of the story. The pieces of this dream must be "related" to one another for the full significance to become clear. Freud explores the nature of his ambivalence and comes to a resolution when he analyzes the second half of the dream, his perilous journey over a shifting terrain. And the most important tool in that analysis is, once again, Freud's establishment of a connection between the details of his dream and the plots of novels—Rider Haggard's *She* (1887) and another Haggard novel he briefly introduces into the analysis, *Heart of the World* (1891). The novels form the link that ties the pieces of the dream together. The "plot" of Freud's authorship of this book is, strangely enough, "derived" from the plots of novels; in them, the royal road to the completion of his book becomes a perilous journey as well. The genesis of this book—together with its theoretical claims about the nature of the self—is based upon his discovery of the plot of his own dissection, the novel that emerges out of his own self-analysis.

While there were "further thoughts" about his conversation with Louise, Freud says, they "went too deep to become conscious" (454). These are the aspects of his character that he will not "give away" but will retain as his own. In place of that information, Freud offers the plots of the two Haggard novels from which "numerous elements of the dream were derived" (454). Increasingly, Freud's own life story becomes interchangeable with this novel of adventure and empire building. Freud tells us that both Haggard novels were concerned with "perilous journeys," both had women as the guides in those journeys, and both involved children who achieved what their fathers had failed to achieve. These details all strikingly correspond to the details of the dream and, more important, to the larger "plot" of Freud's family romance. But in a more immediate way, they are also of vital importance to Freud's purpose in writing this book: its pioneering role in his anticipated adventure of building the empire of psychoanalysis. This adventure has been recounted—like Robinson Crusoe's—by the narrator's censoring, condensing, and revising of his life to resemble a novel of risk and triumph.

Freud has not told us two other important facts about these novels which link them to his own story. They are both presented as documents written by one of the characters in the text, and the journeys they recount are occasioned by the death or disappearance of a father. Like *The Interpretation*, these books are autobiographical; also like it, they serve as evidence that a child had achieved something the father had not been able to achieve. In the case of *She*, the son manages to accomplish (at great risk to his own life) what his father—and generations before him—had failed to do: to reach the legendary, immortal mother of their family. That quest is not only a rite of passage for the son but also a replacement of the father. It is achieved through the production of a narrative that replaces and surpasses the text of the father's will—the very document that urges the quest at the outset of the novel. Freud ascribes the fear that wakes him to the emergence in the dream of a "fresh allusion to the strange novel" that "children may perhaps achieve what their father has failed to" (455). Like his dreams, and like the novels to which they refer, Freud's theory of dream interpretation will allude repeatedly to this fear.

Since Freud is both father and son, the fear works in two directions for him: he is reluctant to surpass and replace his own father and determined not to be surpassed by his own children. In his interpretation of the two previous dreams, Freud first pictures himself replacing his father as a patient, then dramatizes himself as a doctor who both endorses and surpasses a father figure ("a man to whose authority I am readiest to bow") and as a father concerned about the future of his children. Now, Freud expresses how strong an incentive the dream was for him to "reach the goal of my difficult journey" rather than "leave it to my children" (478). At this point, Freud himself is the father in the dream. The goal of his difficult journey is clearly identified with the "work" of self-dissection and analysis, with the writing of this "immortal work," with the book that Freud says in the 1908 preface had "a significance which I only grasped after I had completed it. It was, I found, a portion of my own self-analysis, my reaction to my father's death—that is to say, to the most important event, the most poignant loss, of a man's life" (xxvi).[23]

The writing of the book was a "reaction" to his father's death: it was a consequence of that death and was made possible by it. The novels are only the romantic accounts of this achievement by their fictional authors. But for Freud, the writing of "this present book" is literally the achievement itself, the "thing of his own" by which he makes himself an author and so compensates for the loss of his father. Freud could only realize the "story" of this book—and of his life—when he completed writing it. Only then could he discover that his life had a plot. *The Interpretation of Dreams* may be read as Freud's attempt to find that plot by writing it down. Beyond that, the production of the book is represented in this dream as Freud's performance of the family romance in his own body. The dissection scene provides an identification with the mother through the castration of himself and the removal of the father. The surgery he performs is both self-construction and self-mutilation, the effect of which is the achievement of what his father had failed to achieve: self-mastery by self-authorship. At the same time, it enables Freud to reach the legendary mother, as the novels dramatized. He gets through, that is, to the woman of his dreams (Louise N.) by giving her this immortal book, which both contains and replaces the father even as it gives birth to himself.

Freud addresses the larger implications of the relationship between dreams and authority in the first chapter, when he quotes K. F. Burdach's view that "sleep signifies an end of the authority of the self" (50). There Freud also referrs to F. W. Hildebrandt's theory that a dream "places us in another world and in quite another life story which in essentials has nothing to do with our real one" (9). Freud knew that our uninterpreted dreams

[23]Marianne Krull, *Freud and His Father* (1976), makes a case for the centrality to Freud's work of his conflicts with his father. Specifically and most important, those conflicts accounted for Freud's abandonment of the seduction theory in favor of the Oedipus complex, according to Krull. Krull believes Jakob Freud's "taboo" (in the form of the father's erotic life and his religious aspirations for his son) and Freud's reaction to it find expression in Freud's "big dream" (which Fliess advised him not to include in *The Interpretation*), and in the dream of his father's funeral (where Freud reads a sign requesting him to "close the eyes" of the dead man). See especially pp. 41–43 and 55–56. Sarah Kofman also argues for the importance to the writing of *The Interpretation* of a complicated oedipal relationship of Freud to his father: "Through the publication of this work, Freud was to achieve not only his infantile desire of immortality but also what his father, the Jew Jakob, had been unable to accomplish, so that his son had to accomplish it in his stead" (*The Enigma of Woman: Woman in Freud's Writings*, trans. Catherine Porter [1985], p. 23).

represent threats to the narrative coherence and control of our own experience. His emphasis on the dream work and the dream synthesis, however, made what seemed to be an undermining of our authority over ourselves into an opportunity for that authority to be exercised. One concern repeatedly expressed in the period was that if dreams were not visitations from some "divine agency" which necessitated our accommodation to some "master plot," they might be something even more disturbing—indications that at their foundations our lives make no sense at all. Perhaps neither our lives nor our dreams are leaves of a book but only random scraps of paper.

Freud responds to this concern with a strategy of dream interpretation which offers an alternative to the choice between divine inspiration and absolute meaninglessness. He would claim for the dreamer the responsibility to be both the author of the dream and the one who "assigns" it a meaning by telling it to another. Freud realized, however, that in order to make that claim he needed more than a mechanism to explain the origin of dreams. He also needed a "plot" to explain their significance. Freud's theory of dreams would, therefore, attempt to accomplish two sometimes conflicting goals: on one hand, it would connect the dream to the specifics of the dreamer's particular life experience, and on the other, it would relate that experience to a larger pattern, a plot with authority wider than the story of a particular self. That plot, which would come to be known as "the family romance," could be read as the writing of a new plot both to replicate and to transform a previous one. The new story of the unconscious is a "romance" that can be plotted out in the familiar terms already available to consciousness—a story in which the mind manifests the "symptoms" of "repression" taking place in a psychic "economy."

Two other dreams in *The Interpretation* deal directly with Freud's imposition of this plot on his life story and on the book that tells that story—the Hullthorn dream and the dream of the Bird-Beaked Figures. Freud juxtaposes the first of these immediately alongside the Self-dissection dream. The Hullthorn dream presents Freud crowded into a train car with several other people (including an English brother and sister) when his attention is arrested by some books: "A row of books were distinctly visible on a shelf on the wall. I saw "The Wealth of Nations" and "Matter and Motion" (by Clerk-Maxwell), a thick volume and bound in brown cloth. It seemed as though the books were sometimes mine and sometimes theirs" (456). The last sentence, "It seemed as though the books were sometimes mine and sometimes theirs," describes all the appearances of books in Freud's dreams and his analyses of them, from the dream of the Botanical Monograph onward. To whom the books belong, from whom they proceed, who is author and who owner, whether they are forgotten or remembered—these are the recurring concerns that Freud's dreams pose about the books within them. The inclusion in this dream of a copy of *The Wealth of Nations* is particularly significant since it is the central economic treatise of capitalist ideology, just as Freud wished *The Interpretation of Dreams* to be for psychoanalysis. Adam Smith defined human beings much as Freud did: as fundamentally ego-centric and acquisitive, driven by hidden forces ("the invisible hand") that they could not change but must master. *Matter and Motion* was the equiv-alently dominant text in physics at the time. It defines "work" as the dis-placement of matter by force, whereas *The Wealth of Nations* describes work in terms of personal production and property. For Freud, the dream work is an economy of forces the dreamer could master and a property she or he could own. His book "appropriates" these other master texts by appropriat-ing their diction and by making their disciplines subject to his own. "Some-times," Freud says, these books of "theirs" were "mine." Sometimes, that is, his diagnostic theory is an economics of the psyche; sometimes it is a dy-namics of the psyche; sometimes it is the novel of his life. But in all these cases his theory is necessarily and fundamentally *his* book—a text that in-cludes among its stories the story of his writing it.

"While I was writing the dream down," Freud says in his analysis, "a new piece of it occurred to me, which my memory had tried to pass over" (456). In that piece remembered only in the act of writing, Freud intervenes in an argument between the English couple. He assures them that a particular book whose authorship they are disputing was in fact written by Schiller. But Freud makes a mistake in translating his comments into English, and he accidentally says that the book is "from" Schiller rather than "by" him—a mistake he immediately realizes and corrects. Since *translation* is the key word that Freud uses to describe the dream work in the opening to chapter 6 of *The Interpretation*, it is no mistake that the error he makes in the dream is one of translation. Freud is concerned that dreams be properly translated. But he is also concerned that the dream be given a plot, that it fit into the chain of events in the story of an individual life. In pursuit of the plot of this dream, Freud is led by way of the translation mistake to a pun on the German word for "pious" (*fromm*). He then goes on to interpret this dream about books as "analogous" to a "confession" of impiety by one of his patients, who admitted to harboring "hostile impulses against his father" and his father's "orders" (458–59). The dream is, of course, Freud's confession as well.

Freud's dream recalls to him this patient's memory of "a scene of early childhood in which the child" had "forced his way into his parents' bedroom and been turned out of it by his father's orders" (459). Freud evokes a primal scene reported to him by one of his patients and calls it analogous to the scene in his own dream. He suggests that his dream and its plot possess a universality beyond his own particular life story. This strategy of identifying himself with one of his patients also enables him once more to be both doctor and patient—author and character—in his own story. But the more important point is that Freud again joins the idea of authorship with hostility against the father and access to the mother; his writing is a way to "force" himself into the forbidden territory of the father. It is a replacement of the father, as it had been in the dreams of the Botanical Monograph, Auto-didasker, and the Self-dissection. Freud's book has a plot that tells the story of how he compensates for being fatherless. His book enables him to be both "by" and "from" himself, to be his own father and mother, to repeat and to originate.[24]

The last of Freud's dreams introduced into *The Interpretation of Dreams* consolidates the issues of authority and power I have noted in the previous dreams. This dream is the final point in the "dream plot" of Freud's text, and it performs an important role in that plot. The dream of the Bird-Beaked Figures is Freud's most explicit representation of his own family romance, and his analysis of it extends the significance of the dream beyond his own case and those of his patients to the culture in general. He includes the dream presumably as an example of an "anxiety dream." It is composed of a single scene that suggests that his dream journeys have all led to this anxious moment when his mother arrives in his own room: "I saw *my beloved mother, with a peculiarly peaceful, sleeping expression on her features, being carried into the room by two (or three) people with birds' beaks and laid upon the bed*. I awoke in tears and screaming, and interrupted my parents' sleep" (583). The effect of the dream as Freud describes it is as important as the dream itself. The power of his own voice interrupted his parents' sleep as well as his own. Even the primitive articulation of the dreamer in the form of a scream is a deployment of power, a taking over the sleep of the parents. Moreover, the dream brought his "beloved mother" out of the room where she had been sleeping and "into the room" where the dreamer was. It is difficult to imagine a more explicitly expressed wish for the mother than this picture of her being brought into the room of the dreamer and "laid upon the bed." The vacillation in the dream account between the numbers "two" and "three" expresses the dynamic of the oedipal triangle, especially since the father is not mentioned in the scene. He is and is not present in it, counted but not named. Freud did not seek any more esoteric meaning in the dream than what seems evident on its surface. He simply and discreetly attributed his anxiety over the dream to the "repression" of an "evidently sexual craving

[24]Lukacher sees Freud's development of the idea of the primal scene as a conflation of philosophy, literature, and psychoanalysis since it makes a truth claim that is constituted by an act of recollection which cannot be absolutely distinguished from an act of invention: "The primal scene is a strategic answer to the dilemma of a critical discourse that on the one hand maintains the impossibility of moving beyond interpretation to a discourse of truth but on the other hand has not forgotten that the burden of the truth continues to make itself felt" (*Primal Scenes*, p. 25). He cites the Rat-Man case as showing psychoanalysis to be "closer to a poetics than to therapy" because the provision of a unified narrative seems more important than the patient's recollection of the scene—more important than even his cure (pp. 331–34).

that had found appropriate expression in the visual content of the dream"
(584). But this last dream in Freud's dream plot, in which the dreamer is
united with the mother, expresses yet another desire having to do with
Freud's authorship and its repressed textual content.

For the purposes of the dream plot, the most obvious significant omission
here is the father. Of equal importance is the omission of a book. But both
father and book appear prominently in the analysis of the dream, one implicitly and the other explicitly. Freud's father is, in fact, silently contained
within the book. Freud's first comment on the dream is that its images were
"derived" from illustrations of the Bible, specifically from the Philippson
edition. Ernest Jones reveals an important fact about this edition of the Bible
which Freud does not mention here: although Freud owned the first volume
of this Bible as a child, he did not receive the second volume until his thirty-
fifth birthday, when his father gave it to him. This book, which contains both
pictures and text, recalls another book his father had given him, the last book
in Freud's interpretation of the dream of the Botanical Monograph, the book
his father had "handed over" to him "to destroy." Here, the dream expresses
an erotic desire to replace the father alongside the mother, and in this it
corresponds to the scenes of replacing the father in the other dreams. But
this dream also serves as a culmination of the "narrative plot" of *The Interpretation of Dreams* because it replaces the book Freud's father had given him
with the text of the dream itself. At this point, the father's name does not
even bear mentioning, and the destruction of his book is complete. Freud
has translated the pictures of his father's Bible in this dream into the words
of his own book.[25]

The book implicitly contained within this last dream also recalls another
in Freud's dream plot: the two volumes of that first novel Freud had read as a
child. The novel ended, as he recalled it, with the hero screaming out in his
madness the names of the women who had brought him the most happiness
and sorrow in his life.[26] One of those women, Freud recalls, was "the mother
who gives life," and his interpretation of the dream associates the dream with
the time in his own life "when I was six years old and was given my first
lessons by my mother" (204–5). As he awakens from the dream of this
woman, Freud represents himself calling out, summoning his mother into
his room. With her he summons the essential lessons and images of his life
story into the account he will make of these dreams in *The Interpretation of*

[25]Jakob Freud's inscription in the second volume begins with these words: "My dear
son . . . the Spirit of the Lord began to move you and said to you: Go, read in My Book that I
have written, and there will be opened to you the sources of wisdom, of knowledge and
understanding" (Krull, *Freud and His Father*, pp. 160–61).

[26]Grinstein has shown that this nameless novel was Charles Kingsley's historical romance
Hypatia. See *On Sigmund Freud's Dreams*, pp. 179–92.

Dreams. Most important, the book that his dream account replaces here is Holy Writ. It is the sacred text of the culture which the "text" of Freud's final dream supplants. Freud's own family romance is "derived" from and replaces the book his father gave him; it appropriates and transcribes the culture's religious expressions of the dream into "scientific" terms; and it provides for Freud the story of himself as the man who wrote something valuable and memorable. It gives him a voice of his own which has the authority of a sacred text.

One reason Freud is regarded as the principal scientist of the dream for the nineteenth century is that in its very form *The Interpretation of Dreams* responded to the period's anxious and deep-seated crisis of authority in the most effective way. It established a "solid relation" between the making of a book out of an individual's dream experience and the possession and use of that object as a means of personal authority and power. Freud took as his subject the commonest but the most mysterious and confusing kind of experience, and he managed to make it into a coherent story integrally connected with waking life. In the final chapter of *The Interpretation of Dreams* Freud even claims to have mastered all his competitors' explanations by the "powers of exposition." "I have been able to find a justification for all these mutually contradictory opinions at one point or other of my complicated thesis," he says, "and to show that they had lighted upon some portion of the truth" (588). *Their* partial truths have been made aspects of *his* complex theory by means of his expository and narrative power. He has occupied their territory with the force of his words and turned it into the setting for his own life story.

Freud described the relationship of psychoanalysis and fiction writing as a "partisanship," and he described his interest in "the way in which storytellers make use of dreams" as "intense" (*Delusion and Dream*, 27). The intensity of Freud's own partisanship with novelists is quite clearly demonstrated in the dream plot of his own great theoretical work on dream interpretation. In the remaining chapters of *Dreams of Authority*, I investigate the intensity of that partisanship by tracing the same kind of dream plot in many of the most important novels of the nineteenth century. By focusing on a set of first-person narratives from the gothic, autobiographical, and detective traditions, I point out how these novelistic forms and the dreams they contain served as sites for the production of different discourses for representing the unconscious. One of the primary objectives of the novel during the nineteenth century was to invent new fictions of personal authority to replace the structures of divine and social authority which were rapidly being dismantled. Since dreams present themselves as irruptions of personal and social material that is inherently antiauthoritarian, inherently opposed to all discourses of mastery, they were strategic places for this objective to be pursued and implemented.

Before turning to those novels, I briefly consider three literary dreams that have achieved virtual mythic status in English literature, which present in miniature the issues with which the rest of the book will deal in more detail. In the poet-dreamer of *The Prelude*, the dreaming child of *Alice in Wonderland*, and the nightmare-ridden old man of *A Christmas Carol*, the fundamental psychological insights developed in the nineteenth century about the significance of dreams, and the discourses in which they were conceived, are shadowed forth in concentrated form. These texts demonstrate how deeply certain implicit theories of the mind had penetrated into the popular unconscious and how widely they were circulated. In every case, the dreams foreground the problem of their own representation, and the dreamers' responses to their dreams manifest the very difficulties of converting a dream into a "text" that will prevail throughout the period. Wordsworth's Arab dream is the only poetic text I attend to here, and my reading is intended to define and substantiate fundamental differences between the treatment of dream experience in poetry from that of prose fiction in the period. Not coincidentally, the Arab dream was provoked by the dreamer's reading of a novel, a novel that also features prominently in the dream. In the first-person novels I examine in the remainder of the book, the narrators tell their own life stories to us when they tell us their dreams. Those dreams map out a hidden plot that reveals how narrative privilege was achieved or sacrificed, and they invariably express a form of the same ambivalence that Freud expressed in his "autobiographical novel" *The Interpretation of Dreams*: the desire to resist the imposition of master plots from an authority outside and the conflicting desire to surrender to the sense of order and meaning that such plots provide.

Poetry and Prose in Wordsworth's Arab Dream

> it shall be my pride
> That I have dared to tread this holy ground,
> Speaking no dream, but things oracular.
>   —*The Prelude* XIII:251–53

Comparing the dream work to the writing of a poem, Freud declared that, like poems, the productions of the dream work "are not made with the intention of being understood" (*Interpretation of Dreams*, 341). Rather, they are acts of mystification and disguise whose meanings are intended to remain fragmentary and ambiguous, rich in association, elusive, compressed, distorted. He went on to describe dream interpretation as a demystification and decoding of that hieroglyphic language, analogous to the substitution of the more specific and commonplace language of prose for the mysterious, concrete language of poetry. This association of the dream work with poetic creation is supported by the traditional identification of the poet with the dreamer and, more specifically, by the visionary quality of much nineteenth-century English poetry—stretching from the Romantics to Tennyson to the Pre-Raphaelites. Bakhtin echoes Freud's view when he speaks generally of poetic speech as a form of what he calls the "authoritative word," a discourse with which he claims the novel, as a "dialogic form," is at odds. The authoritative word, he says, is a "prior discourse" that is "given (it sounds) in lofty spheres." "The authoritative word demands that we acknowledge it, that we make it our own; it binds us, quite independent of any power it might have to persuade us internally; we encounter it with its authority already fused to it." Just as Freud had done, Bakhtin associates such "hieratic language" with poetic genres, opposing it to the more "authentic," historical language of prose in the novel: "At the time when major divisions of the poetic genres were developing under the influence of the unifying, centralizing, centripetal forces of verbal-ideological life, the novel—and those artistic-prose genres that gravitate toward it—was being historically shaped by the current of decentralizing, centrifugal forces."[27]

The generalization is problematic, particularly in such cases as Wordsworth's *Prelude*, a text that exists on the boundary between poetry and prose, seemingly designed to occupy both generic positions. But much of the poem is concerned with these very matters—with identifying its form, its purpose, and its source—and therefore, it provides an appropriate place to explore the relationship between the discourse of dreams and the discourses of poetry and prose. In the first book of *The Prelude*, Wordsworth identifies the presentation of "the story of my life" as the object of the poem (639).[28] But his doubts about his ability to write that story, his anxieties about the "vague longing haply bred by want of power" to accomplish this task (239), lead him to take consolation in "a voice / That flowed along my dreams." That voice, he says, was not generated from within himself but was "sent" to him from nature (273–74). These two impulses—the narrative impulse to tell his life as a story in his own voice, on the one hand, and the lyrical impulse to listen to and be spoken through by the "authoritative," rapturous voice of nature on the other—contend throughout the poem. The voices of "native prose" and "numerous verse" come into direct conflict in the account Wordsworth gives in book V of the Arab dream, which, significantly, concerns itself primarily with the preservation of a book of poetry and a book of prose (200).

[27]Bakhtin, "Discourse in the Novel," pp. 342, 272–73.
[28]William Wordsworth, *The Prelude*, in *Wordsworth: Poetical Works*, ed. Thomas Hutchinson (London: Oxford University Press, 1975), cited by book and line number in the text. I have used the 1850 text except where noted.

Wordsworth's characterization of the dream as a voice sent to him from some force external to himself is a benign version of the prevailing contemporary demonic conception of dreams.[29] Almost invariably, the dreams Romantic poets tell are concerned with the source of the dreamer's authority and voice, and they characteristically assume the shape of a demonic possession. Shelley refers in *Alastor*, for example, to enchantment by the "fierce fiend of a distempered dream" (225) and of the veiled dream-maiden's voice that speaks in that dream "like the voice of his [the dreamer's] own soul" (153), yet profoundly distinct from it. In "Kubla Khan" and *Christabel*, Coleridge portrays the dream as a possession, as the irrecoverable and irresistible song of a demon lover. Keats's "Belle Dame sans Merci" shows the dreamer enthralled and seduced by his dream, left "ailing" and powerless by it.

The "ineffable" and "incommunicable" voices that speak in these dreams consistently wield a power over the dreamer, often silencing the dreamer's own voice. Christabel, for example, sees in Geraldine a "sight to dream, of not to tell" (I:253); their dreamlike encounter becomes a spell cast by Geraldine which is the "lord of thy [Christabel's] utterance," captivating her by permitting her "no power to tell" what happened to her (I:268, 473). The literal dream related by the bard in the poem portrays this silencing of Christabel as a strangling by her mysterious night visitor. In *The Fall of Hyperion* (the poem Keats subtitled *A Dream*, which is the most explicit exploration of the relationship between the poet's dreams and his or her authority to speak), the dreamer is struck dumb when he tries to respond to the challenge issued by the mysterious voice that addresses him in the dream:

> I had no words to answer, for my tongue,
> Useless, could find about its roofed home
> No syllable of a fit majesty
> To make rejoinder to Moneta's mourn.
>   (228–31)

Rather than seek to decipher and master the voices in the dream, these poems seem to value their majestic, mystified language. They consistently resist interpretation or translation into common speech. Appropriately, therefore, "Kubla Khan," *Christabel*, and *The Fall of Hyperion*—the romantic poems in which dreams are most important—remain fragments. They are inconclusive, unmastered, unresolved even by their authors. Since the dreamers in these poems never wake from their dreams, the dominant voices speaking in the poems are not those of the dreamers but those that are "sent"

[29]See Alethea Hayter, *Opium and the Romantic Imagination* (1970) for an analysis of the role of dream in romantic poetry.

to them in their dreams. "Poesy," as Keats says in *Hyperion* (the same poem in which the poet is implored to speak his dream), does not dispel the demonic power of dreams; it only imitates their mystifications, responding to their "sable charm" and "enchantment" with another "fine spell of words" (9–11).

The Arab dream presents itself as an exception to this pattern. The dream is told in apparent completeness, and it is contained within the section of the story of the poet's life aptly titled "Books." Throughout, the dream remains deeply ambiguous about the value accorded to its books as preservers of human experience against the flood of time. The Arab's obsession in the dream springs from the absolute necessity of saving the books from some impending deluge. Yet he seeks to accomplish that end by burying the books. In its attempt to preserve the texts from erasure, this plan merely substitutes one form of erasure for another.[30] These seemingly contradictory impulses within the dream parallel Wordsworth's contending attitudes toward authority: he intends to tell his own story in the poem and yet he desires to submit his own powers to the voice that nature sends him in his dreams.[31]

In addition to being a problematic dream about books, placed in the center of a book about the poet's life, the dream itself is directly provoked by the dreamer's reading of still another book. That book is *Don Quixote*, a text distinguished not only as "the famous history of the errant night / Rendered by Cervantes" but also as one of the first great European novels. Even more to the point, the central issue of this novel—like many that would come after it—is the cost of the desire to live in a world of dreams: the errant knight is destroyed because, like Scott's Waverley, he fails to distinguish between the lyrical world of chivalric ballads and romances and the more prosaic world of human history.

The Arab dream, then, provides a case in which the languages of dream, poetry, and novel are placed in complex relation—in a context in which the author of the poem is continually expressing his own uncertainty about the

---

[30]In Geoffrey H. Hartman's reading of book V, Wordsworth "continually displaces or interprets apocalypse as akedah" (*Wordsworth's Poetry* [1971], pp. 225–38); that is, he distorts experiences that separate his own imagination from nature to make them appear as if they bind the two together. This displacement parallels the paradoxical "displacement" of and surrender to authority with which I am concerned here.

[31]Richard Onorato points to the importance of the issue of authority in book V when he speaks of the events in this book, especially the "impending revelation" of the Arab dream, as Wordsworth's attempt to interpret a death in his own past, to come to terms with and replace the loss of a paternal authority and guide (see *The Character of the Poet: Wordsworth in "The Prelude"* [1971], pp. 373–77). Harold Bloom argues that this anxiety haunts the poet's whole career and is specifically directed toward Wordsworth's literary fathers. According to Bloom, the use of memory in Wordsworth's poetry is "a composite defense, a defense against time, decay, the loss of divinating power, and so finally a defense against death, whose other name is John Milton" (*Poetry and Repression*, p. 53). Both critics see this impulse in Wordsworth as what Bloom calls a "primal poetic urge for *divination*" (p. 80).

value of his task and his anxiety about taking authority over the story of his life. As book V of *The Prelude* begins, the poet is questioning his poetic enterprise. Given the cataclysms of history, can the image of human experience be housed in "shrines so frail" as books? Should they be? What will become of "the consecrated works of Bard and Sage" in times of cultural destruction and disorder?

> Where would they be? Oh! why hath not the Mind
> Some element to stamp her image on
> In nature somewhat nearer to her own?
> Why, gifted with such powers to send abroad
> Her spirit, must it lodge in shrines so frail?
>
> (V:45–49)

The Arab dream is presented in book V as a response to these questions. The answer it provides for Wordsworth seems to be that he should bury his own voice. He consequently will define the poet in book V as the one who effectively surrenders to the transcendent voice of nature, rather than speak the "weak words" of the mortal man who expresses "what is already written in the hearts / Of all that breathe" (186–87). Instead of rendering an account of his own particular life in his own words, then, Wordsworth's real theme has a grander scope, to utter "what we are and what we may become" in a miraculous revelation (220). His theme is the story not of himself but of "nature's self, which is the breath of God, / Or His pure Word by miracle revealed" (221–22). What is "peculiar to myself," Wordsworth says, "let that remain / Where still it works, though hidden from all search / Among the depths of time" (196–98). The dream represents Wordsworth's desire—like Quixote's—to be lost in sacred, lyrical time, rather than to take possession of his own peculiar experience in history.[32]

The identity of the voice that speaks in the dream is also put into question by an important variant in the two texts of *The Prelude*. The 1805 edition attributes the dream not to the poet but to a friend who told him about the dream. The 1850 text speaks of the dream in the first person, as if it

[32]Hartman regards the "dangers of confrontation and engulfment" of the poet's own imagination as restricted to "the 'sacred' space of the dream." "The poet himself," Hartman maintains, "stands firmly in nature and narrative" (p. 227). To claim that the poet stands firmly in narrative and that engulfment is a possibility only inside the dream seems to me to be insufficiently aware of Hartman's own insistence that acts of displacement (between what he calls experiences of separation and those of union) permeate the entire poem. J. Hillis Miller also sees the displacements of this dream as consistent with those that characterize *The Prelude* as a whole; he reads the dream as an allegory of the displacement of language by natural signs and the collapse of differences between them ("The Stone and the Shell: The Problem of Poetic Form in Wordsworth's Dream of the Arab," in *Untying the Text: A Post-Structuralist Reader*, ed. Robert Young (1981), pp. 244–60).

occurred to the poet himself. This equivocation repeats the equivocation about authority and voice that operates throughout book V and within the content of the dream as well. The issue is further complicated by the un-likelihood that this dream was dreamed by either the poet or his friend, since it so closely resembles one of the dreams related by Adrien Baillet in his *Vie de Descartes* (1691).[33] But this possibility only makes Wordsworth's use of the dream and his changes in its presentation more interesting. The poet's take-over of the dream in the later text would seem to indicate a development toward owning the material of the dream and giving voice to it. Yet even in the first-person expression of the dream, the dreamer describes himself as passive. He does not produce the dream but is subject to it, "yielding" himself to its power. "Sleep seized me," he says, "and I passed into a dream" (70). This expression of the dream as a taking control of the dreamer has special significance here because the poet passes into the dream immediately after reading the novel that tells the story of the knight who also yielded his entire existence to a dream and who failed to distinguish between poetry and reality. That failure finally cost him his life. But the poet seems to have missed this point. He identifies himself with Don Quixote's mission both in the dream and in its recollection. Even before the dream, at the moment when he closes the novel and begins to muse "on poetry and geometric truth" and on "their high privilege of lasting life," the poet shares the errant knight's confusion between text and world, regarding both as eternal and indestructible, invulnerable to time, "from all internal injury exempt" (67–68).

The dream is presented in book V as a "haunting" on this very subject (56). In it the dreamer finds himself lost in a desert waste when an Arab appears, bearing two objects: a common stone and a shell of "surpassing brightness" (79–80). The dreamer had hoped that the man would be a guide to lead him out of the desert, but instead, the strange objects carried by the Arab present the dreamer with another problem of meaning:

> and while yet
> I looked and looked, self-questioned what this freight
> Could mean, the Arab told me that the stone
> (To give it in the language of the dream)
> Was "Euclid's Elements"; and "This," said he,
> "Is something of more worth"; and at the word
> Stretched forth the shell, so beautiful in shape,
> In colour so resplendent, with command
> That I should hold it to my ear.
>
> (83–92)

[33]On the implications of the literary origins of this dream, see Onorato, pp. 369–70; Timothy Bahti, "Figures of Interpretation, the Interpretation of Figures: A Reading of Wordsworth's 'Arab Dream,'" *Studies in Romanticism* 18 (1979): 608–9.

The poet makes it clear that the explanation of these objects is given "in the language of the dream," and this announcement is important to the explanation of the dream as well. It reveals the poet's desire for the dream to remain as a kind of sacred utterance, as a voice sent to the dreamer and speaking through him, as a mysterious guide who makes "commands" that the dreamer carries out. Only the Arab's words are reproduced in the dream account; he speaks, he interprets, he possesses the things that he identifies as books. The dreamer merely wonders, listens, obeys, follows, prays, and is finally abandoned—left without access to the valorized texts that remain the "twofold charge" of the Arab (134).

The Arab "declared" to the dreamer that his intention is "to bury those two books," which we may regard as the books of science and religion, the body and the spirit, or prose and poetry (102). The two books, it may be said, speak in very different languages: the first in the language of men, the second in the language of the gods. And of the two, the latter is clearly preferred. To give it in the language of the dream, the shell is "something" that is "of more worth." This valuation is quite evident in the descriptions of the two books. The book of the stone is *Euclid's* book: it is written by a man, and it speaks to practical human concerns, connecting "man to man by purest bond / Of nature" according to the 1805 text (104), connecting them by "reason" in the 1850 edition (105). The shell represents an altogether different kind of text: "The other that was a god, yea many gods, / Had voices more than all the winds"(106–07). In other words, the two books represent the contending attitudes toward dream experience in the nineteenth century: a secular, scientific one that seeks to explain the dream and give the dreamer power over it, and a supernatural, demonic one that seeks to mystify the dream "with power / To exhilarate the spirit" of the dreamer (108). While the two positions are in constant tension within *The Prelude*, here the poem firmly allies itself with the latter. The dreamer is commanded to listen only to the divine book, not to the book of man. In that more mysterious book, he hears "an unknown tongue" that "in passion uttered" a "loud prophetic blast of harmony" foretelling the destruction of the children of the earth by an imminent deluge. Ironically, the source of the danger that threatens these texts and demands their burial is itself one of the texts—the divine book, the book of poetry. Significantly, it is at the moment when the dreamer indicates his "desire" to "cleave to this man" who goes to bury the books, when he "prayed / To share his enterprise," that the Arab suddenly appears also to be the deluded dreamer Don Quixote.

> He, to my fancy, had become the knight
> Whose tale Cervantes tells; yet not the knight,
> But was an Arab of the desert too;
> Of these was neither, and was both at once.
>   (122–25)

This confusion between the dreamer, the one who buries the books, and the novelistic character who was lost in his dreams reveals the central desire in the dream to be a longing for escape, for the burial of the dreamer's own "peculiar" voice in the language of the "unknown tongue" spoken by "many gods."

The dream ends with the poet looking back to the "glittering light" of the deluge that pursued the Arab, fleeing with his two books the same deluge that was prophesied by the many gods of the book of poetry. In a direct echo of that ending, book V of *The Prelude* concludes with the poet praising the "glittering verse" of "mighty Poets" because it contains a "visionary power" that is "embodied in the mystery of words" (591–97). The implicit argument of book V seems to accord with Freud's claim that neither dreams nor poems are made with the intention of being understood. They are made, rather, to remain as "mysteries," presenting themselves as "objects recognized, / In flashes, and with glory not their own" (604–5).[34] Wordsworth's dream of the Arab expresses his preference for the dream to be spoken by a voice sent to him over the terror of being lost in a wilderness with no divine guide, even if that choice means he must suppress his own peculiar voice.[35]

Either alternative represents a terror, as the poet seems to recognize when he awakens from his dream:

> I waked in terror,
> And saw the sea before me, and the book,
> In which I had been reading, at my side.
> (138–40)

The sea and the book represent the two choices with which the dream confronts the dreamer—engulfment by the poetic voices of unknown tongues or self-authorship by the secular, demystifying language of the novel he had been reading.[36] But it is "the sea" that lies before the poet's gaze

[34]Cynthia Chase reads book V as another form of opposition: "an opposition between reading and books, and a valuing of texts for their very resistance to reading, their persistence as accidents that elude our reading" (p. 564). According to her view, this opposition between intuitive reading and systematic, rigorous interpretation finally breaks down in the book, leading Wordsworth to value writing as a form of mute disfigurement ("Accidents of Disfiguration," *Studies in Romanticism* 18 [1979]: 547–66).

[35]Bahti sees a tension in book V between nature's attribution of a rhetorical activity to man and man's attribution of a rhetorical activity to nature, alternatives which Bahti believes we must understand as "a paradox or, more properly, an enigma" in the poem ("Figures of Interpretation," p. 622). Rather than a choice between alternative sources of authority, then, Bahti sees book V as "a leveling and involvement of any transcendental author(ity) and script within the common problematic of rhetoric" (p. 622). The sacred language of "enigma" and mystery which the poem so richly partakes in, however, seems to me to elevate at least as much as it levels the "problematic of rhetoric" dramatized in *The Prelude*.

[36]The miraculously "revealed" word of God into which Wordsworth's own peculiar voice disappears in book V corresponds to Bakhtin's characterization of the "authoritative word" (see "Discourse in the Novel," pp. 272–73 and 342–46).

here, and "the book" that remains closed at his side. The scene repeats the gesture of passivity which brought on the dream at the outset: "While listlessly I sat, and, having closed / The book, had turned my eyes toward the wide sea" (63–64). Wordsworth praises poets for their expression of "shadowy things" that are "not their own" (see 595–605). When he praises poets as "dreamers," as "forgers of daring tales," it is because they "make *our* wish, *our* power, *our* thought" into "*a* deed, / *An* empire, *a possession*" (523–528, my emphasis). Poets are "in league," he says, with some "great might" (527); they forge what may have been "ours" into possessions that are no longer our own, into books that remain closed to reason, written in the unknown tongues sent through their dreams. Therefore, it becomes the poet's "pride," as he puts it in book XIII, to distinguish between his own dreams and the prophetic utterances of himself as poet. "It shall be my pride," he says, "that I have dared to tread this holy ground / Speaking no dream, but things oracular" (250–52). Like any good poet, the dreamer of Wordsworth's *Prelude* refuses the book and the language of science, preferring instead to tell his dream in the mysterious voice of the oracle.

Dreams of Power in *Alice in Wonderland*

> I do hope it's my dream and not the Red King's! I don't like belonging to another person's dream.
>
>   —Alice

As the Arab dream demonstrates, a dream may either possess or be possessed by the dreamer. If the poetry of the nineteenth century was oriented toward the former notion, its prose was directed toward the latter. Two of the most enduring mythic figures of the period are dreamers whose dreams are fundamentally concerned with these alternatives. Lewis Carroll's dream-child Alice dreams of the adult world as a chaotic, crazy realm, but also as a territory she wishes to enter and possess as her own. Dickens's Scrooge turns that dream wish around. He dreams of his childhood innocence and desires to repossess certain features of it in his old age. Common to both dreamers is the wish to bring the experience of childhood together with that of adulthood, to see life whole, to transform what threatens to be disjointed and meaningless into a coherent narrative rather than a series of timeless moments, as Wordsworth sought in *The Prelude*. Scrooge and Alice want to take possession of time, and they begin to do so by taking control of the dreams that threaten to dominate them. In both cases, this take-over is an empowering and curative act for the dreamer, as the endings of their two dream narratives reveal. Both end with the dreamers' accession to power, an achievement that is made possible when they translate their mysterious dreams into a language of political or economic mastery.

Alice in Wonderland (1865) and *Through the Looking-Glass* (1872) both question whether Alice "belongs" to another person's dream or the dream belongs to her. The answer is contained in Alice's response to her dreams when she awakens from them and takes verbal control over them. The Alice books are often read as political or psychoanalytic allegories.[37] But their politics and psychology are both joined in their concern with the power of language. In her dreams, Alice is repeatedly faced with linguistic challenges—contests of storytelling, riddle guessing, remembering a rhyme, interpreting a confusing text, identifying herself, or simply engaging in an argument. These contests usually take place between Alice and some figure of political authority, such as a king, a queen, a duchess, or a judge. And the power of those figures invariably rests in their mastery of some verbal maneuver or trick. The connection between the exercise of power and the control of language is made quite explicit to Alice in her conversation with the masterful figure called Humpty Dumpty. "When *I* use a word," he tells Alice, "it means just what I choose it to mean—neither more nor less." "The question is," Alice responds, "whether you *can* make words mean so many different things." "The question is," Humpty Dumpty corrects her, "which is to be master—that's all."[38]

Language is a game of political mastery, and it is presented to Alice in her dreams as just that. When she is told by "the chorus of voices" that she is better off saying nothing because language is too valuable to squander, being worth "a thousand pounds a word," she responds by thinking to herself, "I shall dream about a thousand pounds tonight, I know I shall" (217–18). At this point, Alice begins to acknowledge that the value of language and the mastery it offers to the speaker are the subjects of her dream and the basis of her identity. But it has taken her a long time to realize this. A word is worth a thousand pounds, and as Freud would quite plainly say in *The Interpretation of Dreams*, the pictorial images of any dream will grant the dreamer a purchase on them only when they are converted into the currency of language. The images of Alices's dream are constantly trying to silence her, and as long as she says nothing, she will be powerless to own or disown those images. This is what she dreams about, and what many of the dispossessed dreamers

[37]For a sampling of the range of such interpretations, see the critical anthologies *Aspects of Alice*, ed. Robert S. Phillips (1971), *Lewis Carroll Observed*, ed. Edward Guiliano (1976). See also Daniel Bivona, "Alice the Child-Imperialist and the Games of Wonderland," *Nineteenth-Century Literature* 41 (September 1986): 143–71.

[38]Lewis Carroll, *The Annotated Alice*, ed. Martin Gardner (1960), p. 269, hereafter cited in the text. See Patricia Meyer Spacks, "Logic and Thought in *Through the Looking-Glass*", in *Aspects of Alice*, ed. Phillips, pp. 267–78, on the importance of language in Carroll's dream worlds.

in nineteenth-century fiction dream about. When Freud described his method of dream interpretation as the "translation" of the images of our dreams
into language, he also described the task set before Alice in her confusing
dream of Wonderland.

Early in *Wonderland*, Alice feels as if she is lost in a book of fairy tales. This
idea leads her to express an important wish: "There ought to be a book
written about me, that there ought! And when I grow up, I'll write one" (59).
Being grown up is defined here as writing a book about oneself, as opposed
to being "in" a book written by someone else. And if *Alice in Wonderland* can
be construed as a dream about growing up, it construes growing up as taking
authority over one's own life story, as writing a book "about me." Alice's
escapes from certain verbal and physical structures form the central episodes
of her dream.[39] She is continually being imprisoned in and breaking out of a
room or a house or a joke or a poem in which she does not fit. This pattern
also forms the larger structure of the text. The whole adventure begins when
Alice drifts off to sleep because the book that her sister was reading had no
pictures and no conversation. Alice escapes from the mastery of this text by
"falling" into the images of her own dream and then arising to tell her own
story. When Alice wakes to recount that story to her sister, she provokes the
sister to dream the very same dream. But the sister's version of it ends with a
significant difference—a vision of Alice as a grown woman telling "many a
strange tale" of "the dream of Wonderland long ago" to a group of children,
"remembering her own child-life" (164). The dream becomes the book "that
you have just been reading about," a book of Alice's own which replaces the
one that was being read to her (162). In *Wonderland*, Alice moves from a child
being told a story to a young woman telling her own story, re-membering the
images of "her own child-life." She converts her dream into a book about
herself.

The episode within the story itself which most explicitly dramatizes this
point is the Mad Tea Party.[40] There, the sleeping Dormouse is clearly
intended as an image of Alice. Like her, the Dormouse is both present at the
party and absent from it because it is asleep and dreaming throughout the
event. The significance of the episode lies in its confrontation of Alice with a
narrative problem: time has been "killed" here; it is always the same time,
always the present. There can be no progress, only eternal repetition and
confusion. As Freud would later indicate, this sense of the eternal present is
a characteristic of dreams. The temporal confusion springs in part from the

---

[39]In "Alice's Journey to the End of the Night," Donald Rackin reads *Wonderland* as a subversion of logic and ordinary language, an exposure of the artficiality and inadequacy of linguistic
constructs. Yet, Rackin argues, the book finally affirms those inadequate constructs as necessary
for the preservation of sanity and identity (in *Aspects of Alice*, ed. Phillips).

[40]Spacks claims that language is a theme underlying virtually all the episodes of *Through the
Looking-Glass*.

absence of narrative time. The dream expresses its logical connections not by sequence but by simultaneity and juxtaposition, combining recent memories with old ones. The task of the dreamer, therefore, is to reconstruct the narrative connections that have thereby been obscured in the dream work.

After Alice detects the pattern of the constant movement of guests from seat to seat around the table in a never-ending tea party, she takes up this task within her dream, inquiring what happens when they all get around to the "beginning" again. The Mad Hatter suggests at that point in the conversation that they "change the subject," and he asks Alice to tell them a story (99–100). This exchange implies that part of the "work" of this dream is to "change" the dreaming subject by making her into a speaking subject. The dream of Wonderland eventually serves to bring Alice to a place where she can end the risk of madness and confusion by telling the story of the dream. Then she can answer the question that the dream poses to her over and over again: "Who are *you*?" (68). But at this point, Alice claims to have no story to tell, and the sleeping Dormouse is called upon to do the telling instead. Alice is not yet prepared to tell her story; she is not yet in possession of it. So the Dormouse replaces her in this function and becomes a double for her. He tells her story.

When the mouse is awakened and begins to spin a story out of the confusion of its dream, that story turns out to be a coded version of Alice's dream as well. The mouse's story concerns three children (one of whose names is an anagram for Alice) who lived in a well of treacle (Alice's adventures began when she fell down "what seemed to be a very deep well"). But the tale soon becomes a story about language, as the children learn to "draw" from the well things that have a common linguistic property: "everything beginning with M"—mousetraps, the moon, memory, and finally, muchness. When Alice protests that one can't "draw" things like memory or muchness from a well, she begins to assert her speaking voice in the episode; but her protest also indicates a failure to recognize something equally important. She has not realized that the material drawn out of the well of a dream is a memory, and it has a logic that the dreamer imposes upon it through recollection in language. Alice does not yet recognize this story as a coded version of her own experience—as her dream to master and to tell. "If you can't be civil," the Dormouse challenges her as she interrupts him with complaints about the truth of his story, "you'd better finish the story for yourself" (101). "Finishing the story" is defined here as *not* being "civil"—not obeying, that is, but commanding. This is precisely what Alice eventually will do, but not yet. She will finish the story for herself and command its characters when she declares it finished at the trial. She will do so again when she wakes up and tells it as her story to her sister just before she takes her tea at home. But first, Alice must see that this dream is about her ability to be the master of her words; she must draw them from the well of her own desire and finish her story for herself.

Many of Alice's adventures in Wonderland are trials she must endure in which the control over her own body, her own desires, or even her own psychic health depends upon her ability to interpret coded, confusing information. An actual courtroom trial, presided over by political figureheads whom she must defy, therefore, is an appropriate culmination to Alice's adventures in Wonderland. The key piece of evidence in the trial, brought against the knave accused of stealing, is a document apparently without meaning, without signature, and without author. The document turns out to be another series of verses that weave a confused narrative, the characters of which are pronouns with no specific referents, identities that tumble together in nameless ambiguity. Like Alice's confusion before the caterpillar's inquiries about her identity, the confusion of the poem continues throughout until it ends with a pronouncement about the impossibility of deciphering it: "For this must ever be / A secret kept from all the rest, / Between yourself and me" (158).

This mysterious document repeats the intepretive problem of the entire dream and is, therefore, the central "text" of it. Knowledge of the secret may be had "between yourself and me," in the place where the self recognizes and defines its difference from the other. Alice is right when she declares that there is no meaning in the text. The meaning resides in the one who assigns meaning to it, the one who tells the secret. The king will attempt to do just this. He explicates the document by identifying certain of its pronouns with the defendant, testing how well the words of the text "fit" the characters in the plot as he has told it. Assigning this significance to the words will guarantee the knave's guilt and simultaneously preserve the king's authority. The king's power is defined here as an interpretive authority. He seeks to impose a meaning on a text that has no meaning in itself and to silence any other interpretation of the case. This is the penultimate act in Alice's dream. The last is her take-over of the power and interpretive language of the king. She declares the figures of this trial to be "nothing but a pack of cards." This act usurps the interpretive power of the king because it recognizes, that like the poem, the dream is a text and the figures in it are figures—signs signifying something other than what they appear to be (161). They are part of a kind of political game, a language it is her responsibility to master. In order to be free from the power the dream holds over her, she must see that there is not an atom of meaning—or power—in those figures beyond what she confers upon them. When she realizes as much and acts upon the realization, Alice can awake and tell "these strange Adventures that you have just been reading about" (162).

In *Through the Looking-Glass*, Alice's development is extended along just these lines. From the beginning of the sequel, Alice realizes she is involved in a world defined by game playing, a world of signification which she deliberately enters rather than falls into. She is not put on trial and interrogated by the figures in this world as she was in Wonderland; she tries and interrogates them. She does not refuse or interrupt the game of chess as she does the game of cards; she plays it and wins. She becomes a queen herself and puts the opposing king in check. The text repeatedly suggests that this self-assertion can occur only when Alice recognizes the linguistic aspects of her dream as political power plays. One of her initial acts in this dream is to take the pen from the White King and start "writing for him" in his own memorandum book (190). This act of mastery over the king's book is immediately followed by an act of interpretive mastery when Alice is confronted with another indecipherable poem just as she had been at the end of *Wonderland* (this time, the text is the *Jabberwocky*). Instead of being defeated by the text's apparent meaninglessness as she was at the trial, here she takes control over the words on the page. Alice holds the book up to the mirror, literally turning its words around; and though the book is "rather hard to understand," "somehow," Alice says, "it seems to fill my head with ideas" (197). She may not be sure of what all those ideas are, but one thing is very clear to her about the content of this book: "somebody killed something." The one meaning that Alice can confer upon this text is that it is the scene of a life-and-death struggle—a place where somebody lives and somebody dies.

The dream of Alice and the metaphorical dream of life both present the same problems of desire, mastery, possession, and authority. One reason for the refusal to answer the question of whose dream it was at the end of the book may be that the book is an expression of Lewis Carroll's dream-child; it is the means by which he possesses the little girl Alice Lydell and tells her story.[41] Carroll may be the still-threatening, still-dreaming Red King who competes with her for possession of the dream and her definition of herself. But the action of the Alice books moves toward the breakdown of that possibility and the refusal by Alice to be possessed, as is substantiated by the rules the text itself has set up for interpretation. The dream belongs to Alice because she has the last word—because she asks the question of ownership and mastery, because she expresses the desire.[42] The Red King is checkmated by Alice; he is silenced in his sleep, and he is therefore only a part of her dream. He remains on the other side of the looking glass while she emerges into the realm of consciousness to assert her authority. At the end of *Looking-Glass* Alice becomes a figure of authority herself, in literary and political terms. The reversal that takes place in the looking-glass world for

[41]Jan B. Gordon sees the *Alice* books as decadent adult literature rather than children's literature, connecting Carroll's work with the Victorian impulse to make of the child a little adult and to justify participation in childhood fantasy by adults ("The Alice Books and the Metaphors of Victorian Childhood," in *Aspects of Alice*, ed. Phillips).

[42]In this, the Alice books could be read as feminist texts. Nina Auerbach, however, finds in them "many intense and unexamined feelings about womanhood," together with the conventional Victorian stereotypes of the female: "the demonic energy of the fallen woman" and the "preternatural purity Carroll located in little girls" (167). From *Woman and the Demon: The Life of a Victorian Myth* (1982).

Alice is a completion of the action begun in Wonderland. The final question of this text is not who dreamed it but who tells it, who gives it—or withholds from it—its meaning, who writes the book about "me"? "The question is," as Humpty Dumpty said to Alice, "which is to be master—that's all" (269).

Dreams of Profit in *A Christmas Carol*

A very, very brief time, and you will dismiss the recollection of it, gladly,
as an unprofitable dream, from which it happened well that you awoke.
—Charles Dickens, *A Christmas Carol*

The fundamental claim Freud would make about the origin of dreams is that they are expressions by the dreamer of a wish. The wish may be repressed and hence not immediately recognizable as a wish, and its expression may be disguised for a number of important reasons. But the dream is nevertheless an expression of the dreamer's desires. One of Freud's achievements was to establish the dream as a disguised wish and then to shift the center of the discussion about the significance of dreaming from the question of its origins to the tactics of its representation and decoding. *The Interpretation of Dreams* set out to repeat and undo the distortions and disguises of the dream work in the course of the dream analysis, and thereby to expose the wish at the root of the dream's "expression."

Wordsworth's Arab dream expresses the poet's desire to speak in a transcendent voice from beyond himself, and it portrays the dream as a form of prophetic utterance or supernatural possession. The dream of *Alice in Wonderland* reveals a desire for personal mastery and takes the form of a myth of entrance from the childhood world of fantasy into the adult, secular world of political power. *A Christmas Carol* (1843) is the nineteenth-century myth that expresses the dream in terms of economic power. Dickens's subtitle aptly identifies the tale as *A Ghost Story of Christmas*; it takes the language of ghostly possession and transforms it into one of material possession.[43] Lurking persistently behind the "spectral hand" of the spiritual visitors is the invisible hand of Adam Smith. The manifest plot relates a "conversion," an "exchange" of Scrooge's moral personality from the miser to the philanthro-

---

[43]According to Humphry House, "the language of [Dickens's] religion is all in human metaphors, its charity is confined to the existing scheme of social life and takes its tone from common heartiness. Scrooge does not see the Eternal behind the Temporal, a new heaven and a new earth: he merely sees the old earth from a slightly different angle" (*The Dickens World* [1942], p. 53). I have used the Penguin edition of *A Christmas Carol* in *The Christmas Books*, vol. 1 (1971), cited in the text.

pist. But the term *conversion* has both religious and economic connotations, and Scrooge's dream works the exchange between them. The wishes that are fulfilled in dreams, Freud claims, "are invariably the ego's wishes, and if a dream seems to have been provoked by an altruistic interest, we are only being deceived by appearances" (267). Despite appearances to the contrary, the latent "conversion" resulting from Scrooge's dream is more in the service of mammon than of God, and its effects suggest Dickens's participation in a bourgeois ideology that unconsciously conflates conversion and profit.[44]

The worst fate one of the voices from Scrooge's dream can wish him is that he will awaken to see the path he has chosen as nothing but an "unprofitable dream" (81). But Scrooge will be sure to make his Christmas dream turn a profit for him. Rather than do that by telling his dream after he awakens, as Alice did, Scrooge does it by suppressing the dream—by keeping its unprofitable aspects secret, by ensuring that the "writing" that appears in the dream will be "erased" (108). Alice's dream allows her to enter the adult world and retain some authority and power by mastering the game of language. Scrooge's dream enables him to enhance his place in the economic world and tighten his hold over those in his "service" by understanding that "power lies in words and looks" (78). In his dream, he discovers that words can have as much power when they are strategically withheld as they can when they are spoken. It is important, therefore, for Scrooge's dream and his response to it to "look" like and be decribed in the "words" of moral reform. It must not appear to be motivated by self-interest if it is to be profitable for him.

A Christmas Carol is presented more in the tradition of an allegorical dream vision than as a genuine dream. In contrast to the confusion of Alice's dreams, Scrooge's is tightly structured by the visitation of three apparently supernatural figures, each bearing a clear moral message and each appearing in correct temporal sequence. Their explicit intention is to confront Scrooge with the error of his ways and to urge him to turn from those ways. These are the ghosts that represent and connect his past, present, and future. They show him that the "plot" of his life story will end in an unmourned grave if he persists along his current path. Despite the apparent narrative orderliness of this vision, however, other features of it resemble the dream's confusing "work," as Freud described it. First, Scrooge's is a dream of regression. The persistence of his "forgotten self" in the form of repressed childhood memories and desires is at the heart of the dream material, appearing and disappearing in literal and symbolic forms in all parts of the dream, not just in the dream of Christmas past.[45] Second, Scrooge's dream repeatedly dramatizes

[44]For the limitations of Dickens's representation of moral conversion, see Barbara Hardy, "The Change of Heart in Dickens' Novels," *Victorian Studies*, 5 (September 1961): 49–67.

[45]In *Dickens: The Dreamer's Stance*, Stoehr sees in much of Dickens's fiction a confusion analogous to Scrooge's between belief in what is and desire for what could be (pp. 261–70).

acts of repression, denial, and distortion. It could be accurately described as a dream about censorship, as well as one that practices it. Finally, the central wish of the dream is to extend the dreamer's power and life, a wish that is successfully disguised from beginning to end. According to Freud, the "true significance" of a dream is always overdetermined, and it is always disguised. If the dreamer achieves an instant and complete certainty or clarity about the significance of a dream, a failure—or refusal—to see its complexity is usually present. Scrooge's absolute certainty about the purpose of his dream and its implications for him must be read as an act of repression on his part, repeating his final act in the dream itself, when he expresses his desire to "sponge away the writing on this stone"—to erase, that is, the text he has been confronted with in his dream, to obfuscate the "true" wish expressed in the dream (126).

Each section of the dream concludes with an act of repression. Scrooge ends the first stage in a state of "resistance," wrestling with the ghost, trying to end its haunting of him by pressing the "extinguisher cap" that covered the ghost's head (83–84). Scrooge "pressed it down with all his force" in his attempt to shut out the fragments of images from his past which the ghost cast around him (84). "No more!" Scrooge insists. "No more! I don't wish to see it. Show me no more!" (81). The second visitation also concludes with an act of suppression. The Ghost of Christmas Present shows to Scrooge the two child figures Ignorance and Want and then urges him to "beware them both." "Deny it," he says of the boy, Ignorance, instructing Scrooge to ignore the inscription of Doom on the child's head and to let the "writing be erased" (108). Scrooge seems to take the instructions literally, as is dramatized in the last scene of the final vision, which presents yet another portrait of denial. There Scrooge claims, "I am not the man I was," imploring the ghost to allow him to "erase" the inscription on the stone that spells out his own death (126). Scrooge "escapes" the implications in each part of his dream by denial, erasure, or revision: "Assure me that I may yet change these shadows you have shown me, by an altered life," he says to the final ghost. Scrooge resists his dream and desires to change its content throughout, declaring even after he awakes that "the Spirits of all Three shall strive within me" (126). Their haunting, in other words, is not complete. The conflict within Scrooge is not resolved. It has only been repressed and postponed into the indefinite future, inviting our suspicion of the simplistic moral interpretation Scrooge imposes upon his dream.[46]

Even the narrative sequence of the dream may be read as a deceptive

[46]Citing Scrooge's punning attempt to dismiss his visitation by Marley's ghost as a dream with "more of gravy than of grave" about it, Garrett Stewart identifies Scrooge as one of a series of "escape artists" in Dickens's fiction, figures whose imaginations are "tactical," "narrowly functional," and serve to deflect or fend off reality rather than face up to it (*Dickens and the Trials of Imagination* [1974], pp. 146–48).

product of secondary revision. The sense of time in Scrooge's dream stands in direct contrast to Alice's in Wonderland, where past, present, and future cannot be distinguished and where narratives can never be controlled or completed. But in fact, the stages of Scrooge's dream are not purely of the "past" or "present" either, even though they are announced as such. Scrooge is present either figuratively or literally as both child and adult in every part of the dream. This ambiguity is reflected in the appearance of the specters themselves. The first ghost appears "like a child: yet not so much like a child as like an old man" (68). As the second ghost grows old and begins to vanish before Scrooge's eyes, he is replaced by two young children who appear from beneath his cloak, once again suggesting the persistence of the child within the man. The age of the final ghost, like all his features, is "concealed"; but the continual effort of that spirit is to direct Scrooge's attention toward two other absences: the one caused by the death of the child Tiny Tim and the one caused by the death of Scrooge himself as an old man (110). These conflations of child and old man throughout the dream are effectively acknowledged by Scrooge when he awakens and expresses the regressive desire of the dream: "I'm quite a baby," he says. "I don't care. I'd rather be a baby" (128). Scrooge's dream dramatizes a desire to repossess his childhood world again, much as Alice's figured her desire to control the adult world.

The apparent narrative orderliness and the clarity of the dreamer's progressive moral viewpoint are not the only deceptions in this dream. Early on the tale announces itself as a critique of the ethos of the cash nexus. But the language of that critique within the scenes of the dream itself reveals it to be more of an endorsement. On the day preceding his dream, Scrooge rebukes the man collecting for the poor by quoting Malthusian sentiments on the fortunate demise of the "surplus population" (51). That rebuke is ironically repeated to Scrooge in the dream by the second ghostly visitor, but this admonition is softened when the ghost proceeds to lecture Scrooge that he had been wrong to say such things only because he misunderstood them: "Forbear that wicked cant until you have discovered What the surplus is, and Where it is" (97). The ghost goes on to urge Scrooge to think more seriously about what is of value and what is worthless in the sight of heaven. But these words may be read merely as a corrective rather than a repudiation. The "cant" is "wicked" only if it is wrongly applied. The principle of value remains intact. Scrooge simply needs to view the economics of time from a longer range and to understand that the "value" of a person is a more complicated computation than he has allowed.

Ultimately, the principles celebrated in the dream and applied to the value of individuals are those of the marketplace, as is most clearly dramatized in Scrooge's memory of his old employer Fezziwig. In that scene, Scrooge admires and envies the great dividends of "power" over his employees that a modest investment of capital manages to yield the employer: "He has the power to render us happy or unhappy; to make our service light or burdensome; a pleasure or a toil. Say that his power lies in words and looks; in things so slight and insignificant that it is impossible to count 'em up: what then? The happiness he gives, is quite as great as if it cost a fortune" (78). Scrooge sees before him the tremendous power an employer can have over an employee by simply bestowing the right "words and looks" at the right time. "In things so slight," Scrooge sees, "power lies." This kind of power must lie and deceive to achieve its purposes. It must make "service" that is "burdensome" look "light"; it must make "toil" appear like "pleasure." And by these slight and insignificant strategies of representation, the canny employer can shape the modest desires of his employees and save himself a "fortune" at the same time.

This may well be the point Scrooge refers to when he tells his second ghostly visitor what he learned from the previous ghost: "I learnt a lesson which is working now. Tonight, if you have aught to teach me, let me profit by it" (87). The specter proceeds to conduct Scrooge to the marketplace at Christmastime, where the lessons of profit are best learned. The vision there described offers a stunning rhetorical performance in tribute to the deceptive spectacle of the marketplace and the power of misrepresentation exercised there. The objects for sale are displayed in such a way that they are "urgently entreating and beseeching to be carried home in paper bags" (90). The workings of the market itself are presented as fraudulent and dangerous incarnations of human desire: "The scales descending on the counter made a merry sound. . . . the canisters were rattled up and down like juggling tricks. . . . the candied fruits [were] so caked and spotted with molten sugar as to make the coldest lookers-on feel faint and subsequently bilious" (90). The customers' feelings of faintness are then transformed into a euphoric state of distraction in the exhilarating atmosphere of extravagance and spending: "The customers were all so hurried and so eager in the hopeful promise of the day, that they tumbled up against each other at the door, clashing their wicker baskets wildly, and left their purchases upon the counter, and came running back to fetch them, and committed hundreds of the like mistakes in the best humour possible" (91).

Here the marketplace is not condemned but celebrated as a place where confusion and deception mask the customers' "mistakes" in a flourish of entertaining good humor, where the thrills of exchange and activity hide the subtle "juggling tricks" of commerce. Behind the specious fiction that there is a privilege in simply participating in the market economy, there lurks a desire. At this point in the dream, the marketplace seems to act as the central metaphor for Scrooge's unconscious desire. He is the miser who wishes to be a consumer, who is tempted by the fruits of the marketplace. And in the end, *A Christmas Carol* is more fundamentally an account of the dream as a scene of wish-fulfillment than it is an account of moral reform.[47]

The desire behind the dream is made quite clear in the last scenes of it. Scrooge is most deeply moved not by the prefiguration of his death but by his portrayal as an object of exchange which he does not own. The ghost of the future shows him his clothes, his possessions, and his personal "effects" being sold by his employees to the man in the rag and bone shop. Scrooge literally becomes no more than a series of things for sale. When he hears his charwoman say that the proper end for a man like him is "to profit us when he was dead," Scrooge recoils in horror (117). This is the expression of the "true significance" of the dream for Scrooge: the self is a thing to be owned, if not by oneself, then by someone else. To be owned by others is to die, to cease to be a self. This is what horrifies Scrooge—seeing himself as a commodity possessed and profited from by others than himself.

The ghost that accompanies Scrooge at the end of the dream is different from the other two in one important way: it is absolutely silent. At the outset of this part of the dream Scrooge resolved "to treasure up every word he heard" (113). But the words in this part of the dream are his; he takes over the power of describing and interpreting these scenes to himself rather than let the ghostly visitor have control over those actions. That power becomes a "treasure" for Scrooge to own and bury in secrecy after he awakes. As the third spirit silently glides through the city, past the deathbed, and into the graveyard, it attempts to present Scrooge with the figures of his own death. But Scrooge will not acknowledge that these things could have any relation to him. He describes the events in other terms, as if they concerned someone else. He refuses to lift the sheet that covers his own lifeless face and see it for what it is. By resisting the directives of the ghost and reinterpreting them for himself, Scrooge makes the dream his own, but only superficially so, since he doesn't "own up" to its "true" significance. He rejects what he sees as another's portrayal of him rather than a self-portrayal. When he is finally confronted with a representation he cannot reinterpret—the inscription of his own name on the tombstone—he demands to erase the name.[48]

---

[47]In what remains one of the best analyses of Dickens's politics and economics, House suggests such a reading when he claims that "the rather clown-like exaggerations of Dickens's satire of statisticians and economists are partly to be explained by the underlying doubt whether they might not be right after all" (p. 71). House also points out how the patronization of the poor was in the interests of the middle-class and how in Dickens's work "the beneficent characters have their full return in watching the happiness they distribute, and in the enjoyment of gratitude and power" (p. 111). He cites the cases of Fezziwig and Scrooge as examples of the "phoney" quality of the "good employer in action": "We must, I think, conclude that all these attempts to show the working of the Christmas spirit in the relations between master and man are either cheats or failures—at least that they are so on the employers' side" (pp. 64–67).

[48]This climactic phase of Scrooge's dream and his subsequent awakening correspond to what Albert Hutter calls Dickens's "lifelong fascination with morgues, and tombs, and burial sites" and with resurrection (p. 12). Hutter sees in Dickens's novels a way of managing the terror of

The dream ends when this last silent specter "dwindle[s] down into a bedpost," provoking in Scrooge a sense of elation over his possession of himself: "Yes! and the bedpost was his own. The bed was his own, the room was his own. Best and happiest of all, the Time before him was his own, to make amends in" (126–27). At heart, Scrooge is the miser still, objectifying his self-amendment in terms of these things he possesses. The immediate effect of the dream on him is his listing of this "happy" inventory of the things that are "his own," by which he is able to possess time itself. The dream, moreover, will be his most coveted possession, since it has expressed to him the possibility of owning his time by controlling how it is represented.

But if the dream is his possession, it is not something he has owned as Alice owned her dream. This story ends with the asssurance that Scrooge has learned an important lesson: he now "knew how to keep Christmas well, if any man alive possessed the knowledge" (134). The language of possession applies no longer to Scrooge's occupation alone but to the economy of his psyche as well. And whether we read Scrooge as reformed or simply reorganized, the important point is that his mind is shown to work like a business. The dream and the "knowledge" of it have become "possessions" that he "keeps" as "his own," with the intention of more effectively mastering others rather than himself. The acts of kindness with which Scrooge "keeps" Christmas (the gift of the goose, the new coal scuttle for Cratchit, and the shared glass of punch) are little more than window dressing, a small price for Scrooge to pay to ensure his mastery over the people in his life.[49]

The publishing history of *A Christmas Carol* lends an interesting footnote to the suspicion with which I have read its moral. The book was an instant success at the bookstands and elicited a response from the public not unlike the impassioned enthusiasm described in the book's marketplace scenes. The sales reversed Dickens's very bad showing with *Martin Chuzzlewit*, and provided an economic turning point for his career. *A Christmas Carol* would surely become a classic means by which to "keep" Christmas in England, and it would provide Dickens with a sizable profit as well.[50] But ironically, his

---

death, a way of "resurrect[ing] the corpse [of the past] into a living narrrative, a history" (p. 19). See "The Novelist as Resurrectionist," *Dickens Studies Annual* 12 (1984): 1–40.

[49]In his famous essay "Dickens: The Two Scrooges," Edmund Wilson points out Dickens's introduction of a new kind of character in *Martin Chuzzlewit*, the novel immediately preceding *A Christmas Carol*: the character who does evil while pretending to do good (in *The Wound and the Bow: Seven Studies in Literature* [1978], p. 27). The first symptom of Dickens's benevolence, House claims, is "generosity, in money, and in kindness that costs nothing" (p. 46).

[50]Edgar Johnson's presentation of these events in his biography of Dickens emphasizes the irony here and reads almost as parody. Johnson ends one paragraph with the following sentence: "*A Christmas Carol* is a serio-comic parable of social redemption, and Scrooge's conversion is the conversion for which Dickens hopes among mankind." He begins the next paragraph with this: "The earnings of the *Carol*, he expected, would help make up for the disapppointing returns from *Martin Chuzzlewit*." See *Charles Dickens: His Tragedy and Triumph* (1986), p. 257.

profit would have been much greater had Dickens been able to retain sole possession of his own words. The astounding success of the book led to its widespread piracy by publishers who owned no copyrights and who paid the author no royalties for sales. Dickens's response was rather Scrooge-like. He launched a protracted and expensive lawsuit, which he won but which ended up costing him more money in legal fees than he was able to recover in damages. Nevertheless, he was victorious in the principle of the thing: there is a power in the possession of one's own words, and a profit in them as well.[51]

The form of Scrooge's dream in *A Christmas Carol* might be seen as expressing another of its most profound wishes: the desire for a plot, for a life story that has an ordered sense of past, present, and future, a story that connects the old man with his forgotten childhood self. In this his dream is an inversion of Alice's. It does retrospectively what hers does prospectively. But the form of this dream, like that of Alice's, also shows Scrooge's desire to take over its narrating power, to tell it himself, to erase, revise, and rewrite the story of his own life. Scrooge's increasing involvement as the voice within his dream is the fulfillment of that wish; it is the sponging away of the text of the dream as something visited on him and the replacement of it with another self-authored text after he awakens. We can read Dickens's own excursions into autobiographical writing as a repetition of Scrooge's action. Dickens began writing an autobiography in the late 1840s, but broke off the project, explaining to John Forster that he was so tormented by dreams of his past that he could not continue to write down the "deep remembrances" of those experiences. Dickens would only resume the project in the form of *David Copperfield*.[52] There, he could revise his tormented dreams, mix fact and fiction, and present himself as "the hero of my own life," only to rewrite that story once more in *Great Expectations*.

Together with the dreams in *The Prelude*, the Alice books, and *The Interpretation of Dreams*, *A Christmas Carol* connects the phenomenon of dreaming with the desire for self-possession and self-control, which are achieved by strategies of speaking or being silent, writing or suppressing writing, representing or refusing to represent the "true significance" of the dream. These are the very issues that more elaborately inform the function of dreams in the gothic, autobiographical, and detective novels with which I am concerned in the following chapters. Like any dreams, their images are overdetermined and could be associated with many different kinds of repressed materials from the dreamers' waking lives. But I attend specifically to the problems of

---

[51]See J. A. Sutherland, "Dickens as Publisher," in Sutherland, *Victorian Novelists and Publishers* (1976). Sutherland cites Dickens's experience with the *Carol* as the turning point in the novelist's relationship with publishers (p. 167n).

[52]John Forster, *The Life of Charles Dickens*, ed. J. W. T. Ley (1928), p. 26.

representation as they are manifested in the dreams themselves and in the dreamers' responses to them. The gothic novel has a fundamental interest in these matters since uncanny dream experience is often so central to it. Gothic fiction consistently raises the possibility that the dream originates from some supernatural possession of the dreamer by an alien, uncontrollable force. This possibility, however, invariably becomes entangled with some psychological repression on the part of the dreamer, a repression that disables him or her and is expressed in the dream. Each of the three gothic texts in the next chapter takes the form of a different kind of first-person discourse in which the dreamer attempts to come to terms with the disturbing power of the dream either by taking control over it and recognizing its psychological origins or by denying responsibility for the dream and ascribing it to demonic origin. Like Freud's *Interpretation of Dreams*, these novels are acts of interpretation intended to replace an alien discourse with a discourse of control. Like Wordsworth's Arab dream, the dreams in these texts reveal the seductive power of a supernatural voice. Like Alice's, they express a desire to master the forces that drive us. And like Scrooge's, they result in either the loss or gain of authority over the words in which the self is kept and expressed.

Henry Fuseli, *The Nightmare* (1782)

Horace Walpole saw Fuseli's *Nightmare* at its first exhibition in London in 1782 and called it a "shocking" image. The picture, which established Fuseli's reputation as a painter, is regarded as a precocious example of nineteenth-century Romanticism in its blend of rational and irrational beliefs about the unconscious. Like many gothic novels, the figures in the painting evoke the supernatural and the mysterious along with the erotic and the psychological. The image impressed itself on the public mind in England so strongly that it was reproduced in a number of engravings, was frequently referred to by literati (including Coleridge, Byron, Leigh Hunt, and Mary Wollstonecraft), and was used as the basis for innumerable personal and political caricatures throughout the century. Max Eastman reported seeing a print of the painting hanging in Freud's office in 1926, arranged alongside Rembrandt's *Anatomy Lesson* to express pictorially, perhaps, Freud's intention to render in medical terms what had always been seen as supernatural. Freud's disciple and biographer, Ernest Jones, also used a version of the painting as a frontispiece to his own book *On the Nightmare* (1931). (© the Detroit Institute of Arts. Gift of Mr. and Mrs. Bert L. Smokler and Mr. and Mrs. Lawrence A. Fleischman.)

CHAPTER TWO

Recovering Nightmares:
Nineteenth-Century Gothic

It is within the experience of many medical practitioners, that a patient, with strange and unusual symptoms, has been more distressed in mind, more wretched, from the fact of being unintelligible to himself and others, than from the pain or danger of the disease.

—Samuel Taylor Coleridge, *Biographia Literaria*

The high esteem in which dream-life is held by some schools of philosophy . . . is clearly an echo of the divine nature of dreams which was undisputed in antiquity. . . . For attempts at giving a psychological explanation have been inadequate to cover the material collected, however decidedly the sympathies of those of a scientific cast of mind may incline against accepting any such beliefs.

—Sigmund Freud, *The Interpretation of Dreams*

The author of the first gothic novel in English traced the origin of his story to the recovery and writing down of a haunting dream that disturbed his sleep: "I waked one morning in the beginning of last June from a dream, of which all I could recover was, that I thought myself in an ancient castle (a very natural dream for a head filled like mine with Gothic story) and that on the uppermost bannister of a great staircase I saw a gigantic hand in armour. In the evening I sat down and began to write, without knowing in the least what I intended to say or relate."[1] Here, at the beginning point of English gothic fiction, Horace Walpole joined the experience of dreaming with a question about authority. In recovering his dream, Walpole represented himself as being virtually compelled to write about something outside of his own knowledge and intention, as if he had been forced to write *The Castle of Otranto* (1764) in the strange, gigantic hand of his dream. Authors of many

---

[1]Letter of Horace Walpole to the Reverend William Cole, 9 March 1765, quoted in the Introductory Essay of *Three Gothic Novels*, ed. Mario Praz (1968), p. 17.

71

subsequent gothic tales attributed their origins to dreams, often to emphasize a failure on the part of even the writers to understand and control the
forces that drove their narratives. The stories frequently contain dreams as
well, most often nightmarish dreams of demonic possession.[2] Matthew
Lewis's *Monk* (1796), Mary Shelley's *Frankenstein* (1818), James Hogg's *Private Memoirs and Confessions of a Justified Sinner* (1824), and Charles Matu-
rin's *Melmoth the Wanderer* (1820) all contain dreams of this kind, and the
dreamer is invariably someone who suffers from a state of illness or divided
personality that he or she can explain only as a form of supernatural possession.

These characteristics of the gothic novel make it an appropriate place
for Freud to put into practice his project of replacing a divine interpretation
of dreams with a scientific one. In fact, in *Delusion and Dream* Freud gave an
elaborate analysis of the dreams in an early twentieth-century gothic novel,
Wilhelm Jensen's *Gradiva*. Even though *Gradiva*, like most gothic fiction,
contains many reports of ghostly visitations, Freud did not regard it as a
ghost story at all. He called the novel nothing less than "an entirely correct
study in psychiatry, by which we may measure our understanding of psychic
life, a story of illness and cure which seems designed for the inculcation of
certain fundamental teachings of medical psychology" (*Delusion and Dream*,
64). Freud marveled that the author had somehow "acquired the same
knowledge as the physician," or at least "behave[d] as if he possessed it" (77).
He particularly admired the remarkable ways in which Jensen seemed to
anticipate the talking cure by treating the protagonist's speech and his
dreams as symptoms of a delusion, by tracing these symptoms back to their
origins, and by effecting a "concurrence of explanation and cure" in the
articulation of those origins (110–14). Freud could only conclude that "science leaves a gap which we find filled" by this "story of illness and cure"—
the same gap Freud himself sought to fill with his theories of dream interpretation (75).

Several other nineteenth-century gothic novels also anticipated the claims
of psychoanalysis, especially the concern with replacing supernatural explanations for delusional formations such as dreams with scientific—even
medical—explanations. Although the dreamers of these novels may not always be "cured" by their explanations, they consistently call attention to the
symptomatic aspects of the words they use to describe their dreams. Like

[2]A number of studies of the gothic novel have emphasized its nightmarish quality. See
Elizabeth MacAndrew, *The Gothic Tradition in Fiction* (1979); Judith Wilt, *Ghosts of the Gothic:
Austen, Eliot and Lawrence* (1980); and William Patrick Day, *In the Circles of Fear and Desire: A
Study of Gothic Fantasy* (1985). For a more specific consideration of the dreams of female
characters in eighteenth-century fiction, see Margaret Anne Doody, "Deserts, Ruins, and
Troubled Waters: Female Dreams in Fiction and Development of the Gothic Novel," *Genre* 10
(Winter 1977): 529–72.

Jensen's *Gradiva*, these novels expose a gap in scientific knowledge which needed to be filled by a language that would enable the dreamer's recovery, and they go some distance in helping to fill that gap as well.

The importance that Freud placed upon attributing dreams to the psychic health of the dreamer rather than to some divine intervention is evident in the very beginning of *The Interpretation of Dreams*, where he lines up the forces engaged in the nineteenth-century debate over the signficance of dream experience. In reviewing the current literature on the subject, Freud concluded that the two basic theories then prevailing were not new but already established in the ancient world. On one side were positivists who, like Aristotle, maintained that dreams "do not rise from supernatural manifestations but follow the laws of the human spirit." On the other side were idealists of various kinds who, like Plato, thought of the dream "not as a product of the dreaming mind but as something introduced by a divine agency; and already," Freud goes on to say, "the two opposing currents, which we shall find influencing dream life at every point in history, were making themselves felt" (2–3). These same currents also made themselves felt in the gothic fiction of the nineteenth century. *Frankenstein, Confessions of an English Opium-Eater*, and *Wuthering Heights*, and the dreams in them present themselves through both story and discourse as neurotic symptoms, as attempts at "recovery" centered in the conflict between supernatural and psychological explanations for the uncanny experience of dreaming. At stake for the gothic hero or heroine in this conflict is the recognition of the powerful influence of irrational impulses on behavior and the need to take control over those impulses. The very rise of the gothic novel as a genre may be read as an attempt to recover or reconstruct an account of psychic life in the face of supernatural accounts whose inadequacy was becoming more and more apparent. Even more to the point, these texts expose how supernatural explanations of such events often mask a repressed pathological struggle rooted very firmly in the powers of this world.

The extensive theoretical writing on dreams during the eighteenth and nineteenth centuries was generally directed against supernatural explanations for psychic disturbances. Characteristically, the scholarship took one of two courses: dream theory either deferred to an idealism that tried to rationalize the supernatural element of dreams by attributing them to something like a world soul or collective unconscious, or it sought to explain dreams as purely physiological phenomena that did not reveal anything profoundly important about the dreamer.[3] As the most systematic and comprehensive theory of

---

[3]See Henri F. Ellenberger, *The Discovery of the Unconscious: The History and Evolution of Dynamic Psychiatry* (1970). Ellenberger speaks of the two basic theoretical dispositions toward the mind during sleep as "open" theories (which regarded the dreaming mind as in communication with some mysterious other realm, whether it was a previous life, a disincarnated spirit, or simply some transcendent reality) and "closed" theories (which explained the dream material as

dreams in the period, Freud's *Interpretation of Dreams* offered a third course. For Freud, dreams were neither the manifestations of possession by some spiritual power nor the result of normal somatic processes during sleep. Rather, dreams were to be regarded as symptoms of a neurosis in the dreamer, evidence of a psychic wound or illness. But in regarding the dream as a symptom Freud did not think of it as a "pathological product"; on the contrary, he saw the dream, like any other delusion formation, as "an attempt at recovery, a process of reconstruction."[4]

The common association of physical and psychic illnesses with the dreams and dreamers of gothic fiction suggests some continuity with Freud's description of the dream as a symptom. The rise of gothic fiction during the latter part of the eighteenth century and its flowering during the nineteenth may in fact be read as a symptom on a cultural scale, an expression of a desire for a vocabulary by which to name and control psychic forces in terms of pathology rather than theology. Freud himself offers a direct point of contact between the two discourses not only in his commentary on *Gradiva* but also in his remarkable essay "A Neurosis of Demoniacal Possession in the Seventeenth Century." There Freud analyzes a case of alleged demonic possession which had been recorded in a form strikingly like that of a gothic novel. As is true of such gothic tales as *Frankenstein, Melmoth, Justified Sinner, Dr. Jekyll and Mr. Hyde*, and *Dracula*, for example, the material for this case consists of several documents written in the first person. A series of captioned drawings by the "patient" (who in this instance is a painter) depict his signing of a pact with the devil and his redemption at the shrine of the Holy Mother. Those drawings are combined with a description of the case by a "reverend compiler" (who also includes some lines in verse which contain information about his own life), a deposition by an abbot testifying to the authenticity of the documents, and finally the diary of the patient, which chronicles his possession and exorcism. Freud takes particular interest in the complex textual issues of the case—the contradictions between the pictures and the painter's verbal accounts of them, the inconsistencies within the diary itself, the variations in wording of the patient's two written pacts with the devil, the compiler's attempts at textual reconciliation, and so on. The function of Freud's analysis is to add still another text of reconciliation or reconstruction, a "final" attempt to piece together the inconsistencies by substituting a story of neurosis for one of possession.

---

composed of forgotten memories or sense impressions). He identified four approaches to the function of dreams at the turn of the century which grew out of these two positions: (1) a conservative function (to preserve traces of the past lost to conscious memory); (2) a dissolutive function (to aid in the transformation of once-conscious acts into unconscious, habitual acts); (3) a creative function (to produce lucid expressions of "higher" truths unavailable to the conscious mind); and (4) a mythopoetic function (to create cultural myth—often associated with the activity of mediums and somnambulism). See especially pp. 145–70 and 311–21.

[4]Sigmund Freud, "On the Mechanism of Paranoia," *SE* 12:71.

Freud clearly took up the case in order to demonstrate how phenomena perceived in medieval times as demonic dreams, visions, and possessions could be explained in terms of repressed impulses and psychic forces. "We merely eliminate the projection of these mental entities into the external world," he says; "instead, we regard them as having arisen in the patient's internal life, where they have their abode."[5] But Freud's analysis does much more. His translation of the incident from a theological into a medical vocabulary dramatizes exactly what is dramatized in the dreams of many gothic texts: fundamentally, dreams and visions are sites of interpretive power where dreamers are actually attempting to resist or surrender to the notion that an authority from the outside is governing their lives. Furthermore, these struggles for authority take place on the level of language—in the giving or witholding of a dream account. In both cases, dreams and visions must be seen as symptoms that serve as attempts at recovery, and thus are actions taken by the dreamer, not actions taking him or her over from the outside. Like the case Freud analyzes here, gothic fiction commonly evidences this assertion of authority in the production of the texts themselves—in the writing of pacts in blood, in the retraction of those pacts through confession and exorcism, in the revision of inconsistencies to preserve the authority of the church, and most important, in the patient's composition of a diary that seeks to bring together the fragmented pieces of a life threatened by a divine or demonic usurpation.

This particular case has a special fascination and significance for Freud since he is able to trace the patient's morbid anxiety to the recent death of his father and the paralyzing melancholia that resulted from this loss of parental authority. Not only does this scenario follow the pattern of Freud's own experience in writing *The Interpretation of Dreams*, but it corresponds to the set of forces commonly operating in the gothic novel as well—problems of inheritance, incest, parricide, entombment, ghostly hauntings from the past, and so on. In Freud's view, this patient never fully recovered from his neurosis because he never recognized his visions as symptoms of this anxiety. Rather, he merely substituted one form of "possession" for another, replacing his father's authority first with that of the devil, then with that of the church. "He wanted all along simply to make his life secure. He tried first to achieve this with the help of the devil at the cost of his salvation; and when this failed and had to be given up, he tried to achieve it with the help of the clergy at the cost of his freedom and most of the possibilities of enjoyment in life" (104). This failed self-recognition in the desperate attempt to find the "security" of some transcendent authority is the fate of many gothic dreamers as well, and it reflects a larger crisis of authority in the nineteenth

[5]Freud, "A Seventeenth-Century Demonological Neurosis," *SE* 19:72, hereafter cited in the text.

century—a crisis of which the rise of the gothic novel is itself a symptom.

The acceptance of a secular interpretation of dreams as originating in the individual psyche demands that the dreamer be the source of the significance as well as the haunting images of the dream. Any authority the dream might have for the dreamer is based upon her or his own recognition of it as a self-portrayal, rather than a revelation from the divine world. If, as T. S. Eliot claimed, one consequence of this assumption is that the "quality of our dreams suffers," another consequence is that the quality of the dreamer's account of the dreams becomes that much more important.[6] In many gothic texts, acts of self-representation are presented as acts of self-discovery and healing, and acts of secrecy or repression are part of a pattern of illness and psychic disturbance. When the narrator of *Justified Sinner* complains of having "such dreams that they will not bear repetition," for example, he either fails to understand that his refusal to repeat his dreams keeps him "troubled" and "enchained" by them, or he admits that he wants to maintain his illusions about himself by censoring the thoughts that are behind the dreams.[7] Stories like this narrator's consistently dramatize how dreams take shape and reveal themselves as symptoms only when they are put into words and connected with the dreamer's waking life.

This conflict between the "two opposing currents" of dream interpretation divided Freud from Jung more subtly than from his other opponents. Though Jung shared Freud's conviction that the dream was essentially a self-portrayal by the dreamer, he maintained that dreams had a higher, objective value as well. Jung's interest in symbol and archetype led him to conceive of the dream as transcending the personal ego and participating in a historical pattern external and inexplicable to the self. For Jung, the symbolic content of the dream had its own value and meaning, which could not be imposed by the individual dreamer. Ultimately, that symbolic significance was inexpressible in words: "A symbol does not define or explain," he said; "it points beyond itself to a meaning that is darkly divined yet still beyond our grasp, and cannot be adequately expressed in the familiar words of our language."[8] Jung's use of theological language is significant here, and this kind of statement fundamentally distinguishes him from Freud, who argued that dreams are nothing more than our symptomatically disguised desires, which we can understand and control only when we translate them into the "familiar words of our language."

[6]T. S. Eliot, "Dante," *Selected Essays of T. S. Eliot* (1960), p. 204.

[7]James Hogg, *The Private Memoirs and Confessions of a Justified Sinner* (Oxford: Oxford University Press, 1981), p. 214.

[8]C. G. Jung, "Spirit and Life," *The Collected Works of C. G. Jung*, ed. Sir Robert Read, Michael Fordham, Gerhard Adler, William McGuire, trans. R. F. C. Hull, vol. 8: *The Structure and Dynamics of the Psyche* (1953), p. 336. For a fuller discussion of the relation between Freud's and Jung's theories on dreams, see Liliane Frey-Rohn, *From Jung to Freud: A Comparative Study of the Psychology of the Unconscious*, trans. Fred E. Engreen and Evelyn K. Engreen (1976).

Jung's views represented a compromise between the traditional religious belief that dreams have their origins and significance in a realm "higher" than the dreamer and the more scientific and biological orientation of Freud, who related them to the personal life history of the dreamer. But as Freud indicated, what he regarded as an entirely "pre-scientific" viewpoint was not without its adherents in the nineteenth century, not only the "pietistic and mystical writers" of the period but a number of "clear-headed men" as well: "It would be a mistake to suppose that the theory of the supernatural origin of dreams is without its supporters in our own day," Freud cautioned in *The Interpretation of Dreams*. "One comes across clear-headed men, without any extravagant ideas, who seek to support their religious faith in the existence and activity of superhuman spiritual forces precisely by the inexplicable nature of the phenomena of dreaming" (4). In this latter category Freud placed P. Haffner, Friedrich Schelling, and Johann Fichte, who saw dreams either as representative of some "complementary" reality, as "divine in nature," or simply as separate in important ways from waking life. Freud consistently made it a point to associate such views with the demands of religious faith and to oppose them to a truly "scientific" attitude of mind. While such claims may have overstated the case, these thinkers did consider dreams to be part of some complex of forces outside the spheres of rational and empirical inquiry, forces that we conventionally align with the gothic and romantic strain of nineteenth-century literature.

But the role of the dream in gothic fiction is much more complicated than that. The gothic use of dreams may be more properly understood as expressing the uneasy tension in the period between scientific and religious explanations of dream experience. The dreamers in these stories tend to be wounded figures suffering from some physical and psychological disturbance and some visionary experience that they commonly explain in terms of the supernatural. Those explanations, however, usually contend in the text with a desire for a more "psychological" explanation that connects the dream to some undisclosed repressed material, some traumatic experience, or some crisis in authority experienced by the dreamer. The conflict between these two viewpoints becomes apparent when the dreamer chooses either to convert the dream event into the common words of our language or to submit it to the uncommon language of the divine.

One of the more dramatic fictional examples of this situation occurs in Sheridan LeFanu's *Carmilla* (1870). The narrative begins with a terrifying dream experience recounted by the young woman who narrates the story. In her dream she is visited by a female figure who first comforts and caresses her until the dreamer feels a terrible pain in her breasts. Then the dream figure disappears beneath the bed. The narrator, Laura, initially dreams this dream as a child, and it provokes a nervous disorder from which she never entirely recovers. The dreams continue, and they develop into a series of

voices that haunt the narrator in her dreams; one of these she recognizes as
the voice of her mother mysteriously warning her to avoid her "assassin"
(308). The warning seems not only to refer to the father in the tale but also to
reinforce the sense that these dreams are efforts toward recovery and self-
preservation on the part of the dreamer. She is told by various authorities
that these dreams are either visitations of evil spirits, the product of a fever in
the body, or finally, the haunting of a vampire. Eventually, her father destroys
this monster and presumably solves the mystery, appropriately, in an old
Gothic church.

But since the destruction of the supposed vampire does not cure the
narrator's illness or alleviate her recurring dreams, this supernatural explanation is called into doubt. That the trauma of the childhood dream had
obliterated Laura's memory of everything that preceded it strongly suggests
that the dream serves as an agency of repression for her and her father as
well.[9] Her dreams are also continually associated with the loss of her dead
mother (whom Laura cannot remember), with the awakening of her own
sexuality, and with the domination of her life by her father. Together with the
father's repeated attempts to dismiss the significance of the dreams and to
obscure crucial events in Laura's past, these details indicate that her dreams
may screen the memory of a childhood seduction or primal scene. But these
"symptoms" are never fully understood in *Carmilla* because they are never
allowed to be expressed. Rather, they remain unrecovered, uninterpreted
memories for the patient, who is still plagued by her dreams, her illness, and
her overbearing father at the end of the story.

Like William Godwin's *Adventures of Caleb Williams* or like *Melmoth, Justified Sinner, Frankenstein, Wuthering Heights*, and many other gothic tales,
Carmilla represents a narrator's attempt to recover from a disordered state—
a condition that not only is often physically debilitating but proves to be
psychologically crippling as well. This disability almost invariably takes the
form of a loss of personal control, a usurpation, a denial, or a willing abandonment of personal authority over and responsibility for one's actions.
States of dream, trance, madness, and possession provide the appropriate
psychological conditions to investigate (or explain away) this problem. Typically, this project takes place in complex, embedded narratives that serve
both to suggest the buried psychological origins of dreamlike materials and
to designate the dynamics of the telling as essential to understanding the
meaning of the condition. Bram Stoker's *Dracula* (1897), for example, represents a further development of the plot and structure of a typical gothic text
such as *Carmilla*. Count Dracula's victims can never clearly distinguish their
own dreams from the vampire's nocturnal visitations. The dreamers embed

---

[9]On repression in *Carmilla*, see also Day, pp. 88–89; and William Veeder, "'Carmilla': The
Arts of Repression," *Texas Studies in Literature and Language* 22 (Summer 1980): 197–223.

their dreams in a strange legend composed of their own diaries, journals, case histories, letters, medical reports, telegrams, newspaper stories, and the transcripts of phonograph recordings made by a doctor about his patients, all of which are employed to project the dreamers' fears and desires onto an exotic, monstrous ghoul as an alternative to accepting them as symptoms of their own psychic disturbances.

These gothic novels anticipate many of the features of Freud's speaking cure and his emphasis on rendering an account of the images of our dreams in the familiar words of our language. But by also continuing to evoke the atmosphere and rationale of the supernatural in these tales—even if sometimes discrediting supernatural explanations as strategies of denial or repression—gothic fiction reenacted the debate that raged in England throughout the nineteenth century over the source and significance of dreams. Fashionable groups of secular and religious spiritualists argued that dreams were miraculous events that permitted communication with a divine realm, while positivist theorists maintained that dreams were explainable phenomena governed by natural law.[10] The scientific community in England was most deeply influenced by the theories of the rationalists of the previous century, who based their description of dreams on the laws of association, the effects on the mind of recent sense impressions and ideas, and the state of the body during sleep. This positivistic tradition was carried forward into the nineteenth century by such theorists as Dugald Stewart (*Elements of the Philosophy of the Human Mind*, 1814) and Robert Macnish (*The Philosophy of Sleep*, 1838), and later others in England, including F. W. H. Myers and James Sully, who began to look more seriously at the psychological significance of dreams and to suggest the importance of what Freud would later identify as the unconscious.

Myers is a particularly interesting figure for the period, since he founded the Society for Psychical Research in order to oppose the tide of positivist thought in England and on the Continent. He maintained that positivist explanations of strange psychic events such as dreams and schizophrenia were often reductive and tended to minimize, manipulate, or ignore evidence that was contrary to their theories. His organization collected thousands of case studies and first-person reports of mysterious dreams, visions, telepathy, sleepwalking, and related occurrences, concluding that this sort of experience proved the immortality of the human soul. In his influential book *Human Personality* (1903), Myers cogently expressed the characteristic double vision of the scientific and literary communities in the nineteenth century: "The permanent result of a dream, I say, is sometimes such as to show that the

---

[10]For treatments of the relation of morals to dream theory in England, see Bernard, "Dickens and Victorian Dream Theory"; and Werner Wolff, *The Dream—Mirror of Conscience: The History of Dream Interpretation from 2000 B.C. and a New Theory of Dream Synthesis* (1952).

dream has not been a mere superficial confusion of past waking experiences, but has had an unexplained potency of its own,—drawn like the potency of hypnotic suggestion, from some depth in our being which the waking self cannot reach."[11] In a gesture typical of nineteenth-century ambivalence on the subject, Meyers simultaneously emphasizes the importance of explaining the hidden logic of the dream and the impossibility of doing so, comparing the dream logic to the mysterious "potency" of hypnotic suggestion. Like Jung, he forges a fragile compromise between the dictates of science and those of religion. The gothic novel of the period poses the issue more decisively: the dreams and their recollections are the sites of a struggle to gain authority over the self through language. At stake is a necessary choice between conceiving of the psyche as a supernatural soul facing damnation or redemption, on the one hand, and a medical subject capable of illness or recovery, on the other. Despite certain equivocations, however, figures like Myers and Sully anticipate the claims of psychoanalytic theory more faithfully when they trace dreams back to both immediate and distant memories and find them to be inextricably associated with current wakeful thoughts. These considerations also parallel the gothic preoccupation with the problems entailed in remembering and representing dream experience and in distinguishing it from waking life. Eventually, Freud would respond to this confusion raised independently by scientists such as Sully and Myers and novelists such as Mary Shelley and Emily Brontë. The realization that conscious thoughts "will be apt to be unconsciously read back into the dream" and become part of the dreamer's memory of the dream is transformed by Freud into a form of confusion which contributes to, rather than detracts from, understanding the significance of a dream.[12] For him, the language of disguise becomes the language of revelation, at once a symptom of psychic distress and a sign of psychic recovery.

The dream accounts that permeate *Frankenstein*, *Confessions of an English Opium-Eater*, and *Wuthering Heights* anticipate this interpretive turn. They are all told by a narrator recovering from some illness or disabling event, and they all express a profound psychological conflict. Not only do these three texts offer a representative range of gothic conventions, they also foreground an essential characteristic of the genre: the narratives exist primarily as symptoms of an attempt to recover from a disordered state of mind which is most dramatically manifested in the narrator's dreams.[13] *Frankenstein* began as the "waking dream" of Mary Shelley, which she proceeded to turn into a

[11]Frederick W. H. Myers, *Human Personality and Its Survival of Bodily Death* (1954), 1:126.
[12]F. W. H. Myers, Edmund Gurney, and Frank Podmore, *Phantasms of the Living*, quoted in *The World of Dreams*, ed. Ralph L. Woods (1947), pp. 278–79.
[13]For a more general treatment of the importance of acts of writing in the gothic conception of character, see Eve Kosofsky Sedgwick, *The Coherence of Gothic Conventions* (1986), chaps. 3 and 4.

"ghost story" for her husband and friends during a holiday in Switzerland. But most of the text itself takes the form of a deathbed narrative told by an ailing scientist trying to explain away his own obsessive dream as a form of demonic possession. Thomas DeQuincey's *Confessions of an English Opium-Eater* recounts its narrator's recovery from a paralyzing illness and addiction to opium, and it is written to "display the marvelous agency" of the dreams associated with that illness as well as to recover the dreamer's health (114). The *Confessions* demands attention not only because of its importance for the medical literature on dreams in the period but also because of its thematic and formal affinities with the gothic and autobiographical novel.[14] Finally, the uncanny, disturbing events of *Wuthering Heights* can be said to grow out of the bewildering nightmares of its narrator who is stricken ill at the beginning of the tale and is nursed back to health during the course of it. His dreams seem mysteriously and irresistibly to connect him to the other dreams and dreamers in the story and to compel him to question his own authority over his experience, just as they do.

In each of these cases, the giving of the dream account is not only a part of the recovery from an illness but also a literal act of authorship—the production of a text. Beneath the manifest plots of these novels, then, is another plot—a plot of "recovery" or "reconstruction" that determines the narrative structure of the texts and reveals the attitudes that the narrators take toward the materials they dream and write about. These plots take a different form in each of the books, reflecting fundamentally different responses to the crisis of personal authority which haunted the period. But of central concern to all of them is the attempt to discover an appropriate language with which to represent and master the unsettling experience of their dreams. As Freud said of *Gradiva*, these gothic novels were all "working over the same material" that he would theorize about. They were merely using "a different method" to express it (*Delusion and Dream*, 117).

Demons and Disease in *Frankenstein*

> I had retrod the steps of knowledge along the paths of time and exchanged the discoveries of recent enquirers for the dreams of forgotten alchemists.
>
> —Victor Frankenstein

[14]In the introductory essay to the Penguin edition of DeQuincey's *Confessions* (1978), Alethea Hayter claims that with this book DeQuincey "brought to the art of prose autobiography something entirely new, and his influence has been felt by every self-conscious English writer, whether of reminiscences or of autobiographical novels, ever since" (p. 24).

Frankenstein is an extended, elaborate account of its author's remarkable dream. In her description of the dream in the Author's Introduction to
the novel, Mary Shelley equivocates about the exact nature of the experience.
She regards her dream, on the one hand, as something she created—as the
product of her own "imagination" and "fancy." But on the other hand, she
refers to it as an alien presence—as "the spectre which had haunted my
midnight pillow," a "phantom" that "possessed" and "haunted" her.[15] These
two very different characterizations signal one of the central issues of the
novel into which Shelley transposed her dream. The language with which
Victor Frankenstein speaks about his own dream reveals the extent to which
he is willing to take responsibility for his desires and actions. The connection
between Mary Shelley's dream and Frankenstein's is made explicit when the
author places the manifest content of her dream into a scene in the novel in
which Frankenstein himself awakens from a dream only to be confronted
with its terrible reality. Paradoxically, whereas Mary Shelley immediately
transformed her dream into her "ghost story," the dreamer within the tale
struggles through most of his story to keep his dream from being told.
Frankenstein is, then, an elaborate weaving together of the activities of dreaming, invention, repression, and storytelling. It links by means of a dream
event the issues of personal origin, authority, and power in a manner that
establishes this novel as a myth of self-making for the dreamers that pervade
nineteenth-century fiction. The gothic novel Mary Shelley called the "transcript" of her dream may be read as a symptom—a text that expresses the
desire for an adequate language to describe the mysterious forces that produced it.

Frankenstein is a story about storytelling, as its dependence upon and
allusions to "The Rime of the Ancient Mariner" attest. Critics often note
that *Frankenstein* is not a single story but a complex of stories, one embedded
within another, and that the relationship among these Chinese-box narratives is important for understanding the novel.[16] But it should also be noted

---

[15]Mary Shelley, *Frankenstein, or the Modern Prometheus*, the 1818 text, ed. James Rieger
(Chicago: University of Chicago Press, 1982), 227–28, hereafter cited in the text. Variant
quotations from the 1831 text, also in Rieger's edition, will be noted.

[16]See for example Peter Brooks, "Godlike Science/Unhallowed Arts: Language, Nature, and
Monstrosity," in *The Endurance of "Frankenstein": Essays on Mary Shelley's Novel*, ed. U. C.
Knoepflmacher and George Levine (1979); Richard J. Dunn, "Narrative Distance in *Frankenstein*," *Studies in the Novel* 6 (Winter 1974): 408–17; and Harold Bloom, "*Frankenstein, or the
Modern Prometheus*," in Bloom, *Ringers in the Tower* (1971). Brooks describes each tale within the
tale as touched by "the taint of monsterism . . . leaving us with only a text, a narrative tissue that
never wholly conceals its lack of ultimate reference" (p. 219). Dunn also sees the narrators as
analogous with one another but argues for a hierarchy of narrative success and failure based
upon the degree of "communicative interchange" achieved between teller and listener, the
monster being the least successful (p. 417). My reading of the narrative structure coincides
more closely with that of Bloom, who cautions that the monster cannot be compared to his
creator as narrator since he is "the nightmare actualization of Frankenstein's desire" (p. 127).

that the novel is not only a collection of stories; it is also a collection of personal documents that contain stories—letters, journals, diaries, notes, transcripts, and so on. We are constantly reminded of these components by a number of devices and events within the text: the epistolary notations and conventions of Walton, the presentation by the monster of the DeLaceys' correspondence as evidence to prove his case, Frankenstein's subsequent handing over of those letters to Walton, the monster's discovery of his origins in Frankenstein's journal, Clerval's reproof of Frankenstein for failing to write to his family, and finally, Frankenstein's insistence that the notes made by Walton be "corrected and augmented" so that a "mutilated" version of himself not be passed on to "posterity" (207). This repeated representation of the narratives as sources of power underscores their value for their possessors. Moreover, such events as Frankenstein's demand to edit his own story, his fear of mutilation by Walton's narrative, and his terror of the influence of the monster's story reveal the relationship among the various narratives as one of conflict.

What is often ignored about these documents is that the first piece of the narrative fabric is not Walton's letters but Mary Shelley's introduction. Although it was added more than a decade after the first publication of the novel, the introduction becomes the beginning of the tale, since it presents, as Mary Shelley says, an "account of the origin of the story" (222). It is as if the telling of this story of authorial origin were the purpose for which the entire text was written—its end as well as its beginning. In a novel that tells a whole series of conflicting dreams of origin, this dream account takes its place as the fundamental one and provides an interpretive frame for the others. It both surrounds the other tales as their source and forms their center as well. Like the accounts given in the novel by Walton, Frankenstein, and the monster, Mary Shelley's account of the origin and authorship of the story is also an account of the origin and authorship of herself. Each successive narrator within the novel begins his tale as Mary Shelley begins her introduction—by recounting certain crucial facts about his childhood, his parentage, and the origin of his desires. At the heart of Shelley's introduction to her tale, is her dream about another dreamer who awakens to find his dream real, but at the margins, she provides the provocative dream thoughts that compose that dream: an autobiographical sketch of her own childhood, an account of her development as a writer who was the "daughter of two persons of distinguished literary celebrity," and a view of the ordeal she struggled through as the wife of another literary celebrity to achieve the narrative authority necessary to create the novel she called "my hideous progeny" (222, 229).

This paradigmatic story of authorship and competition is essential to understanding the role of dreams in *Frankenstein*. Mary Shelley begins it with a description of herself as a child—a child distinguished by an important pair of attributes: she liked to "write stories" and to "indulge" in "waking dreams" (222). Here at the very outset, she indicates that her writing was always at odds with and inferior to her dreaming. "My dreams were at once more fantastic and agreeable than my writings," she claimed. In her writing, she laments, she was merely "a close imitator—rather doing as others had done than putting down the suggestions of my own mind" (222–23). Though she could assert, "My dreams were all my own; I accounted for them to nobody," she had to admit that her writing was *not* her own (223). Such statements pinpoint an essential conflict in the mind of the young Mary Shelley. The constraint she experienced as a writer made her an imitator rather than an author, while in her more authentic dream experience she was unfettered by any precedent or pattern. It was as if Mary Shelley's dreams themselves were potential narratives that contended with the existing rival narratives of her predecessors which governed her imagination. Those dreams remained suppressed during her childhood, "accounted for" to nobody, stories that were unrealized because they were never told. This narrative conformity has special significance for Shelley in light of her earlier references in the introduction to her parents as accomplished writers and the complicated admiration she would subsequently express for Percy and Byron as her rivals in storytelling.[17]

Following this piece of self-analysis about her literary heritage, Shelley relates the well-known incident in Switzerland which led directly to the writing of *Frankenstein*. She mentions Byron's proposal that each of his guests "write a ghost story," a suggestion posed immediately after they had together read a gothic tale in which the ghost of "the sinful founder" of a family returned to kill all the the sons of his ill-fated house (224). Then, in recounting the invention of her own ghost story, Shelley describes the project in competitive terms, speaking of her desire "to rival those which had excited us to the task" (225–26). By juxtaposing the traditional gothic tale of a deadly threat from the past with her own desire to "rival" such a tale, Shelley introduces the notion of contending narratives which becomes a characteristic of her story—the struggle for authority and originality which is a contest not only for narrative competence but for the right of self-definition. The author's rivalry here seems to be not only with past writers but specifically

[17]In *The Madwoman in the Attic: The Woman Writer and the Nineteenth-Century Literary Imagination* (1979), Sandra M. Gilbert and Susan Gubar point out that Mary Shelley studied her parents' writings intensely just before she wrote *Frankenstein*, "like a scholarly detective seeking clues to the significance of some cryptic text" (p. 223). Gilbert and Gubar read the novel as an attempt to come to terms with both her parents' writings and Milton's—a "psychodrama reflecting Mary Shelley's own sense of what we might call bibliogenesis . . . a version of the misogynistic story implicit in *Paradise Lost*" (p. 224). See also U. C. Knoepflmacher, "Thoughts on the Aggression of Daughters," in *The Endurance of "Frankenstein,"* ed. Knoepflmacher and Levine, for an interpretation of the novel as a daughter's rage against her parents.

with the writers of patriarchal tales, a culture of fathers who rival and threaten their own sons and daughters.[18]

The implication is reinforced by Mary's account of her painful struggle trying to compose her story in the context of the embarrassment she felt as a "silent listener" to the tales of Byron and Percy (227). "I felt that blank incapability of invention which is the greatest misery of authorship," she says (226). This sense of authorial competition is also present later in the introduction when Mary makes a "declaration" that Percy had nothing to do with the content or feeling of the novel, except for the preface, which, "as far as I can recollect," she concedes, was "entirely written by him" (229). The story itself, however, was entirely written by her.[19] The culmination of this conflict and of Shelley's account of the origins of her story occurs when she relates her climactic "waking dream" of an "artist" and inventor: "I saw the pale student of unhallowed arts kneeling beside the thing he had put together. . . . He sleeps; but he is awakened; he opens his eyes; behold, the horrid thing stands at his bedside, opening his curtains and looking on him with yellow, watery, but speculative eyes" (228). After giving this account, Shelley then tells how much her dream terrified her and how she managed to conquer that fear, implicitly recognizing her dream as a symptom of her failure as an author, prescribing that she give an account of it to cure her of its horror: "Swift as light and as cheering was the idea that broke upon me. 'I have found it! What terrified me will terrify others; and I need only describe the spectre which had haunted my midnight pillow.' On the morrow I announced that I had *thought of a story*. I began that day with the words, *It was on a dreary night of November*, making only a transcript of the grim terrors of my waking dream" (228). By putting her dream into words, she transforms it from the alien "spectre" that haunted her into *her* waking dream and the story *she* conceived. This act also transforms her from a silent listener into a powerful—even terrifying—narrator. She has realized that the terrified has the power to terrify. Finally, the dream reveals to Mary Shelley that the conflict she had earlier posed between her dreams and her writing could be resolved only by uniting them, by making her writing out of her dreams. By recognizing her dream as her own production and as something she had herself imagined—as a "thing" she had "put together"—she established herself as an author rather than an imitator of others.[20]

[18]See William Veeder, *Mary Shelley and "Frankenstein": The Fate of Androgyny* (1986), and Margaret Homans, *Bearing the Word*, for two full accounts of Shelley's complaint against patriarchy in *Frankenstein*.

[19]In his Introduction and notes to the University of Chicago Press edition of the text, James Rieger maintains that Percy's contribution to the tale was more extensive than Mary admits here; if so, her assertion of authority is that much more significant (see pp. xviii, xliv, and xxiii).

[20]Mary Poovey takes a different view in *The Proper Lady and the Woman Writer: Ideology as Style in the Works of Mary Wollstonecraft, Mary Shelley, and Jane Austen* (1984). Poovey maintains that

Two important aspects of this introductory dream account explicitly connect it with the major concerns of *Frankenstein*. First, like the story of *Frankenstein*, the account of Mary Shelley's dream relates the activity of dreaming
to the recovery from a state of psychological paralysis through an act of
"invention," a recollection of personal "origins," and the "creating" of something new "out of chaos" (226). Second, the content of Shelley's dream is
transplanted into the novel at a point when Frankenstein—a man of speculative science and a failed student of medicine—awakes from a disturbing
dream, discovers that the project that had been his "dream" now terrifies and
repulses him, and perceives his own work as a supernatural possession that
he must keep secret. His refusal to tell his story here is as significant as Mary
Shelley's insistence on telling hers.[21] The original version of the novel as told
to Lord Byron and Percy Shelley was, in fact, described by Mary Shelley as
"only a transcript" of her dream. Since the entire novel that emerges from
that transcript is a series of stories told by someone to someone else, Victor
Frankenstein's elaborate act of narrative repression must be regarded as
unnatural indeed.[22]

George Levine has remarked that the "realism" and "secularity" of
Frankenstein are evidenced by the lack of supernatural content in Victor's
dream. Levine places the author of Frankenstein in the tradition of such
nineteenth-century thinkers as Darwin, Freud, Marx, and Feuerbach, whose
common project it was "to discover in matter what we had previously attributed to spirit."[23] This phrase accurately describes both what Frankenstein attempts in creating his monster and what Mary Shelly attempts in
transcribing her dream. The gothic customarily deals with a situation more
like the one summarized in Shelley's introduction, in which a curse or a
secret from the past returns to the present to assert its power in the form of a
ghost or specter. But *Frankenstein* is the account of a curse that springs from
the inside rather than the outside of a man, and then recoils on him with the

Mary Shelley "finds that she cannot escape the 'hideous phantom' except by 'transcribing' her
'waking dream.' In other words, she can exorcise the specter of her own egotistical imagination
only by giving in to it as if to a foreign power—no matter how guardedly, with no matter what
guilt" (p. 142). Whereas Poovey sees Shelley's transcription as a way to disown the dream, I see
it as a way to own and master the dream, which distinguishes her from Frankenstein and his
denials.

[21]Poovey reads Victor as a gothic victim and sees in Shelley's revisions of the novel an
increasingly clear portrayal of him as "a helpless pawn of a predetermined 'destiny,' a fate that is
given, not made" (p. 133). Certainly, this is how Victor portrays himself but not necessarily how
Shelley regards him. Poovey is correct that the revisions make this case more persistently; but it
is Victor who is making the case, and his increasingly shrill protestations against his own
responsibility do not make them any more convincing—only more desperate.

[22]See David Ketterer, *Frankenstein's Creation: The Book, the Monster, and Human Reality*
(1979), on the importance of textuality in the novel and for an exploration of the other texts it has
"embodied."

[23]George Levine, "The Ambiguous Heritage of *Frankenstein*," in *The Endurance of "Frankenstein,"* ed. Knoepflmacher and Levine, p. 7.

greater violence because he permits it to remain a specter. On the one hand, *Frankenstein* is a story of a man's self-authorship and self-determination rather than his determination by some conspiracy of the past or by supernatural forces beyond his control. On the other hand, it is a story about a man who denies just this self-creation. Critics have commonly spoken of the supernatural events in gothic fiction as allegories for psychological phenomena.[24] But *Frankenstein* differs from this pattern in that it presents dreams as quite clearly humanly generated and then has their self-deceived dreamers speak of them in supernatural terms. *Frankenstein* succeeds by exposing a dreamer's failure to understand the psychological significance of his own dreams and by expressing the need for a new explanatory discourse through which to interpret those dreams. This feature of the novel is not so much a critique of nineteenth-century ideologies of self-authorship and self-assertion as it is a demand for more appropriate terms in which to express that ideology.

Even though Frankenstein is almost continuously sick in body and mind from the moment he creates his monster, he does not recognize that the monster is not only the embodiment of his dream; it is a symptom of a neurotic condition that he must understand and from which he must recover. After the monster murders Frankenstein's most beloved friend, Clerval, Frankenstein is again stricken by a fever in which his whole past life appears to him as a "frightful dream" (180–81). In the course of his "recovery from the fever," Frankenstein describes himself as being "possessed" by frightening dreams that figure his psychological paralysis and connect it with a failure to articulate: "My dreams presented a thousand objects that scared me. Towards morning I was possessed by a kind of night-mare; I felt the fiend's grasp in my neck, and could not free myself from it; groans and cries rung in my ears. My father, who was watching over me . . . awoke me" (181). With each death of a loved one, the pattern is repeated. Frankenstein becomes ill and plagued by dreams of his monster, dreams that he describes as demonic possessions. Then he is nursed back to health by another intimate, a parental figure from whom he keeps the dream-monster a secret for fear of being declared mad.[25] Finally, that very person becomes a potential victim of the violence of Frankenstein's repressed nightmare. Walton is his last nurse and his final auditor, and the entire novel becomes the tale of repression the scientist relates to the navigator. As Victor finally fails to "recover" through telling his tale, Walton is placed in danger as well. He too risks becoming a

[24]See, for example, MacAndrew, *The Gothic Tradition in Fiction*; Day, *In the Circles of Fear and Desire*; and Robert Kiely, *The Romantic Novel in England* (1972).

[25]See Veeder's extensive treatment of the "negative Oedipus" in the novel and his exploration of the significance of Victor's desire to kill and replace his father (*Mary Shelley and "Frankenstein,"* pp. 137–53).

casualty of Frankenstein's nightmare. Though Frankenstein has finally revealed his secret to someone, he never makes the vital connections among the dream, his illness, and the monster; so he dies in his sickbed with his dream still presiding over him.

Frankenstein's manmade man functions both literally and figuratively as his dream in the novel, even in his own account. The monster is at first presented as the embodiment of Frankenstein's desires, his grand romantic dreams and aspirations; it is his remaking of himself. But as such, the monster is also his failure to deal with himself as he is, and the dream therefore becomes a nightmare to him as soon as it becomes a reality. "Now that I had finished," he concedes upon first seeing the creature he had made, "the beauty of the dream vanished, and breathless horror and disgust filled my heart" (52–53). Frankenstein immediately seeks refuge from his accomplishment in sleep ("to seek a few moments of forgetfulness"), but his sleep is disturbed by "the wildest dreams," which awaken him and remind him of the monster's reality: "Dreams that had been my food and pleasant rest for so long a space, were now become a hell to me" (53–54). His desire to forget the implications of his dream enables it to imprison him and results in a chronic state of mental illness, which even he refers to as "the sickness of fear" (54). Frankenstein's refusal to face the psychological realities behind his dream, however, give the monster a power over him and lead him to continue dreaming in a literal and obsessive way. As Frankenstein's repressed story of himself, the monster is driven to violence only by Frankenstein's continual attempts to maintain its secrecy. When we first meet Frankenstein he is, like the Ancient Mariner to whom he compares himself, anxious to tell his tale. But the narrative he offers to Walton actually chronicles his continued, calculated suppression of that narrative. His story, then, is at least implicitly a confession of this narrative failure, an admission of his long resistance to offering his story and taking control of his own life and dreams. It is also an acknowledgment of his abandonment of science for superstition. "I had retrod the steps of knowledge along the paths of time," Frankenstein admits, "and exchanged the discoveries of recent enquirers for the dreams of forgotten alchemists" (from the 1831 text, 241).

The cost of this exchange of knowledge for dream is most dramatically registered at the crucial moment in the novel when Frankenstein tries to escape the reality of his completed dream project in sleep, only to be confronted by that reality in the form of another dream. This is also the place where Shelley has placed the "transcript" of her own dream of authority, calling attention to it as the crucial moment of narrative opportunity for the dreamer. What seems most important about the dream is that it occurs when it does—just as Frankenstein finishes his invention, when "the beauty of the dream vanished" and he is attempting to repress its reality. His dream is conspicuously not about the monster he has made, at least not in its manifest content, but his desire to repress the monster distorts its representation in revealing ways:

> I slept indeed, but I was disturbed by the wildest dreams. I thought I saw Elizabeth, in the bloom of health, walking in the streets of Ingolstadt. Delighted and surprised, I embraced her; but as I imprinted the first kiss on her lips, they became livid with the hue of death; her features apppeared to change, and I thought that I held the corpse of my dead mother in my arms; a shroud enveloped her form, and I saw the grave-worms crawling in the folds of the flannel. I started from my sleep in horror. (53)

The dream is not about the fiend Frankenstein has made but about the fiend he has made of himself. Yet the dream encodes the sense that the monster is Frankenstein, that Frankenstein's dream is his symptom. Frankenstein directly causes Elizabeth's transformation from a woman "in the bloom of health" to a corpse shrouded in graveclothes. He is the source of a deadly illness. Elizabeth dies, he tells Walton, "as I imprinted the first kiss on her lips." Both his mother and his fiancée, his past and his future, are conflated into a single image of betrayal and death at the instant his desire is expressed in the form of the "imprinted" kiss. The dream appears to contain both a memory of guilt for the death of his mother and a prophecy of guilt for the murder of Elizabeth, merged in an image of the grave—the place where the pieces of his own invention originated. That both figures in the dream are female, that they are his own mother and the potential mother of his children, also suggests a subconscious awareness of the horror of his desire to create a man by himself—without a mother. Feminist critics have regarded this feature of the dream as symptomatic of Frankenstein's patriarchal exclusivity, which seeks to devalue and eradicate women even in the area of sexual reproduction. But Victor's preoccupation might also be read as yet another manifestation of his battle against just this sort of social authority, in this case as it is manifested in the restrictive controls exerted on him by the conventional family structure.[26]

Frankenstein had said of his monster in the course of making it that he "desired it with an ardour that far exceeded moderation" (52). The dream shows that Victor's immoderate desire to be a self-made man has required him figuratively to murder his family and lover, to eliminate the traces of his "natural" origins. In the remainder of the novel, this dream will become a

---

[26]Margaret Homans reads the novel (and the dream) as a portrayal of "the situation of women obliged to play the role of the literal in a culture that devalues it," and as centrally concerned with the "death and obviation of the mother" (p. 100). On the importance of the mother, see also Marc A. Rubenstein, "'My Accursed Origin': The Search for the Mother in *Frankenstein*," *Studies in Romanticism* 15 (Spring 1976): 165–94; and Barbara Johnson, "My Monster/My Self," *Diacritics* 12 (Summer 1982): 2–10.

reality. As Frankenstein stifles the expression and interpretation of the dream, he will gradually eliminate all the people in his life who might inhibit his self-mastery in any way. Earlier, Frankenstein admits that he "forgot" his friends and neglected "all that related to my feelings of affection until the great object . . . should be completed" (50). This neglect denies him the very intimacy that the monster so deeply desires. The result is that Victor becomes "oppressed by a slow fever" and "nervous to a most painful degree" just before the monster is completed. Then he dreams his terrible dream (51). But even though he is a man of science, Victor views his dream as a visitation from another world, a "spectre," a "fiend," and a "demon"—"my own vampire, my own spirit let loose from the grave" (72). He still will not recognize it as a symptom of his disordered state of mind.

Frankenstein's repeated use of supernatural language to describe psychological conditions signals a linguistic crisis that the novel enacts. Victor presents himself as a scientist committed to a scientific world view, and yet he continues to represent his achievements in debased theological terms. The use of such language not only indicates Frankenstein's refusal to take responsibility for his own creation but also reveals his desire to replace divine authority with his own. His representation of himself to Walton can be read as a text in which these two vocabularies come into conflict. Frankenstein is a scientist, but he seeks to create "a new species" that would "bless" him as "its creator and source" (49). His approach to science does not demystify a superstitious world view. It only mystifies science. The young Frankenstein's fascination with mystical and occult practices exposes this internal conflict early in his career. He is attracted by the "unlimited powers" of science rather than by any truth about the world or about himself which science might teach him. He pursues those powers, he says, with "an almost supernatural enthusiasm" (42, 46). One of his more modern and realistic professors advised Frankenstein that the essential task of modern science was "to give new names" to the knowledge the occult scientists had articulated (43). But Frankenstein keeps resorting to the old names, especially in describing his own state of mind. Despite his commitment to science, Frankenstein fails to realize what Mary Shelley realizes in her introduction: in the modern world, human beings are not spoken to in dreams; they are speaking to themselves. The dream does not invade the dreamer; it is invented by the dreamer.

Frankenstein completes his first grand project of defying heaven and making a man very early in his narrative. At that point he commences his second project, which occupies much more of the novel and is perhaps an even more ambitious enterprise: suppressing the reality of his first accomplishment. Once "the beauty of the dream vanished," Frankenstein attempts to disown it. His determined suppression of the story of his nightmarish creation evidences itself right at the outset, on the morning after he awakes from his dream and encounters the monster once more in his room, this time in the presence of his friend Clerval. When Clerval implores Frankenstein to tell him what has caused his obvious disturbance of mind, Frankenstein responds with a reproof: "Do not ask me." Then, imagining he sees the "dreaded spectre" before him, Frankenstein gestures wildly at it, screaming to Clerval, "*he* can tell," as he falls into another fit of unconsciousness (56).

This is the first of Frankenstein's many refusals to own his dream and the first time he explicitly identifies the monster as a potential teller of a tale. Indeed, Frankenstein comes to fear this threat more than any other, and it is the monster's tale that he struggles most intensely to suppress. His repeated warnings to Walton to avoid listening to any tale told by the persuasive monster are central features of Frankenstein's narrative of repression. The novel stages a competiton between his creation story and the monster's version, a competition that Walton must finally judge. Though Frankenstein presents his narrative as a contest between two stories, their fates are bound together, as the monster warns the disbelieving creator when he claims they are "bound by ties only dissoluble by the annihilation of one of us" (94). Frankenstein admits that there is power in the monster's story which moves him deeply, but he does not recognize himself as the source of that power. The monster, however, has a better grasp of his creator's narrative connection to him, demanding to tell his own story as adamantly as Frankenstein insists on not telling his. "Hear me," the monster warns several times in his first meeting with Frankenstein, "or become the scourge of your fellow-creatures and the author of your own speedy ruin" (95–96). The monster reminds Frankenstein that he is the "author" of the material that constitutes his own life story and that a denial of his own actions by calling them demonic will eventually ruin him. This information is precisely what Frankenstein wants to repress, as he indicates when he responds to the monster in words that express his desire to "forget" the responsibilities of his own authorship: "Why do you call to my remembrance circumstances of which I shudder to reflect, that I have been the miserable origin and author?" (96).

The monster's tale is also a story of desire. But his desire is to express himself in language. As Frankenstein's dream, the monster paradoxically acts both as a sign of the dreamer's repression and an expression of his desire to tell. As the monster tells it, his personal history is an exact reversal of Frankenstein's. The monster records his progress from uttering "inarticulate sounds" to becoming a "master of the language," all in the pursuit of the kind of self-understanding and human community that Frankenstein has shunned (99, 114). The monster's resentment of his creator originates, significantly, in his discovery and reading of Frankenstein's private journals. They contained, he said, "the minutest description of my odious and loathsome person . . . in language which painted your own horrors, and rendered mine ineffaceable" (126). In the person of the monster, the dream material declares itself here as ineffaceable, despite Frankenstein's effort to erase or paint over his connection to the dream as soon as he generated it. As the embodiment of the dream, the monster reminds Frankenstein of this ineradicability, relentlessly seeking the "ineffaceable" explanation of himself through the "godlike science" of language (107). The monster implicitly recognizes that language may be godlike, but it is not God-ordained. It is a tool of science, not a mysterious means of invoking or exorcising spirits. Appropriately, the first dream the monster tells to Frankenstein is about the power of telling his own story. In that dream, he overcomes the "disgust" of Felix and his family and wins their friendship through the efficacy of his own "conciliating words" (110).

From the beginning Frankenstein possesses an intense interest in the mysteries and secrets of nature. "The world was to me a secret which I desired to discover," he says of the quest for knowledge which took him away from his family and eventually from the whole human community (30). But clearly he is intent on repressing the secret desires of his own nature rather than bringing those secrets to light. He performs his grand project in complete secrecy, and during that time he acknowledges having received frequent reprimands from his family for not writing to them and accounting for his long absences. This failure as a correspondent must be significant in a novel that includes so many letters and is itself written in epistolary form. Frankenstein exhibits symptoms of his nervous disorder when Clerval raises the subject of writing home to his family. "Compose yourself," he counsels. "I will not mention it, if it agitates you; but your father and cousin would be very happy if they received a letter from you in your own hand-writing. They hardly know how ill you have been, and are uneasy at your long silence" (58). Frankenstein's silence is consistently associated with his illness and his refusal to "compose" himself by expressing it in language is always a symptom of that illness.

The first victim of Frankenstein's silence is his brother William, whose death Victor intuitively but inexplicably knows was caused by "his" monster. When Victor returns to his family to grieve over William's death, he considers telling his family his strange tale but finally resists. "I paused when I reflected on the story I had to tell," he says, claiming that he kept silent because the improbablity of the story would make his family think him insane (72). This refusal to own his dream, to identify the monster's action as as his own, is precisely what is driving him insane and causing the "nervous fever" from which he suffers (72). But he refuses to contemplate this possibility. "These reflections determined me," he says, "and I resolved to remain silent" (73). This resolution Victor makes several more times, and each time he causes the death of someone close to him. His silence assures Justine's unjust conviction and execution. Just prior to Clerval's murder, Frankenstein again decides to withhold his story from his family and keep his promise to make a mate for the monster as a secret condition of his marriage to Elizabeth. Once more he rationalizes this silence as a gesture of concern for his friends and family, even though he knows the strategy is dangerous: "I knew that a thousand fearful accidents might occur, the slightest of which would disclose a tale to thrill all connected with me with horror."[27] Again, just before his marriage to Elizabeth and her subsequent murder, Frankenstein avoids explaining his bizarre behavior to his family, so they will not think him mad: "I avoided explanation, and maintained a continual silence concerning the wretch I had created. I had a feeling that I should be supposed mad, and this for ever chained my tongue, when I would have given the whole world to have confided the fatal secret" (182). Frankenstein does not realize that what makes his secret fatal is that it is kept secret. He promises to divulge this "one secret" and "confide this tale of misery and terror" to Elizabeth only on the day after they marry. But it is a promise that—as his nightmare revealed—he would never have to keep (187).

Frankenstein's calculated effort to stifle his story is the most articulate symptom of his "incurable disease" (182). Its neurotic and compulsive character is suggested on the occasions when, despite his vigilance, "words" about his past which he refuses to explain "escape to my lips, as a half stifled sigh" (183). "I was in reality very ill," Frankenstein admits as soon as he has created his monster (57), and he alternately describes himself as suffering from "nervous fever," "insanity of the heart," "delirium," or some other form of illness from that moment on. Even as Frankenstein tells his tale, Walton is nursing his physical and emotional infirmities. But Frankenstein has neither the will nor the words to understand the symptoms of his own pathology. The language of psychological illness is "painted" over by the language of supernatural fatalism in Victor's account of himself, and he therefore cannot arrive at any understanding of his fears and desires.[28]

In this sense, Frankenstein never does succeed in becoming the narrator of his life story. Even as he speaks to Walton he continues to surrender his authority to the "fate" that he interprets as embodied in his dream. From beginning to end, Frankenstein refers to himself not as self-determined but as under the control of supernatural forces outside himself, forces he finally associates with the very dreams and desires from which he dissociates himself. Early on in the "record" he metaphorizes his "tale of misery" in a way

[27]The quotation is from the revised text of 1831. See page 252 of the Rieger text I have used throughout.

[28]Like Poovey, Levine regards Frankenstein as "removed from direct personal responsibility even for his own ambitions: for the most part he is described as passively consumed by energies larger than himself or as quite literally unconscious and ill when his being conscious might have changed the course of the narrative" ("The Ambiguous Heritage of *Frankenstein*," p. 10). The passive constructions in Levine's prose here may obscure exactly what Frankenstein himself desires to obscure. We must remember that it is Frankenstein who is doing the describing and providing the self-justifying narrative in the text.

that makes its driving force seem to spring from the outside, even though he relates the origin of that force to a "passion":

> In drawing the picture of my early days, I must not omit to record those events which led, by insensible steps to my after tale of misery: for when I would account to myself for the birth of that passion, which afterwards ruled my destiny, I find it arise, like a mountain river, from ignoble and almost forgotten sources; but swelling as it proceeded, it became the torrent which in its course, has swept away all my hope and joys.
> Natural philosophy is the genius that has regulated my fate. (32)

Frankenstein is "ruled" by "that passion" he has objectified, whose sources he has conveniently forgotten. His tale is an abandonment to fate rather than a record of his desires. The effects of his own desires (his "hopes and joys") have been "swept away" in his own self-alienating diction. Toward the end of his narrative, when he describes his life as a confusion of dream and waking, Victor's language explicitly turns his own passions and impulses into the agencies of heaven: "At such moments vengeance, that burned within me, died in my heart, and I pursued my path towards the destruction of the daemon, more as a task enjoined by heaven, as the mechanical impulse of some power of which I was unconscious, than as the ardent desire of my soul" (202). Here Frankenstein's attribution of his actions to the super-natural forces of heaven and hell keep him from assuming any control over the unconscious desire that he permits to be understood merely as an "im-pulse" issuing from some divine machine.

Frankenstein's refusal to assume the authorship of his own story, then, carries with it a cost for himself as well as for the victims of his creation. Even before he dies, he loses his life in a metaphorical sense—by losing control of it. His failure to give an account of his dream turns his entire existence into a nightmare that haunts and possesses him, as Mary Shelley's dream did before she told it. "The past appeared to me in the light of a frightful dream," he says after being accused of Clerval's murder, which occurs ap-propriately, while Frankenstein sleeps in his boat on his way to an intended meeting with his friend (180–81). "The whole series of my life appeared to me as a dream; I sometimes doubted if indeed it were all true, for it never presented itself to my mind with the force of reality" (175). The confusion of dreams and reality is Frankenstein's own doing, his own failure to associate the forces in his dreams with those in his waking life. He prefers to conceive of himself as a gothic character haunted by a fiend or a phantom, a ghost he has been cursed with. This mastery by external forces Frankenstein identi-fies with the recurring nightmare by which he claims to be "possessed," in which he is engaged in a struggle with the "fiend," from which he cannot free himself: the monster's hands grasp his neck and he is silenced, just as William, Clerval, and Elizabeth were silenced (181).

Victor as much as admits responsibility for his infirmities when he says that it was "by the utmost self-violence" that he "curbed the imperious voice of wretchedness, which sometimes desired to declare itself to the whole world" (183). His detachment from his own voice here, speaking of it as a thing apart from his will and power, underscores the harm that his failure as a narrator has inflicted on him. He is wounded by the secret he keeps even from his own consciousness. The single effort he makes to tell his "tale of horrors" before meeting Walton occurs when he goes to the magistrate after Clerval's murder. But even this is not a confession of guilt but rather an act of revenge in which Frankenstein still seeks to project responsibility for his crimes on an agency outside himself. He comes to the magistrate declaring he has "an accusation" to level, and in the course of arguing for the truth of his account he explicitly denies that the monster is his dream. "The story is too connected to be mistaken for a dream," he pleads (196–97). But the unacknowledged *dis*connectedness of the story is exactly what confirms it as a dream. Frankenstein laments that the judge "heard my story with that half kind of belief that is given to a tale of spirits and supernatural events" (197). Of course he did. This is precisely how Frankenstein has repeatedly represented his dreams and his neuroses. He explains away his "phrenzy" while telling his story as the "haughty fierceness, which the martyrs of old are said to have possessed." He refers to his "appearance of madness" during the narrative as an expression of his deep "devotion" and "heroism" (198). As he has throughout his career, Frankenstein takes refuge in a theological language in which his madness can be regarded as heroic and his "self-violence" can appear as martyrdom.

Frankenstein's self-deception may be seen either as an expression of the repressed romantic-gothic overreacher or as representative of a more widespread cultural problem. As a psychological case, Frankenstein, like the painter in Freud's case "A Seventeenth-Century Demonological Neurosis," might be understood as suffering from a crisis of authority which exhibits itself as a rage against his parents, as paranoia, schizophrenia, and egomania. Frankenstein's project at the outset is quite clearly associated with the death of his mother, his confused family history, and the failure of his father to guide him properly. He defines his scientific aspirations in Promethean terms as a human assumption of divine attributes—the creation of a race of beings that will worship him as creator. But upon completing his project, Frankenstein discovers, among other things, that he is only a man who has taken on divine responsibilties, whose scope terrifies him. He fears the implications of replacing his father and mother with a family romance enacted in his own mind. Early in his narrative, Victor criticizes his father's curt dismissal of his interest in the occult and even suggests that had his father been a better guide, he might "never have received the fatal impulse that led to my ruin" (33). These issues emerge again when the father explicitly requests that

Victor marry Elizabeth at the same time as the monster requests he make a female mate. Frankenstein meets both requests with "horror and dismay," seeing each "solemn promise" as necessarily excluding the other, instead of recognizing them as parallel demands of the erotic life (149). Rather than accept the consequences of his essentially modern and secular situation, then, Frankenstein once more rejects responsibilty for it and for himself. At the same time, he rejects the world of science for the more secure world of religion, failing in the project to "give new names" to the phenomena of human experience (43).

But Frankenstein's failure to give "new names" to psychological phenomena may also be read as a larger cultural accusation by Mary Shelley. Put another way, her dream text may be seen as expressing a desire for a scientific language to identify and explain human psychology, a language to mediate between the only alternatives Frankenstein could imagine to represent his condition: hopeless, incurable madness or supernatural possession. In this reading, *Frankenstein* becomes a text that asserts the existence of a powerful inner life and laments the lack of an adequate vocabulary to identify and control the sometimes terrifying psychic forces that drive that life. Our dreams are monstrous specters until they find a language by which they can be effectively integrated into our waking experience. Without such a language, they remain repressed, denied, or projected onto a transcendent world of spirits and demons. It is for this reason that the monster, as Frankenstein's dream, devotes himself so absolutely to a quest to master language, a quest that may be read as a request for a form of psychoanalytic discourse with which to work through the dream specters and translate them into what Freud called the familiar language of our dream thoughts. Frankenstein's failure is his frustration of that quest, his devotion of himself "to the annihilation of those visions on which my interest in science was chiefly founded" (41). The monster remains as a sign of Frankenstein's now-abandoned scientific interests. Yet, even the monster represents a threat, because the wish for a scientific discourse in the novel is qualified by a suspicion. Victor's own course demonstrates that medicine wrongly applied can produce Faustian overreachers and can, by way of a scientific and professional elitism, mystify the nature of the self as profoundly as any religion.

The monster's final appearance in the novel reinforces the ambivalence about the desire he represents. Walton is the last person to see the monster, and he is the only acquaintance of Frankenstein's who encounters the monster and lives. Walton is, of course a double for Frankenstein: both are engaged on a grand quest; both have abandoned home and friends for that quest; both have violated the will of their fathers in pursuing their great projects; and both have their stories to tell. Walton even describes his project in terms that echo Frankenstein's when he calls the polar expedition his "favourite dream" and describes it as imbued with "an enthusiam which elevates me to heaven" (10). When the dying Frankenstein asks Walton to "undertake my unfinished work," he makes an ominous request (215). If Walton is to succeed where Frankenstein fails, he must recognize the dangerous analogy between himself and the dying scientist, and he must recognize what his predecessor did not—that the monster may be the projection of his own "favourite dream." His project has brought Walton, like Frankenstein, face-to-face with a monster, which he encounters in his bedroom. In order to psychically survive that experience he must tell his own tale of self-recognition rather than repeat Frankenstein's story of self-repression.

When the monster reappears to Walton after his creator's death, he begins his final account of himself by posing an important question: "And do you dream?" (217). The question remains unanswered by Walton, as it was by Frankenstein. The quality of Walton's response when he completes his own account of himself will determine whether or not his story will substantially differ from Frankenstein's. Walton's letters to his sister are not the end of his story, though they do represent a hopeful sign of commitment to the familiar world abandoned by Frankenstein. But his decision to forsake his journey is imposed on him by his crew, rather than freely taken by himself. He remains vulnerable to Frankenstein's lofty rhetoric and to "the power of his eloquence," referring to him as a "godlike" and "glorious spirit" (208, 210, 216). Walton, however, *is* also moved by the monster's last words, which work in the direction of self-understanding rather than self-justification. The monster acknowledges that his passions drive him, but he takes responsibility for those passions: "I had cast off all feeling, subdued all anguish to riot in the excess of my despair. . . . I had no choice," he goes on to say, "but to adapt my nature to an element which I had willingly chosen. The completion of my demoniacal design became an insatiable passion" (218). Whereas Frankenstein converts his passions to the mechanisms of demonic or divine intelligence and resists their psychological reality, the monster's demoniacal designs "become" for him the expression of his own passions. He acknowledges the need to adapt himself to the elements of the nature he was at least partially responsible for bringing into being. For Walton to survive his encounter with Frankenstein's monster and to finish what was left unfinished by his double, he must judge between these two accounts of the self and formulate out of his dream a story that takes responsibility for the desires and passions within it.

Frankenstein raises issues central to the development of the nineteenth-century novel. It is a book simultaneously concerned with constructing a self and with becoming, or failing to become, a responsible narrator—projects that the novel portrays as essentially related. Edward Said has identified a tension in the novel between what he calls "authority" and "molestation," between the powers and the limits of self-origination. Said's description of this tension is so appropriate to the specifics of its plot that *Frankenstein* seems to become a model for the novel so defined: "The common pattern here is the initial rejection of natural paternity in the narrative, which then leads to a special procreative yet celibate enterprise, which in turn yields to death and a brief vision of what might have happened had the narrative and the initial act of self-isolation never been undertaken."[29] *Frankenstein* is the archetypal tale of a literal "procreative yet celibate enterprise" for the nineteenth century. Its plot is what Peter Brooks describes as the fundamental plot of any novel—an account of aberration from a prescribed pattern, of deviance, abnormality. According to Brooks, the novel characteristically follows a course of error which seeks to correct itself by conforming to a divine "master text."[30] Much as Freud had defined the dream event, Brooks defines the novel as a kind of cultural symptom that is also a part of the process of recovery.

Brooks claims, however, that "if the master text is not available, we are condemned to the reading of erroneous plots . . . to repetition, rereading in the knowledge that what we discover will always be that there was nothing to be discovered."[31] This is the most pessimistic view of the secular, recuperative project of the novel. The genre can also be described as expressing, as *Frankenstein* does, a continuing quest for a new discourse to replace the missing divine master text in the explanation of the self. The publication of a host of novelistic and quasi-novelistic autobiographies during the nineteenth century represents a sustained experiment in formulating such discourses. "Once translated from images into interpretative language," Said says of Freud's speaking cure, "the plot of the dream, and hence its image, loses its effective power to dominate one's attention."[32] The terrifying image of Frankenstein's monster has no power over one person in the novel—the blind DeLacey. This is the case, of course, because for him the words of the monster's story necessarily replace his fearful image. "I am blind, and cannot judge your countenance," DeLacey says to the monster, "but there is something in your words" (130). The finding of that "something" in the words of the narrators in these autobiographical texts constitutes their recovery from a disordered or inadequate vocabulary of the self. DeQuincey's *Confessions of an English Opium-Eater* is just such a text. It drifts across the boundaries of gothic fiction, autobiography, and the autobiographical novel in a unique way, and it appropriately recounts the narrator's literal recovery from the domination of an addiction and its accompanying dreams of terror. By directly associating dreams, illness, and the process of recovery, DeQuincey's *Confessions* deepens the desire for a medically based discourse of dream interpreta-

[29]Said, *Beginnings*, pp. 83, 145.
[30]Peter Brooks, "Repetition, Repression, and Return: *Great Expectations* and the Study of Plot," *New Literary History* 11 (Spring 1980): 503–26.
[31]Ibid., p. 525.
[32]Said, *Beginnings*, p. 167.

tion as it was expressed in *Frankenstein*. At the same time, by parodying and debunking the discourse of religious conversion and confession, the *Confessions* also reveals the exhaustion of the ability of theological language to account for our dreams.

Symptoms and *Confessions of an English Opium-Eater*

I now pass to what is the main subject of these latter confessions, to the history and journal of what took place in my dreams; for these were the immediate and proximate cause of my acutest suffering.
—Thomas DeQuincey

Thomas DeQuincey ends the "Preliminary Confessions" of his *Confessions of an English Opium-Eater* with an address to his wife: "Thou wilt read these records of a period so dolorous to us both as the legend of some hideous dream that can return no more."[33] Like Mary Shelley and Horace Walpole before him, DeQuincey traces these "records" of his illness to a dream account—or, more precisely, to the "legend" of a dream. By characterizing his project as the making of a readable legend out of his hideous dreams, DeQuincey implicitly acknowledges that his dreams were symptoms of a life story in disarray. Later in the *Confessions*, he identifies the "main subject" of the narrative as "the history and journal of what took place in my dreams," because the dreams were "the immediate and proximate cause" of the infirmities that demanded the narrative be written (102). But De-Quincey's dreams are symptoms not only because they manifest a disorder but also because they enable a recovery. The story, he claims, once composed out of the dream, will order his past in such a way as to give each event its proper place, releasing the reader and the writer from the painful hauntings that will "return no more." The whole of the *Confessions* is an account of this transfer of power from the dream to the dreamer, or more accurately, to the teller of the dream. If *Frankenstein* expresses the desire for a new discourse with which to explain and integrate dream experience into the construction of a self, DeQuincey's *Confessions* provides a framework for that project to begin.

"As an essayist and autobiographer, Thomas DeQuincey was a great Gothic novelist," Eve Kosofsky Sedgwick attests. "The subjects he ap-

---

[33]Thomas DeQuincey, *Confessions of an English Opium-Eater*, ed. Alethea Hayter (Harmondsworth, Eng.: Penguin, 1978), p. 69, hereafter cited in the text. This edition uses the text as it was first published in the September and October 1821 issues of *London Magazine* (vol. 4, nos. 21:293–312 and 22:353–79).

proached with the most characteristic sympathy were certain heightened versions of a privation and immobilization: dreams and trances, submergence under a massive space, the unspeakable."[34] But as is also typical of much gothic fiction, DeQuincey's *Confessions* strives to speak the unspeakable language of the dream. Describing the "higher key" into which his work sometimes rises, DeQuincey reminds the reader of "the perilous difficulty besieging all attempts to clothe in words the visionary scenes derived from the world of dreams, where a single false note, a single word in a wrong key, ruins the whole music."[35] From the very beginning of the *Confessions*, the choice of the particular kind of discourse with which the narrator constructs the legend of his dreams and articulates the unspeakable is the urgent concern. DeQuincey opens the book with a section addressed directly "To the Reader" in which he firmly declares that "my self-accusation does not amount to a confession of guilt" (30). Despite the title of the book, then, the language and intention of this narrative is to be distinguished from a traditional confession. In opposition to the moral language of guilt and innocence, DeQuincey employs the medical terms of illness and health. His confession seeks "remedies" for "infirmity and misery," which, he maintains, "do not, of necessity, imply guilt" (30). At the same time, he also wants to distinguish his narrative from the sensationalizing "spectacle" of "public exposure" engaged in by the "spurious and defective sensibility of the French," who indiscreetly flaunt their "moral ulcers or scars" for the purpose of defying moral conventions (29). Unlike such writers, DeQuincey is no more interested in subverting the "decent drapery" of moral standards than he is in endorsing it. His project is to provide a different kind of discourse with which to talk about psychic experience. In writing this narrative, DeQuincey wishes to "render" a "service" to the "scores of cases" that suffer from this same "infirmity" (31). Like the opium about which it is written, the narrative itself is presented as a kind of medical treatment "aiming at the bare relief of pain" (30).

In the final paragraph of this introductory address to the reader, DeQuincey defers to the authority of "medical writers" as the "greatest enemies" of opium, who, even so, recognize its "fascinating powers" (32). Later, he refers to the authority of doctors and surgeons in the *Confessions*, often lampooning them for their unfounded superstitions about opium. Nevertheless, much as Freud would do in *The Interpretation of Dreams*, DeQuincey aligns himself with the medical profession in this book, and he

[34]Sedgwick, *The Coherence of Gothic Conventions*, pp. 27, 37. See also Karen M. Lever, "DeQuincey as Gothic Hero: A Perspective on *Confessions of an English Opium-Eater* and *Suspiria de Profundis*," *Texas Studies in Literature and Language* 21 (Fall 1979): 332–46. Lever demonstrates the "fictionality" of the narrator of the *Confessions* and relates him to several gothic heroes.

[35]Thomas DeQuincey, *The Collected Writings of Thomas DeQuincey*, ed. David Masson (1889–90), 1:9, 14.

presents himself as a case study in which he is both doctor and patient, the "medical writer" who corrects and augments the prevailing views of dream experience by writing his own life story into an inquiry about the "extensive power of this drug" and the meaning of the dreams it provokes (32).

Michel Foucault speaks of the "medicalization of the effects of confession" as one of the crucial cultural transformations of the nineteenth century. He demonstrates how new forms of discourse were generated in the period out of the "interference" that existed between the "procedures of confession" and those of "scientific discursivity."[36] Not only did these new discourses contribute to the shaping of contemporary notions of the self, but they also generated new rituals of self-definition which culminated in the language of psychoanalysis at the end of the century. De Quincey's *Confessions* participates in this process. In the following passage, for example, the narrator asserts his "authority" against that of a surgeon on the intoxicating effects of opium, only to plead for a more scientifically accurate "diagnostics" of the self:

> I confess, however, that the authority of a surgeon, and one who was reputed a good one, may seem a weighty one to my prejudice: but still I must plead my experience . . . and, though it was not possible to suppose a medical man unacquainted with characteristic symptoms of vinous intoxication, it yet struck me that he might proceed on a logical error of using the word intoxication with too great latitude, and extending it generically to all modes of nervous excitement, instead of restricting it as the expression for a specific sort of excitement, connected with certain diagnostics. (76)

With scientific precision, DeQuincey explains his experience with opium as a medical phenomenon. The movement in the sentence from the "I confess" with which it begins, to the expression of concern about the accuracy of the doctor's language, then to an appeal by the narrator to his own experience, and finally to a call for the specificity of more "certain diagnostics" provides a concentrated case of the discursive development that Foucault envisions as taking place across the century.

The *Confessions* is generally regarded as a text without a structure or as having, at best, a fuguelike structure in which themes blend, build upon one another, and reappear in modified forms.[37] This organic, improvisational

---

[36]Foucault, *History of Sexuality*, 1:67, 64–65.

[37]See Alethea Hayter's Introduction to *Confessions*. J. Hillis Miller relates the structural confusion of the book to DeQuincey's desire to combine the literature of "power" with the literature of "knowledge" (*The Disappearance of God: Five Nineteenth-Century Writers* [1975], pp. 45–46). The disintegrative structural aspects of the book may also be related to Freud's later insistence on the "disintegrative" work of dream interpretation—the necessity of seeing the dream first in its disparate pieces, of bypassing plot in favor of verbal analysis. The apparent lack of narrative structure here allows for the material of the dreams to be dissolved back into its contradictions before meaning is imposed on it. See Philip Rieff, *Freud: The Mind of the Moralist* (1959), pp. 118–36.

quality is certainly present in the narrative, and DeQuincey explicitly describes much of the text as necessarily spontaneous and "disjointed. "I have
not been able to compose the notes of this part of my narrative into any
regular and connected shape," he says at the opening of the crucial "Pains of
Opium" section (96–97). He apologizes that the events could not be put into
proper sequence but must remain in a state of "horrors" because of the
"palsying effects on the intellectual faculties" of the opium and its dreams
(97–98). These announcements are part of the case DeQuincey is presenting of a life in narrative disorder, symptoms of the disease the narrative is
intended to heal. In addition, they are indications of the unavailability of the
specific interpretive strategies he requires to accomplish his diagnostic goals.
In this section, which contains his literal dream accounts, DeQuincey apologizes that his "way of writing" has been simply "to think aloud" in order to
make "some record of a time, the entire history of which no one can know
but myself" (97). But these apologies are also recognitions that his writing is
itself a symptom and that his text is the presentation of a case study that
requires a kind of talking cure. When DeQuincey identifies himself as a
dreamer seeking to make sense out of the confusion of his "disjointed" and
"disconnected" mental life, he underscores his desire to make his private
experience knowable to someone else. His narrative of self-reproduction is
also a form of self-exposure, then, a turning inside out by the writing subject
in order to reconstruct himself as a coherent entity with a narratable inner
life.

Rather than actually deny a structure to the text, passages like these
foreground the struggle to achieve one. The narrative is, as DeQuincey calls
it several times, a "record." It records the process of making dreams into
language, of turning from dreamer into author. It records the history of a self
inventing the language to describe its private life. The "plot" of this narrative
is appropriately represented as an escape plot, then. It recounts the narrator's "untwist[ing]" of "the chain that fettered him," his release from silence
into speech (30).[38] His dreams, DeQuincey claims, were accompanied by a
deep "melancholy" that was "wholly incommunicable by words" (103). But
this narrative of the inexpressible recounts his discovery of the "assuaging
balm" of "eloquent opium," which offers him a "potent rhetoric" by which
he creates a "new character" for himself (83, 88).[39]

---

[38]For a broader analysis of the importance of language in DeQuincey's writings, see Sedgwick's chapter on DeQuincey, "Language as Live Burial," in *Gothic Conventions*.

[39]In the 1856 edition, DeQuincey's revision of the opening of the "Pains of Opium" section
underscores the centrality of the translation of dreams into language in the *Confessions*: "The
main phenomenon by which opium expressed itself permanently, and the sole phenomenon that
was communicable, lay in the dreams (and in the peculiar dream-scenery) which followed the
opium excesses. . . . The final object of the whole record lay in the dreams" (also in Hayter's
edition, p. 205).

The characterization of the text as therapy makes it both resemble and differ from a religious conversion tract. The *Confessions* tells the story of "a sort of physical regeneration" but not a spiritual one (115). In fact, De-Quincey describes his message as fundamentally secular; it directly opposes the message of conventional religious texts. "This is the doctrine of the true church on the subject of opium," he proclaims, "of which church I acknowledge myself to be the only member—the alpha and the omega" (75). In this book, DeQuincey writes a heretical, Byronic scripture of the first person. The "I" is the only authority in this church, seeking to accomplish "what I never yet heard attributed to any other man" (30). In this scientific gospel, a human being can achieve what previously was attributed only to God. Here, when DeQuincey frees himself from "the accursed chain that fettered" him, he performs a "self-conquest" that is a conquest *by* the self rather than a conquest over it (30). One aspect of this release from opium addiction is its simultaneous release from the power of religious language and a religious world view as well. No wonder that DeQuincey says he takes such pleasure in reading aloud the Satanic speeches from *Paradise Regained*.

The frequent references to *Paradise Lost* and *Paradise Regained* invoke the religious allusiveness of many gothic novels, and they are central to the legend the *Confessions* seeks to create. In this book, DeQuincey rebels against religious conceptions of the self by reinventing himself as a specifically secular, self-authorized agent. He gives birth to a new self and to a general cultural notion of the subject as well. In writing the legend of his own psyche, we might say that he is medicalizing the soul. Appropriately, the dual enterprise of "self-reproduction" and dream interpretation begins with the recollection of certain crucial experiences of DeQuincey's childhood which center around the loss of his parents. He includes this material because it is "necessary" to "an author's purposes" in several ways (33). First, these memories explain why "any reasonable being" would "fetter himself with such a sevenfold chain" as opium addiction. DeQuincey then claims that the childhood material is also included to provide a "key" to the account of the dreams he will later tell and that these recollections are meant to create in the reader some "interest of a personal sort in the confessing subject" (33). DeQuincey's project of unlocking the meaning of the dream material, in other words, is always connected with both diagnosis and treatment: establishing "plausible" narrative explanations by reconstituting a past, and constructing a relationship between author and reader (29, 33).[40] In what might appear to be a description of his own psychoanalysis, DeQuincey seeks to

[40]See Terrence Doody, *Confession and Community in the Novel* (1980). Doody says the occasion for a confession stems from the attempt to resolve a crisis of exclusion by creating a confessor to enable the connection to some community. DeQuincey's attention to the reader in the text and his addressing the book to his wife are consistent with this impulse toward intimacy.

reengender himself by way of a speaking cure—by remembering and writing down the story of his lost parents. This, he asserts, is the key of entry into his unarticulated dream-self.

DeQuincey's account of his youth contains several important details that make this period fundamental to the "narrative plot" of achieving self-authorship. Most striking is his direct linking of the death of his father with the original "pain" that the opium was intended to "remedy." The narrator traces his first use of opium to his desire to ease a "pain in the severest degree" which attacked him at the age of twenty-eight. He then follows the memory of this pain to a specific incident that took place some ten years earlier. Finally, he recalls its first occurrence, caused by the "extremities of hunger suffered" in an earlier time—"in my boyish days" (35). But De-Quincey suggests that these more vaguely remembered pains are caused by more than physical hunger. When he recounts the "youthful sufferings which first produced this derangement," the first event he mentions is that "my father died when I was about seven years old and left me in the care of four guardians" (35). How DeQuincey characterizes his resistance to this loss and to these substitute parents reinforces the sense that his project of self-reproduction began here, with the birth pangs that followed his father's death.[41]

This association of physical and psychological symptoms leads to De-Quincey's first dream descriptions and to the story of the origins of his book as well. The story begins with DeQuincey's attempt to obtain some of the inheritance his father left him in order to attend the university. The effort is met with the uncompromising "authority" of one of his tyrannical guardians, who refuses his charge's request and demands "unconditional submission" to his will (36–37). The young DeQuincey then tried to borrow the money against his expectations from his father's estate and the moneylenders questioned his identity as his father's son. Their suspicion prompts DeQuincey to question the matter himself. "*Was* I that person?" he asks. "It was strange to me to find my own self, *materialiter* considered . . . , accused, or at least suspected, of counterfeiting my own self, *formaliter* considered" (55). This fear of being a self-counterfeit provokes his decision to earn the money with which to buy back his authority over himself—by writing and selling his *Confessions*.

The writing of the *Confessions* is DeQuincey's resolution of a crisis in his identity by returning to but refusing to be determined by the "text" of his past. The magazine publication of his story provided him with an income that made him financially independent and the author of "a new character"

---

[41]V. A. DeLuca reads the *Confessions* as fundamentally a quest for love, emphasizing De-Quincey's portrayals of himself in the text as the forlorn child, the abandoned lover, the ailing husband (*Thomas DeQuincey: The Prose of Vision* [1980], 17–19).

(88).[42] That effort, however, produced dreams that "haunted" him during this period of his life, dreams that he says were "as ugly, and as ghastly phantoms that ever haunted the couch of an Orestes" (68). These dreams remain phantoms for DeQuincey. They bind, dominate, and torture him as much as his unyielding guardians did and as much as his addiction to opium would. He never reveals the content of those dreams, only that they were associated with the pains and traumas that produced the book. It is enough at this stage of the narrative that the dreams are regarded as "ghostly" and are likened to the hauntings of Orestes—another son who suffered from the consequences of his parents' deaths, for which he was in part responsible. The dreams are symptoms of the "derangement" DeQuincey's narrative project is intended to remedy; they contain the "hieroglyphic meanings of human sufferings" which he says his dreams encode, meanings that are only decoded when the dreams are placed in this narrative of his life (52).

In order to move from this considersation of his dreams as ghostly haunt-ings to a fuller understanding of their psychological significance, DeQuincey notices several "facts" about dreams. Chief among them is that dreams have the power to record accurately, to "revive" the "minutest" yet most critical "incidents of childhood" (104). This aspect of dreaming he likens to a "book of account" in which we can read the "secret inscriptions on the mind," which he says, "remain for ever." This "secret," or repressed, narrative is what the *Confessions* sets out to reveal by offering a language with which to decipher the "hieroglyphs" of the psyche, which Freud would name the unconscious. The resemblance of DeQuincey's dream "facts" to Freud's conception of distortion, condensation, and revelation-by-censorship in the dream work attests to the role that this kind of literature had in the formation of a medicalized vocabulary to control by language what had previously been controlled by faith. But beyond that, it anticipates Freud's bringing together of the acts of invention (or fantasy) and recollection to reach a psychological "truth" about the self. The *Confessions of an English Opium-Eater* is both the "legend" and the "history" of what took place in its author's dreams.[43]

Not until the final part of his narrative does DeQuincey make the transi-tion from speaking about his dreams as "incubus and night-mare" (102) to regarding them as a "power of endless growth and self-reproduction" (106). This is also where he actually provides detailed accounts of his dreams,

[42]DeQuincey's first success as an imaginative writer was the *Confessions*. It became a sensa-tion, brilliantly opening his career in popular journalism and saving him from financial ruin.

[43]Sedgwick cautions that writing should not be given any privileged status here, since dreams are seen to correspond to many things besides writing in the *Confessions* (such as plays, paint-ings, forgotten music, rooms within the brain). Such correspondences she identifies as gothic in that they "recreate parallel representations at a distance from the original, subject to more or less frightening distortions" (*Gothic Conventions*, p. 63). These other analogies are certainly drawn, but DeQuincey resorts to writing and language most prevalently in his attempt to control those frightening distortions, giving them privileged status among the other "correspondences."

instead of referring to them obliquely and keeping their specific content to himself. But even here, the dreams themselves are terrifying events that pose a threat to the dreamer until they become part of the narrative of the *Confessions*. DeQuincey gives several dream accounts in this chapter, each of which involves some struggle for power. The final dream is the most elaborate representation of such a struggle, and in important ways it represents the culmination of the entire project of the *Confessions*. The dream shows the dreamer engaged in a great conflict that is paradigmatic of the role of dreams in the book as whole:

> Somewhere, I knew not where—somehow, I knew not how—by some beings, I knew not whom—a battle, a strife, an agony, was conducting . . . with which my sympathy was the more insupportable from my confusion as to its place, its cause, its nature, and its possible issue. I, as is usual in dreams (where, of necessity, we make ourselves central to every movement), had the power, and yet had not the power, to decide it. I had the power, if I could raise myself, to will it; and yet again had not the power, for the weight of twenty Atlantics was upon me, or the oppression of inexpiable guilt. (112–113)

Here the dreamer is at the center of a battle for power which only his will can decide. "As is usual in dreams" he both is and is not in possession of that power. This dream is the clearest representation of what is true of all these dreams—that they are sites of power the dreamer must occupy if he is to avoid being preoccupied and overwhelmed by them. But this is a dream of confusion and defeat. The final images mount into a torrent of human faces, a swirl of familiar female forms, a vision of "heart-breaking partings, and then—everlasting farewells" (113). This is how the dream and its account end, and the dreamer is left with the haunting "sense that all was lost."

This is a disturbing dream account with which to end this book. Yet, despite the narrator's apparent loss of the battle that took place within the dream, the sequence of dream accounts that lead up to it implies a kind of plot for what the narrator refers to on the next page as the achievement of his "triumph" (114).[44] Somehow, DeQuincey turns the apparent defeat within this dream into a triumph for his narrative. The remarkable feature of this final section of the book is DeQuincey's failure to interpret his dreams despite all the preparations he has made in the text to do exactly this. While he has managed to give a case history of himself and an account of several

---

[44]DeLuca sees this last cycle of dreams as figuring a failed effort at imaginative integration on the part of DeQuincey, and he emphasizes the narrator's "sense of loss" at the end of the text: "He is incapable of willing the victory into being, because he cannot master its operative forces, and this because he has lost faith in his power of supplying vital connections" (pp. 27–33). This loss and failure, however, DeQuincey regards as his triumph, and in the sense that they represent a fulfillment of his desire to make a precise diagnosis of a condition, they are imaginative triumphs.

dreams, he makes no actual effort to interpret or analyze the images of the dream in light of the life story he has presented. He simply puts them side by side. It is as if the vocabulary and techniques for such analysis were not available to him, and he could only take his interpretation this far. In fact, the content of the dreams themselves suggests something very close to this state of affairs. The *Confessions* reveals itself in its treatment of these dreams to be a fuller, more direct, and more articulate expression than *Frankenstein* of the desire for a therapeutic explanatory system rooted in the whole life of the dreamer. The triumph of the book is its expression of this desire and its first modest steps to fulfill it. On the final page of his book DeQuincey virtually states as much: "Medical account, therefore, of my emancipation I have not much to give: and even that little, as managed by a man so ignorant of medicine as myself, would probably tend only to mislead" (115). What the book initially conceives as its project—the forging of a more "certain" and more medically sophisticated "diagnostics"—has only begun to be achieved. But this beginning is its victory.

The final dream in DeQuincey's *Confessions* appropriately, then, portrays a battle whose outcome is not yet decided. The dreamer both does and does not have "the power to decide it" (113). Up until this point, DeQuincey's struggles with his desires and guilt over his self-authorship have been evident. But in this last dream of struggle, along with the other dream accounts immediately preceding it, the desire for self-authorship finds expression in the "sympathetic ink" of DeQuincey's unconscious, where he is giving birth not only to himself but to a strategy with which to explain the imagery of dreams. Like the final dream, the two dreams that precede it dramatize a struggle for power associated with the dreamer's separation from a woman, much as the initial pains that led to his opium dreams were associated with his separation from his father. The pathos of the dreamer's separation from "female forms," which appears in the final dream, pervades the entire book as much as the pain over the father's death does (113). In the "Preliminary Confessions," for example, DeQuincey records a vivid memory of the day he left school for the last time, which may have furnished one of the latent thoughts for this pattern in his dreams and which also indicates how central to his thinking these images are:

> I wept as I looked round on the chair, hearth, writing-table, and other familiar objects, knowing too certainly, that I looked upon them for the last time. Whilst I write this, it is eighteen years ago: and yet, at this moment, I see distinctly as if it were yesterday, the lineaments and expression of the object on which I fixed my parting gaze: it was a picture of the lovely _____, which hung over the mantlepiece; the eyes and mouth of which were so beautiful, and the whole countenance so radiant with benignity, and divine tranquillity, that I had a thousand times laid down my pen, or my book, to gather consolation from it, as a devotee from his patron saint. Whilst I was yet gazing upon it, the deep tones of _____

clock proclaimed that it was four o'clock. I went up to the picture, kissed it, and then gently walked out, and closed the door for ever! (38–39)

This emotional leave-taking from a portrait of a "divine" and saintly woman who remains unnamed anticipates the images of separation from female figures in these last dreams and repeats his abandonment of religious authority throughout the text. It marks both an end and a beginning for De-Quincey, his passing away and rebirth associated in his memory with his act of transcribing a vision into language.

Each of these final dreams in the book combines images of birth and separation with verbal reconstitutions of the self. The next detailed dream account DeQuincey gives is the dream of Ann, which is perhaps the most elaborate example. The dream occurs directly after the narrator describes his oppressive architectural visions of Piranesi-like labyrinthine spaces and his monster-filled Oriental dreams. These are presented as recurring dream patterns rather than as specific dream events, and both are dominated by images of entombment in womblike spaces.[45] The elaborately described dream of his reunion with Ann presents these materials in very different form. The dream occurs in two discrete parts, and in each part the dreamer is afflicted by the object of his "gaze," and he recovers by the power of his own words:

> I thought that it was a Sunday morning in May, that it was Easter Sunday, and as yet very early in the morning. I was standing, as it seemed to me, at the door of my own cottage. Right before me lay the very scene which could really be commanded from that situation, but exalted, as was usual, and solemnized by the power of dreams. . . . no living creature was to be seen, excepting that in the green churchyard there were cattle tranquilly reposing upon the verdant graves, and particularly round about the grave of a child whom I had tenderly loved, just as I had really beheld them, a little before sun-rise in the same summer, when that child died. I gazed upon the well-known scene, and I said aloud (as I thought) to myself, "It yet wants much of sun-rise; and it is Easter Sunday; and that is the day on which they celebrate the first-fruits of resurrection. . . . with the dew, I can wash the fever from my forehead, and then I shall be unhappy no longer." (111)

The sadness and malaise caused by the death of the child in the dream is characterized here as an illness—a fever cured by the dreamer's act of articulation: "I said aloud . . . I can wash the fever from my forehead, and then I shall be unhappy no longer." The child's grave recalls the entomb-

---

[45]Miller points out a recurrent motif in DeQuincey's writings which represents the mind trapped in some form of thought which is repeated forever—the constant threat of narrative impasse. He gives the name of this vertigolike motif "the Piranesi effect" (*Disappearance of God*, p. 67).

ments of the previous dreams, and the appearance of the grave at the door of the dreamer's own cottage suggests that the death is also his own. His recovery from the fever is, then, a kind of resurrection, or rebirth, of himself, "commanded" and "solemnized by the power of dreams."

The second part of the dream repeats the same "talking cure." Here the reunion with Ann, the beloved companion of his youth in the streets of London, is effected by an articulation of his desire:

> Immediately I saw upon the left a scene far different; but which yet the power of dreams had reconciled into harmony with the other. The scene was an Oriental one; and there also it was Easter Sunday, and very early in the morning. And at a vast distance were visible, as a stain upon the horizon, the domes and cupolas of a great city—an image or faint abstraction, caught perhaps in childhood from some picture of Jerusalem. And not a bow-shot from me, upon a stone, and shaded by Judean palms, there sat a woman: and I looked; and it was—Ann! She fixed her eyes upon me earnestly; and I said to her at length: "So then I have found you at last." I waited: but she answered me not a word. Her face was the same as when I saw it last, and yet again how different!

The dream ends with the disappearance of the whole scene and its replacement by a vision of the dreamer, no longer separated from Ann in a strange land but walking together with her in the familiar streets of London, "just as we walked seventeen years before, when we were both children" (111–12).

This part of the dream might once again be read as a second birth. It represents the recovery of childhood and the reunion of the child with the "female form" of Ann, both of which are enabled by the dreamer's articulation of his desire within the dream: "So then I have found you at last." Like the utterance in the earlier part of the dream, this is both an expression of the dreamer's wish and an exertion of his will over the images of the dream. DeQuincey had strongly identified himself with Ann earlier in the *Confessions*, portraying her both as a surrogate mother and as another orphan of the London streets he called his "stony-hearted stepmother" (67). After he had parted from Ann and searched for her in vain for some years, he finally "wish[es] to see her no longer; but think[s] of her, more gladly, as one long since laid in the grave." He would rather imagine she has died than envision the "injuries and cruelties" of the world, which might have "blotted out and transfigured" the image he had of her in his mind (65). In this dream, the deeper wish is fulfilled: the parting with the orphan-mother becomes unnecessary. She is restored to life—a child like himself—by the dreamer's own words. Just as DeQuincey had overcome the loss of his father by writing his *Confessions*, he overcomes his parting with the woman by the words he speaks in his dream. Together, these articulations enable him to recuperate, and author, himself. When the streets of Jerusalem that witnessed one resurrection turn into the London streets in which the narrator gives new life to himself, the shift from a religious to a secular setting for the authority in the dreamer's life is enacted within the images of the dream.

The architectural and Oriental dream accounts that DeQuincey includes in this section are more gothic in character and are not described in nearly so great detail. These earlier dreams, like the Orestes visions, are dreams of haunting, and significantly, the dreamer remains silent within them. He does not give voice to his desires within the dream itself, as he does in the dream of Ann. "I was buried, for a thousand years, in stone coffins," he recalls of the Oriental dreams. "Over every form, and threat, and punishment, and dim sightless incarceration, brooded a sense of eternity and infinity that drove me into an oppression as of madness" (106, 109). These dreams assume their terror from their endless unrepresentability in words. The architectural dreams in particular seem to refer directly back to his descriptions of his earlier "baffled efforts" to write a single, great work on the operations of the mind: "This was now lying locked up, as by frost, like any Spanish bridge or aqueduct, begun upon too great a scale for the resources of the architect; and, instead of surviving me as a monument of wishes at least, and aspirations, and a life of labour dedicated to the exaltation of human nature . . . , it was likely to stand a memorial to my children of hopes defeated, or baffled efforts . . . of the grief and ruin of the architect" (99). In the dream of Ann, however, the dreamer escapes from the tombs of time and space. He speaks and relieves the fever of his madness, restoring to his life what had been lost—or buried—in the vast, silent spaces of the others. Together, this sequence of dreams expresses the desire for the words to master the dream images, for the making of a book in which to contain them, and for the remedy of the psychological disorder and bafflement of which they are symptoms.

DeQuincey includes one more dream about the apparently lost struggle for power in his book. Like the others, it too ends with a verbal assertion of release. This time, however, the utterance does not occur within the dream itself: "And I awoke in struggles," the dreamer says, "and cried aloud—'I will sleep no more!'" (113). These words allow him to escape the "struggles" of unconsciousness and to move into the conscious state where he can conquer them through analysis and interpretation. They reassert the signficance of his assuming a voice in the narrative by which to command his dreams. These words also form the bridge to the end of DeQuincey's narrative. His very next statement calls for the conclusion: "I am now called upon to wind up a narrative which has already extended to an unreasonable length" (113). But that the narrative has now been so abruptly "brought to its crisis" demands some apology and explanation by the narrator: "The reader is already aware [from a passage near the beginning of the introduction to the first part] that the opium-eater has, in some way or other, 'unwound, almost to its final links, the accursed chain which bound him.' By what means? To have narrated this, according to the original intention, would have far exceeded the space which can now be allowed" (113). This acknowledgement of a fundamental gap in the narrative makes two important points. First, the narrator admits that the therapeutic goal of the narrative has not been fully reached. The cure of his opium addiction and his dreams is only "almost" complete. Second, the intended narrative goal of the piece is not fully achieved either. The narrator could not say all he wanted. These two failures are, of course, the same. The narrator's inability to interpret and associate the images of his dreams with the events of his life precludes his absolute mastery over their "fascinating power" (114). The most striking feature of the *Confessions* is where it stops. It "displays" but does not explain its dreams because it *cannot* explain them. It can only express the desire for a language that completes what the words within his dream began.

Despite his failures, DeQuincey can nevertheless assert, "I triumphed," once he refers to himself as an "author" who has thrown off the "empire" of his opiate "spells" by giving an account of his past and his dreams. His triumph is the production of this narrative that implicitly connects his conscious and unconscious life, even if he could not integrate them completely (114). "The object was to display the marvelous agency of opium," he says in explaining the omission of the details of his escape. "If that is done, the action of the piece has closed" (114). The "marvelous agency" he has displayed is the "agency" of dreaming, as DeQuincey restated in the *Suspiria*. But even here in the *Confessions*, he has clearly shown that dreaming is a "faculty" the dreamer can own and connect with his waking life. That has been the "action of the piece," the critical event in the plot of escape. The narrative is "closed," then, but not completed. It represents only what the narrator was capable of doing with the knowledge—and discourse— available to him. The mastery of the dreaming and interpreting faculty must remain more a wish than an achievement in these *Confessions*.

"One memorial of my former condition still remains," he says in closing. "My dreams are not yet perfectly calm: the dread swell and agitation of the storm have not wholly subsided: the legions that encamped in them are drawing off, but not all departed" (115–16). In the *Suspiria*, DeQuincey would admit to having "mastered" the forces of his addiction and his dreams some three times, revealing the provisional character of his "triumph" and the incompleteness of his cure in the *Confessions*. The third "prostration" before opium, he says, almost reduced him to permanent silence (235). But even if his dreams are not "calm," they have become his possessions, the "memorials" of his assuming a power once perceived to be entirely outside his authority. In these last pages of his account of the medicalization of his soul, DeQuincey acknowledges that it is "as painful to be born as to die" (115). "My sleep is still tumultuous," he says in the closing words, comparing his dreams to the fiery visions of "our first parents" in *Paradise Lost,* when they looked back to the gates of the Eden from which they had been expelled (116). In this final image, DeQuincey provides a figure of his own achievement and of its limitations. His book is poised between the confidence of a religious explanation of dream experience and the uncertaintly of an as-yet-incomplete scientific one. DeQuincey has clearly emerged from the former but has not yet fully entered the latter. That world is still all before him and the other writers—both literary and scientific—who will attempt to "clothe in words the visionary scenes derived from the world of dreams." One of the most ambitious such efforts is Emily Brontë's *Wuthering Heights,* in which dreams and illness are again explained alternately as demonic possessions or psychological symptoms and where the dream account is shown to be as potentially repressive as it can be expressive.

Dreams and Disorders in *Wuthering Heights*

> I've dreamt in my life dreams that have stayed with me ever after, and changed my ideas; they've gone through and through me, like wine through water, and altered the colour of my mind. And this is one—I'm going to tell it.
>
> —Catherine Earnshaw

At age seventeen, Emily Brontë was sent away to school along with her sister Charlotte. Emily's attachment to her home at Haworth was apparently so deep that she became seriously ill when she was separated from it. Charlotte's memoir of the experience describes how Emily's illness was accompanied by haunting dreams of home, which she dreamed just as she awoke each morning: "Every morning when she woke, the vision of home and the moors rushed on her, and darkened and saddened the day that lay before her. Nobody knew what ailed her but me—I knew only too well. In this struggle her health was quickly broken; her white face, attenuated form, and failing strength threatened rapid decline. I felt in my heart she would die, if she did not go home, and with this conviction obtained her recall."[46] These symptomatic dreams of longing for the moors and for home are replicated by Catherine in the novel that Emily would write some ten years after her return home. *Wuthering Heights* may be read as the extended account of Emily's childhood dreams of grief. It is presided over by the dreams,

---

[46]This passage is from the Biographical Notice Charlotte composed as a memoir of her sister for her publisher, quoted by Winifred Gérin, *Emily Brontë: A Biography* (1978), p. 55.

illnesses, and unfulfilled longings of a number of its characters. During the illness in which Catherine dreams of her childhood on the moors, her nurse Nelly Dean speaks of her patient's "delirium," "frenzy," and "madness" as resembling a state of "half dream."[47] Cathy's dreams during this period— like Emily's—are clearly symptoms of the disturbance of her mind. "I dread sleeping," she says. "My dreams appal me" (124). But she is equally appalled by the behavior of her husband, who responds to her illness by retreating into his library and the "society" of his books. "Among his books!" she protests to her nurse when she learns of his whereabouts. "What in the name of all that feels, has he to do with *books*, when I am dying?" (121, 122).

In *Wuthering Heights*, books and narratives are matters of life and death, and they are repeatedly set against passion, dream, and illness. Whereas in *Frankenstein* the dreamer refuses to tell the story of his dreams and in *Confessions of an English Opium-Eater* DeQuincey expresses the need for a discourse to tell such a story effectively, *Wuthering Heights* dramatizes how the narrative of one's life and dreams can be a repression as well as a release or revelation. The Brontë family produced three novelists whose work may be read as offering alternative psychological visions for the sometimes repressive authority of their clergyman-father's theology. Emily's only novel is perhaps the most direct effort to substitute the secular for the sacred.[48] Just as Catherine replaces the Testament in *Wuthering Heights* with the diary she titles "Catherine Earnshaw, her book," Emily's novel replaces the absolute authority of Scripture with a subversive, secular text of her own, which contains and expands upon her dreams of longing. The subversiveness of the novel is perhaps most deeply felt in its attack upon the notion of the self as a unified and coherent entity—as an independent, immortal soul. In this respect, *Wuthering Heights* extends the psychological implications of Mary Shelley's and DeQuincey's conceptions of the invented self, recognizing that human personality is most accurately represented not as a single immortal soul but as a complex of psychological forces held in a tenuous, shifting configuration. This novel seeks to counteract the psychological danger played out in its characters' dreams and in their discourse on these dreams. That danger is not so much the failure to integrate the forces of the personality in a narrative act as it is the failure to recognize that an overly mastering

[47]Emily Brontë, *Wuthering Heights*, ed. Hilda Marsden and Ian Jack (Oxford: Oxford University Press, 1981), pp. 120–31. The text is that of the Clarendon edition of 1976. Hereafter cited in my text.

[48]See Miller, *The Disappearance of God*, for a fuller discussion of the religious aspects of the novel. Miller regards *Wuthering Heights* as "an attempt to reconcile two irreconcilable requirements: the need for a source of spiritual power outside oneself, and the need to be self-sufficient" (p. 158). At the conclusion, he says, "God has been transformed from the transcendent deity of extreme Protestantism, enforcing in wrath his irrevocable laws, to an immanent God, pervading everything" (p. 211). See also Gilbert and Gubar, "Looking Oppositely: Emily Brontë's Bible of Hell," *The Madwoman in the Attic*, pp. 248–308.

narrative may repress the vital, irrational aspects of the personality, especially if that narrative is sought from an outside authority—sacred or secular— rather than from within.

The dangers of such a repressive narrative are most apparent in the first narrator, Lockwood, and his reaction to the dreams in the paneled bed that once belonged to Catherine Earnshaw. There Catherine had dreamed as well, had carved her name into the wooden panels, and had preserved parts of her childhood in a diary. And there Heathcliff would also dream, finally dying triumphantly in the very chamber where Lockwood had dreamed of Cathy struggling to enter. The setting for these dreams makes up part of their content: the paneled bed and its window appear as images not only in Lockwood's dream of entrance and exclusion but in Cathy's feverish dreams of her childhood and in Heathcliff's final visions of Cathy as well. The site and substance of these dreams represent a psychic center for the novel, coloring all its events. Lockwood's dreams, like his entire experience at the Heights, present a challenge to his sense of himself, a challenge he may either explore or repress. He may see the dreams as symptoms of his own repression or dismiss them as ghosts and appropriate them as part of his repressive mechanisms. Dorothy Van Ghent has remarked that even the form in which much of the novel is told resembles a dream in its displacement of events into the past through the alternately censoring, indulging, and revising voice of Nelly Dean.[49] Yet both Lockwood and Nelly fail to recognize that their narratives repeat that distortion, and they never understand what their dreams have to tell them.

Lockwood's narrative begins with a dream that wounds and disables him—a dream for which the narrative presents itself as the cure. The problem for Lockwood, though he does not recognize it as a problem, is that the majority of this text that is his own diary is told in the words of someone else. The story Nelly tells as she nurses Lockwood back to health seems intended to enable his recovery, to provide the crucial element in the healing of his illness and in the recovery of control over his dreams. In that story Lockwood apparently seeks to comprehend and master the disordering experiences at the Heights which brought on his illness in the first place. "Keep your fingers from that bitter phalanx of vials," he orders Nelly when she is about to give him one of the medicines the doctor has prescribed for him. "Draw your knitting out of your pocket—that will do—now continue the history of Mr. Heathcliff, from where you left off, to the present day" (90). When Nelly's narrative is interrupted by the visit of a doctor to treat Lockwood's ailment, Lockwood again speaks explicitly of Nelly's story as an alternative to the medicine that the doctor is likely to provide: "I reflected as the good woman descended to receive the doctor; and not exactly of the kind which I

[49]Dorothy Van Ghent, *The English Novel: Form and Function* (1953), p. 160.

should have chosen to amuse me; but never mind! I'll extract wholesome medicines from Mrs. Dean's bitter herbs" (154).

Although Lockwood clearly recognizes in these statements that his disorder is not purely physical and that it demands some kind of narrative therapy, he mistakenly perceives Nelly as dispensing a miraculous treatment for his mental disturbances, which he need simply swallow like a pill. Lockwood may technically be the primary narrator of the novel, but he is obviously not the most important or powerful narrator. As he himself concedes, Nelly Dean is "a very fair narrator" on her own, and he finds it sufficient to give the story "in her own words, only a little condensed" (155). By his own admission, he exercises his narrative prerogatives over his experience only minimally, esentially handing over Nelly Dean's account as she offered it to him. This is not a tale that is told by the narrator at all but a tale in which the narrator seeks someone else to do the telling for him. In terms of the psychoanalytic model, which defines the talking cure as a joint venture enabling mutual discourse, the narrative pattern in this novel is a therapeutic failure.[50] That Lockwood is a listener rather than a teller, however, is not his real failure. Even though he is presumably writing "his book," Lockwood errs by looking for the meaning of his experience not in an analysis of the experience itself or within his own life history but entirely in the words and experience of someone else. He remains an invalid through most of the text, subject to an overly intervening analyst who fails to recognize that the patient's dreams are symptoms that contain the basis for his recovery. Instead, Nelly employs her "wholesome medicines" like an anaesthetic. But if the narrative therapy of *Wuthering Heights* serves Lockwood as an agency of repression, it performs the same function for its speaker Nelly Dean. The final dream recounted in the novel is not Lockwood's, nor is it Cathy's or Heathcliff's. It is Nelly's. And that dream account reveals her entire narrative as an elaborate strategy of repression which disguises her own desires and fears even from herself.[51]

We learn of Lockwood's dreams and his ensuing illness in his own words in the short three-chapter passage that forms the first narrative frame for the novel. Whereas Nelly's narrative is at least manifestly given as a form of conversation with her ailing "master" on his sickbed, the purpose of Lockwood's narrative is less obvious. He affixes two dates to it, one at the very beginning and the other toward the end, when he resumes his account after a

[50]See Said, *Beginnings*, p. 174.

[51]In *Laughter and Despair: Readings in Ten Novels of the Victorian Era* (1971), Knoepflmacher notes the similarity of Lockwood and Nelly as narrators, emphasizing their common "passivity" (p. 89). But both may also be seen as active repressers and manipulators of information. James Hafley has gone so far as to identify Nelly Dean as the "villain," ambitiously plotting to gain control of the two estates. See "The Villain in *Wuthering Heights*," *Nineteenth-Century Fiction* 13 (December 1958): 199–215.

hiatus of several months, at least suggesting that the narrative is some kind of journal in which he has simply recorded his strange experiences at Wuthering Heights strictly for his own purposes. Unlike Walton's letters in *Frankenstein* or DeQuincey's *Confessions* to his wife, Lockwood's journal recognizes no reader or listener and makes no attempt to address or acknowledge such a person. This omission figures strategically in such a novel as this, in which the narrative structure and situation are worked out in such careful and complex ways. Lockwood's narrative seems to be intended as a purely private document, a recording of events meant for no one's eyes but his own. This way, he can use it to reinforce his own delusions about himself.

As is true of the documents that make up *Frankenstein*, the stories, letters, and other documents of *Wuthering Heights* often contradict and compete with one another. And all of them, by her own admission, Nelly alters through her acts of narrative repression and revision. She alternately secretes and confiscates the letters and books exchanged by the younger Cathy and Linton Heathcliff, for example. She is reproached by Edgar Linton for keeping silent when she should have spoken in some cases, and she is rebuked for "bearing tales" when she should have been more discreet. Over the course of the novel, Nelly shows herself to be more—and less—than the "fair narrator" of Lockwood's description. She becomes a more and more shrewd manager of information and a more and more skillful—if unreliable—narrator.[52] But this skill is of a particular kind, put to a particular use. It is, in fact, more of a detriment than an advantage in psychological terms, since the narrative Nelly produces is employed as a tool of repression rather than understanding. While Nelly's and Lockwood's narrative styles and their relationships to those narratives vary, they have the same effect. Her diction represents Nelly as direct and unaffected, even if she presents herself as a manipulating character within her own tale. Lockwood remains supercilious and formal, as distanced in his diction as he is in his relation to the content of his tale. Yet the two conspire to produce a narrative of control which protects them from the subversive material within the narrative and denies the threatening forces within themselves and their dreams.

The first characteristic that connects Lockwood's dreams with his pattern of misreading and misinterpreting signs and symptoms in *Wuthering Heights* is that the images of the dreams emerge directly from Lockwood's listening to and his misreading of still another narrator. In the paneled bedchamber where Lockwood has taken refuge for the night, he discovers and begins to read Catherine's account of her own life—first as it was carved into the windowsill itself and then as it was scrawled in the margins and blank pages

---

[52]See Gideon Shunami, "The Unreliable Narrator in *Wuthering Heights*," *Nineteenth-Century Fiction* 27 (March 1973): 449–68. On the more general problem of the "unreadability" of the figures in the novel, see J. Hillis Miller, *Fiction and Repetition: Seven English Novels* (1982).

of the Testament to which she had given her own name (18). The very existence of the book and its retitling testify to Catherine's refusal to accept an external authority and her insistence upon asserting her own authority in its stead. Her rebellion is thus first made known in the form taken by her written account of herself. She essentially replaces the printed text with her own manuscript, replaces a sacred book with a secular one. "Scarcely one chapter had escaped a pen-and-ink commentary—at least the appearance of one—," Lockwood notes, "covering every morsel of blank that the printer had left" (18). The content of the narrative bears out this impression of the rebellious Catherine, as Lockwood "decyphers" from her "faded hiero-glyphics" the account of her and Heathcliff's decision "to rebel" against the "tyrant" Hindley and his zealous agent Joseph (18–19). That rebellion is signified by their kicking of Joseph's religious books into the dog kennel and their conspiring against Hindley's orders of confinement and separation by planning to take an illicit "scamper on the moors" together (20). In the writing of Catherine's book, rebellion takes the dual form of rejecting a sacred text and trespassing into forbidden territory.

Lockwood's reading of Catherine's book is connected with his dreams not only because one directly precedes the other but because her book provides the manifest content for his dreams. In fact, Lockwood falls asleep while reading the text as he notes the conflict between Catherine's "manuscript" and the "print" of the text itself. "I began to nod drowsily over the dim page," Lockwood recalls; "my eye wandered from manuscript to print. I saw a red ornamented title . . . 'Seventy Times Seven, and the First of the Seventy First. A pious Discourse delivered by the Reverend Jabes Branderham, in the Chapel of Gimmerden Sough'" (20). The dream that follows seems to be drawn directly from the "print" of the text, since it has to do with the sermon announced by the red ornamented title. The second dream appears to be a product of Catherine's manuscript, since it involves her frequenting of the moors. But in fact, the two dreams are one dream that, like Lock-wood's gaze, wanders between manuscript and print, combining the images of both in order to reveal the moral and psychological implications of Lock-wood's refusal to engage and master his own experience and to accept re-sponsibility for narrating it. The dream dramatizes a choice between two ways of regarding the nature of dreams, a choice between two kinds of "text" for constructing the story of one's life: a text that is given (in print) or one that is self-constructed (by hand). The first is sanctioned by religion; the second is hostile to it.

Lockwood is portrayed as a listener in both parts of the dream, just as he is in the narrative scheme of the novel itself. In the first part, Lockwood says that he "was condemned to hear" the sermon of Branderham, a "discourse" intent upon having the sinner who commits the unforgivable "First of the Seventy First" sin "publicly exposed and excommunicated" (21). Since

Lockwood has come to the country to ensure his own isolation from human contact, the sentence of excommunication seems appropriate and desirable for him. Yet, since he also clearly does not wish to be publicly exposed, the dream represents a threat as well. That the dream is primarily concerned with the making of texts and the act of interpretation is indicated by the situation of the dream, in which the "discourse" is an explication of still another text, namely, the phrase from Saint Matthew which calls for per- petual forgiveness of the offending brother so long as he asks for forgiveness, even if he asks "seventy times seven" times. This phrase, Lockwood tells us, the preacher "had his private manner of interpreting" (21). In the course of the long sermon, Lockwood becomes so impatient at being a passive listener forced to accept Branderham's explication of the text that he rises to assert his own interpretation and to accuse the preacher of the unforgivable four hundred and ninety-first sin. But what appears to be rebellion against the preacher's interpretation of the text in fact shows Lockwood adopting it.

The point of the biblical text is that there is no limit to the number of times forgiveness should be granted to the one who asks for it, that no sin is unforgivable. Branderham, however, has interpreted the text literally and established the figure of seventy times seven as the upper limit of grace.[53] Lockwood effectively accepts this interpretation as correct and simply turns the implications on Branderham. When Lockwood echoes the accusation of his accuser, he begins to wrestle with Joseph and sets off a violent mob scene in which the community is effectively "excommunicated" en masse (21). What initially appears as an assertion of order by Lockwood is, like his narration itself, only a surrender to the "private interpretation" of another. But this surrender is also an act of violence to himself, an act of isolation and self-repression. The dream may be read as an expression of Lockwood's desire to remain unexposed, to suppress the dream by seeing—as he saw in the biblical phrase—only its manifest "text" without making any attempt to penetrate to the latent dream thoughts behind it.

This acceptance of a rigid textual interpretation is precisely what Catherine and Heathcliff refuse. They recognize that Joseph's cruel and narrow interpretation of these texts is motivated by a desire to control them. They prefer to go their own way and write their own book. But throughout his narrative Lockwood continually accepts Nelly Dean's "private manner of interpreting" as he has Jabes Branderham's in his dream. This is what Cathy and Heathcliff adamantly refuse to do, insisting on their own interpretation of their own experience, in defiance of every custom and law that would keep them from doing so. Their community together survives the tests of their own betrayals, the divisions and accusations of their families, and—as is

---

[53]William A. Madden considers forgiveness the central issue in the novel. See "*Wuthering Heights*: The Binding of Passion," *Nineteenth-Century Fiction* 27 (September 1972): 127–54.

suggested in their dreams—even their deaths. Catherine, moreover, as her dreams indicate, refuses to accept a purely rational, stable model of the self which does not accommodate the fundamental irrationality and desire that drive it. Immediately after she has told Nelly her dream of escape from heaven back to the moors, she goes on to claim that Heathcliff is "more myself than I am" (80). When she does so, Catherine is at the very least challenging the categories by which the self was conventionally defined.[54]

Lockwood's dream, however, is a desperate "self-defence," which is how he describes its final image (22). Analogously, his treatment of the entire dream is a defense of his conception of himself. The manifest dream content never reveals the "First of the Seventy First" sin, only that Lockwood is guilty of it in the eyes of the preacher. Lockwood's resistance to the sermon is not his transgression, since Branderham forgives him that failing. "This is human weakness," the preacher says; "this also may be absolved" (22). Nevertheless, Branderham still holds Lockwood accountable for the un- named, unforgivable sin. That sin is not revealed to him until the second part of his dream, when Catherine Linton effectively exposes Lockwood's crime as his failure to make the testament of his dream into his book. The second part begins when the sounds of a fir tree outside Lockwood's window dis- solve into the clawing sounds of Catherine's hand clutching at that same window and her "melancholy voice" implores to be let in. The child Catherine, then, effectively replaces the preacher Branderham as the speak- ing voice of the dream. In contrast to the previous vision, this part of the dream shows Lockwood immediately attempting "to silence" the voice, "to exclude" the words that Catherine repeatedly wails to him: "Let me in—let me in" (23). This request is the message that Lockwood absolutely refuses to hear, and it provokes him to another uncharacteristic act of violence. Though he has endured four hundred ninety parts of James Branderham's sermon, Lockwood cannot endure these three words of Catherine's because they represent a far more profound accusation than that leveled by the preacher. "I must stop it," he insists feverishly, crashing through the window, grabbing the hand of the child, and scraping it over the broken glass until her blood drenches his sheets.

Lockwood "must stop" Catherine's request for admission because it rep- resents forces he believes he must deny. Most obviously, the dream figures his refusal to permit passion and intimacy into his life. The bloody scene of penetration and exclusion manifests a desire for erotic experience which is overcome by a repressive fear of it. This violent exclusion of the female figure from his bed recalls the attraction Lockwood has already admitted for the younger Cathy Linton and the failed love affair from which he has

---

[54]Leo Bersani reads the novel as a representation of "the danger of being haunted by alien versions of the self" (p. 208). See *A Future for Astyanax: Character and Desire in Literature* (1976).

recently fled. But in a deeper sense, to shut out the child at his window is to shut out his own past, the "me" Lockwood will not let in. Like the first part of the dream, the second is also a self-defense. Lockwood attempts to maintain a conception of himself as independent and self-sufficient by repressing anything about himself he fears he cannot control. The goal of every action Lockwood performs within the dream is to silence and exclude. His behavior is finally unforgivable because by its very nature it precludes acknowledgment of the self and confession to another.[55] But his failure goes farther in the dream by literally dramatizing how the forces of the unconscious can be as effectively suppressed within the "text" of a dream account as they can be exposed. Lockwood himself describes his struggle within the dream as an attempt to "disengage myself," and his obfuscating account of the dream to Heathcliff when he wakes up functions to "disengage" him from his own dream as well (23).

In his desperate attempt to "exclude" the child from his dream and to wall it out of his consciousness, Lockwood employs the books in the room to create a protective buffer between himself and the forces of his unconscious. Perhaps the most deftly constructed image of repression in this dream is this picture of Lockwood when he "piled the books up in a pyramid" against the broken window "and stopped my ears to exclude the lamentable prayer" (23). Paradoxically, Lockwood uses Catherine's own books to exclude her voice, the very books that record both her refusal to accept what was printed in them and her determination to articulate her own passions. Nevertheless, Lockwood converts these texts into agencies of repression. Whereas Catherine is an author whose "manuscript" rebels against and supersedes the "print" that it surrounds, Lockwood's journal reveals him to be a passive reader dominated by the narrative of someone else—as long as the content of that narrative does not touch him in any personal way. He allows the "print" of Nelly's text to go unrevised, unexplained, and unexplored by any "manuscript" of his own. Just as he excludes the child from his dream, he manages to produce a narrative that effectively excludes and "disengages" himself as well.

The two parts of Lockwood's dream demonstrate his lack of desire to comprehend it and to provide an interpretation that mediates between his conscious and his unconscious self. This failure is manifested when his shouts of terror wake him and he gives the partial account of his "frightful nightmare" to Heathcliff. Lockwood's descriptions of his dream are expressed in the conventional "gothic" terms of possession: he dismisses its images as a swarm of "ghosts and goblins," speaks specifically of the image

---

[55]Edgar F. Shannon's essay "Lockwood's Dreams and the Exegesis of *Wuthering Heights*" emphasizes the importance of passion in the dreams and in the novel, regarding it as the "ethical eye of the storm" in both cases (*Nineteenth-Century Fiction* 14 [September 1959]: 99). I emphasize the psychological more than the ethical aspects of the dreams and the novel.

of Catherine as a "little fiend," a "changeling," and a "spectre," and he regards the entire dream as nothing more than "another proof that the place was haunted" (24, 25, 27). These superstitious denials and projections distinguish Lockwood from the other important dreamers of the novel— Catherine and Heathcliff—who treat their dreams as serious statements about themselves and at least attempt to come to terms with the claims of those dreams and to incorporate them into their understanding of themselves.[56] But Lockwood's attitude perfectly aligns him with Nelly, who admits to being "superstitious about dreams" because they only succeed in "conjuring up ghosts and visions to perplex us" (79). The images and actions in her dream of repression, which occurs later in the narrative, directly recall this dream of Lockwood's (330). Like Victor Frankenstein, Lockwood and Nelly prefer to think of their unconscious experience as something alien and unrelated to them, and their stories are committed to preserving this illusion. Also like Frankenstein, they make use of a supernatural explanation of their dreams, in the course refusing to consider those dreams as symptoms or to think of their dream accounts as ways to understand those symptoms.

When he leaves Wuthering Heights for the last time, Lockwood pauses before the graves of Catherine and Heathcliff directly after listening to and feeling "irresistibly impelled to escape" from the final story told to him by Nelly of the young shepherd boy's encounter with the lovers' phantoms on the moors. Lockwood's flight from that story repeats his denial of the implications in all he had heard and dreamed about at Wuthering Heights. When Nelly says "I saw nothing" in response to the shepherd boy's claims, she speaks for Lockwood as well; and though Lockwood has spent so much time listening, he has really heard nothing either (336). In the very last sentence of the novel, and presumably the last entry in his journal, Lockwood still portrays himself as a listener who does not hear: he "listened," he says, "to the soft wind breathing through the grass; and wondered how anyone could ever imagine unquiet slumbers for the sleepers in that quiet earth" (338). Once again bereft of human contact, Lockwood is shown listening only to the wind, excluding with the last words of his journal the possibility of intimacy and self-knowledge as insistently as he excluded Catherine's prayer to be "let in" in his own unquiet slumbers. Thanks to his—and Nelly's—narrative, Lockwood's world remains as quiet as the earth he cannot imagine otherwise. And though he has recovered physically, he leaves Wuthering Heights as psychologically damaged as when he arrived.

But Catherine and Heathcliff have never slept quietly. They do not narrate the text in the way that Nelly and Lockwood do. They "interrupt" Nelly's

[56]James H. Kavanaugh sees Lockwood as "a weak or even inverted analogue of Heathcliff, an 'antitype' whose function in the text is to register a difference from Heathcliff and to display much of what Heathcliff is not" (p. 18). Kavanaugh's *Emily Brontë* (1985) presents a Marxist-psychoanalytic-oriented reading of the novel.

narrative as she interrupts Lockwood's. And they dominate her narrative as much as she does his. But they do so very differently from Nelly. Catherine and Heathcliff make Nelly their listener as Lockwood makes her his narrator. Just as Lockwood submits himself to Nelly's care and manipulation, Catherine and Heathcliff rebel against her didactic moralizing and reject her interpretation of their dreams. As is true of Lockwood's dreams (and of Frankenstein's and DeQuincey's as well), Catherine's and Heathcliff's dreams are associated with their psychic illness. The dreams become symptoms and efforts at recovery. But the similarities end here. Catherine and Heathcliff both refuse the ministrations offered by Nelly when they are sick, just as they refuse her dismissal of the import of their dreams. They will not repress their dreams, even if the only firsthand account of them we have is the book of Catherine's which is suppressed within Lockwood's.

Catherine and Heathcliff both die in Lockwood's narrative, and their deaths may be read as implicit affirmations of Lockwood's and Nelly Dean's strategies of repression, as a warning of the danger of recognizing and indulging the passions that drive the psyche. But the conflict between the two points of view the novel dramatizes—between civilization and its discontents—may also be read as an incipient critique of the Victorian "theory of repression," which demanded a choice between absolute capitulation to the extreme repression of culture and mad surrender to intense passion—a choice that the discourse of psychology and psychoanalysis sought to mediate. My reading of the novel affiliates *Wuthering Heights* with the other gothic texts I examine here in that it too calls attention to the costs of not having a discourse in which to perform this act of mediation. Catherine and Heathcliff become victims of a cultural conception of personality which denies rather than integrates passion and irrationality in the formation of the self.[57]

This interpretation is supported by the final words of one of the key figures in this novel of recovery—the doctor, Kenneth. Kenneth is a pervasive character in Nelly Dean's narrative. He treats all the sick persons in the novel, including not only Catherine and Heathcliff but also Mr. and Mrs. Earnshaw, Hindley, Edgar Linton, Linton Heathcliff, and even Nelly and Lockwood. In his last appearance in the novel, the doctor examines Heathcliff just before he dies and "was perplexed to pronounce of what disorder the master died" (336). Indeed, Kenneth presides over at least seven deaths during the course of the novel and is perplexed to explain any of them. This perplexity evidences Kenneth's diagnostic limits, his inability to understand the symptoms of his patients. The language required to accomplish what Catherine and Heathcliff desired and dreamed of did not yet exist. As a

[57]For a Freudian reading of the role of passion in the novel, see Madden, "*Wuthering Heights*," pp. 148–49.

result, Lockwood can continue to regard these two figures of passion as "ghosts" in his last visit to the Heights, just as he had regarded Catherine as a ghost in his dream.

But like DeQuincey's *Confessions*, *Wuthering Heights* not only demonstrates this need for a discourse; it seeks to fill that lack as well. Charlotte Brontë's defenses of her sister's novel often deal directly with the nature of its language. In the course of mounting those defenses, Charlotte indicates that Emily may have succeeded in breaking new ground in the development of a discourse to explain psychological experience. In her Biographical Notice on her two novelist sisters, Charlotte compares the critics of *Wuthering Heights* to the superstitious "mob of Astrologers, Chaldeans, and Soothsayers gathered before the 'writing on the wall' . . . unable to read the characters or make known the interpretation." Then, in the preface Charlotte wrote for the second edition, she once again diagnoses the failure to understand the novel as a linguistic failure by the culture that reads the book. She defends the "rough, strong utterance" and "harshly manifested passions" of the novel against those who "have been trained from their cradle to observe the utmost evenness of manner and guardedness of language."[58] Charlotte recognizes the problems and passions of the book as essentially diagnostic and linguistic: the prophetic writing that Emily's strange hand had etched on the wall of culture remained mysterious and unreadable to Victorian readers, whose language was too heavily guarded and too refined in manner to represent the passions at the heart of *Wuthering Heights*. In opposing its publication and insisting on preserving the secret of her authorship of *Wuthering Heights* right up to her death, Emily seemed to know in advance that her book would remain as subversive and scandalous as the one written by Catherine Earnshaw.

This very problem is reenacted within the novel when Catherine tells her first dream to Nelly and reveals the "secret" of her deep love for Heathcliff. Her love is a secret because it has to do with a reality that Nelly Dean does not know and cannot comprehend, a reality that the culture sought both to suppress and to mystify.[59] The reality of that inner life seems "very strange" to Nelly; faced with Catherine's discourse about it, Nelly admits that she "cannot make it out" (79). When Catherine tries to "explain" her secret, she laments that she "can't do it distinctly" (79). Only by telling Nelly a dream can Catherine convey "a feeling of how I feel" (79). She recognizes that her

[58]Charlotte Brontë, Biographical Notice of Ellis and Acton Bell (dated 19 September 1850), p. 362, and Editor's Preface to the New Edition of *Wuthering Heights*, p. 365.

[59]See Foucault, *History of Sexuality* 1:17–35. Foucault argues that the "repressive hypothesis" actually generated more and more ways of talking about sexuality instead of repressing it. "What is peculiar to modern societies," he says, "is not that they consigned sex to a shadow existence, but that they dedicated themselves to speaking of it *ad infinitum*, while exploiting it as *the* secret" (p. 35).

dreams constitute a language that can convey the otherwise "secret" aspects of herself in a way prohibited by conventional social intercourse. She does not perceive her dreams as hauntings of her mind by a demon or a specter as Lockwood does. Rather, they are sources of truth about her own mind which she heeds and integrates into her conception of herself. Catherine makes these claims directly to Nelly as she introduces her dream: "I've dreamt in my life dreams that have stayed with me ever after, and changed my ideas; they've gone through and through me, like wine through water, and altered the colour of my mind. And this is one—I'm going to tell it—but take care not to smile at any part of it" (79). In addition to representing her dream as something she both produces and is altered by, Catherine also acknowledges here that the telling of her dream is vital to it. When Nelly tries to silence Catherine's dream account because dreams are nothing more than the "conjuring up of ghosts and visions," therefore, Catherine responds with a simple insistence that her dream be told: "I shall oblige you to listen" (79).

Like Lockwood's dream, Catherine's begins with an exclusion. But unlike his, it develops into a dream of entrance. Also like Lockwood's, her dream deals—at least on the manifest level—with religious material. But whereas he dreams he is in a chapel listening to a sermon, she dreams she is in heaven angering the angels: "Heaven did not seem to be my home; and I broke my heart with weeping to come back to earth; and the angels were so angry that they flung me out, into the middle of the heath on the top of Wuthering Heights; where I woke sobbing for joy. That will do to explain my secret" (80). Catherine "explains" to Nelly that this dream is no conjuring of ghosts but a representation of her "secret" self, a picture of the difference between her desires for Edgar and for Heathcliff. "He's more myself than I am," she says of Heathcliff, distinguishing him from Edgar. "Whatever our souls are made of, his and mine are the same, and Linton's is as different as a moonbeam from lightning, or frost from fire" (80). Cathy has nevertheless decided to marry Edgar because she recognizes and accepts the compromises she must make for the sake of convention and practicality. But she will not allow this capitulation to diminish her love for Heathcliff in any way, nor will it alter her intention to remain close to him. "Nelly, I *am* Heathcliff— he's always, always in my mind—not as pleasure, any more than I am always a pleasure to myself—but, as my own being—so, don't talk of our separation again" (82).[60]

---

[60]There is no critical consensus on these difficult passages. Bersani reads them as evidence of "the self as the potentiality for metamorphoses . . . which has renounced not only the closed circle of family repetitions, but also the limiting definitions of individuality" (p. 212). Miller interprets them as claiming that "no human being is self-sufficient, and all suffering derives ultimately from isolation. A person is most himself when he participates most completely in the life of something outside himself" (*Disappearance of God*, p. 172). Gilbert and Gubar read these passages as manifestations of the "psychic split" caused by patriarchal systems, which demand acts of anxious self-denial from women like Catherine (pp. 273–83).

At the very minimum, these statements indicate that Catherine's dream has profoundly "changed" her "ideas" about herself, has "altered the colour of [her] mind," has brought her into another way of describing her "soul," has caused her to reevaluate the role of pleasure in her life, and has generally increased her knowledge of who she believes herself in essence to be. One clear implication of her claim that she *is* Heathcliff is that Catherine sees herself as at least partly constituted by the object of her desire. Such remarks make plain that the most dramatic distinction between her dream and Lockwood's is the degree to which their dreams inform them about themselves. This essential difference is reflected in the way each regards and speaks about the dream event afterward. Lockwood dreams about himself and other people, and in his account of the dream turns the other people into ghosts and specters—from whom he must then flee in terror. Catherine dreams about herself and angels, and in her analysis of the dream proceeds to convert those supernatural beings into images of the people who figure in her own waking desires. What is an opportunity for self-discovery and self-revison for Catherine remains an occasion for self-defense and denial by Lockwood. His dream is employed to reinforce his sense of what is inside and outside of himself; Catherine's dream opens up and realigns those boundaries.

This dream of Catherine's anticipates another that she obliges Nelly to hear. After she marries Edgar and he demands that she never see Heathcliff again, Catherine becomes seriously ill and in her delirium has dreams that appall her. She is not too appalled to tell them, however, as she proves by describing to Nelly one dream in which she imagines herself to be a child again, sleeping in her own paneled bedchamber back at the Heights:

> Most strangely, the whole last seven years of my life grew a blank! I did not recall that they had been at all. I was a child; my father was just buried, and my misery arose from the separation that Hindley had ordered between me and Heathcliff—I was laid alone, for the first time, and rousing from a dismal doze after a night of weeping—I lifted my hand to push the panels aside, it struck the table top! I swept it along the carpet, and then, memory burst in—my late anguish was swallowed in a paroxysm of despair." (125).

Catherine yearns to hear the same "wind sounding in the firs by the lattice" which a frenzied Lockwood had tried to silence by breaking the window. Lockwood's reinforcement of his confinement is again opposed by her desire to overcome it. In a related way, Catherine's dream opposes Lockwood's, both in the way she regards it and in the way she goes about uncovering its latent content. Even in her delirium, she recognizes that the images of this dream encode her past and its relation to her present.

As she begins to explicate the dream to Nelly, Catherine immediately connects her repressed childhood desires for Heathcliff as they are represented in the dream with the conditions of her marriage to Edgar and with her current confusion about who she is. The dream shows her that she is not a single, unified person but subject to a number of traumatic internal and external forces, which demand that she be different persons at different times and under different circumstances. The analogy she draws between her dream and her experience has, she says, deeply "unsettled" her: "Supposing at twelve years old I had been wrenched from the Heights, and every early association, and my all in all, as Heathcliff was at that time, and been converted at a stroke into Mrs. Linton, the lady of Thrushcross Grange, and the wife of a stranger; an exile, and outcast, thenceforth, from what had been my world—You may fancy a glimpse of the abyss where I grovelled!" (125). This is, of course, essentially what did happen to Cathy, and what happened to most young women when they married. Her dream indicates that the "conversion" from child to woman is never absolute, that "the child and the child's impulses live on," as Freud put it, within the adult (*Interpretation of Dreams*, 191). When in her fever after the dream Catherine asks Nelly, "Why am I so changed?" (126), she might just as well have asked, "Why am I so unchanged?" "Why do I still feel like a child?" These questions cannot be fully answered within the discourse of this novel; they remain repressed, etched only in the shadowy figures of the charcters' dreams and the unreadable script of Catherine's book.

When Edgar denies the seriousness of Catherine's state of mind and escapes into his books, he appalls Catherine and aligns himself with the repressions of Lockwood. Edgar insulates himself in his library in order to wall himself off from the implications of Heathcliff's and Catherine's more deeply felt desires, just as Lockwood will do first with the books in his dream and once again with the journal in his waking life. Books have already played a central role in the relationship between Edgar and Catherine, for their exchanging of books and their literary discussions make up much of their courtship and succeed in alienating Heathcliff from Cathy as well. But now Edgar's literary life has become monstrous to Cathy because, rather than use books to express emotion, he uses them to repress it. When Catherine asks Nelly, "What in the name of all that feels, has he to do with *books*, when I am dying?" she directly opposes the forces of passion to those of textuality (122). She knows that these books represent the forces in the culture which are killing her, setting up the very divisions within herself that still her voice, waste her spirit, separate her from the object of her desire, and make her into a stranger to herself—unable even to recognize her own image in the mirror.

I have argued that Brontë's novel expresses a desire for a more adequate medical language to replace the rhetoric of religion and to mediate more effectively between irrational emotional states and the demands of practical life. In Edgar's retreat into his library, just as in Joseph's tyrannical use of the Bible and in Lockwood's repressive use of books, the novel demonstrates the risk of mediating strategies that do not sufficiently come to terms with the very forces they are intended to confront. Books become important aspects of the plot twice more in the novel: when the younger Catherine reads to Linton Heathcliff in an unsuccessful attempt at treating his illness and at the conclusion when Catherine reads with Hareton and raises the promise of finally resolving the conflict that has raged between the forces within novel from the outset. The books in these scenes are employed more responsibly than Lockwood's and Edgar's, and they respond more effectively to Heathcliff's compulsive repetition of the plot of revenge. Heathcliff's compulsion is also dispelled in the set of dreams that immediately precede his death. Those dreams take place as Catherine and Hareton come together through the mediation of a set of texts that offer the promise, at least, of a language that expresses rather than represses the forces that drive the unconscious.

Linton Heathcliff's arrival at Thrushcross Grange begins the second half of the story of *Wuthering Heights*, just as his father's arrival began the first half. The younger Heathcliff is ill when he appears there, and so he remains for the rest of his short life. Heathcliff exploits his son's illness, using it to lure Cathy to the ailing child to complete his plot of revenge. "He pines for kindness, as well as love," Heathcliff tells Cathy, "and a kind word from you would be his best medicine" (234). Heathcliff's plea for curative language is more appropriate than he realizes. Her loving words do seem to sustain the sickly child, and when Catherine is prohibited by her father from seeing Linton, she sends books as substitutes for her presence with love letters hidden within them. And when she does succeed in visiting Linton, she usually spends her time reading books or reciting ballads to him as part of her treatment of his sickness. But his health does not improve under her ministrations, and in one scene the source of his protracted illness is symptomatized in a dream. Linton suddenly "started from his slumber in bewildered terror, and asked if anyone had called his name" (263). Apparently "under the spell of the imaginary voice" of his father, Linton repeatedly dreams of his father calling his name. Linton never acknowledges any other content to these dreams but remains under their spell just as he is under his father's imperious spell in his waking life. The ballads and stories he demands from Cathy are only diversions from this manipulation, momentary relief from the repressive authority of his father's voice. They perform the same function as Nelly's palliative tale to Lockwood, who is also unable to relate the narrative to his own symptomatic dreams or to master the forces that speak within them.

The intricate pattern of dreams that emerges from the paneled bedchamber of Wuthering Heights is completed by the imaginary speaker of that voice—Heathcliff, in his fitful dreams of Catherine just before he dies. These dreams occur immediately after he painfully witnesses Cathy and Hareton's developing intimacy and he identifies himself with them. The children's relationship is based on books: they exchange them as gifts, and Cathy teaches Hareton to read them. "Do you ever dream, Hareton?" Cathy asks him just before their intimacy begins. "And, if you do, what is it about? But, you can't speak to me!" (311). In this remark, Cathy indicates that her love and instruction of Hareton are both directed at giving him the power of articulating his desires to her, at teaching him how to tell her his dreams.

But Heathcliff seems to benefit from this instruction at least as much as Hareton. Nelly repeats Heathcliff's account of the night he disinterred Catherine as part of his plan to join his body with hers, and then dreamed about her. He explains to Nelly how his longing for Cathy had driven him to having her grave opened to fulfill his dream of "sleeping the last sleep, by that sleeper, with my heart stopped, and my cheek frozen against hers" (289). He then reveals how after visiting Cathy's grave, he felt compelled to return to the paneled bed, convinced he would meet her spirit there:

> When I slept in her chamber . . . I couldn't lie there; for the moment I closed my eyes, she was either outside the window, or sliding back the panel, or entering the room, or even resting her darling head on the same pillow as she did when a child. And I must open my lids to see. And so I opened and closed them a hundred times a-night—to be always disappointed! It racked me! I've often groaned aloud, til that old rascal Joseph no doubt believed that my con-science was playing the fiend inside of me. (290–91)

Heathcliff's dream connects directly to Lockwood's and Catherine's in its placement of the dreamer at the same threshold of entry and exclusion. Heathcliff welcomes the same visitor whom Lockwood had so violently ex-cluded. But for Heathcliff, the dream figure is both adult and child, present and absent, inside and outside the window. And while this dream hardly qualifies as a moment of profound psychological insight for Heathcliff, its effect upon him is to relieve a state of mental desperation rather than to create one as it had for Lockwood. "Now, since I've seen her, I'm pacified— a little," he tells Nelly, echoing the claim he had made a moment before that when he saw Catherine's dead body in the grave, "a sudden sense of relief flowed from my heart" (291, 290). Heathcliff's strong conviction that at least in his dreams Catherine's spirit is with him, even if her body is not, indicates that to some degree he shares the idea her dreams had suggested to Catherine: the self is partially constituted by the object of its desire.[61]

[61]See Sedgwick (*Gothic Conventions*) on Heathcliff's double discourse as revealing the felt absence of continuity between the internal and the external: "On the one hand there is the elaborate and unquestionably authentic self-revelation, and on the other there is an unbreach-able sense of separate and secret power that somehow remains undiminished" (p. 109). I read the novel as straining at this frontier of language, seeking to bridge the gap between the private and the public.

Moreover, Heathcliff sees the dream as an expression of something from "inside" him, not the "fiend" of "conscience" he speculates Joseph would consider it.

Nevertheless, Heathcliff is tormented by this dream of "disappointment" just as Catherine had been in her later dreams. Like hers, this dream is a symptom of a deepening mental depression that will lead to death. Just before he dies, Heathcliff recalls Catherine's earlier dream of heaven and the opposition it dramatized between spiritual and psychological interpretations of the self. When Nelly attempts to make him read his Bible and confess his sins, Heathcliff corrects her. "I have nearly attained *my* heaven," he says, "and that of others is altogether unvalued and uncoveted by me" (334). Heathcliff's inability to explain his death drive here resembles Catherine's in dramatizing the cultural inability to describe psychological reality in any effective way. But his achievement resembles Catherine's as well. Both discredit the "heaven" of religion and prefer to seek after a realization of the desires of their own minds. Nelly speaks for a society that finds repression the best way to deal with such experience when she responds to Heathcliff's dream account with the same resistance that marked her response to Cathy's. "I maintained silence," Nelly says; "I didn't like to hear him talk" (291). In a deeper way than she intends, Nelly is right when she says that Catherine died "in a gentle dream." Catherine and Heathcliff both end their lives as they had lived them—according to the unarticulated truth of their dreams—while the narrators of the novel survive by refusing to listen to or talk directly about their dreams.

"Thus ended Mrs. Dean's story," Lockwood says, as he introduces his own brief postscript to it. "Notwithstanding the doctor's prophecy," he continues, "I am rapidly recovering strength" (298). Lockwood's "recovery," however, is only physical, just as Heathcliff's and Catherine's deaths are only physical. His listening to "Mrs. Dean's" story could not cure the illness of which his dreams of terror were symptoms. He wanders away from Wuthering Heights, the solitary misanthrope he came. His real cure can only take place in the telling of *his* story, not Mrs. Dean's. The dream plot of *Wuthering Heights* is therefore appropriately completed by her dream, which she tells Lockwood in her "sequel of Heathcliff's history" (309–10). Nelly recounts this sequel at the very end of the novel, when Lockwood returns to Wuthering Heights after an absence of several months. Lockwood is again confused and disturbed by his visit to the Heights. This time he is bewildered by the absence of Heathcliff and the sudden rapport between Cathy and Hareton as she teaches him to read.

In response to his confusion, Nelly resumes her narrative and informs Lockwood that Heathcliff has died. Then, in the course of explaining the details surrounding her master's death, she tells her dream. As Heathcliff grew more and more seriously ill, he would compulsively retreat into the paneled bedchamber. On the night before he died in that spot, Nelly began to reflect upon Heathcliff's origins and on her long association with him. "Is he a ghoul, or a vampire?" she asks herself, speculating about where "the little dark thing" they called Heathcliff could have come from. Finally, as Nelly remembers how she has "followed him almost through his whole course," and as he takes his place in the dream center of the novel, she dreams a dream of her own that reveals the depth of her feelings about him:

> I dozed into unconsciousness. And I began, half dreaming, to weary myself with imaging some fit parentage for him; and repeating my waking meditations, I tracked his existence over again, with grim variations; at last, picturing his death and funeral; of which all I can remember is being exceedingly vexed at having the task of dictating an inscription for his monument, and consulting the sexton about it; and, as he had no surname, and we could not tell his age, we were obliged to content ourselves with the single word, "Heathcliff." (330)

Nelly's waking speculations about Heathcliff's demonic character are transformed in the dream into fantasies of his birth or even of his conception ("imaging some fit parentage"), and then into a desire for his death and burial ("picturing his death and funeral"). In its manifest content, then, this is the most explicit dream representation of the merging of the erotic and morbid impulses that have driven all the characters in the novel and, Freud would claim, always drive the unconscious. But beyond that, the dream also manifests Nelly's desire to repress those impulses under the "single word" of her dictation, to bury them with her text.

In Nelly's dream, the "little dark thing" Heathcliff is the figure of desire he has been for everyone throughout the novel. He first arrived in Wuthering Heights as the father's substitute fulfillment of the desires of Catherine, Hindley, and Nelly. This "fatherless child" replaced the gifts Earnshaw had promised to bring them from the city, just as his name, taken from Earnshaw's son who had died in childhood, marks Heathcliff as a figure of Earnshaw's desires as well (36). Heathcliff occupies virtually every role in the psychic economy of the novel: he is dispossessed orphan and tyrannical father, servant and master, victim and tormentor, husband and lover, the embodiment of brutality and the soul of sentiment. He finally acquires power over everything and everyone in the world of Wuthering Heights, then dies of some self-induced illness. He consistently acts as an expression of uncontrolled individualism, ultimately subversive to all forms of social authority— legal, familial, religious, even medical. Perhaps Heathcliff's most scandalous action is also the one that most clearly represents his function in the novel. When he digs Catherine's body up and exposes her to decay, he breaks down the final structure in which her culture sought to contain her. Heathcliff first arrives at Wuthering Heights speaking a language that sounds like "gibberish" to Nelly Dean, a language that "nobody could understand" (35). Throughout the novel, Heathcliff remains the cipher about whom everyone in the novel speculates—the other whose language no one is able to understand and who challenges and subverts their conceptions of themselves as well.[62]

The erotic scenes sketched out in Nelly's dream account show Heathcliff to be the "dark thing" that she too has "followed through his whole course," the secret object of her own fears and desires, as he has been for all the other characters. But the dream goes farther to show how Nelly has buried her desire, repressed it with a linguistic strategy, erased it by literally "dictating" another text resembling the one she dictates to Lockwood. Like the story she tells Lockwood, the narrative she has the task of inscribing in the dream is a "history" of Heathcliff's life. This too is a narrative of censorship, though in this case it contains only one word—"Heathcliff"—and the date of his death. Much as Lockwood had used the books in his dream to keep out the voice of his desires, Nelly uses this "text" to lay the voice of her dreams to rest, literally to mark the grave of her desire. The dream reveals Nelly's wish to preserve the indecipherability of the principle subject of the text, the "he" who is "more myself than I am," as Cathy put it. In her dream, Nelly buries the same force that in her story she disinters. The same perplexity Kenneth feels in trying to diagnose Heathcliff's illness and determine the cause of his death precludes Nelly Dean from speaking the psychological truth about her desires. She makes no comment on the significance of her dream to Lockwood or anyone else. Like him, she takes refuge in silence instead, allowing the origins of the unspeakable dark things that drive her unconscious to remain in the mysterious realm of her dreams.

Just as Emily Brontë's novel deals with the same dream material that accompanied her illness as a young woman, the course of the illness that finally took her life bears uncanny resemblances to the disorders that preceded the deaths of Catherine and Heathcliff. Like her fictional protagonists, Emily seems to have suffered from a self-induced disease. Also like

---

[62]Again, contradictory critical interpretations of Heathcliff abound outside the novel as well as within it. Gilbert and Gubar see him as "'a woman's man,' a male figure into which a female artist projects in disguised form her own anxieties about her sex and its meaning in her society. . . . Heathcliff incarnates that unregenerate natural world which must be metaphorically cooked or spiritualized, and therefore a raw kind of femaleness that, Brontë shows, has to be exorcised if it cannot be controlled" (p. 294). Kavanaugh, on the other hand, notes the "phallic, patriarchal images surrounding Heathcliff," which figure him "as an implicit imaginary substitution for the Father" (p. 39). Bersani says that "Heathcliff is so radically the other that he is almost the beastly or even the inanimate" and that he represents "the alienating possibilities of Wuthering Heights" (pp. 210–11).

them, she refused the attention of her family and the doctors they consulted, both of whom were bewildered as to the cause of Emily's distress. In a letter written on the day Emily would die, Charlotte seems to echo the words of Nelly Dean on Dr. Kenneth's diagnosis of Heathcliff. She observes in dismay that "the physician's opinion was expressed too obscurely to be of use" in helping them to care for Emily. "He sent some medicine which she would not take," Charlotte says with resignation.[63] Like the sufferers in *Wuthering Heights*, Emily suffered at least in part from this "obscurity" with which her society understood and expressed her symptoms. Her sickness was surely related to the cold she caught at her brother's funeral, which was the last time she left the house before she died. But even before that cold developed into a more serious inflammation of the lungs, Emily inexplicably began to retreat into herself and withdrew behind a veil of almost complete silence, "too ill to occupy herself," according to Charlotte, "with anything but reading."[64] Most frustrating for Charlotte and the family was Emily's absolute refusal to speak about her illness: "She resolutely refuses to see a doctor; she will not give an explanation for her feelings, she will scarcely allow her illness to be alluded to."[65] In her novel, Emily had already dramatized the costs of an inability to "give an explanation" of deep feelings. With her last audible words she finally agreed to allow a doctor to see her. But she died before he came, and before her culture could produce a medical discourse to explain her feelings and the still-uninterpreted dreams in which they were expressed.

These very different gothic texts, *Frankenstein*, DeQuincey's *Confessions*, and *Wuthering Heights*, all present the narrative of a life suffering from some disorder, that inhibits the presentation of the narrative itself. All three texts dramatize the convergence of disturbing dreams, physical and mental illness, and either an unavoidable inarticulateness about or a determined suppression of the exact nature of these subjects. The possibility of regarding the dream as an expression of the dreamer's desire is in each case opposed by the diction of supernatural possession, which enables the dream to be disowned as an alien presence. But the choice of the supernatural alternative is consistently shown as regressive in these texts, invariably producing a deformed narrative of some kind—a narrative that remains as a scar, a sign of the failure of the narrator to master the forces within his or her own tale. To varying degrees, these narrators are all failed autobiographers, then, who

---

[63]Letter from Charlotte Brontë to Ellen Nussey written on the day of Emily's death, 19 December 1848, quoted by Gérin, *Emily Brontë*, p. 259.

[64]Letter from Charlotte to George Smith, 7 November 1848, ibid., p. 248.

[65]Letter from Charlotte to Ellen Nussey, 23 November 1848, quoted ibid., p. 250. See the final chapter of Gérin's biography for a fuller account of Emily's silence and her resistance to medical attention in her last days.

have been unable to become the authors of a complete life story of recovery from their disordered state. But their failure has succeeded in expressing a need for a language that can accomplish that goal, for the terms in which the symptomatic confusion of the dream can be diagnosed. Their collective achievement is the rearticulation of the Victorian self as a psyche subject to disease rather than a soul subject to demons.

These gothic texts represent only one set of the many popular narrative attempts to deal with this problem in the nineteenth century, efforts at reconstructing a notion of individual identity with a language that could give new names to and organize the forces that drive the self. Nelly's inability to name Heathcliff's origins in her dream indicates her inability, or refusal, to name the origins of her own desires, the origins of the essential forces that shape her own life story. This discursive failure provokes what Foucault has called a "discursive explosion" in the nineteenth century, which culminated in the discourse of psychoanalysis. As evidence of the "medicalization" of the confession during this period, Foucault notes the simultaneous "metamorphosis" in literary form and taste: "We have passed from a pleasure to be recounted and heard, centering on the heroic or marvelous narration of 'trials' of bravery or sainthood, to a literature ordered according to the infinite task of extracting from the depths of the self, in between the words, a truth which the very form of the confession holds out like a shimmering mirage."[66] But this literary metamorphosis in turn may be said to have shaped the very medicalization to which Foucault attributes it. As Freud was to admit in his first full-length analysis of a case of hysteria (1892–1894), the narrative forms of fiction provided the explanatory models that led to his own shift from a physiological to a psychological understanding of hysterical symptoms: "I have not always been a psychotherapist. Like other neuropathologists, I was trained to employ local diagnoses and electroprognosis, and it still strikes me myself as strange that the case histories I write should read like short stories and that, as one might say, they lack the serious stamp of science. . . . The fact is that local diagnosis and electrical reactions lead nowhere in the study of hysteria, whereas a detailed description of mental processes such as we are accustomed to find in the works of imaginative writers enables me, with the use of a few psychological formulas, to obtain at least some kind of insight into the course of that affection."[67] The stamp of Freud's science and the stamp of gothic fiction bear profound resemblances. Of the gothic tale of illness and cure he treated in *Delusion and Dream*, Freud said that he merely "reproduce[d] it in the technical terms of our science" (66).

---

[66]Foucault, *History of Sexuality* 1:17, 59.
[67]From Freud's analysis of the case of Fraulein Elisabeth von R. (*SE* 2:160–61).

It should be noted, however, that the gothic texts I have examined here also provided examples of the potentially repressive power of a medical discourse for the self. In *Wuthering Heights*, for example, where the association of dream experience with medical discourse is most directly called for, the professional physician in the text is as much a tool of repressive social forces as the clergyman. As modern feminist critiques of psychoanalysis have shown more dramatically, even a medical language can be deployed to "subject" individuals rather than free them. John Kucich's study of repression in Victorian fiction also speaks directly to this issue by emphasizing a more subversive and productive use of repression in the nineteenth-century novel. Rather than restrict the expression of identity, repression as understood in these terms could help serve the individual by establishing and valorizing a secret, libidinal interiority that could resist the incursions of social monitoring.[68] Novels like *Wuthering Heights* actually dramatize a dialectic between two opposing Victorian uses of repression, setting the forces of an insistent privacy and self-defense, on the one hand, over against the impulses of revolt and self-liberation by a boundaryless self, on the other. When the dynamic of the novel is viewed in this way, as such Marxist critics as Terry Eagleton have done, its demands for a mediating language might be construed in political or economic rather than medical terms. In fact, as Freud (and the novels treated in the next chapters) would demonstrate, the discourses of medicine, politics, and economics were not always separable in the representation of the self in the nineteenth century. More often than not, they were inextricably bound together.

In *Jane Eyre* and *Great Expectations*, like any number of nineteenth-century novels that take the form of autobiographies, the forces of the gothic are absorbed and redeployed in more conventional settings and plots. The affiliation between the intentions of these novels and those of the gothic is as plain as their common reliance upon the confessional form. At one point in her fictional autobiography, Jane Eyre even refers to a monstrous dream figure in her life—Bertha Mason—as a "vampyre," whereas in his account of his life, Pip compares himself to a Frankenstein who has made a monster of his own existence. Like the gothic texts produced throughout the period, the fictional autobiography poses the central question of authority in the life story through the narrator's discourse about his or her dreams and the voices that are understood to be speaking through those dreams. Here the dream operates less as a symptom of an illness than as capital in the psychic economy of the self. The production of a dream account comes to represent something like a psychic "cost" of ownership which the narrator must pay in

[68]See Kucich, *Repression in Victorian Fiction*.

order to produce and take possession of his or her "self." The dominant discourse of mastery with which the self is represented and recovered in these texts, therefore, derives not so much from medical science as from economics. The narrator's goal is not to heal the self by telling these stories but to own the self and the raw materials of the unconscious.

R. W. Buss, *A Dream of Dickens* (1875)

This unfinished canvas was based upon the well-known photographic portrait of Dickens in his study by C. Watkins. Characters from his work, taken directly from the original illustrations of the novels, swarm around the author. The painting portrays Dickens's teeming imagination as a virtually limitless unconscious resource through which he—like David Copperfield and Pip Pirrip—invented himself as a successful author by transforming the images of his dreams into the written words of his books. The unfinished state of the painting only makes it a more suggestive portrayal of the mastery of language over image in Dickens's dreams, the figures becoming fainter and fainter until they dissolve into the author's writing desk and the very books on his shelves. (Reproduced by permission of the Dickens House, London.)

CHAPTER THREE

Capitalizing the Unconscious:
Nineteenth-Century
Fictional Autobiography

As to sleep, I had dreams of poverty in all sorts of shapes.
—David Copperfield

What alone was wanting to the realization of a vast fortune, he considered to be More Capital. Those were the two little words, more capital. Now it appeared to him that if that capital were got into the business, through a sleeping partner, sir—which sleeping partner would have nothing to do but walk in, by self or deputy, whenever he pleased, and examine the books—and walk in twice a year and take his profits away in his pocket, to the tune of fifty per cent.—it appeared to him that that might be an opening for a young gentleman of spirit combined with property, which would be worthy of his attention.
—Great Expectations

I need not sell my soul to buy bliss.

—Jane Eyre

When Dickens gave up writing his autobiography and decided instead to compose the story of his life in the form of the novel *David Copperfield*, he was responding to his deep ambivalence about recollecting and directly confronting certain painful events of his past. In his dreams, he relived the humiliation of his family's poverty, his father's incarceration in debtor's prison, and the degrading work he had to perform to help support his family:

No words can express the secret agony of my soul. . . . The deep remembrance of the sense I had of being utterly neglected and hopeless; of the shame I felt in my position; of the misery it was to my young heart to believe that, day by day, what I had learned, and thought, and delighted in, and raised my fancy and my

137

emulation up by, was passing away from me, never to be brought back any more; cannot be written. My whole nature was so penetrated with the grief and humiliation of such considerations, that even now, famous and caressed and happy, I often forget in my dreams that I have a dear wife and children; even that I am a man; and wander desolately back to that time in my life.[1]

The trauma of Dickens's poverty left him without words to express it. He could only say of that time that it "cannot be written" about. But it could be—and was—dreamed about. As also became true of the dreams of David Copperfield, these dreams gave Dickens's poverty "all sorts of shapes" and took away his sense of himself in the present. With "no words" to express it, Dickens's past retained a destructive power over him. So he abandoned writing what became known as his "Autobiographical Fragment" and converted the images of his dreams and his life story into the history of a novelist named David Copperfield instead.

But eleven years later, when Dickens wrote the second of his novels in the form of an autobiography, he gave its hero and narrator dreams of gentility and affluence rather than poverty. In *Great Expectations* Dickens transformed the shape of his own past with a much freer hand than he had in *David Copperfield*; the details of his own life were not nearly as recognizable. But in the greater distance between fact and fiction in *Great Expectations*, Dickens may have approached a different truth about himself and about the process of writing a life story. *David Copperfield* ends with the hero's emergence as a successful, accomplished novelist. *Great Expectations* also ends with its narrator developing into a professional writer. But Pip is not a novelist. He is an accountant whose career involves writing numbers instead of letters, and his life becomes inscribed in the terms of others' financial affairs rather than in the imagined events of a novel. That Pip practices his profession not in Copperfield's London but in Cairo—which would become known as the "master key" of the British Empire in the 1870s—reinforces, among other things, the continuity of his profession with a worldwide capitalist system. Dickens's revision of the identity of the autobiographical narrator from professional novelist to professional capitalist exposes what is repressed in *Copperfield*: the writer of the fictional autobiography is not only a dreamer; he is an entrepreneur who organizes, manufactures, and markets the material of his past as a commodity of power and profit.

These aspects of Dickens's fictional autobiographies are characteristic of this genre, which commonly presents the individual subject as a commodity in the marketplace—or, as Pip is called, "a spirit combined with property." In these texts, the self is a property that is produced and at least potentially owned by the narrator-hero. That David Copperfield dreams of the shapes

[1]Forster, *Life of Dickens*, p. 26.

of his poverty and Pip of one-pound notes indicates how much their unconscious minds are shaped by that same market system and expressed in its
terms. This interpenetration of psychology and economics is reinforced by
the knowledge that what haunted Dickens's dreams and drove him to write
David Copperfield was his family's humiliating poverty and their insistence
that he become a "labouring hind" in a London factory. When Freud later
refers to the dream wish as a "capitalist" providing the "psychological outlay"
for the dream, he may be using the conception of the self sketched out in
this, his favorite Dickens novel.[2] Freud's use of the language of the marketplace to describe the functioning of the unconscious provides another
important discursive model for his theory of dream formation and interpretation, a model equally central to the biographical and autobiographical novel
in the period. Psychoanalysis, as Freud describes it, is not only a therapeutic
system designed to give medical treatment and to offer the possibility of a
cure for the patient. It is also intended to be a productive science by which
the "psychic economy" of the subject can be reorganized and made functional through an elaborate process of psychic investment, exchange, and
transfer.

The development of psychoanalysis in the nineteenth century and the mat-
uration of the biographical novel during the same period are both commonly
linked to the bourgeois virtues of individualism and privacy and, at least
by implication, to the economic values that made use of those virtues. The
rise of the novel as a literary form is often associated with the rise of capitalism in Europe. "The 'spirit of capitalism' is," according to Mikhail Bakhtin,
"reflected in artistic language, specifically in the language of a particular
variety of the novelistic genre." These remarks concern Dostoevsky, but they
refer to the type of novel that emphasizes the subjectivism and individualism
especially prominent in the first-person autobiographical novel of the nineteenth century, in which, Bakhtin says, the "unsubjugated" subject attempts
to transform the "forced loneliness" of capitalist society into a "proud soli-
tude."[3] Ian Watt's account also traces the development of the novel to the
advent of industrial capitalism and to the attendant capitalist virtues of individualism, private ownership, and specialization. He cites *Robinson Crusoe*
(1719), one of the first great fictional autobiographies in English, as the
classic example of Adam Smith's individualistic conception of "economic
man."[4] Fredric Jameson aligns the novel with the development of capitalism
in Europe as well, citing its central role in what he calls the "bourgeois
cultural revolution—that immense process of transformation whereby popu-
lations whose life habits were formed by other, now archaic, modes of pro-

[2]Ernest Jones, *The Life and Work of Sigmund Freud* (1953), 1:174–75.
[3]Mikhail Bakhtin, *Problems of Dostoevsky's Poetics*, trans. R. W. Rotsel (1973), pp. 15–16.
[4]Ian Watt, *The Rise of the Novel* (1974), pp. 60–70.

duction are effectively reprogrammed for life and work in the new world of market capitalism."[5]

The characteristic form and plot of the biographical novel support this affiliation with capitalism. Such a novel typically spans the life story of its protagonist from infancy to adulthood, the period normally required for the hero to progress from a condition of desire, dependence, or exploitation to a position of self-fulfillment, independence, or control. That movement is often figured as a journey from poverty to relative affluence—hence the preponderance of orphan protagonists, inheritance plots, and bourgeois success stories. In the case of *Jane Eyre* and *Great Expectations*, the novels with which I am concerned in this chapter, the protagonists must resist the allure of a genteel world to come to more realistic terms with the world of market capitalism as they move toward self-knowledge. Jane Eyre repeatedly refuses Rochester's offers of gifts and insists on receiving from him only the money she has earned as a governess in his employ. Later, she gives away most of the inheritance she receives from her uncle, preferring to earn her own way in the world as a teacher instead. Pip's whole life story is an account of the deception contained in the working-class dream of gentility, a dream that is more properly fulfilled by his entry into the new world of market capitalism as an accountant. While Pip must recognize the illusion of living in an aristocratic world free of the constraints of the marketplace, he must also resist those like his uncle Pumblechook who would reduce him to a "sleeping partner" in an enterprise in which he would only be able to "examine the books" that account for his investment but would have no control over the accounts that appear in those books. These choices all associate psychological maturity with economic responsibility, implying a model of the psyche fashioned after the realities of the marketplace.

Robinson Crusoe's transformation of his barren wilderness island into a profitable estate provides the paradigm for these plots. His venture into the wilderness essentially enables him to remake himself and then to return home as a rich, masterful man in possession of a new world of profit: "I was now master, all on a sudden, of above 5,000£. sterling in money, and had an estate, as I might well call it, in the Brasils, of above a thousand pounds a year, as sure as an estate of lands in England: and in a word, I was in a condition which I scarce knew how to understand, or how to compose my self for the enjoyment of it."[6] Here, Crusoe acknowledges that his successful composition of himself, his self-possession, is evidenced in the success of his capitalistic venture, in the material possessions he has accrued and converted into private property for his own pleasure. As Marx would note in the first

---

[5]Fredric Jameson, *The Political Unconscious: Narrative as a Socially Symbolic Act* (1981), p. 152.
[6]Daniel Defoe, *Robinson Crusoe* (Harmondsworth, Eng.: Penguin, 1965), p. 280, hereafter cited in the text.

chapter of *Capital*, Crusoe's representiveness as the capitalistic "independent man" is best expressed in his desire to "keep a set of books" which translate his labour into its exchange value: "His stock-book contains a catalogue of the useful objects he possesses, of the various operations necessary for their production, and finally of the labour-time that specific quantities of these products have on average cost him."[7] This stock book of Crusoe's becomes the model for the book of his life; a catalogue of the products of his labor essentially defines who he has become.

But in the story of Robinson Crusoe, material acquisition is also accompanied by the acquisition of self-knowledge. This psychological achievement finds one form in the identification and articulation of desire, often as it is expressed in the protagonist's dreams and in his or her response to those dreams. Crusoe views his dreams as divine signs, providentially visited upon him for his instruction, but he also recognizes in them an economic imperative. As soon as Crusoe awakens from his dream of a savage visitor who becomes his servant and assists his escape from the island, for example, he makes a revealing interpretation of the dream: "I made this conclusion, that my only way to go about an attempt for an escape was, if possible, to get a savage into my possession" (203). The acquisitive, mastering forces that drive the unconscious have no clearer expression than the wish the entrepreneurial Crusoe recognizes in his dream—the desire to "possess" the savage forces within him that will enable him to master his world. To master himself, he must own a servant.

The same features of the fictional autobiography which align it with the capitalist emphasis on private ownership and the individual as commodity also align it with the development of psychoanalysis—itself often regarded as a product of bourgeois capitalism. Bakhtin, who acknowledged that the "polyphonic novel could, indeed, have come into being only in the capitalist epoch,"[8] also wrote a critique of "Freudianism." Ironically enough, he based that critique on some of the very social conditions that produced the polyphonic novel, on Freud's "abiding and profound expression of certain crucial aspects of European bourgeois reality," notably the desire for a fabricated individual life history that "competed" with and acted as a "surrogate" for a broader conception of social history.[9] In fact, the analogy Freud chooses to account for the part played in dreams by the unconscious wish demonstrates how deeply the language of the capitalist marketplace had penetrated his understanding of unconscious processes. "A daytime thought may very well play the part of *entrepreneur* for a dream," he says, "but the *entrepreneur*, who, as people say, has the idea and the initiative to carry it out, can do nothing

[7]Karl Marx, *Capital*, trans. Ben Fowkes (1977), 1:170.
[8]Bakhtin, *Dostoevsky's Poetics*, p. 16.
[9]Bakhtin published this, and some other works, under the name V. N. Volosinov. See *Freudianism: A Marxist Critique*, trans. I. R. Titunik (1976), pp. 8, 11.

without capital; he needs a *capitalist* who can afford the outlay, and the capitalist who provides the psychical outlay for the dream is invariably and indisputably, whatever may be the thoughts of the previous day, *a wish from the unconscious*" (*Interpretation of Dreams*, 561).

Freud would go on to define psychic processes as an elaborate economic system, portraying dreams as the productions of the dreamer, productions that the dreamer is required to own in order to master and make useful. Freud describes the operation of this system in terms of a fluid marketplace, where the various agencies shift their functions according to the needs of what he calls "the economic situation": "The *entrepreneur* may himself make a small contribution to the capital; several *entrepreneurs* may apply to the same capitalist; several capitalists may combine to put up what is necessary for the *entrepreneur*. In the same way, we come across dreams that are supported by more than one dream-wish" (*Interpretations of Dreams*, 561). Freud theorizes about the repetition of traumatic situations in his patients' dreams: "It shows us the way to what we may call an *economic* view of mental processes. Indeed, the term 'traumatic' has no other sense than an economic one."[10] Here and elsewhere it is apparent that Freud's use of the economic model to explain mental operations as the balance of psychic payments extends beyond his treatment of dream formation into his general conception of unconscious processes. He characterizes the relationship between the sexual instincts and the instincts of self-preservation as "one of those considerations which deserve to be described as *economic*," and of the sources of symptom formation, Freud warns that "a merely *dynamic* view of these mental processes is insufficient; an *economic* line of approach is also needed."[11] To one of his major works on the subject of masochism he gives the title "The Economic Problem in Masochism."

As such statements indicate, economics serves Freud not merely as an analogy for his theory of the unconscious but as one of the fundamental structural models for it. The appearance of Adam Smith's *Wealth of Nations* in Freud's account of his own Hullthorn dream in *The Interpretation of the Dreams*, and his reference to the book as "sometimes mine" manifest that Freud's own acquisitive desires might have taken the form of envying the authorship of Smith's text. Those desires may also have been realized by Freud's entrepreneurial use of Smith's work as part of the "capital" of his own dream book. His account of this dream strongly implies that he acknowledged the relationship between the invisible hand of profit, which Smith says motivates the marketplace, and what Freud himself called the hidden "motive force" behind the dream (561). It is especially fitting, then,

[10]Sigmund Freud, "Fixation to Traumas—the Unconscious," *Introductory Lectures on Psychoanalysis, SE* 16:275.

[11]Freud, "Some Thoughts on Development and Regression—Aetiology," ibid., *SE* 16:356. Freud, "The Paths to the Formation of Symptoms," ibid., *SE* 16:374.

that when Freud composed *On the History of the Psycho-Analytic Movement*, he likened himself at the time of writing *The Interpretation of Dreams* to Robinson Crusoe, enjoying his "splendid isolation."[12]

But even before Freud, the unconscious was seen as a stage for the play of economic forces. When DeQuincey was plagued by the dreams provoked by his opium addiction, he described his memory as a "book of account" in which each entry "remains forever" (104). During this chaotic period of his life, DeQuincey claimed to have found pleasure in reading only one book: David Ricardo's *Principles of Political Economy and Taxation*. The treatise seemed to provide DeQuincey with a supreme sense of order and explanatory power, as well as a model for what he had himself hoped to accomplish with his dream experience: it had adumbrated a set of principles "which first gave a ray of light into the unwieldy chaos of materials, and had constructed what had been but a collection of tentative discussions into a science of regular proportions" (100–1). So taken was he by Ricardo's book that DeQuincey, though unable to exert himself in any other way during his addiction, dictated his own version of economic science, which he titled *Prolegomena to All Future Systems of Political Economy*. Because of business considerations, however, DeQuincey did not complete or publish it until many years later (*Confessions*, 101). Instead, he composed and published the *Confessions of an English Opium-Eater*, a book that gave an account of the production of his dreams in the place of an account of political economy. As we have seen, this book was itself a prototypical theory of the unconscious as well as a source of quick cash. DeQuincey's use of both medical and economic terms to describe his dream experience demonstrates how some of these texts employ more than one kind of professional discourse to secularize supernatural interpretations of dreams. In many fictional autobiographies, for example, it is as imperative for the dreamers to recognize their dreams as symptoms of their mental state as it is for them to manage their psychic economies. As is most apparent in *Jane Eyre*, both forms of explanation are often placed in tension with supernatural or simply naïve explanations of psychic life.

Both DeQuincey and Freud embed economic treatises within their own dream theories, and both represent the dream as an economic system of production in which aspects of the dreamer's mind perform the functions of entrepreneur, labor, and product as well. Freud's theory of dream formation and interpretation formalizes what DeQuincey suggested: that the dream produces a new version of the dreamer's past by combining repressed materials from the unconscious with images of more recent experience. This combination of materials is broken down and distorted in the dream work, reassembled in the dream synthesis, and then refined into a coherent form in

[12]Freud, *On the History of the Psycho-Analytic Movement, SE* 14:22.

the dream account. "Dreaming is another kind of remembering," Freud says in explaining his use of the dream material in the Wolf-Man case. "It seems to me absolutely equivalent to a recollection if the memories are replaced (as in the present case) by dreams, the analysis of which invariably leads back to the same scene, and which reproduce every portion of its content in an inexhaustible variety of new shapes."[13] In dreams, then, dreamers reproduce their own past and present it to themselves in a variety of new shapes which it is their task (by way of the dream account and analysis) to incorporate into their present understanding of who they are. Dreamers remake themselves by remaking their history. The many shapes of poverty in David Copperfield's dreams and recollections, for example, are transformed into new shapes in the pages of his story, shapes that trace out the progress of his career and enable him (along with Dickens himself) to become the affluent "hero" of his own life. In this novel and in Freud's theory as well, the dream event is the dreamer's rewriting and reappropriation of his or her own history, what DeQuincey in his *Confessions* calls the dreamer's "power of endless growth and self-reproduction" (106).

Central to the production of a dream interpretation—and of an autobiographical novel—is the basic problem of adequately representing the experience to be encoded, of discovering the means by which to give form and coherence to the flood of random but significant fragments that are, beneath the chaotic surface of the manifest, deeply connected. At the origin of narrative, according to Roland Barthes, is desire, and the "allure" of the autobiographical narrative in particular is that whereas its messages "appear to float freely, to form a galaxy of trifling data," they are "in fact saturated with pseudological links, relays, doubly oriented terms," elaborately arranged in a heavily encoded system.[14] Freud speaks of the origin and function of dreams in much the same way—as wish fulfillments that appear "meaningless" and "absurd" on the manifest level but have in fact been "constructed by a highly complicated activity of the mind," in which everything means something (*Interpretation of Dreams*, 122).

The dream and the fictional autobiography share another desire, which may compete with the desire for representability. The choice to write an autobiographical novel rather than an ordinary autobiography reflects the potentially contradictory desires of the author at once to discover the truth about who she or he is and to justify what she or he has become. In this dual concern for self-revelation and self-justification, both dream and novel simultaneously conceal and reveal the meaningful antecedents that have led up

[13]Freud, "From the History of an Infantile Neurosis," *SE* 17:51.
[14]Roland Barthes, *S/Z*, trans. Richard Miller (1974), pp. 22, 118.

to the present moment of speaking.[15] The language in which they are expressed may simultaneously serve as a tool of repression and of revelation as well, then, and the two opposing projects become inseparably joined. "In and behind the agencies of repression," says Freud, in *Delusion and Dream*, "the material repressed finally asserts itself victoriously" (56).

Just as the agencies of repression and censorship in a dream reveal themselves in the very disguises they employ, the manifest plot of the autobiographical novel both hides and reveals its repressed plot. The position of narrative voice is entrepreneurial, achieved through a competitive struggle. To occupy that position is to act as manager of the narrative, to be the presiding consciousness through which the experience of every other character, as well as that of the narrator, is processed—converted, as it were—into capital for the production of the narrator's story. The goal of any narrator who is also a character in the story is to achieve this position of power and privilege, to acquire the narrative voice, to secure the right to tell. The record of this acquisition is the repressed plot of any such narrative, and therefore, its end is paradoxically its beginning. That repressed plot recounts the takeover of the means of the story's production, and its outcome is revealed on the first page when the speaker assumes possession of the narrative voice. What remains in the subsequent pages is an account of the costs exacted by this process. When David Copperfield begins his history by proclaiming that "these pages must show" whether he or someone else will turn out to be the hero of his life story, he has already revealed the outcome, since he is in possession and control of the very pages that will do the showing. David has only to reveal the price he has had to pay for managing this enterprise, and the new "shape" he will give to his poverty.

Mikhail Bakhtin describes any act of speech in the novel as an "appropriation" by the speaker of words at least partially owned by others, as a take-over of the meanings and intentions of those words, a "transformation [of them] into private property." "One must take the word," he says, "and make it one's own."[16] In an autobiographical novel, whose primary act of speech is the telling of the story itself, this act of appropriation saturates every event. In such a text, every character theoretically represents a potential narrator, a would-be "I," a rival for the position of final authority. The one who tells the tale and gives shape to it is analogous to the dreamer who performs the work of dream synthesis and interpretation by which he or she "owns" the

[15]In *Design and Truth in Autobiography* (1960), Roy Pascal says the "interplay" and "collusion between past and present" in autobiographical writing is more significant as a revelation of the present situation than as an uncovering of the past (p. 11). See also Elizabeth W. Bruss, *Autobiographical Acts: The Changing Situation of a Literary Genre* (1976).

[16]Bakhtin, *The Dialogic Imagination*, pp. 293–94.

psychic material of the dream and its latent content. The narrator of a fictional autobiography is the dreamer who has emerged from the fragmented, opaque dream of life to give a coherent account of it, an account that is also a remaking of her- or himself. The other characters then become mere objects in the narrator's plot, pieces of the narrator's dream, the private property of the narrator's account. They too may tell tales, but those tales will be part of and subordinate to the narrator's life story, subject to his or her management, distortion, revision, and censorship. The repressed plot of acquiring the narrative voice locates the fictional autobiography, then, at the very point that Freud locates the dream: at the intersection of force and meaning, simultaneously in the semantics of desire and in the semantics of interpretation.

Jane Eyre (1847) and *Great Expectations* (1860–1861) are written in this autobiographical form and can be read as struggles on the part of their respective narrators to produce and own themselves by appropriating the language in which their actions will be represented. In each case, the narrator as character is confronted with a field of competing narrative voices— other characters seeking to acquire narrative control and to subordinate all other voices to their own. Rival plots contend for dominance, and alternative accounts of other selves are proposed.[17] A fundamental distinction exists between the way Jane Eyre deals with her competitors, however, and the way Philip Pirrip deals with his. From the outset, Jane recognizes that her project of self-possession is a labor she must perform herself rather than a gift that can be given to her. When she desires to escape from her job as a teacher at Lowood, she longs not for release from her labors but only for a new setting in which to work her way toward self-possession. "Those who want situations must advertise," she tells herself. "You must inclose the advertisement and the money to pay for it under a cover directed to the Editor of the Herald."[18] In one of Jane's first written expressions of herself, then, she converts herself into an advertisement in a newspaper. She represents herself in the form of a commodity involved in a competitive marketplace where she has a price and where she must advertise to command that price. The entire novel may be seen as emulating the model of this advertisement, with Jane continually establishing the terms of her own value, resisting other competitors who wish to represent her and fix her price.

In his narrative, however, Pip seeks to repress this economic and psychological necessity. He dreams of some benefactor who will magically trans-

[17]Barbara Hardy argues that "most novels" are "concerned with the nature of narrative" and that they "create tensions between narrators." I would add that the fictional autobiography is a special case in which "tensions" between narrators—or potential narrators—are heightened to competition, the outcome of which produces the text and determines the shape it will take. See *Tellers and Listeners: The Narrative Imagination* (1975), p. 22.

[18]Charlotte Brontë, *Jane Eyre*, ed. Richard J. Dunn (New York: W. W. Norton, 1971), p. 75, hereafter cited in the text.

form him from a laborer into a gentleman. When his dream comes true, Mr. Jaggers is the bearer of the news and temporarily becomes the teller of Pip's story, informing Pip at once of his good fortune and of the reshaping of his life that his good fortune demands. But even Jaggers is only an agent, hired for a price by this other, unnamed narrative power: "'I am instructed to communicate to him,' said Mr. Jaggers, throwing his finger at me sideways, 'that he will come into a handsome property. Further, that it is the desire of the present possessor of that property, that he be immediately removed from his present sphere of life and from this place, and be brought up as a gentleman—in a word, as a young fellow of great expectations.'"[19] Pip is himself represented as a piece of property here, the control of which is to be put in the hands of the narrative voice identified only as the "possessor of that property." Pip's willing response to the offer and his accession to its terms are characteristic of the attitude he assumes toward telling his life story: he repeatedly seeks out other "narrators" to tell it for him, constantly attempting to subordinate his plot to some grander one, allowing himself to become the portable property in some secret scheme. His eventual profession as accountant is an apt fulfillment of his narrative career: he is merely the recorder of financial transactions that are not his own.

Although both Jane and Pip end up composing autobiographical narratives, then, those narratives grow out of very different desires and self-conceptions, which are directly related to the ways Jane and Pip deal with the forces of the marketplace. These different desires also express themselves in the dreams Jane and Pip relate to us and in their opposing attitudes toward their dreams. Jane strives to understand and work through her dreams, seeking to take control of the productive forces of her unconscious and use them for her own benefit—to achieve the desires expressed in her dreams. Pip struggles to remain within the illusions and expectations of his dreams, hoping to find himself transformed into a gentleman exempt from the realities of economic life. In this enterprise he fails, of course, as becomes clear to him when he awakens to discover that he has been a "sleeping partner" in a plot of forgery, thievery, and extortion. The accounts that Jane and Pip give of their dreams in the course of narrating their life stories, then, reveal two fundamentally different repressed plots of narrative voice. And the two narratives they compose represent two distinct types of fictional autobiography, each with a different view on the costs of acquiring or failing to acquire entrepreneurial control over the terms in which their experience is represented. Both share a common assumption, however: the protagonist's dreams manifest the workings of a volatile psychic economy.

[19]Charles Dickens, *Great Expectations*, ed. Angus Calder (Harmondsworth, Eng.: Penguin, 1978), p. 165, hereafter cited in the text.

The Advertisement of *Jane Eyre*

I shall advertise.

—Jane Eyre

Promise me one thing. . . . Not to advertise: and trust this quest of a situation to me. I'll find you one in time.

—Edward Rochester

You, sir, are the most phantom-like of all: you are a mere dream.

—Jane Eyre

"We had very early cherished the dream of one day becoming authors," Charlotte Brontë wrote about herself and her two younger sisters in a preface for *Wuthering Heights*. "This dream never relinquished," she added, "it took the character of resolve."[20] The dream was especially dear to Charlotte Brontë, whose persistent and aggressive marketing of her own and her sisters' manuscripts to publishers—sometimes in direct opposition to Emily's wishes—was largely responsible for making the dream come true. Even after her considerable efforts as literary "agent" managed to secure an agreement with a publisher, Brontë insisted that more than the normal amount of money be spent on advertising, agreeing to deduction of that amount from the authors' expected royalties.[21] But this dream of authorship was not the only one that drove her. Through much of her life her sleep was disturbed by a recurrent dream of her two elder sisters, Mary and Elizabeth, both of whom had died at Cowan Bridge School, the model for what would become the Lowood School of *Jane Eyre*. This dream and Charlotte Brontë's response to it are not unrelated to her consciously cultivated "dream" of becoming an author, and they may even provide a basis for understanding that dream and the dreams she later introduced into the book that made her the successful writer she so deeply desired to be.

Brontë first gave an account of her dream as a young girl, to her friend Mary Taylor, who later described the incident to Elizabeth Gaskell:

---

[20]Memoir of Ellis Bell prefixed to the Smith, Elder posthumous edition of Emily Brontë's *Works* (1850), quoted in Winifred Gérin, *Charlotte Brontë: The Evolution of Genius* (1967), p. 306.

[21]See Gérin, *Charlotte Brontë*, p. 308. Charlotte wrote to Aylott and Jones 11 May [1846], urging them to spend more than the agreed £2 on advertising, "especially as the estimate is increased by nearly £5, in consequence, it appears of a mistake. If you do not object, the additional amount of the estimate can be remitted when you send in your account at the end of the first six months." The authors eventually agreed to contribute £31 10s. 0d. toward cost of publication (and later added another £5) and agreed to pay £2 for advertising in literary journals.

She had told me, early one morning, that she had just been dreaming: she had been told that she was wanted in the drawing room, and it was Maria and Elizabeth. I was eager for her to go on, and when she said there was no more, I said, "But go on! *make it out.* I know you can." She said she would not; she wished she had not dreamed, for it did not go on nicely; they were changed; they had forgotten what they used to care for. They were very fashionably dressed, and began criticizing the room, etc.[22]

Brontë's refusal—or inability—to relate this dream fully was finally overcome when she wrote *Jane Eyre*, the novel she subtitled *An Autobiography*. Writing *Jane Eyre* provided Brontë with the opportunity to express her anger at the role the Cowan Bridge School played in her sisters' deaths. She was able to expose the cruelty of the institution and to purge it through its fictional incarnation as Brocklehurst's Lowood School. But in writing *Jane Eyre* Brontë was also able to tell a story in the first person of a young woman who—like her sisters in the dream—became rich and independent after lowly beginnings. By the end of the novel, Jane Eyre is not only an heiress; she is an entrepreneur as well, who has earned and advertised her way to financial and psychological independence. "I shall advertise," Jane informs Rochester when she mistakenly believes she will have to get another situation because he is to marry someone else (197). She had come to Thornfield by advertising herself, and by advertising herself she would leave it. But though Jane never has to take out another advertisement in the newspaper, when she returns to Rochester at the end of the novel, she is still advertising her independence to him: "I told you I am independent, sir, as well as rich," she says. "I am my own mistress" (383).

Jane's story of becoming her own mistress consistently links psychological independence and financial success. The literal accumulation of wealth becomes a metaphor for Jane's psychic development; she increasingly conceives of her own psychological processes in terms of an economic system. Jane's success on both counts turns on one critical avoidance: the marriage to Rochester does not take place, presumably because Jane discovers that Rochester is already married. For her to marry him would be a violation of law, and in terms of the dream of authorship and the hidden narrative plot, the marriage would also violate Jane's struggle to gain authority over her life by winning psychological and economic independence from all her "masters." Jane's equation of psychological well-being with financial security is evident in her declaration to Rochester about how she will function once they are married. "I will not be your English Céline Varens," she declares. "I shall continue to act as Adèle's governess; by that I shall earn my board and lodging, and thirty pounds a year besides. I'll furnish my own wardrobe out

---

[22]*The Brontës: Their Lives, Friendships, and Correspondence in Four Volumes*, ed. Thomas J. Wise and J. Alexander Symington (1933), 1:91. Quoted in Helene Moglen, *Charlotte Brontë: The Self Conceived* (1984), p. 23.

of that money, and you shall give me nothing but . . . your regard: and if I give you mine in return, that debt will be quit" (237). Whether she is describing her material or her moral disposition, Jane consistently represents her life as a series of such debts and payments, for which she makes the terms. Her dreams—two of which she insists on telling Rochester on the eve of the ill-fated wedding day—become the private capital upon which she draws to settle those bargains. They are an "inward treasure," providing her with the self-knowledge that ensures her own regard for herself and acquits her of any debts to anyone else (177).

Jane Eyre's dreams can become useful in the project of self-authorship only when she converts them into verbal representations of herself, when she makes them into personal "accounts." Jane's determination to tell her dreams to Rochester before marrying him contrasts dramatically with Charlotte's reluctance to tell a friend her childhood dream about the visit of her fashionable and contemptuous sisters. Whereas Charlotte's friend had to urge her to "go on" and "make it out," Jane demands that Rochester allow her to tell him her dreams, despite his active interference. "Let me talk undisturbed," she warns him; "hear me to the end" (246, 248). It is as if in *Jane Eyre* Charlotte Brontë was finally able to "make out" the dream that remained so unapproachable to her through much of her life. In writing her novel, she realizes with Jane that her most precious possession is her voice, her power to articulate her own story of herself from beginning to end without fearing competition from those who would disturb her tale or sell it short.[23] Brontë's reluctance to tell her disturbing dream seems to be rooted in the shame she felt when her apparently affluent sisters judged her as inadequately "fashionable." Brontë worked through that shame by writing this autobiography as a Cinderella story and a capitalist myth, the story of the dispossessed orphan child who earns her way to respectability and learns to give voice to the unconscious desires encoded in her dreams.

Critics have viewed Jane Eyre's story of acquiring power and independence from a number of perspectives. Terry Eagleton links the dialectical patterns of Jane's desire for mastery and her resistance to it with the social structures of capitalism. Helene Moglen has connected these desires to specific relationships in Brontë's family, and Dianne Sadoff has extended the analysis to the larger oedipal structures of desire operating in the nineteenth-century family. Sandra Gilbert and Susan Gubar, Margaret Homans, and other feminist critics have interpreted these issues as expressions of a feminist counterattack on an oppressive patriarchal system. Gayatri Spivak, however, interprets the politics of the novel as essentially repeating

[23]See Rosemarie Bodenheimer's valuable analysis of the way Jane places her story within a variety of fictional forms that are "partly to be used, partly to be exorcised and denied as limitations in the scope of Jane's character or Brontë's narrative powers" ("Jane Eyre in Search of Her Story," *Papers on Language and Literature* 16 [Fall 1980]:387–402). See also Jerome Beaty, "*Jane Eyre* and Genre," *Genre* 10 (Winter 1977): 619–54.

the model of imperial conquest practiced economically by the Masons and personally by Rochester's family in Jamaica.[24] I believe that the critique of desire central to all these interpretations is made possible because the novel conceives of and represents the self in essentially economic terms— specifically, in terms of a competitive marketplace of the mind. Over the course of her narrative, Jane increasingly comes to think of the dreams and desires of her "inner self" as entities in a marketplace over which she struggles to gain entrepreneurial control. This thinking not only reflects the dominant economic realities of Jane's life; it also anticipates the bourgeois model of the psyche which will be formalized by Freud at the end of the century.

The now-famous December 1848 review of *Jane Eyre* in the *Quarterly Review* condemned the author's "tone of mind and thought" as the same kind of thinking that had "overthrown authority" abroad and "fostered Chartism and rebellion at home."[25] This description of the author's psychology in terms of a radical economic movement is useful for understanding the dream psychology implicit in *Jane Eyre*. In the 1840s the debate over the English economy led to a controversy that eventuated in, among other things, the transformation of the problem of poverty from a social condition to a psychological state. Increasingly in this debate, the discourse of the mind became intertwined with the discourse of money. In *The Idea of Poverty* Gertrude Himmelfarb demonstrates how developing *ideas* about the meaning of poverty largely eclipsed the *material fact* of poverty in nineteenth-century England. She traces an intricate ideological conflict that raged through the first half of the century among moralistic, sentimental, and scientific treatments of economic problems and among the competing models of Adam Smith, Thomas Malthus, and Henry Mayhew for what was more and more regarded as the wasted productive resource of the poor. Ironically, Himmelfarb concludes, "just at the time when the poor were finally relieved of the stigma of pauperism," Mayhew came along at midcentury "with the most laudable of intentions and the most generous of sympathies" and "inflicted upon the poor a new stigma," the interpretation of economic poverty as a "moral, psychological, and cultural poverty" that was even more debilitating than the harsh material conditions the poor suffered.[26] This conception of one's economic condition as a state of mind led directly to the conception of one's state of

[24]See Terry Eagleton, *Myths of Power: A Marxist Study of the Brontës* (1975); Sadoff, *Monsters of Affection;* Margaret Homans, "Dreaming of Children: Literalization in *Jane Eyre*," in her *Bearing the Word;* Moglen, *Charlotte Brontë;* Gilbert and Gubar, *The Madwoman in the Attic;* and Gayatri Chakravorty Spivak, "Three Women's Texts and a Critique of Imperialism," *Critical Inquiry* 12 (Autumn 1985): 243–61. My reading employs the work of all these critics, shifting the emphasis to the rhetoric by which the self is "conceived" in the novel and the language and plot forms that embed an idea about how the psyche works.

[25]Elizabeth Rigby, Review of *Jane Eyre*, *Quarterly Review* 84 (December 1848): 174.

[26]See Gertrude Himmelfarb, *The Idea of Poverty: England in the Early Industrial Age* (1985), p. 370.

mind as an economic condition. In *Jane Eyre*, the "tone of mind and thought" adopted by the narrative voice in making her life story out of her dream accounts, reflects (as Freud would later say) "an *economic* view of mental processes."[27]

Jane's identification of herself as a figure in the marketplace—at once capital, labor, and commodity in a series of economic exchanges—not only acts as a representation of a material fact and as a metaphor for the psyche. It is expressed in the narrative form her novel assumes as well. In each of the settings where her story takes her, Jane is confronted with a narrative competitor who attempts to take her story from her. In every case those narrators seek to silence Jane and assign her a passive role in the story of her life, subordinating her to their own designs, absorbing her in narratives in which she serves their ends. Like Rochester, these linguistic competitors are also always economic superiors who wield their verbal power over her by virtue of some financial advantage they possess.

Jane is first abused by her "benefactress" Aunt Reed, then maligned by the "treasurer and manager" of Lowood School, deceived and exploited by her master and employer, and finally manipulated by her "charitable" clergyman cousin. Jane's resistance to these narrative competitors and her reversal of their financial advantage constitute the hidden plot of *Jane Eyre*. She overpowers each of them when she refuses and exposes their false narratives and, at the same time, reconfigures the terms of their economic relationship with her. In every case, the reversal is accompanied by a dream or dreamlike vision to which Jane gives voice and by which she defines herself.[28] The business of Jane's self-narrated novel aims at giving an account of these dreams and thereby taking and retaining possession of the privilege of telling her own story. In the dream of her dead sisters, Charlotte Brontë is "told that she is wanted" in the drawing room. In the dream accounts of *Jane Eyre*, the dreamer does the telling and finally determines where she is wanted and what she wants. Just before Jane recounts her two disturbing dreams to Rochester on the eve of the wedding that will not take place, she tells him that he is "a mere dream" (245). By so identifying him, she takes control over him and his mystifications of her. But she also takes control of her own unconscious, implicitly recognizing that Rochester is the embodiment of her desires as well as the obstacle to achieving them. In his present position of mastery, he is a force she must manage if she is not to be managed by him.

---

[27]Freud, "Fixation to Traumas—the Unconscious," *Introductory Lectures on Psychoanalysis, SE* 16:275.

[28]Robert Heilman's influential essay "Charlotte Brontë's 'New' Gothic" (reprinted in *The Brontës*, ed. Ian Gregor [1970]) maintains that the "new dimension of Gothic" that Charlotte Brontë discovered is at least partially evidenced in the use she makes of "strange, fearful symbolic dreams" in *Jane Eyre*, in which Brontë is "plumbing the psyche, not inventing a weird decor" (p. 99). Though I believe many gothic texts do the same thing, I agree that Brontë has extended this process considerably.

The hidden plot of competition for the right to be the author of the story is made known on the very first page of the novel when Jane is ostracized by her adoptive family for the things she says and the way she says them. Mrs. Reed identifies herself as the first narrative competitor in the first words spoken to Jane in the novel, when her aunt reprimands Jane for being a "caviller" and a "questioner," commanding her: "Until you can speak pleasantly, remain silent" (5). The injunction to silence is the fundamental threat Jane faces throughout the novel, and it is consistently tied to her financial dependency. "You are less than a servant," one of the servants reproves her, "for you do nothing for your keep" (9). Another servant immediately reinforces the reproof and urges Jane to keep her thoughts to herself. "You ought to be aware, Miss, that you are under obligations to Mrs. Reed: she keeps you: if she were to turn you off, you would have to go to the poor-house" (10). "They will have a great deal of money," Jane is told of the Reed children, "and you will have none: it is your place to be humble, and to try to make yourself agreeable to them" (10).

For Jane, this "reproach of my dependence" is "painful and crushing." She recognizes from the start that her silencing is a function of this impoverishment. So she resolves very early that she will neither "do nothing" nor be "kept." She will live her life on her own terms, whatever the cost. Eventually, she reverses the prophecy of her poverty. Jane returns to this household when her benefactress is dying and her tyrannical cousin John has already died in bankruptcy. Her summons to the house comes after she dreams a recurrent dream in which she is accompanied by a phantom infant whose wailing she silences. When she arrives at Gateshead, her tormenting cousin, John Reed, has been silenced; he has slit his own throat. Driven to distraction by her dissolute son's incessant demands for money, Mrs. Reed confesses her cruelty to Jane and dreams on her own deathbed of her son with that mortal wound in his throat. Jane's fortunes, however, are on the rise; and she proceeds to dream of her own increasing eloquence as the Reeds are rendered more and more silent. Throughout the novel, this pattern of a dream of silence, an articulated dream account, and a financial reversal by Jane continues to bring her into possession of her own voice and fortune. Like the dreams of *Frankenstein* or *Wuthering Heights*, Jane Eyre's dreams embody the desire for a language to express them. Unlike the dreams of those novels, however, these manifest a desire for a language that profits the dreamer instead of merely healing her.

As is the case with all of Jane's narrative rivalries, her battle with the Reeds takes place most profoundly on the level of language. When Jane rebels against their mastery, she is reproved by Mrs. Reed's "emphatic voice," which confines her to her room and forbids her to "utter one syllable" (23). Jane cannot bear this unjust prohibition; she challenges Mrs. Reed "as if my tongue pronounced words without my will consenting to their utterance:

something spoke out of me over which I had no control" (23). The whole of Jane Eyre's story relates how she gains control over this "something," how she comes into possession of this voice that speaks out of her unconscious. Here at the outset of her tale, Jane seems already to be naturally aware of the issue that will form the center of her dreams—the importance of preserving her own voice and of refusing others' descriptions of her and her experience.

Later, when Jane is interrogated by Brocklehurst, and Mrs. Reed banishes her once more to silent confinement in her room, Jane again "retaliates" with words. "*Speak* I must," she declares, and she "launches" a single "blunt sentence" that asserts the truth of her own self-description and the deceit of the Reeds (30–31). Jane describes this verbal counterattack in military terms as "the hardest battle I had fought and the first victory I had gained" (32). She is provoked into it, she says, by Brocklehurst's presentation to her of a book about the "awfully sudden death" of a young girl who is "addicted to falsehood and deceit" (30). By rejecting this book, which Brocklehurst and her aunt imply is a prospective narrative of her own fate, Jane rejects both their accusations and their threats to reform her. "I am not deceitful," she declares to Mrs. Reed. "If I were, I should say I loved you; but I declare I do not love you . . . and this book about the liar, you may give to your girl, Georgiana, for it is she who tells lies, and not I" (30–31). Throughout her story, Jane insists on being the only source of truth about herself. This incident is fundamental because in it she refuses a book in which her life is threatened and the truth of her voice is questioned. In the psychological terms of Jane's story, these two things are equivalent. When Jane declares that Georgiana must play the character of the liar in this book, she assumes authority over her usurpers. Then, having made her eloquent defense by telling a narrative of her life in which she accuses her "benefactress" of cruelty and deception, Jane explicitly declares her narrative power and warns her accusers, "I will tell anybody who asks me questions this exact tale" (31). "This exact tale" becomes a chapter in the book Jane writes and in which she plays the truth-telling hero rather than the lying victim.

This successful claim to authority is preceded by a dream, setting the pattern for the rest of Jane's story. At the climax of her panic when she is confined in the red room by Aunt Reed, Jane falls asleep and has the first of her dreams, a terrifying nightmare of which she never gives a complete account. "I suppose I had a species of fit," she says at the end of the second chapter; "unconsciousness closed the scene." "The next thing I remember," she says in opening the following chapter, "is waking up with a feeling as if I had had a frightful nightmare, and seeing before me a terrible red glare, crossed with thick black bars" (15). The nightmare Jane refers to but does not tell is locked behind those bars, inaccessible even to her. Its content is hidden in the blank space between these two chapters of her life. But Jane's verbal assault on the Reeds after she awakens may be regarded as the dis-

placed account of this dream. A voice, Jane says, "spoke out of me over which
I had not control" (23). The fantasies Jane indulges in immediately before
her dream suggest that her suppressed dream is concerned with the preservation of this voice. As she is about to go to sleep in the dreamlike space of
the red room, Jane sees a beam of light move across the wall: "I began to
recall what I had heard of dead men, troubled in their graves by the violation
of their last wishes, revisiting the earth to punish the perjured and avenge the
oppressed. . . . I wiped my tears and hushed my sobs, fearful lest any sign of
violent grief might waken a preternatural voice to comfort me. . . . This idea,
consolatory in theory, I felt would be terrible if realised: with all my might I
endeavored to stifle it—I endeavored to be firm" (13–14). What Jane fears
most in this fantasy is a voice, an alien voice, which, even though theoretically
reassuring, in fact threatens her. Jane "endeavored to stifle" the voice that
would direct her like Hamlet's ghost, just as she stifles the dream that follows
it. Since she has been the victim of so many tyrannical voices already, she
instinctively refuses the wishes even of a benevolent voice here. Unlike
Hamlet, who pursues his ghost and bids it, "Speak, I am bound to hear"
(1.5.7), Jane will be bound by no speech but her own. She censors the
content of this alien, "preternatural voice" from her consciousness as well as
from her readers.

Jane begins the chapter that recounts her exile and nightmare in the red
room by saying, "I resisted all the way" (9). This resistance to authority
provokes the dream, and it also causes her to censor it. Whatever the manifest content of the dream, the entire dream event bespeaks Jane's resistance
to an authoritative voice from outside herself and the assertion of her own.
Specifically, Jane resists the interpretation of her dream as a *ghostly* voice, as
the utterance of some "spirit" or "preternatural voice" that originates "in the
church vault, or in the unknown world of the departed" (13).[29] The meaning
of the nightmare for Jane is clear even though it remains unspoken: she
refuses the gothic dream of an alien presence and transforms it into an
expression from her own "unconsciousness" which empowers her to speak
for herself. Jane proleptically identifies this as a dream of her own authority
when she sees herself in the mirror, immediately before the dream, in the
form of a fiction to be narrated: "All looked colder and darker in that

[29]According to Herman Rapaport, in "*Jane Eyre* and the *Mot Tabou*," *Modern Language Notes*
94 (December 1979): 1093–104, the ghostly voices in *Jane Eyre* can be traced to the absent
"collective mother" of the text. "If one were to pursue a poetic of hauntedness," he claims, "of a
text that disclosed disembodied voices, perhaps the voices of ancestors or departed lovers or of
the damned, one might turn to Charlotte Brontë's *Jane Eyre*" (p. 1093). Rapaport sees the Reed
ghost as "death re-inforced, at the same time that it is negated, revenged, mastered. And the
ghost, that necessary accomplice, is acting here as signifier of desire, an imaginary agency
facilitating the achievement of pleasure" (p. 1094). My reading is consistent with Rapaport's,
except that I see Jane as making those disembodied voices her own through repression and
rearticulation, and thereby essentially "mothering" herself.

visionary hollow than in reality: and the strange little figure there gazing at me with a white face and arms specking the gloom, and glittering eyes of fear moving where all else was still, had the effect of a real spirit: I thought it like one of the tiny phantoms, half fairy, half imp, Bessie's evening stories represented as coming out of lone, ferny dells in moors, and appearing before the eyes of belated travellers" (11). Jane's realization of herself as a character, as a being from a story, provokes her unconscious determination also to be the teller of her story and thereby to control the part she plays in that story. By resisting the phantom voice, she resists being the "tiny phantom" these narrative competitors try to make her. If Jane is to have any authentic identity of her own, she will have to escape the control and manipulation of the Reeds—and everyone else who tells her who she is—by defining herself. As Jane demonstrates in her treatment of the dream in the red room, to define oneself is not necessarily to reveal oneself; rather it is to have control over the information by which one presents oneself to the world.[30]

Jane tells us that her vision of herself in the mirror caused the "violent tyrannies" of the Reed family to roll through her "disturbed mind like a dark deposit in a turbid well" (11, 12). She resents Georgiana's deceptive beauty, which is able to "purchase indemnity for every fault," and John's cruel greed, which "spoiled" his own family without any cost to himself (12). Jane figures this "deposit" of resentful dream thoughts in economic terms, and she seems to convert them in her nightmare into psychological capital that she invests in her own self-assertion, first to the sympathetic doctor Mr. Lloyd and then to Brocklehurst and the Reeds themselves. "Poverty looks grim to grown people," Jane reflects to herself as she tells the doctor her story of abuse; "still more so to children: they have not much idea of industrious, working, respectable poverty; they think of the word only as connected with ragged clothes, scanty food, fireless grates, rude manners, and debasing vices: poverty for me was synonomous with degradation" (20). But Jane's poverty is a state of mind as well as a material condition. When she adds that she "was not heroic enough to purchase liberty at the price of caste," she equates her liberty with her psychological enrichment and continues to establish a sense of self that is construed in economic terms, as a series of purchases, deposits, and payments. Whereas Jane's self-assertion after her nightmare results in another banishment—this time to Lowood School—what seems like a defeat for her in the manifest plot is a victory in the hidden plot. Her strong statement enables Jane to escape the exploitative voices of the Reeds, educate herself, and gain a profession. When she returns to the Reeds she is

[30]In this regard, I agree with John Kucich's treatment of the role of repression in Charlotte Brontë's novels. "In fundamental ways," he says, "expression and repression cooperate and enhance each other by being identically opposed to direct self-revelation" (*Repression in Victorian Fiction*, p. 47). As I show in this chapter, Jane's strategic use of dream accounts sometimes takes the form of expression and sometimes of repression.

earning a living. They are not only impoverished but dead or dying or confined. Jane stifles their voices in her nightmare and as her subsequent dream accounts indicate, also converts her encounters with them into the material that allows her to speak for herself.[31]

The red-room scene in which Jane dreams of resisting an alien voice and subsequently deploys her own voice to preserve herself is played out in a more dramatic dream event at Lowood School, when Jane goes to sleep beside the dying Helen Burns and awakes alone. The account of this event, like the one that preceded it, is strategically presented by Jane. She reveals her strategy at the opening of the chapter in which she records the results of that event: "This is not to be a regular autobiography," she admits. "I am only bound to invoke memory where I know her responses will possess some degree of interest" (72). Jane recognizes that *she* will determine what accumulates interest in this account and that the privilege of representing or refusing to represent her past is *her* possession. Jane's account of the death of Helen is a case in point: it accomplishes the disempowerment of Brocklehurst in Lowood, Jane's assumption of professional authority in the institution, and her eventual independence from it as well. Helen Burns is a kind of dreamy double for Jane throughout her time at Lowood; her removal from the text at the moment of Jane's awakening is a sign of Jane's complete rejection of this oppressed voice. The image of Helen may remain with Jane and be resurrected in the form of her subsequent nightmares of infantile helplessness, but as quiet and harmless as Helen Burns appears, she must be stifled as firmly as Jane's other oppressive nightmare.

Helen, who has put her faith in a heavenly economy, has no investment in the earthly one. "Hush, Jane!" she says in response to Jane's criticism of Brocklehurst; "the sovereign that created your frame, and put life into it has provided you with other resources than your feeble self" (60). But Jane is convinced that her only resource is herself. When Helen adds that "besides this earth, and besides the race of men, there is an invisible world and a kingdom of spirits," Jane hears the ghostly voice of her red-room dream, a voice she knows she must resist and convert into a resource for her own voice. But Helen chooses to divest herself of her own resources. She accepts the "untidy" badge that defines her as a "Slattern," which Miss Scatcherd forces her to wear "like a phylactery" around her forehead (64). Helen merely repeats this one-word story of her life. She even urges Jane to take the same course. "Learn from me," she instructs Jane, "not to judge from appearances. I am, as Miss Scatcherd said, slatternly; I seldom put, and

---

[31]Gilbert and Gubar assert that Charlotte Brontë intended the red-room incident as "paradigm of the larger drama that occupies the entire book," largely because Jane so often recalls the incident at crucial moments in her career (p. 341). I want to point out that its recollection is connected with dream experience in each case, and it is paradigmatic in linking dream events with issues of authority (note both sets of dreams at Thornfield).

never keep, things in order; I am careless; I forget rules; I read when I should learn my lessons; I have no method; and sometimes I say, like you, I cannot bear to be subjected to systematic arrangements. This is all very provoking to Miss Scatcherd, who is naturally neat, punctual, and particular" (48). Helen adopts Miss Scatcherd's voice and vocabulary here in accounting for herself, sacrificing her own words in favor of those systematic arrangements that "the sovereign" has placed over her. As far as Helen is concerned, she is "as Miss Scatcherd said" she is. When she is falsely accused, she refuses to make any explanation to exonerate herself. No wonder the outspoken Jane "wondered at her silence" (46).

Even before she dies, Helen collaborates with her erasure from this world by withdrawing from it into a dream world. During her lessons, she tells Jane, "I fall into a sort of dream" (49). "When I should be listening to Miss Scatcherd, and collecting all she says with assiduity, often I lose the very sound of her voice." But the sound of Miss Scatcherd's voice and of the others that dominate Helen are the places in which she has lost herself. They have made Helen begin to speak of herself in the third person, writing herself out of her own life story. Helen is not only Jane's silenced dream-self, she is an example of something that Jane must not allow her dreams to become: mere escapist fantasies unconnected to her desires in this world. Appropriately, then, both Helen and Jane fall asleep in the same bed, but only Jane awakes. "I was asleep, and Helen was —dead," Jane says, seeming to draw a causal relation (72). Like Helen, Jane had been given a sign to wear at Lowood, a sign whose text had again questioned her authority over herself: it read "Liar." But unlike Helen, Jane resisted and transformed her sign of humiliation into a symbol of heroism. She retaliated on its author, Brocklehurst, by "telling all the story of my sad childhood" to Miss Temple, both vindicating her authority and exposing Brocklehurst as the liar (62). Jane retaliates once again when she awakens from the dream during which Helen dies; this time she helps provoke an inquiry that eventually costs Brocklehurst executive and financial control over the institution. Because of his "wealth and family connections," unfortunately, he remains treasurer of the school, but because Jane relies on the resources of her own story, he no longer exploits the school financially (72). In fact, he eventually puts Jane on the payroll.

The most severe potential threat Jane faces, however, is not Helen Burns but Bertha Mason. In an even more extreme way than Helen, Bertha is a silenced narrator, locked away, unable to tell her own story except in the occasional shrieks and cries that escape the attic at night. She is also a commodity, the "wealthy marriage" bargained for by Rochester's father to keep his son from being "a poor man" (268). The daughter of his father's business acquaintance, the beautiful but presumably insane Bertha Mason comes to Rochester with a fortune of thirty thousand pounds. For this sum she is sold to him, and the disinherited Rochester (who says he was "piqued" by his "competitors" to marry her) is bought off (269).[32] In Bertha Mason economic dependency and psychological incapacity are given their most literal equation. She is only Rochester's mad money, not the "partner" he had sought in marriage (268).

Like Helen, Bertha is a dream-self for Jane whose first view of her, like her last view of Helen, is in the bedroom—this time in the reflection of her own mirror. Bertha is seen putting on and then destroying the veil Jane was to wear as Rochester's bride. This visitation occurs directly after Jane has dreamed two foreboding dreams about her marriage to Rochester, and we learn of it when she tells those dreams to him. Rochester even tries to explain the vision of Bertha away as another dream of Jane's. He may, unwittingly, be close to the truth. Jane wakes from her dream to the dreamlike appearance of her silenced predecessor, warning her of the cost of marrying Rochester. This warning seems to act out the implications of the tapestry covering the doors that lead to Bertha Mason's cell, a depiction of Judas's betrayal of Christ for thirty pieces of silver. This silent narrative becomes Rochester's cover story for Bertha's life. Potentially, Jane is warned, it could also be hers. Like Jane's dreams, the tapestry signifies the reduction of the person who marries Rochester to a prisoner with a price on her head.

Even before her climactic dreams, Jane seems to be aware of this possibility. Immediately after his proposal, Jane notes that Rochester looks on her like a sultan viewing "a slave his gold and gems had enriched" (236). But Jane refuses to be commodified in this way as an object purchased by Rochester's wealth: "Don't consider me an equivalent for one; if you have a fancy for anything in that line, away with you sir, to the bazaars of Stamboul . . . and lay out in extensive slave-purchases some of that spare cash you seem at a loss to spend satisfactorily here" (236–37). The terms of Jane's and Rochester's cash relations have been strained from the start. As her employer, he seeks to control her by giving her less money than he owes her or to manipulate her by giving her more. He tries to get his money back when he learns she will use some of it to advertise for a new position after he marries. Unable to persuade her to surrender her wages, he tries to extort from her a promise that she will *not* advertise but allow him to find her a new place. But Jane maintains control of herself, refusing his gifts and insisting on her due. After offering to be her "banker" for some of the money he owes her, Rochester asks Jane at least to let him "look at the cash" he has just paid her. But she holds firm: "No sir," she says; "you are not to be trusted" (197–98).

The essential economic configuration of Jane and Rochester's relationship is given symbolic form by Rochester himself when he masquerades as a

---

[32]See Spivak, "Three Women's Texts."

gypsy fortune-teller and charges Jane a shilling for the privilege of hearing her life story told for her. He proposes to "read" Jane's face and hands for a sum, to treat her as a "customer" with whom to make "deals" (172). At the same time, he refers to her as a mysterious text that tells a silent "tale" only he can narrate (176). In so doing, Rochester reveals his deep intentions. He desires to be the voice of Jane's experience, to represent her life before it is lived, and thereby to gain ownership of it. He admits as much when, in the voice of the gypsy, he anticipates Jane's resistance to the fortune he reads in her. Looking into her eyes, he articulates what she might be thinking when he affirms her need for a partner in love. "I need not sell my soul to buy bliss," he hears her saying. "I have an inward treasure, born with me, which can keep me alive if all extraneous delights should be withheld; or offered only at a price I cannot afford to give" (177). Rochester is on the mark. Jane does not resist thinking of her inner self as an economy; she only refuses to be sold short or overcharged. Jane herself describes this entire event as "a kind of dream" in which the gypsy's words sounded like "the speech of my own tongue." "Did I wake or sleep?" she asks herself. "Had I been dreaming? Did I dream still?" (175, 177). Thus far, all Jane's dreams and quasi dreams offer her either a silenced person (Helen or Bertha) who is a threatening model for herself and whom she must therefore resist or the opposite, a powerful voice (Mr. Reed's ghost or Rochester) that might speak for her and therefore must be suppressed if Jane is to be author of her own story. Jane's literal dreams throughout the novel increasingly enable her to realize what these earlier dreams and dreamlike events figure for her: she desires to dictate the terms of her psychological independence herself, to make her "inward treasure" her own "fortune."

This desire becomes explicit in the central dream events of the novel, narrated by Jane to Rochester on the night before they are to marry. Jane begins her account by telling Rochester her thoughts on the day before she dreams, explaining her resentment and anxiety over his attempts to manipulate her with his wealth. Jane tells him how when she opened his gift of an expensive wedding veil, she realized it was intended to "cheat me into accepting something as costly" as the previous gifts, which she had refused. "I smiled as I unfolded it, and devised how I would tease you about your aristocratic tastes, and your efforts to masque your plebeian bride in the attributes of a peeress" (247). Jane knows that the veil only masks the reality of an economic barrier between them and that the economic reality corresponds to a psychological barrier that divides them as well. Despite Rochester's attempts to interrupt and dismiss her narrative, Jane insists he let her "talk undisturbed," and she begins to tell the first of her dreams, in which she pictures this "barrier dividing us":

On sleeping, I continued in dreams the idea of a dark and gusty night. I continued also the wish to be with you, and experienced a strange, regretful consciousness of some barrier dividing us. During all my first sleep, I was following the windings of an unknown road; total obscurity environed me; rain pelted me; I was burdened with the charge of a little child: a very small creature, too young and feeble to walk, and which shivered in my cold arms and wailed piteously in my ear. I thought, sir, that you were on the road a long way before me; and I strained every nerve to overtake you, and made effort on effort to utter your name and entreat you to stop—but my movements were fettered, and my voice died away inarticulate; while you, I felt, withdrew farther and farther every moment. (247–48)

The barrier, of course, is in one sense the fettered Bertha Mason, whose voice, once purchased, has also died away inarticulate (and, incidentally, whose financial victimization foreshadows Jane's). The child that Jane has charge of in the dream seems in its inarticulate wailing to warn Jane against following Rochester and suffering Bertha's fate. The child also connects this dream to the others Jane dreamed just before she returned to, and triumphed over, the Reeds. In addition to representing her desire to cease being an inarticulate and dependent child, this dream-child has a number of other resonances: it could represent the new self that Jane will become in marrying Rochester or Jane's own neglected childhood or even the silenced Helen Burns. According to Margaret Homans these multiple associations suggest that the threat the dream represents is tied not to any particular part of Jane's self the child represents, but to the general danger of Jane's self-fragmentation.[33] I concur, but wish to emphasize that Jane's fragmentation here is attributable, as it has been before, to the thing that Jane's dream-self and her dream-infant have in common: their inability to speak authoritatively and articulately.

Jane's second dream of the unknown child and her presentation of it to Rochester both emphasize this point. Before Jane is able to tell her second dream to Rochester, he interrupts her again by urging her to repeat his own teasing words of love; she meets this request with an assertion of her right to tell her own story first: "I will tease you and vex you to your heart's content, when I have finished my tale," she tells him, "but hear me to the end" (248). Jane knows that she must articulate her inner fears and desires, and the second dream she tells is really an elaboration of the first, an expression of her desire that her voice not die away without articulating her own independence, financial and psychological:

I dreamt another dream, sir: that Thornfield Hall was a dreary ruin, the retreat of bats and owls. I thought that of all the stately front nothing remained but a shell-like wall, very high and very fragile-looking. I wandered, on a moonlight night, through the grass-grown enclosure within: here I stumbled over a marble hearth, and there over a fallen fragment of cornice. Wrapped up in a shawl, I still carried the unknown little child: I might not lay it down anywhere, however

[33]Homans, *Bearing the Word*, p. 92.

tired were my arms—however much its weight impeded my progress, I must retain it. I heard the gallop of a horse at a distance on the road; I was sure it was you; and you were departing for many years, and for a distant country. I climbed the thin wall with frantic, perilous haste, eager to catch one glimpse of you from the top: the stones rolled from under my feet, the ivy branches I grasped gave way, the child clung round my neck in terror, and almost strangled me: at last I gained the summit. I saw you like a speck on a white track, lessening every moment. The blast blew so strong I could not stand. I sat down on the narrow ledge; I hushed the scared infant in my lap: you turned an angle of the road: I bent forward to take a last look; the wall crumbled; I was shaken; the child rolled from my knee, I lost my balance, fell, and woke. (248–49)

The child that "wailed piteously" in Jane's ear, an emblem of her own threatened narrative voice, is still cradled protectively by Jane in this second dream. "However much its weight impeded my progress," Jane tells Rochester, seeming to intuit the significance of this unknown "charge," "I must retain it." This dream is more than a symbolic representation of her present danger and her determination to retain possession of her narrative voice. The dream also expresses Jane's desire for the "ruin" of Rochester—the very leveling of their economic differences that will later be accomplished by Bertha Mason's rage. When Jane reaches the summit in her dream, she sees Rochester "lessening" as she rises; in this she seems both to desire and to predict Rochester's payment of the charges incurred by his veiled dealings with her. In her dream, Jane sees what she will be told about later: Rochester amidst "an immense quantity of valuable property destroyed" (375).

The two desires appear inextricably linked in the dream. Jane must be financially independent of Rochester in order to maintain her narrative control over her life. But the dream also figures a conflict in Jane's desires. She remains tempted by his mastery over her—she wants to follow him down the road he travels.[34] Jane feels a perilous attraction to surrendering her life to his authority. But to this seduction she does not yield. The cost of giving in to such a desire would be the loss of the child and the strangling of Jane's own voice. The child's destiny has consistently been identified with Jane's, and in this dream she falls to the ground as the child falls from her grasp. The more powerful desire expressed in the dream is Jane's desire to retain possession of this child and her own voice, superseding even her desire to be with Rochester. This stronger desire was already expressed in an earlier dream in which Jane sees Miss Ingram "closing the gates of Thornfield against me and pointing me out another road" (213). Eventually, Jane must take that other road—away from Thornfield, the symbol of her economic and psycho-

---

[34]In *Monsters of Affection*, Sadoff gives an elaborate and compelling psychoanalytic reading of the "dialectic of master and slave" in Brontë's work, which Sadoff connects with the persistent Brontëan figure of the punishing father whom the daughter wishes to please.

logical servitude. And when she sees Rochester in this dream as "lessening every moment," she sees his power and fortune as diminished to precisely the degree they will be at the end of her story.

Rochester seeks to silence Jane as soon as she has narrated the two dreams, dismissing them first as "unreal" and then as, at best, confused notions, "half dream, half reality" (250–51). But Jane persists in valuing her dreams as integral aspects of her reality: the dreams have been, she says, "all the preface, sir; the tale is yet to come" (249). And as Jane tells of Bertha Mason's appearance in her looking glass (knowing, somehow, that the incident must follow her dreams as the text to which they were the preface), she recalls her nightmare in the red room and challenges Rochester to identify the strange visitor. Once he reassures (or warns) Jane by saying, "I must be careful of you, my treasure," Rochester tries to pass off the mysterious guest as the servant Grace Poole. But Jane is not satisfied, and will not be until she learns the true identity of her visitor the following day. Jane's attention to her dreams as *her own* psychic treasure helps protect her from becoming another treasure in the possession of Rochester. In this dream, she retains what Freud would call "the capital" of her "unconscious wishes" by asserting the power of her own voice in the place of the alien voice she had repressed in the red-room dream. She makes out of her own mind what she earlier had expressed a desire for in financial terms. "If I had ever so small an independency," she had wished to herself, "if I had but a prospect of one day bringing Mr. Rochester an accession of fortune, I could better endure to be kept by him now" (236). In her account of this dream, Jane asserts her independence and makes both a "treasure" and "fortune" of herself.

The next dream Jane recounts occurs immediately after she has discovered the truth about Bertha Mason's identity. Her marriage made impossible by the discovery of another Mrs. Rochester, Jane must decide whether to leave Thornfield and follow her own path or accept Rochester's latest offer—to keep her as his mistress. Now she dreams of herself in the presence not of an unknown and "piteously wailing child" but of a radiant and articulate female form:

> I dreamt I lay in the red-room at Gateshead; that the night was dark, and my mind impressed with strange fears. The light that long ago had struck me into syncope, recalled in this vision, seemed glidingly to mount the wall, and trem-blingly to pause in the centre of the obscured ceiling. I lifted up my head to look: the roof resolved to clouds, high and dim; the gleam was such as the moon imparts to vapours she is about to sever. I watched her come—watched with the strangest anticipation; as though some word of doom were to be written on her disk. She broke forth as never moon yet burst from cloud; a hand first pene-trated the sable folds and waved them away; then, not a moon, but a white human form shone in the azure, inclining a glorious brow earthward. It gazed and gazed and gazed on me. It spoke to my spirit: immeasurably distant was the tone, yet so near, it whispered in my heart—"My daughter, flee temptation!"

"Mother, I will."
So I answered after I had waked from the trance-like dream. (281)

The fear of the "word of doom" does indeed recall the patriarchal, "preter-natural voice" that Jane stifled in the red-room nightmare. It also recalls the powerful, passionate voice with which Rochester tried to persuade Jane to remain in Thornfield as his "best reward" (281). But those male voices are transformed here and replaced by a female voice. The two female figures in the dream—a mother and a daughter—recall Jane's more recent dreams of a woman and child. As an orphan, Jane has no mother; she is her own "au-thor." And this dream-mother whom Jane has dreamed up is herself, the mother of her voice, the guardian of her power to resist the voices that seek to own her. In this dream, as in the others, Jane is both mother and daughter. But now she speaks clearly as an independent adult; she is no longer the helpless, sobbing infant. Now Jane is the resplendent self she has created from the light that flickered on the wall in the red room; and the word of doom which had to be stifled there has now become a word of salvation which Jane speaks to herself—whispers, as she says, "in my heart."

The gradual formation of Jane's vision of herself in this dream was antici-pated in the paintings of female figures which she had earlier shown and described to Rochester. The images of those paintings are as surreal and fantastic as her dream, and Rochester even speculates that they are things Jane "must have seen in a dream" (111). One of the paintings depicts a "woman's shape" that resembles the "white human form" of the dream in startling detail: "The dim forehead was crowned with a star; the lineaments below were seen as through the suffusion of vapour; the eyes shone dark and wild; the hair streamed shadowy, like a beamless cloud torn by storm or by electric travail. On the neck lay a pale reflection like moonlight; the same faint lustre touched the train of thin clouds from which rose and bowed this vision of the Evening Star" (110).

Jane paints as she dreams—in images of power. She shows these female figures "crowned" in one case "with a star" and in another "with a ring of white flame" in the "likeness of a Kingly crown" (110–11). Yet, like the images of a dream, they were not available as sources of self-understanding or power for Jane. "In each case," she laments," I had imagined something which I was quite powerless to realise" (111). But the voice spoken in the last dream seems to enable Jane to realize that power in her life. The continuities between the images articulated in Jane's dream accounts and those pictured in her paintings converge in the final verbal assertion that concludes this last dream, an assertion by which she assumes control of her own life: "I will." Jane's final dream account in the novel ends with the words that both awaken her and affirm her power to act independently. The same words that could have been spoken as a wedding vow to Rochester, declare her independence from him instead. Here, they literally reduce her to poverty, but psychologically they bring her into possession of herself.

Jane finds it almost impossible to recount the ensuing period of economic destitution which was the cost of her decision to leave Rochester. She attributes the difficulty of relating this part of her tale not so much to physical suffering as to the attendant "moral degradation" brought by her poverty. Once again, Jane translates her economic condition into a metaphor for her psychological condition. She explains that the old woman who refused her offer to exchange a handkerchief for a loaf of the woman's bread might be right—"if the offer appeared to her sinister, or the exchange unprofitable" (289). Jane has herself recently refused a sinister and, she knows, ultimately unprofitable offer from Rochester. But her refusal has been costly and has strained her stock of psychic capital. "I am sick of the subject," Jane says as she begins to recount this period of her poverty. "Let me condense now" (289). In her dream accounts, Jane has already provided a condensed narrative of her psychic economy. In the condensed narrative that follows those dreams, Jane realizes both her material and her psychological fortune.

When Jane is finally saved from destitution by the "charity" of the Rivers family, she makes it clear from the outset that she must be "independent" of it as soon as possible: "Show me how to work, or how to seek work: that is all I now ask" (306). Like the other figures Jane must resist in her journey toward self-possession, St. John Rivers endangers Jane on more than a merely economic level: he threatens her authority over herself. Indeed, his is a more radical threat than Rochester's because the plot in which he attempts to absorb Jane would not only change her name but deny her access to her own desires and invert the terms by which she has learned to define herself. The "religious plot" St. John espouses is the most fraudulent of all, a more sophisticated version of the divine economy of Brocklehurst and Helen Burns. "I can offer you but a service of poverty and obscurity," he tells Jane. "*You* may even think it degrading," he says, recognizing her equation of poverty with psychic degradation. He then proceeds simply to turn the equation around. For the "Christian labourer," he explains to her, "the scantier the meed his toil brings—the higher the honour" (311). But the hypocrisy of this inversion is exposed in St. John's rhetoric when, after Jane has become an heir, he urges her to leave her job as a teacher—"turning to profit the talents which God has committed to your keeping" (344). Then, when he argues against her dividing her inheritance with him and his sisters, he bases his appeal upon the "importance twenty thousand pounds would give" in attracting a husband.

Jane knows that more than her bank account would be stolen away under such circumstances and she sees that St. John is commodifying her with his remarks just as Rochester did to Bertha: "I will not be regarded in the light of a mere money speculation," she reproves him (341). Finally, when he proposes to Jane that she marry him and prudently invest her riches by joining his mission to India, St. John's deceptive masking of the discourse of capitalism with the sentiment of Christianity is made clear: "A part of me you must become," he tells her; "otherwise the whole bargain is void" (359). With this, Jane is able to see through this "bargain" and recognize its cost. It is an "offer" motivated by a "counterfeit sentiment," she tells him. "I scorn you when you offer it" (359). His spirituality is exposed as a counterfeit currency with which St. John seeks to purchase her authority over herself, and Jane will not be taken in by it.

Yet, despite her strong resistance to his offer, St. John almost prevails in getting Jane to agree to the bargain. She frees herself from his uncanny power only after she has another dream and makes another verbal assertion of her authority over that dream. Like her other narrative competitors, St. John expressed a linguistic threat. He begins by compelling her to learn Hindustani, the exotic language that only he speaks, so Jane may speak only to him. "He acquired a certain influence over me that took away my liberty of mind," Jane confesses as she begins to speak the new language. "I could no longer talk or laugh freely when he was by" (350). His voice clearly gains ascendancy over her own as Jane realizes that his "freezing spell" is produced by the words he speaks. "I trembled to hear some fatal words spoken which would at once declare and rivet the spell," Jane says when St. John almost persuades her to take up his offer (354). And when she responds to his coercion with the reply, "My heart is mute," his "deep relentless voice" claims, "Then I must speak for it" (354).

As in *Frankenstein* or *Wuthering Heights*, the religious language that would "speak for" an unarticulated self must be resisted and replaced by another explanatory vocabulary. Here, however, the cleric St. John even indicates what that other language might be—the language of the marketplace. This economic discourse is perhaps most dramatically demonstrated when he informs Jane of her inheritance. He reveals that he knows her true identity and offers her the legacy of twenty thousand pounds in the course of telling her own life story for her: "I find the matter will be better managed by my assuming the narrator's part, and converting you into a listener," he tells her (334). It is as if the family inheritance is being offered to Jane at the price of "converting" her from the author of her own story into a listener to it, and the conversion is "managed" by the clergyman-executor St. John. Jane seems to sense the danger in this arrangement, noting that the way she has learned this information is "a very strange piece of business" (337). Her decision to divide the inheritance with her cousins is not only a mark of her own generosity and gratitude but a strategy by which she can both accept the money and retain control over her business. Once again, she dictates the terms of the agreement. Later, when Jane is once again at the brink of succumbing to St. John's plan for her life, he repeats the same offer in a subtler and more powerful form, reading to her from Scripture the promise that those who follow Christ "shall inherit all things" if they acknowledge their names to be "already written in the Lamb's book of life" (367). This time, a *spiritual* inheritance is offered. But once again, it is offered in exchange for authority over Jane's self, for the privilege of writing her name.

Only Jane's voice stands between her and this final threat. And only the intervention of the powerful voice that calls her name enables Jane to avoid St. John's pressure. Strangely enough, Jane at first identifies the mysterious yet familiar voice as belonging to Rochester, miraculously summoning her across the miles that separate them. His inexplicable account of the same night seems to reinforce this uncanny interpretation. At this critical point in the narrative, the novel seems to be its most traditionally "gothic." But Jane manages to convert her supernatural hypothesis into a psychological one when she realizes that this voice that speaks only her name "seemed in *me*— not in the external world" (371). She finally theorizes that it must have been some "nervous impression" or "delusion" from her own mind which "opened the doors of the soul's cell" and "wakened it out of its sleep" in the form of this voice (371). Jane interprets the voice as the awakening and freeing of her inner self, then, the expression of her own unconscious desires, which instinctively spoke out of her dreams from the start. The voice articulates her demand that she be free to be herself—to be Jane and not Mrs. Rivers *or* Mrs. Rochester. Through the agency of Jane's dream plot, the "preternatural voice" of her first dream has been converted into *her* charge, *her* possession, *her* authority over herself.

Her interpretation of the mysterious inner voice that Jane had initially thought to be Rochester's is also a delayed dream account. The final dreams of her autobiography occur just a few pages earlier. In a series of "strange" and "agitated" dreams, Jane finds herself involved in "some exciting crisis," "amidst unusual scenes, charged with adventure, with agitating risk and romantic chance." Then she dreams that she meets Rochester, that in "hearing his voice . . . the hope of passing a lifetime at his side, would be renewed, with all its first force and fire" (323). In her climactic encounter with St. John, Jane projects the repressed desire expressed in her dream into her waking life. She hears Rochester's voice again and then converts it into an expression of her own identity. At this moment of crisis, Jane assumes the role of narrative voice in her own life, taking up all the voices that have sought to speak for her and making them aspects of her own hopes and desires.

Jane comes into her financial inheritance because she unconsciously writes her real name on the cover of her portrait pad, thus revealing her true identity to St. John. She comes into her narrative "inheritance" when she unconsciously speaks that name, simultaneously releasing herself from the bondage of St. John's voice, accounting for her dreams, and subsuming all other narrative voices to her own. In both cases, she has unconsciously "advertised" herself, as she had done intentionally in the newspaper advertisement that garnered her her first job. Jane's first written narrative of herself is in terms of a commodity in the marketplace. Her final verbal account in her autobiography is as a person in possession of herself. When Jane rejoins Rochester and announces to him, "I am independent, sir, as well as rich: I am my own mistress," her authority over her psychic and economic self is assured (383). Rochester acknowledges as much when he asks Jane to give him "the narrative of [her] experience" (387). Her "autobiography" is the account of her acquisition of the power to represent that experience as her own. Jane even describes her subsequent marriage to Rochester as an extended act of narration in which she manages his life as she has her own— by putting it into words: "For I was then his vision, as I am still his right hand. Literally, I was (what he often called me) the apple of his eye. He saw nature—he saw books through me; and never did I weary of gazing for his behalf, and of putting into words the effect of field, tree, town, river, cloud, sunbeam—of the landscape before us; of the weather round us—and impressing by sound on his ear what light could no longer stamp on his eye" (397). Here Jane essentially equates her marriage to Rochester with her writing of the book of his life together with her own. All their shared experience is mediated through her eyes and words. The story is entirely hers to tell, and Rochester is her character now. In completing this narrative, Jane has succeeded in fulfilling her long-held ambitions of being financially independent and telling her tale to the end. At the same time, Charlotte Brontë has managed to fulfill her dream of one day becoming an author by writing a book worthy of its advertisements.

But there is something unsettling about the product. The formulation of a self in terms of a competitive economic model incurs tremendous costs. The marriage of Jane (the wealthy narrator) to Rochester (the bankrupt and disabled listener) represents more a split than it does a union.[35] Jane has not really undermined the pattern of economic and psychological monopoly which characterized her earlier life; she has simply gained control of the means of its production. The plot of the novel has been arranged in such a way that for Jane to win the position of narrative power, Rochester must either die (as Mrs. Reed, Helen Burns, and St. John Rivers must) or surrender that position of power to Jane—at the cost of his fortune, his eyesight,

[35]In "The Place of Love in *Jane Eyre* and *Wuthering Heights*," Mark Kinkead-Weekes links the limitation of the relationship between Jane and Rochester to the "remorseless concentration on the first-person creation of Jane," which denies Rochester a sense of being a "self in his own right" and reduces him to a "projection" or "focus" for Jane (p. 78). I believe that the essentially "capitalistic" psychic economy of the novel demands the same for all the other characters—that Jane either manages the capital of the story or is managed by someone else in it (see *The Brontës*, ed. Ian Gregor [1970]).

and his hand. "He cannot read or write much," Jane notes laconically at the end (397). So she does it for him, both literally and figuratively. She may be a benevolent manager of Rochester's life, but benevolence, as Jane has already learned from St. John, may itself be a form of economic and psychological tyranny. The model of the unconscious mind as an entrepreneur seeking to earn and invest the capital of its own desires appears in *Jane Eyre* to be based upon a model of psychic scarcity in which self-interest necessarily destroys all competition and precludes anything like a just marital partnership. The world outside the self and all the individuals in it are thought of either as competitors that must be converted into suppliers or as consumers of the product the self manufactures and markets independently.

Jane Eyre may just as well be Charlotte Brontë's implicit critique of the social and economic oppression of women which characterized the patriarchal world in which she lived. It may even be a shout of radical protest against the more general injustice of the existing economic order in England in the period of the Chartist rebellions. But Brontë's novel may take part in a political act of another kind: the domestication and neutralization of political and economic forces (like Chartism) by psychologizing them, by turning the materials of history into the materials of consciousness.[36] Regardless of the level of conscious control we can impute to Brontë and the political implications she may have intended for the novel, her deployment of the rhetoric of capitalism to represent the inner self in *Jane Eyre* clearly attests to the increasing power of the nineteenth-century bourgeois conception of the psyche as a commodity in a marketplace, and to the troubling consequences of that conception as well. Bakhtin would maintain that Freud's theory of the unconscious "very distinctly reflects the behavioral-ideological point of view of a petit bourgeois" and that the "inner speech" of the Freudian unconscious is "founded on the economic being" of the whole culture.[37] Brontë's novel of self-construction is a part of that cultural discourse, and the interpretation Brontë gives to the dreams of *Jane Eyre* anticipates those of the scientists in profound ways. Dickens, Freud's favorite English novelist, explores the same problem in *Great Expectations,* another novel written as an autobiography. But Dickens approaches the subject from the viewpoint of a laborer who misunderstands the role of work in the psychic and social

---

[36]Nancy Armstrong argues this point effectively for the Victorian novel in general. She reads the novelistic creation of a language for the psychologically knowable self as a "feminization" of the subject, designed to "enclose certain cultural materials within a structure of consciousness that would further decontextualize and remove these materials from history" (*Desire and Domestic Fiction,* p. 225). Desire, she contends, becomes displaced in the novel from the political into the domestic, the sexual, and the psychological. But as we have seen in *Jane Eyre,* even these displacements can be encoded within a language that exposes the very political and economic conditions that are supposed to be suppressed.

[37]Volosinov [Bakhtin], *Freudianism: A Marxist Critique,* pp. 89–90.

economy and whose dreams of becoming a gentleman render him the personal property of a thief instead.

Balancing Accounts in *Great Expectations*

All other swindlers on the earth are nothing to the self-swindlers, and with such pretences did I cheat myself. Surely a curious thing. That I should innocently take a bad half-crown of somebody else's manufacture, is reasonable enough; but that I should knowingly reckon the spurious coin of my own make as good money!

—Pip

If I ain't a gentleman, nor yet ain't got no learning, I'm the owner of such. All on you owns stock and land; which on you owns a brought-up London gentleman?

—Magwitch

Like Jane Eyre, Philip Pirrip is a dreamer who thinks of his dreams and his inner life in economic terms. Unlike Jane, however, he does not consistently treat his dreams as expressions of psychic capital to be put to use in the development of a more authentic, independent self. In fact, Pip usually sees himself as the property of his dreams rather than the other way around. If the crucial event in the life of Jane Eyre is an act of psychic and economic resistance (in refusing Rochester's offer) the crucial event for Pip is an act of psychic and economic surrender. He allows himself to be made into a gentleman by a forger and a thief at the cost of making and accounting for himself. Pip does not agree to provide the capital for his opportunist uncle Pumblechook's seed business as "sleeping partner" in it; but when Pip accepts Jaggers's terms for the money he receives from his unnamed benefactor, he has already agreed to do essentially the same thing (181). Pip as much as offers himself as the capital for Magwitch's dream of becoming the "owner" of a "brought-up London gentleman" (339). In so doing, he betrays his own dreams and becomes the property of someone else—a "self-swindler," as he finally describes himself, who eventually is employed to record the accounts of imperial traders and investors, having no capital to invest in himself (247). The most apt figure for his own psychic life Pip can imagine is a forged coin: he may be exchanged for a great deal but has no value in himself.

Pip's unconscious life resembles Jane Eyre's in that the essential points in his life story are also punctuated by dreams that reflect the economic policy by which he lives.[38] Yet whereas Jane's dreams provide her with occasions to assert her own authority over her competitors and enable her to come into possession of her own desires, Pip largely misunderstands his dreams and fails to exploit them. Rather than use his dream events to help him recognize and resist his competitors, Pip ignores his dreams for most of his life and treats his rivals as his legitimate owners, acceding to their terms for his life rather than insisting on his own.

In the very first scene of *Great Expectations*, Pip shows himself to be subject to the "authority" of a previously written account, namely, the letters engraved on the tombstones of his parents (35). In seeking out the source of his own name, he misreads the signs on his parents' graves as literal rather than figurative representations of the mother and father he has never seen: "The shape of the letters on my father's gave me an odd idea that he was a square, stout, dark man, with curly black hair," while the "character and turn of the inscription, 'Also Georgiana Wife of the Above'" suggested the "childish conclusion that my mother was freckled and sickly" (35). Throughout his career Pip suffers from this textual confusion, accepting the terms he is offered at face value, failing to recognize what is implicit—and dangerous—in them. In this paradigmatic incident, Pip then stares at the tiny graves of his five little brothers and he connects his interpretive failure with economic failure. Each of the brothers appears to him to have given up trying "to get a living, exceedingly early in that universal struggle" (35). Pip then adds that he is "indebted" to the shape of these graves for his belief that those brothers had all been born "with their hands in their trouser-pockets, and had never taken them out in this state of existence." Here Pip's literalizing of the symbolic makes him think of himself as "indebted" to the world outside for an economic idea he has made up himself. Through most of his life, Pip repeats in his own career what he sees as a family characteristic: he stubbornly resists making a living for himself. And even when he is freed from that obligation after he realizes his great expectations, his pockets remain empty. As a young London gentleman, Pip finds himself—both literally and figuratively—in more debt than he can ever escape. And the terms of indebtedness come to characterize Pip's mental state as well, as he increasingly realizes how he has been complicit in a psychic economy in which he has turned himself into the "the spurious coin" of his own making (247).

These musings of Pip's which open the novel are interrupted and then restated by the "terrible voice" that dictates the terms of the rest of his life.

---

[38]Barbara Hardy correctly cautions that "dreams in novels are images which express the waking lives of the dreamers more lucidly and rationally than the real dreams of our sleeping lives outside of fiction" (*Tellers and Listeners*, p. 33). Dreams in novels are, she says, "acts with consequences," which is certainly true in the case of Jane Eyre. But because of Pip's failure to take them seriously, his dreams act upon him more often than they work as acts by him.

As Magwitch appears from behind Pip's parents' tombstones, his first words to Pip consist of an injunction not to speak ("Hold your noise!") and a threat permanently to deny him the power to do so if he does not comply ("or I'll cut your throat," 36). Magwitch is a thief, and here he steals Pip's freedom to speak for himself. The theft immediately involves Pip in a plot in which Magwitch demands that Pip steal for him and "never dare to say a word or to make a sign" to anyone about it (38). Pip obeys. He agrees to become someone else's property and then to acquire more property for him. This is the same bargain that Pip is offered throughout his life, and this is how he characteristically responds: he accepts a plot from outside himself and silently agrees to take part in a narrative of another's making. Indeed, he even begins to seek out such plots, desperately desiring to be made into a gentleman by someone who will bestow the gift upon him.[39]

Pip's subordination to the voice of the thief and his relinquishment of authority over himself are inscribed on his unconscious as well. The encounter with Magwitch is replayed that very night in a dream in which the threat to Pip's autonomy takes the form of a wish as well as an anxiety. The interpenetration of Pip's conscious and unconscious experience is underscored by his uncertainty as to whether or not he is even sleeping when he dreams of himself "drifting down the river," "a ghostly pirate calling out to me through a speaking trumpet, as I passed the gibbet-station, that I had better come ashore and be hanged there at once, and not put it off" (39). Although Pip never consciously makes the crucial connection between this dream and his encounter in the graveyard, the relationship is apparent. When he first sees Magwitch, Pip describes him as a "pirate come to life," and the connection is reinforced by the surreal amplification of the ghostly pirate's voice through the speaking-trumpet (39). Despite the pirate's loud calls, however, Pip is silent. His voice seemingly stolen away as it had been by the thief in the marsh, he drifts passively down-river, realizing that the orders the pirate gives him threaten his life but unaware that they do so for the same reasons that Magwitch's orders threaten him: they deny him possession of his own voice. The dream does not show how Pip responds to the pirate's imperatives, but his actions when he awakens do. He steals the food and the file and keeps quiet about it, just as he was told.

The dream portrays the same deal offered to Pip by each of the narrative pirates in his life, all of whom wish to make him into a possession for their own profit, whether they "bind" him as an apprentice, exploit him for their own revenge, or own him as a fantasy self. The economy of *Great Expectations*

---

[39]I am indebted to Brooks, "Repetition, Repression, and Return." In this important essay Brooks describes Pip in the first half of the novel as "in search of a plot" and in the last half as involved in a "subversion and futilization of the very concept of plot" (pp. 506, 521). I give a different emphasis to the ending by regarding it as Pip's take-over of the plotting of his life (albeit in a problematic way) rather than his subversion of it.

is in this sense more vicious than that of *Jane Eyre*. With the notable exception of his relationship with Joe, virtually all the financial transactions in which Pip is engaged take an illegal or deceptive form, culminating in Pip's becoming the heir of a thief. In her story, Jane's earning of her own way culminates in her becoming the legitimate heir of an Eyre, and the value of her labors is confirmed by the inheritance that bears her name. All the property circulating in *Great Expectations* seems soiled, however, and all the money has the signs of forgery or theft attached to it. Until the end of his story, Pip never earns any wages, with the possible exception of the few shillings he earned doing odd jobs as a boy. Even that money was confiscated by Mrs. Joe, leaving Pip with only "the impression that [my earnings] were to be contributed eventually towards the liquidation of the National Debt. . . . I know I had no hope of any personal participation in the treasure" (74). Psychologically, Pip fails in the same way. Not until the end of the novel does he actively participate in the "inward treasure" of his own self-possession; he remains for the most part entirely unendowed with anything resembling Jane Eyre's conviction that she could safely claim an independent mind only if she had an independent income. Pip behaves in his conscious life as he does in this dream—as a drifter, subject to the mysterious pirates and princes who will rob or reward him as they see fit.

The linkage of Pip's anxiety about money and property with his inability or failure to articulate and "own" his psychic experience seems to be a direct displacement of the elements that led to Dickens's own mental crisis over writing his autobiography. Dickens's nightmarish dreams about the humiliation of his family's debt and his own physical labor dissuaded him from writing his life story. "How much I suffered," he insisted; "it is, as I have said already, utterly beyond my power to tell."[40] He anticipates Pip's failure to take narrative control over his life story and Pip's preoccupation with his economic status. "From that hour until this at which I write," Dickens confided to Forster, "no word of that part of my childhood which I have now gladly brought to a close, has passed my lips to any human being" (35). Seemingly driven by the dreams of "rescue from this kind of existence," the novelist wrote novel after novel about the poor orphan who realizes that dream of a miraculous rescue (29). Yet Dickens could never bring himself to return to the marketplace where the warehouse he had worked in was located until, he says, "after my eldest child could speak" (35). Even then, Dickens could still not find words adequate to express the experience: "In my walks at night I have walked there often, since then, and by degrees I have come to write this. It does not seem a tithe of what I might have written, or of what I meant to write" (35). While *Great Expectations* is certainly not a complete expression of this material, it may be the most personal and complex repre-

[40]Forster, *Life of Dickens*, p. 29, hereafter cited in the text.

sentation Dickens succeeded in making of the profound ways in which economic anxieties shaped his life and his mind.[41]

Like his creator's, Pip's psychic economy was forced on him from early in his childhood. In this, Dickens's use of the language of the marketplace to account for the development of the psyche in *Great Expectations* is more complicated than Charlotte Brontë's. *Jane Eyre* seems intuitively to understand and operate within the psychological economy of her society as if it were a natural state of being, but Pip remains an uncomprehending figure within the "economy" of his family relations. His very obtuseness about that economy exposes it as an arbitrary and artificial system.[42] When Pip recounts the Christmas dinner that takes place on the day after his meeting with Magwitch, he exposes his family's commodification of him through language. Mr. Wopsle, whose primary distinction for Pip is his "deep voice," transforms the parable of the prodigal son into a story about the "gluttony of the Swine" rather than the welcome return of the son, and he turns the force of the narrative directly against Pip ("What is detestable in a pig, is more detestable in a boy"). Then, the tale becomes a description of Pip himself as Wopsle identifies him with the "Squeaker" of the revised parable: "You would have been disposed of for so many shillings according to the market price of the article, and Dunstable the butcher would have come up to you as you lay in your straw, and he would have whipped you under his left arm, and with his right he would have tucked up his frock to get a penknife from out of his waistcoat-pocket, and he would have shed your blood and had your life" (58). According to Wopsle, "Many a moral for the young might be deduced from that text" (57–58). The moral that Pip should have deduced is that if he allows the story of his life to be rewritten into the texts and the terms of these rival narrators, they will have his life and reduce him to a piece of property with a price on his head as well.

Pip seems to be aware that these voices mean him wrong, but he does nothing to resist their plotting out his life for him. After his family contrives to hire him out as a companion for Miss Havisham, for example, and then

[41]See Alexander Welsh, *From Copyright to Copperfield: The Identity of Dickens* (1987) on the relative autobiographical elements in *Copperfield* and *Great Expectations*. Welsh suggestively describes the later novel as "a model for psychoanalysis" (p. 180).

[42]See Julian Moynihan, "The Hero's Guilt: The Case of *Great Expectations*," in *Victorian Literature*, ed. Robert O. Preyer (1966), pp. 126–45. Moynihan quite properly calls Pip "Dickens's most complicated hero" because he is "victimised by his dream and the dream itself, by virtue of its profoundly anti-social and unethical nature, forces him into relation with a world in which other human beings fall victim to his drive for power" (p. 143). I concur, but disagree that Pip's "ambition" and "unbridled individualism" are what are regarded as purely "criminal" here. Though Dickens is by no means uncomplicated about it, he clearly portrays Pip's "reform" at the end of the novel as at least partly an acceptance of his individualism and his need to be more economically and psychologically responsible for himself. See also F. R. Leavis and Q. D. Leavis, *Dickens the Novelist* (1970): "Pip's moral sensibility is shown to be the product in fact of the very conditions that made his sufferings" (pp. 330–31).

asks him to describe the experience, Pip does not relate his meeting with her as it happened at all but as a fabulous invention designed to satisfy his auditors' fantasies. "I was perfectly frantic," he says about his interview with his sister and his Uncle Pumblechook, "a reckless witness under the torture—and would have told them anything" (97). Instead of describing the decay and corruption around Miss Havisham as he saw it, Pip represents her according to his family's expectations—as living in fantastic luxury and wealth. Having told this lie, Pip then makes a telling confession of the truth to Joe which summarizes his whole life story: "I don't know what possessed me" (99). The entire novel will repeat this narrative of Pip's ignorance about the forces that "possess" him. Already, when he tells his story in the terms his avaricious family prescribes, they have taken possession of him for the price with which Miss Havisham will eventually "bind" him to them. But like Dickens himself, Pip chooses not to express directly the perniciousness of the system that has subjected him, and so remains unrescued from it. And like Scrooge, whose dreams were manifestly about the forces of the marketplace, Pip's dreams reflect the power of the marketplace to shape the subjects that participate in it.[43]

These instances of Pip's verbal and financial exploitation do not merely manage his material life, then. They are also the forces by which what he calls his "inner self" is "composed" (71). That they are becomes increasingly clear in Pip's experience at Satis House, where he begins to think of Estella and Miss Havisham in the very fairy-tale terms he had invented for the sake of his family. Just as Pip adopted his family's words to describe his experience there, he adopts Estella's and Miss Havisham's denunciations of him as a "stupid, clumsy, labouring boy" (90). From this point onward, Pip can no longer bear the prospect of working for a living—a "condition of mind," he says, whose origin he could not determine: "How much of my ungracious condition of mind may have been my own fault, how much Miss Havisham's, how much my sister's, is now of no moment to me or anyone" (134–35). In fact, this is a matter of the greatest moment to Pip. As he embraces the fiction of Satis House gentility, he begins to despise the whole notion of labor and to expect that the grotesque Miss Havisham will make his fortune for him. Consequently, he becomes increasingly alienated from the desires of his "inner self" as he gives up responsibility for articulating those desires and working to achieve them. "What I wanted, who can say?" he ponders. "How can *I* say, when I never knew? What I dreaded was, that in some unlucky hour I, being at my grimiest and commonest, should lift up my eyes

---

[43]David E. Musselwhite points to Dickens's writing of *Dombey* as the "massive act of self-management and self-promotion" that led to his retreat from a decentered conception of the self to the more "concentrated and privileged identity" of the self as a commodity characteristic of the later novels (*Partings Welded Together: Politics and Desire in the Nineteenth-Century English Novel* [1987], p. 145).

and see Estella looking in at one of the wooden windows of the forge. I was haunted by the fear that she would, sooner or later, find me with a black face and hands, doing the coarsest part of my work, and would exult over me and despise me" (135–36). When Pip adopts Estella's repulsion for work, it replaces any quest for knowing his own desires. The abandonment of that quest freezes him in fear and denies him the possibility of realizing the "capital" of his unconscious.

During this period of his life, Pip (like Dickens himself) is "possessed" by dreams that represent the "condition of mind" which leads to his self-hatred and his failure to know and articulate his desire. But his inclination to surrender control over his inner life to the authorities who claim it denies him the possibility of profiting from the knowledge these dreams might offer him. After the strange man who visits the tavern has identified himself has an emissary from Magwitch by showing the file Pip had once given the convict, he bestows two one-pound notes on Pip in a gesture that comes to symbolize how Pip is bought off throughout his life. Pip tells us that this money became "a nightmare to me, many and many a night" (107). The recurrent dream image of the bank notes is combined with another nightmare: "I was haunted by the file too. A dread possessed me that when I least expected it, the file would reappear. I coaxed myself to sleep by thinking of Miss Havisham's, next Wednesday; and in my sleep I saw the file coming at me out of a door, without seeing who held it, and I screamed myself awake" (108).

Characteristically, Pip does not take these dreams seriously enough to try to understand what they mean. Instead of regarding them as coded expressions of his "inner self," of the desires he is convinced he cannot know or articulate, he fears his dreams and tries to put them out of his mind. Pip dreams of a file (the symbol of his labor at the forge) and of money (the symbol of his not having to work at all). He sees the genteel world of Miss Havisham's as a refuge from the world of work, the symbol of which keeps reappearing in the hand of a figure he cannot see. That hand represents, presumably, the convict (to whom he had given the file) and himself as well. Together, the images of these dreams and Pip's reactions to them figure what he does not recognize about himself: that he is more possessed by the money than he is the possessor of it, and that the blacksmith's file may free him in a way that his dreams of money and gentility never will.[44] Later on, when Magwitch identifies himself to Pip as his convict and benefactor, Pip discovers that the same hand that holds the file holds the money. These images are, of course, overdetermined, and the displaced erotic motives behind the con-

---

[44]In *Charles Dickens: The World of His Novels* (1958), J. Hillis Miller claims that at the center of this novel "is a recognition of the bankruptcy of the relation of the individual to society as it now exists, the objective structure of given institutions and values. Only what an individual makes of himself, in charitable relations to others, counts" (p. 277). I see the novel as deeply conflicted on this issue, especially with regard to the contradiction between "charity" and "self-making."

junction of hand and file are suggestive (as such motives may be in all of Pip's or Jane Eyre's dreams). But the more general truth that Pip represses here is that even his libidinal self is consistently composed in the economic images of capital and labor. By understanding how his mind works he might possess the forces that drive his unconscious, rather than be possessed by them. Pip chooses not to know what or who possesses him, however, and in material terms he replaces the ideal of working to earn his living with the ideal of being made into a gentleman by someone else.

Pip's dreams of money and labor revise David Copperfield's dreams of "poverty in all sorts of shapes" (387), which in turn had revised Dickens's own miserable dreams about his poverty and forced labor as a child in the blacking factory. In addition to simply expressing Dickens's childhood traumas over his poverty, these repetitive dreams within his two fictional autobiographies and his own "Autobiographical Fragment" may also manifest a basic conflict in Dickens's thinking about an "economic psychology." Dickens was an outspoken critic of the harsh economic theories of the Malthusians and utilitarians. Many of his novels reflect this antipathy, and in *Hard Times* he subjects those economic philosophers to rather savage parody. *Hard Times* was written in 1854—exactly midway between the publication of *David Copperfield* (1849–1850) and *Great Expectations* (1860–1861). There (and elsewhere) Dickens critiqued as cruel and inhumane the economic philosophers' ideas of driving the poor into the exercise of "economy" and hard work through the terror of the failure to practice responsible domestic "economy." In condemning the arbitrary administration of the Poor Laws, Dickens continued to advocate as an alternative what Walter Bagehot called a "sentimental" radicalism, which encouraged the very things the Malthusians had discouraged—private and institutional charity. Dickens refused to make the harsh judgments urged by the philosophers between the deserving and undeserving poor, based upon their ability and willingness to work. He rejected, that is, the implicit Malthusian understanding of the psychology of the marketplace because it ignored individual cases of suffering in favor of an abstract ideal of "political economy," which made fear into the only incentive for thrift and productivity.[45]

But the implications of the "charity" exercised by Magwitch in *Great Expectations* seem to support, rather than contradict, a Malthusian psychology. Magwitch's plot to reward Pip is eventually exposed as nothing more than the well-intentioned corruption of the boy. The convict's charity in fact precludes Pip's economy and helps make the child into a spendthrift, a victim, and an unwitting collaborator in a marketplace in which he performs

[45]Walter Bagehot, "Charles Dickens" (1858), in *Literary Studies* (London, 1898), p. 157. The best treatment of Dickens's conflicting attitudes toward domestic and political economy is in House, *The Dickens World*. See also Himmelfarb, *The Idea of Poverty*.

no productive role. Humphry House speculates that "the rather clown-like exaggerations of Dickens's satire of statisticians and economists" in such novels as *Hard Times* "are partly to be explained by the underlying doubt whether they might not be right after all." House maintains that Dickens's opinions on political economy were more likely "expressing wishes rather than convictions."[46] *Great Expectations* reinforces the theory that Dickens may have been more persuaded by the Malthusians' and utilitarians' seemingly harsh analyses of human behavior than his sentiments and memories allowed him to admit.[47] Like Jane's, Pip's story demands that he recognize some forms of benevolence as fraud, that he refuse such gifts and work for a living. The cost of his earlier failure to realize these truths is that he surrenders all knowledge of and responsibility for himself. Pip fails to see how his own mind is economically configured, and therefore he has "cheated" himself (as he can say only when he writes his life story afterward) by taking as "good money" the "spurious coin" of his own self-deception (247).

Together with Pip's first dream of himself drifting down the river while a ghostly pirate usurps his power to speak, his nightmares about work and money link Pip's failure to know and articulate the structure of his psychic economy with his lack of control over it. In relation to his narrative competitors, Pip drifts from being "bound" by one authority to being exploited by another.[48] He tells us, for example, that his uncle Pumblechook often "laid hold" of him "to be read at" and to be written into whatever text Pumblechook might be reading to him. On one occasion he bullies Pip by identifying him with the newspaper story of the Barnwell murder, and on another he tries to curry Pip's favor by writing a thinly disguised story for the paper about Pip's "rise in fortune" in which he takes credit for engineering his nephew's success (144). Pip also tells us that he is constantly being "severely mauled" by Mr. Wopsle's "poetic fury," which reduces him to a "dramatic lay figure" in his tutor's theatrical performances. Pip is "contradicted and embraced and wept over and bullied and clutched and stabbed and knocked about in a variety of ways" in the service of Wopsle's self-dramatizing designs (137). Together with Mrs. Joe and her "rampaging tirades," each of these adult characters verbally bullies Pip and tries to profit

[46]House, *Dickens World*, p. 71.

[47]In "Expectations Well Lost: Dickens' Fable for His Time," G. Robert Stange compares Dickens to Stendhal and Balzac in their common "horror of a materialist society," combined with an "admiration for the possibilities of the new social mobility" (*College English* 16 [1954–55]: 10).

[48]Elliot L. Gilbert, " 'In Primal Sympathy': *Great Expectations* and the Secret Life," interprets this conflict in the novel as "the conflict between Romantic solipsism and an equally self-serving Victorian materialism" (*Dickens Studies Annual* 11 [1983]: 99). Gilbert's convincing argument can be further complicated, I believe, by attending to the additional level of conflict within Victorian materialism itself.

financially from him.[49] Unlike the soft-spoken Joe who remains committed to the "virtue of industry" and the autonomy of Pip (135), they think of Pip merely as capital for their own investment. And increasingly, so does Pip. While he recognizes their subjection of him into their own "plots" as abusive, he fails to recognize how his fantasies about being made into a gentleman are only more refined versions of the same thing. His willing complicity in such "master plots" becomes clear in his encounter with the next ghostly pirate distinguished by his verbal powers, Mr. Jaggers.

Jaggers enters the story as a narrative usurper whose primary interest is money, and he plays that role for Pip from the beginning of their acquaintance. Jaggers comes into the tavern in search of Pip just as Wopsle finishes reading aloud a newspaper account of a popular murder. Jaggers proceeds to retell the story and give it precisely the opposite interpretation that Wopsle had given it. In Wopsle's narration of the tale, the tavern patrons had taken on the roles of the principals in the case, performed the trial, and convicted the murderer. When the mysterious Jaggers intrudes, however, his powerful voice captivates the crowd, intensifies their belief and involvement in the case, and persuades them to reverse their judgment and acquit the fictional defendant. The scene parodies Pip's confusion about who possesses the authority over his life. He immediately perceives Jaggers as an "authority not to be disputed," in possession of "a manner expressive of knowing something secret about every one of us that would effectually do for each individual if he chose to disclose it" (163). In this observation Pip once again locates the knowledge of his inner life outside of himself, this time in the man to whom he effectively transfers authority over his life in return for the fortune the stranger promises to deliver.

Jaggers "discloses" to Pip that he has "unusual business to transact" with him. He is the "bearer of an offer," he claims, that comes in the form of a "communication" for Pip (164). "And the communication I have got to make is that he has great expectations" (165). But like his legal services, Jaggers's communication to Pip is not without its costs. The price of Pip's "fortune" as it is spelled out by Jaggers is strangely reminiscent of the price Pip had to pay the convict he met on the marsh and the pirate he met in his dreams: he must sacrifice his right to account for himself. Specifically, he must first agree always to bear the name of Pip (which is the sign of his inability to speak his full name and to acquire his full identity); and second, he is "positively prohibited from making any inquiry, or any allusion or reference" as to the source of his fortune (165). The "unusual business" of Pip's "rise in fortune" is that

[49]For a fuller treatment of the linkage between Pip's entry into the world of language and his entry into the world of market capitalism, see Murray Baumgarten, "'Calligraphy and Code': Writing in *Great Expectations*," *Dickens Studies Annual* 11 (1983): 61–72.

it demands his silence and his ignorance (164,166). But he willingly pays the price. "My dream was out," he says; "my wild fancy was surpassed by sober reality; Miss Havisham was going to make my fortune on a grand scale" (165). Pip does not realize what his own words suggest. His dreams *are* bearing themselves out. In accepting Mr. Jaggers's terms for entrusting his fortune to a stranger, Pip submits himself not only to Miss Havisham but to the pirate of his dreams. The great expectation of Pip's life has been his dream of gentility, of having his destiny magically made for him by the intervention of some powerful figure from outside himself. But regardless of the revealing content of his literal dreams, Pip has not associated his conscious illusions about gentility with the unconscious piracy behind them. The night before he leaves for London to begin his genteel life, Pip dreams of himself as a passenger taking "fantastic failures of journeys," "going to wrong places" in a coach being pulled by a variety of strange beasts and men (185). But though he seems to recognize the dream as a warning, as well as a wish to give up authority over himself, he ignores it and chooses to remain a passenger in a coach driven by someone else.

As Pip takes up residence in London, two important developments bring him to a consciousness of the economy of his "inner self." First, his increasingly strained monetary circumstances conspire with the shocking revelation of his benefactor's identity to make Pip face the implications of his own role in an undisclosed economy. He begins to see that his mind has been as profoundly shaped by financial matters as has his standard of living. Second, Pip begins to decipher the meaning of his dreams, dreams that continue to connect his financial dependency with his failure to articulate and control his inner life. Pip's realization of the connection between his financial and his interior life enables him to come to terms with Magwitch's disclosure. It also earns him the right to tell the story of his own "inner self," even if that right has come at a rather high price.

Pip's inclination to adopt the aspirations of others as his own consistently corresponds to his reluctance to speak his mind and, in particular, to his silence about his dreams. Unlike Jane Eyre, who actively uses her dreams to manage moments of conflict in her life, Pip never recounts a dream to another character. And although he informs the reader that he dreamed very frequently, he rarely describes the contents of those dreams with much detail or attention. He even announces on several occasions that his sleep was broken by wild and fearful dreams, but he characteristically sacrifices the opportunity of giving an account of the dreams and discovering any truth they might contain about himself.

The set of dreams Pip dreams in London, however, show a change in this attitude. Even before Magwitch returns to confront Pip with the knowledge that he has become a criminal's stolen property, Pip begins to discover the economic "properties" of his own mind. In the first of his London dreams,

Pip registers his unconscious awareness of a psychic indebtedness even more profound than his financial debts. On the day before this dream, he is talking with his friend Herbert Pocket, expressing his anxiety over his financial circumstances and his hopeless attraction to Estella. Pip reiterates to Herbert what he had told him before, that it was impossible for him to separate his desire for her from all his "wretched hankerings after money and gentility" (257). Yet Pip is disturbed by the psychological implications of these linked desires. By denying him work, they deny him any sense of who he is. "I know I have done nothing to raise myself in life," he admits with some shame to Herbert, "and that Fortune alone has raised me" (269). "I was a blacksmith's boy but yesterday; I am—what shall I say I am—to-day?" In the same conversation, Herbert discloses that he himself, in addition to looking about for some "Capital," has found a prospective wife in Clara. "The moment he began to realize Capital," Herbert informed Pip, "it was his intention to marry this young lady" (273). As Pip muses on the difficulty of either of them ever attaining any capital, he reaches his hands into his empty pockets and discovers only the playbill advertising Wopsle's performance of Hamlet that night, a performance which they then attend. Later that night, Pip's dream repeats his conflation of the desire for capital and and the desire for romance and interweaves with them details from the play: "Miserably I went to bed after all, and miserably thought of Estella, and miserably dreamed that my expectations were all cancelled, and that I had to give my hand in marriage to Herbert's Clara, or play Hamlet to Miss Havisham's Ghost, before twenty thousand people, without knowing twenty words of it" (278–79).

The dream is quite obviously made up of distortions and displacements of much of the psychic material behind Pip's conversation on the previous day. The form of Pip's dream resembles that of his waking life in that it derives its "plot" from another text, which remains unknown to him. In his life he wonders what he is; in the dream, he plays the part of an actor playing a character who is himself a player of parts. In his waking life Pip is, of course, really playing Hamlet not to Miss Havisham's ghost but to Magwitch's, although her ghost does possess him in the sense that it was Miss Havisham who stimulated his "wretched hankerings after money and gentility." Pip's marriage to Clara in the dream may also express a contending desire—the desire to "realize capital" (since this is the condition of marrying Clara), rather than to remain the unrealized gentleman he is, hopelessly longing for marriage to Estella. Once again, the erotic is displaced into the economic. But of more immediate importance than the interpretation of the dream images is the nature of the images themselves. The dream shows Pip's fortunes being canceled because he does not know the lines he is supposed to speak. He cannot speak them because they are not his. Since he has "done nothing to raise himself," Pip is not yet able to recognize his "daytime thought" as the "entrepreneur" for his dream, and he cannot make use of the "capital" of his unconscious (*Interpretation of Dreams*, 561). Like Hamlet, he is haunted by the instructions of some ghostly authority, indebted to a plot that he seems unable to execute, and unable to find the words with which to own and profit from his dream.

After the dream, Pip's actual financial indebtedness begins to appear to him more and more as a figure for his psychological state and to offer the terms through he can take control of himself. He begins to take account of his life by keeping an account of his debts. Unable to live within the allowance afforded him, Pip decides along with his friend Herbert to start keeping careful written accounts of all the money they owe:

> I would then take a sheet of paper, and write across the top of it, in a neat hand, the heading, "Memorandum of Pip's debts." . . . Each of us would then refer to a confused heap of papers at his side, which had been thrown into drawers, worn into holes in pockets, half-burnt in lighting candles, stuck for weeks into the looking glass, and otherwise damaged. The sound of our pens going, refreshed us exceedingly, insomuch that I sometimes found it difficult to distinguish between this edifying business proceeding and actually paying the money. In point of meritorious character, the two things seemed about equal. (295)

Here Pip mistakenly equates the mere keeping of accounts on paper with the settling of those accounts with his creditors. But he is also quite properly equating a mental operation with a financial transaction, acknowledging that when he gathers together the scraps of his accounts he is making psychological "compensation" for actually paying them. As futile and self-deluding as these gestures toward economy seem, they do mark Pip's first awareness of the symbolic nature of the marketplace and the need to be responsible for himself in it. They also indicate a deeper consciousness on his part about how his mind works. So completely does the keeping of his financial accounts become a model for the operation of Pip's own mind that he claims to start thinking of himself as "a Bank of some sort, rather than a private individual" (296). This account keeping also becomes a model for the writing of *Great Expectations* itself. If *Jane Eyre* was an "advertisement" of its protagonist's worth, this novel amounts to Pip's final balancing of all the accounts of his life, seeing where others have deposited their dreams and desires in him and acknowledging where he has incurred the debts for which he finally has to be forgiven.

The climax of *Great Expectations* occurs when Magwitch visits Pip in his rooms and identifies himself as Pip's "second father" (337). "Words cannot tell what a sense I had . . . of the dreadful mystery that he was to me," Pip says. "I doubt if a ghost could have been more terrible" (353). The event seems in many respects to combine the unconscious realizations of Pip's dream with the conscious realization of his financial straits. As Pip must read a script in his dream, he is reading a book when Magwitch approaches his rooms. As he cannot speak his lines in the dream, he is struck dumb by his visitor's description of himself as both the author and the owner of his life. "I've made a gentleman on you," Magwitch informs Pip, and then adds: "If I ain't a gentleman, nor yet ain't got no learning, I'm the owner of such. All on you owns stock and land; which on you owns a brought-up London gentleman?" (337, 339). Instead of "realizing capital," Pip has become the private stock of this stranger. In the horror of confronting his indebtedness to Magwitch, Pip correctly declares, "I had lost my self-possession" (334). But Pip has never really been in possession of himself. Magwitch has been buying him up ever since Pip agreed to the conditions of his fortune. In contrast to the analogous scene in *Jane Eyre* in which Jane is told about Rochester's past, the effect of this revelation is to bind Pip more securely, not to prompt him to make himself independent as Jane does after she hears Rochester's tale. The difference is that whereas Rochester is merely telling his own illicit life story, Magwitch is telling Pip's secret story too, the account of which Pip has previously managed to ignore or repress.

His "ownership" of Pip is established by the narrative Magwitch tells about the details of his criminal life—"swindling, handwriting forging, stolen bank-note passing, and such like" (362). As he listens to the tale, Pip becomes aware of the fact that he has simply allowed himself to become Magwitch's latest forgery, but he learns something else even more important: that the telling of a life story can give "form and purpose" to what otherwise remains hidden. "A new fear had been engendered in my mind by his narrative," Pip says, "or rather his narrative had given form and purpose to the fear that was already there" (367). The fear Pip identifies here is that Magwitch's life may be endangered by his enemy Compeyson, whom Pip recognizes as another ghostly plotter hidden within Magwitch's story. But the fear refers equally to Pip's growing realization that he has squandered the narrative of his own life. While Pip's unconscious life is still being given its form and purpose by the narrative of another here, he is learning that there is a power in articulating one's fears and desires. Such an articulation can aid him in understanding and possibly even mastering the forces that otherwise simply drive him unconsciously.

Pip's linkage of self-expression with self-possession is reinforced in his account of his next dream. Having begun to give form and purpose to his unspoken desires and fears by giving up his charade of gentility, Pip does some plotting of his own by attempting to help Magwitch escape the country and getting Herbert set up in business. After seeing to these plans one evening, Pip receives a note from Mr. Wemmick which contains only the words "Don't Go Home." Pip takes the warning seriously and seeks refuge in a rooming house. As he drifts off to sleep, his consciousness begins to be filled with the sound of "those extraordinary voices with which silence teems," all echoing the same phrase—"Don't Go Home" (380).

When at last I dozed, in sheer exhaustion of mind and body, it became a vast shadowy verb which I had to conjugate. Imperative mood, present tense: Do not thou go home, let him not go home, let us not go home, do not ye or you go home, let not them go home. Then, potentially: I may not and I cannot go home; and I might not, could not, would not, and should not go home; until I felt that I was going distracted, and rolled over on the pillow, and looked at the staring rounds upon the wall again (381).

The dream dramatizes Pip's life as a series of voices speaking in the imperative, all telling him how to conduct his life. Like the the unspoken lines from *Hamlet* in the last dream, the well-intentioned words borrowed from Wemmick in this dream indicate the degree to which the voices of others have shaped Pip's mind. The content of the note also manifests the cost of Pip's acceptance of this influence. Home is where one belongs and—as Mr. Wemmick knows very well—where one's belongings are. "The difference between the property and the owner," Wemmick informs Pip, is that the property can be "saved" (461). Pip is without a home because over and over he has failed to make the distinction between *owning* property and *being* property. He has no home to go to because nothing belongs to him. By his own choice, he has silently agreed to become the property of another man instead of belonging to—and knowing—himself. In this dream about the power of language to control and determine action, Pip's psychological and financial dependency are implicitly associated with his dependence on others' desires for him. In this dream, he doesn't even appear in a disguise; he is entirely replaced by the words of someone else.

But Pip's subsequent actions suggest his resistance to this dream scenario. The dream itself may serve both as a warning and an incentive to him, for the rest of the novel charts Pip's efforts to take on the voice of his experience and to make himself financially and psychologically independent of those who have until now provided the "imperatives" for his life.[50] He does so by confronting each of the figures to whom he has given some power and demanding that they tell him their secret stories, stories that he in turn converts into the material for his own story of becoming "unbound." Pip becomes the narrator of his life, then, as he rejects the ideal of an externally given, genteel identity and becomes a self-made man, an accountant in the marketplace of British capitalism.

The last part of *Great Expectations* recounts Pip's taking power over the stories of his tyrants by confronting them and "owning" his part in their

---

[50]This might be regarded as the moment when what Brooks describes as Pip's desire for plot is replaced by the counteracting desire to subvert plot, or what Kucich refers to as Dickens's divided desires for self-negation and self-promotion (*Repression in Victorian Fiction*, pp. 207–8, 243). In the "economic" psychology of the novel, however, the shift is more precisely Pip's evidencing of a desire to be self-possessed and self-authored, rather than the forgery produced and owned by another.

stories.[51] He then makes their narratives into "capital" for his own life story, instead of allowing himself to continue as a character in theirs. When he tells Magwitch, Jaggers, and Miss Havisham what he has found out about each of their secret financial relations with him, he also manages to extract deeper secrets from them which he is able to put to use in composing the story of his life. At the same time, he becomes free of their financial hold over him. He surrenders his rights to any more of Magwitch's money. He alters his financial agreement with Jaggers to benefit Herbert. He turns down Miss Havisham's offer of financial restitution for her deception of him. Then, he sells his "portable property" to pay off his debts. And most important, he gives up his illusions of gentility and takes a job as a clerk in the business he has helped to set up for Herbert. In this strange repetition of his own benefactor's secrecy, Pip is taking control, but this time according to a capitalistic rather than a genteel myth. He is providing the capital for Herbert's and his own fulfillment of the bourgeois virtues of industry and "self-possession." Even before he knows it, Pip is becoming an entrepreneur and a laborer in an economy in which he is a productive member rather than a mere piece of property.

The confrontations that enable this change in Pip are accompanied by his account of one final, clarifying dream. In taking authority over his narrative competitors, Pip has watched Miss Havisham literally go up in flames, seen Magwitch go down beneath the waves of the Thames, and faced his nemesis and tormentor Orlick, who is finally safely locked away in prison. Then, just as he is about to be carried off to debtor's prison himself, Pip is taken ill, thereby forestalling that measure. In his delirium, he has one more series of dreams that recapitulate his narrative failures yet also suggest that he is overcoming a prolonged confusion about his identity:

That the time seemed interminable, that I confounded impossible existences with my own identity; that I was a brick in the house wall, and yet entreating to be released from the giddy place where the builders had set me; that I was a steel beam of a vast engine, clashing and whirling over a gulf, and yet that I implored in my own person to have the engine stopped, and my part in it hammered off; that I passed through these phases . . . I know of my own remembrance, and did in some sort know at the time. That I sometimes struggled with real people, in the belief that they were murderers, and that I would all at once comprehend that they meant to do me good, and would then sink exhausted in their arms, and suffer them to lay me down, I also knew at the time. But, above all, I knew that there was a constant tendency in all these people—who, when I was very ill, would present all kinds of transformations of

[51]Taylor Stoehr, in *Dickens: The Dreamer's Stance*, demonstrates the ways in which the structure of Dickens's novels resembles the structure of dreams. Repeatedly, however, Pip himself fails to see the connection between the text he is writing and the dreams he recounts. In this phase of his account, he finally begins to tie the two together.

the human face . . . sooner or later to settle down into the likeness of Joe.
(471–72)

Pip's desire to have the many faces of those who threaten him replaced by
"the likeness of Joe" is joined in this dream with his desire to be "released"
from the elaborate plots that have reduced him to a part in an engine driven
by someone else or a brick set by others in an elaborate building. "Joe had a
strong sense of the virtue of industry," Pip had said of him, "and I know right
well, that any good that intermixed itself with my apprenticeship came of
plain contented Joe" (135). The dream seems to release that repressed
"good" in Pip which is identified with "the virtue of industry" and to express
the ideas of work which have (thanks to Joe) been "intermixed" with Pip's
understanding of who he is from the beginning.

This is the first of Pip's dreams that shows him speaking for himself. "I
implored in my own person to have the engine stopped," he says; he "entreat[ed] to be released" from these bonds and asserted over and over what
he "knew" about himself as well as what he didn't know. Pip's assertions of
self-knowledge, that is, are accompanied by his desire to be his "own person"
and to speak his own words. Earlier, Pip laments how little he knew about
"managing" himself as a young man, and he confesses that "the little I knew
was extremely dear at the price" (153). In this dream, however, Pip indicates
that he knows much more, even if the price he has paid has been dear
indeed. Pip's dreams have shown him moving from a place of death, failure,
fear, and blind obedience, to the desire for release, self-expression, and
independence. But in the process, he has lost a good deal of time by "con-
founding impossible existences with [his] own identity" and failing to know
who he was in his "own person." In his account of this dream, he finally
begins to "remember" and take possession of himself.[52]

In the exchange of narratives between Pip and his competitors which
closes the novel, Pip's newfound authority enables him to get the better of
the voluble Mr. Jaggers by silencing him for the first time and then to witness
the more permanent silencing of Magwitch and Miss Havisham by death.
His achievement of narrative power coincides with their loss of it. But this
novel does not end with a triumphant conclusion to parallel that of *Jane Eyre*.
As we have seen, Pip's rise to a position of authority over himself has come
late and at great cost. Ironically, his autobiography is the account of his many
failures to be the author his life story. The tone of the last pages is one of

---

[52]Catherine A. Bernard, in "Dickens and Victorian Dream Theory," places Dickens's treatment of dreams in the context of nineteenth-century scholarship on the subject. In arguing for
Dickens's anticipation of Freud, she shows how crucial childhood scenes are to these dreams
and their essential autobiographical nature. Here, for the first time, Pip seems to recognize that
his dreams have this autobiographical character, that the images of "all these people" represent
transformations of himself.

repentance, evocative of the last words spoken by Miss Havisham in her final interview with Pip, when she asks him to do for her what she could not do— finish writing her will: "Take the pencil and write under my name 'I forgive her'" (415).[53] Pip, as he later narrates this episode, may be taking her story over from her; but he is saying her words as well. Like Miss Havisham, Pip is both asking for and offering forgiveness in writing this scene, since he has complied with the plots that have exploited him and put him in the position of having to ask that his considerable and unpayable debts be forgiven.

Both versions of the final scene of the novel are also marked by repentance and incompleteness. Even in the more optimistic revised ending, Estella and Pip are shown sadly reviewing their lives in the ruins of the "poor, poor old place" where they first met. His union with Estella seems anything but assured at the end. And since Pip's job as an accountant demands that he live abroad, he still has no home and ends the story as a wanderer. But Pip is nevertheless able to make one modest affirmation in response to Estella's inquiries about his state of mind at this point: "I work pretty hard for a sufficient living, and therefore—Yes, I do well" (492). Pip's logic is a stark affirmation of the bourgeois capitalist ideal: I work, therefore I am. It is also a cogent summary of the bourgeois capitalist psychology: I work hard for a living, therefore I am well. At the same time, however, Pip's assertion of this credo seems to lack conviction, and it suggests the limitations of his reform. Pip can only become a kind of imitator of the bourgeois ideal. His psycho- logically (and economically) responsible actions come so late in the novel that they fail to form a really convincing alternative autonomy for him. Pip not only imitates Magwitch in his secret sponsorship of Herbert, he imitates Joe in his frustrated desire to marry Biddy, and Wemmick in the splitting apart of his professional life (in Cairo) from his emotional life (in London). In many respects, Pip remains to the end little more than a capitalist-poseur—the counterfeit coin of the realm he considers himself much earlier.

Despite the many ways in which they differ, *Great Expectations* resembles *Jane Eyre* in its complicity with an essentially capitalist psychology. The early part of the novel seems critical of such characters as Pumblechook, who try to make economic and narrative "capital" out of someone else. Yet Pip ends his story by doing just that, by capitalizing on his narrative competitors' secrets and profiting from Britain's version of such exploitation on an inter- national scale. Like Brontë, however, Dickens does not offer an uncritical endorsement of that model. Just as the rather grotesque marriage at the end of *Jane Eyre* questions the implications of representing the mind as a mar- ketplace in which competing forces struggle for dominance, the equally

---

[53]For more on the "confessional" character of *Great Expectations*, see Robert Tracy, "Reading Dickens' Writing," and John O. Jordan, "The Medium of *Great Expectations*," both in *Dickens Studies Annual* 11 (1983): 37–59 and 73–88. A larger study of the subject is Barry Westburg's useful book, *The Confessional Fictions of Charles Dickens* (1977).

grotesque figure of Mr. Wemmick challenges both the psychological and the economic capitalism of *Great Expectations*. Jaggers's cashier and clerk lives a perfectly schizophrenic life in which his mind is fully invested in matters of business when he is in his London office and is absolutely committed to a childlike sentimentality when he is at home in Walworth: "My Walworth sentiments must be taken at Walworth; none but my official sentiments can be taken in this office," he informs Pip. "They must not be confounded together" (310). So absolutely does Wemmick separate the structures of his thinking in each place, that when Pip accompanies him on one of his trips from Walworth to London, he can see the strange process of "materialization" Wemmick undergoes daily: "By degrees, Wemmick got dryer and harder as we went along, and his mouth tightened into a post-office again. At last when we got to his place of business and he pulled out his key from his coat-collar, he looked as unconscious of his Walworth property as if . . . [it] had all been blown into space" (232). In London, Wemmick's "unconscious" is so fundamentally committed to the acquisition of "portable property," rather than the sentimental properties of home and family, that he coldly identifies all his clients as whatever piece of property they might offer him. Mr. Wemmick's split personality parodies the division in Pip between the limited "success" of his professional life and the lonely "failure" of his private life at the end. In order to finish the bargain made with his criminal benefactor, as Pip says, he must "transfer" to Magwitch the "romantic interests" he had previously invested in Estella (420).

But Wemmick also parodies the division in Dickens's own mind about the psychology of economics and the economics of psychology. Like Wemmick, Dickens seemed able to maintain the conflict between his competing loyalties—to a public policy of sentimental radicalism, on the one hand, and an entrepreneurial theory of psychological self-possession, on the other—only by not allowing the two to be "confounded together." Pip's profession as at once a clerk in the imperial economy and the secret benefactor of his friend might be regarded as another uneasy compromise on Dickens's part between these two positions. Pip can take on neither Joe's untainted, non-competitive capitalism nor the more aggressive self-interest of the would-be capitalists Magwitch and Pumblechook. In much the same way, Dickens tries to have it both ways psychologically, by setting the tone of Pip's emotional resignation at the end of the novel against his command as its narrator. The somber tones in which Pip's exile in Cairo is painted (like the funereal note on which *Jane Eyre* ends with the letter from St. John in India) betray an anxiety over the practical and political implications of an economic psychology. I shall examine that anxiety more fully where it is more fully manifested—in British detective fiction. In many of those texts, the economic repression exercised on the colonies came home to England in the form of dark, criminal dreams of a divided empire and an equally divided self.

In reading *Jane Eyre* and *Great Expectations* together, it is worth noting that the female protagonist more successfully imagines her selfhood as something to be achieved, whereas the male protagonist is inclined to think of it as something to be endowed. It may be argued (as Nancy Armstrong does) that unqualified individualism like Jane's is generally more acceptable in nineteenth-century women because it is less threatening, safely removed as it is from the aggression and competition of the public domain into the realm of the emotional and domestic.[54] These texts suggest that the Victorian novel helped to generate a "female" ideal, then, which transforms definitions of the self for both men and women from economic terms into domestic terms (as Jane's story recapitulates), fostering the cultivation of an interior self that is politically and economically sentimentalized and domesticated.

Jane Eyre and *Great Expectations* are, of course, not the only fictional autobiographies that Charlotte Brontë and Charles Dickens wrote. If the forces in these novels operate in the gendered way I have just described, they do so in a complicated fashion that crosses the lines dividing male and female protagonists. The story of Pip's predecessor David Copperfield may be a more direct imitation of Dickens's life simply because it tells the "history" of a successful novelist and includes more clearly recognizable figures from the author's own history. But Copperfield's story of double marriage and unqualified personal and professional success—which joins domestic and professional accomplishment in equal parts—reflects Dickens's wishes more than the facts of his life. David ends his narrative as "the hero" and the author of his own life with the ideal Victorian woman; Pip is more like an exiled penitent, modestly keeping the books for his and Herbert's accounting firm in Cairo, still drifting with Estella in some unachieved romantic shadowland. *Villette*, the later and more literal reworking of Charlotte Brontë's life, is more like *Great Expectations* than is *Jane Eyre*, for *Villette* also tells a story of a tortured and lonely penitent, working hard for a modest living. Unlike Jane Eyre, Lucy Snowe is no triumphant protagonist who happily marries her lover in the end.[55]

As is true of Jane and Pip, the inner lives of David Copperfield and Lucy Snowe can be traced out in the dreams they recount in their texts. The same can be said of those nineteenth-century biographical novels that were not (and arguably *could* not have been) written in the first person. In *The Mill on the Floss* and *The Return of the Native*, for example, dreams figure importantly in the protagonists' lives, manifesting their failures to "possess" themselves and manage their life stories. Both of these novels are very much concerned

[54]See Armstrong, *Desire and Domestic Fiction*, p. 8.

[55]Dianne Sadoff sees both of Dickens's autobiographical novels as attempts by the sons to "confront or deny, to love and to accuse, their figurative fathers." She properly distinguishes between them, however, by arguing that David Copperfield "celebrates" his "self-engenderment in language," while Pip "criticizes" his (*Monsters of Affection*, p. 39).

with deploying language to return to and master experience, and in both cases that power becomes too great a burden for the figures that have it. Together with the oppressive forces of the marketplace, these psychological failures eventually take the lives of the protagonists in these novels. It is a situation possibly given its most complete form in George Gissing's *New Grub Street* (1891). Like Copperfield, Gissing's Reardon is a novelist and a dreamer, but unlike him, he cannot convert his dreams of poverty into literary success or psychological health. His life ends in tragedy. As is true of all these texts (in all of which the author's life story closely resembles that of the main character), the failure of the characters to become the interpreters of their own dreams and the authors of their "inner lives" is reflected in their failure to be the narrators of their life stories. The plots into which these dreamers' stories are written demand that they define themselves as figures in a marketplace if they want to survive. To know themselves, they must think of themselves as labor and capital in an enterprise in which they are either the entrepreneurs of their own unconscious wishes or the property of someone else's. This conception of the self as a form of property may be one reason why the detective novel gained such prominence late in the period. If people are property, detective plots center on what may be construed as the analogous crimes of theft and murder. It may also explain why, as we shall see in the next chapter, those crimes and their solutions are often first conceived in dreams.

The linkage of the discourse of the marketplace with a description of the unconscious mind in these autobiographical novels may also partially explain Freud's special attraction to a book such as *David Copperfield*. Freud's reading of this favorite novel by one of his favorite authors was discriminating. He distinguished *Copperfield* from some of Dickens's other novels, which often demonstrated what Freud saw as a weakness in Dickens—"his easy toleration of feeble-mindedness, represented in almost every novel by one or two blockheads or crazy people." As the best example of this defect, Freud offered only the character of "the philanthropist, who has such a frightful lot of money and is available for any noble purpose. *Copperfield*," he adds in praise of it, "has the least of this."[56] Freud's association of the "crazy" person with the wealthy philanthropist who has no need to be a discriminating entrepreneur accords with his own "capitalistic" theory of the unconscious, particularly as he described it in *The Interpretation of Dreams*.

As an avid reader of the autobiographical novel, and of gothic and detective fiction as well, Freud must have recognized how these literary forms transcribed the discourses of the culture to represent the inner workings of the human subject. What Freud said of the novelist in *Delusion and Dream* is especially applicable to the autobiographical novelist. "He learns from him-

---

[56]Quoted by Ernest Jones, *The Life and Work of Sigmund Freud*, 1:174.

self what we learn from others—what laws the activity of his unconscious must follow. But he does not need to express these laws, need not even recognize them clearly; they are, as a result of the tolerance of his intellect, contained incarnate in his productions." Freud then made his debt to the novelist explicit: "We deduce these laws through an analysis of his fiction" (117). Freud was a great admirer of the fiction of Arthur Conan Doyle, as well as that of Dickens, and his "deduction" of the "laws" of the unconscious as "repressing agencies," therefore, may have been equally indebted to his reading of the dreams in detective novels. There, dreams figure importantly as well, not only as sites where illicit desires are expressed and enacted but as places where the laws of social repression are inscribed and enforced. The psyche in these texts is not so much capital to be owned and invested as a state divided—at once fomenting a rebellion against authority and repressing the agents of that subversion.

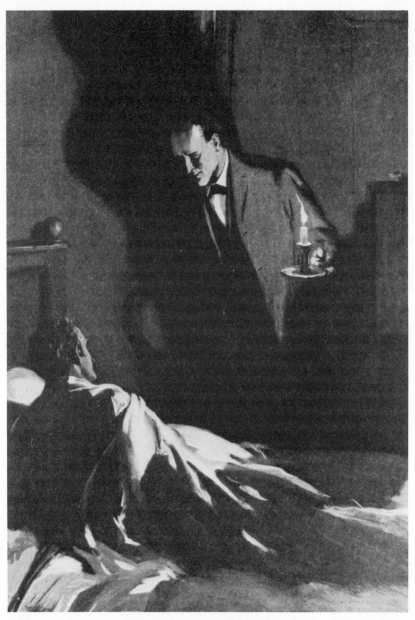

Frank Wiles, illustration for Arthur Conan Doyle, "The Valley of Fear" (*Strand Magazine*, December 1914)

In several of the Holmes stories the detective awakens Dr. Watson either to involve him in a case or to announce its solution. Here, Wiles represents Holmes as both a mysterious figure haunting Watson's dreams and the force that illuminates them. Like many nineteenth-century literary detectives, Holmes repeatedly serves the dual function of bringing a representative figure such as Watson into a confrontation with the dark underworld of crime and protecting him from it by means of ingenious (and insistently "scientific") explanations.

CHAPTER FOUR

The Policing of Dreams:
Nineteenth-Century Detection

Upon the winding up of the tragedy involved in the deaths of Madame
L'Espanaye and her daughter, the Chevalier dismissed the affair at once
from his attention, and relapsed into his old habit of moody revery.
Prone, at all times, to abstraction, I readily fell in with his humour; and
continuing to occupy our chambers in the Faubourg Saint Germain, we
gave the Future to the winds, and slumbered tranquilly in the Present,
weaving the dull world around us into dreams.
—Edgar Allan Poe, "The Mystery of Marie Roget"

Once we happened to speak of Conan Doyle and his creation, Sherlock
Holmes. I had thought that Freud would have no use for this type of
light reading matter, and was surprised to find that this was not at all the
case and that Freud had read this author attentively.
—The Wolf-Man, "My Recollections of Sigmund Freud"

Here, then, in the briefest outline, are the riddles for which the analysis
had to find a solution.
—Freud, "From the History of an Infantile Neurosis"

It is not unusual for Doctor Watson to discover Sherlock Holmes in a
drug-induced dream out of which the detective emerges to impose order on
the confusion of an unsolved crime. The detective's custom is then to de-
scend back into his dreamy state once the crime has been solved. In Watson's
concern for his friend's health, he does not recognize that this pattern is
more than a sign of aberrant social behavior or an instance of the master
detective's eccentricity. It is a model for the entire project of crime and
detection itself. Dreaming is as central to the fundamental texts of detection
in the nineteenth century as the language of detection is to Freud's theory of
dream interpretation. The mysterious theft in the first full-length English
detective novel—Wilkie Collins's *Moonstone* (1868)—takes place during a
dream. *The Mystery of Edwin Drood* (1870) opens in the fevered dreams of

193

John Jasper, in which the dreamer presumably rehearses and replays the unsolved murder in Dickens's last and unfinished novel. The transformation of the respectable physician Dr. Jekyll into a violent criminal takes place, he says, "partly in a dream"; and it is in a dream that the detective figure, Utterson, first sees the twisted form of the murderous Mr. Hyde. In these and many other detective stories, the detective is as deeply involved in the world of dreams as the criminal. Dr. Watson notes with some concern the signs of this dark collusion in his own partner's delinquent behavior. "He had risen out of his drug-created dreams," Watson says suspiciously of Holmes in the beginning of "A Scandal in Bohemia," "and was hot upon the scent of some new problem."[1]

But the victim of the crime is often as deeply implicated in the dark underworld of dreams as the criminal or the detective. In the first of the Sherlock Holmes stories, *A Study in Scarlet* (1887), Holmes solves the case only after he discovers a crucial piece of evidence about the victim, who was apparently murdered while he was dreaming his last dream: at the victim's bedside was a novel he had been reading and an ointment box containing two pills. The key to this case is Holmes's realization that one of the pills was deadly poison, the other was not. The novel at the bedside, like the text of *A Study in Scarlet* itself and like the operation of the detective within it, is analogous to the box containing those two pills: it contains and controls the poison of the deadly dream not by eliminating it but by explaining it and sorting it out. The detective story might be said to contain a drug—a form of therapy and escape—as well as a form of enforcement and power. Like Holmes, it has a dual nature. It both threatens and heals. The story reveals what the dream of the crime had disguised, exposing what—or who—has disappeared in the crime, disciplining its perpetrator, and reestablishing the authority of the one who uncovers the criminal.

Having been through the remarkable analysis of his own dream with Freud, the Wolf-Man should not have been surprised to learn that Freud was an attentive reader of detective literature in general and of the Sherlock Holmes stories in particular. Freud explained dream interpretation as a "reconstruction" of "the process by which the dream was formed" and "the restoration of the connections" between the fragments of the dream which have been obscured by the dream work. The analogy between the methods of Freudian dream theory and those of the master sleuths of detective fiction has subsequently been noted not only by Freud's most famous patient but by literary critics and psychoanalytic scholars as well.[2] As the detective story

---

[1]Arthur Conan Doyle, *The Complete Sherlock Holmes*, 2 vols. (Garden City, N.Y.: Doubleday, 1930), 1:160–61, hereafter cited in the text.

[2]See, for example, Peter Brooks, *Reading for the Plot*; John G. Cawelti, *Adventure, Mystery, and Romance: Formula Stories as Art and Popular Culture* (1976), pp. 94–96, 103–4; Albert D. Hutter, "Dreams, Transformations, and Literature: The Implications of Detective Fiction," *Victorian*

"reconstructs" a crime and provides the missing explanatory links between apparently unrelated events, psychoanalysis reconstructs the web of dream thoughts that lead up to a dream, identifying the logic—or motive—that connects those thoughts. In both cases obstacles to the reconstruction must be overcome, obstacles Freud would refer to as the agencies of resistance, repression, and censorship. These terms, drawn from the world of law and politics, rather than the discipline of medicine, indicate how much Freud's therapeutic model is also a model of social enforcement, just as Holmes's model of law enforcement also serves a therapeutic function.

When Freud uses the discourse of politics to describe the processes operating in the individual subject's dreams, he represents the psyche as a kind of self-contained society intent upon both violating and policing itself through its dreams. This "political" portrayal of the self is the basis of a fundamental similarity between the claims of psychoanalysis and the criminal psychology of early detective fiction. These texts demonstrate that a "political" conception of the individual subject served to explain the dual nature not only of the criminal mind but of every mind. In addition to linking these civil and psychological concerns, moreover, the first great detective stories in England also managed to express anxiety over national crimes for which there was no simple political solution, exposing the same state of conflict within the national unconscious that existed within its individual citizens.[3]

Freud's most elaborate discursive linkage of political and psychological processes occurs in his explanation of the work of censorship in dreams. To describe censorship accurately, he says, he sought out a "social parallel to this internal event in the mind" and found it in the "political writer who has disagreeable truths to tell to those in authority" (*Interpretation of Dreams*, 141):

> If he presents them undisguised, the authorities will suppress his words—after they have been spoken, if his pronouncement was an oral one, but beforehand, if he had intended to make it in print. A writer must beware of the censorship, and on its account he must soften and distort the expression of his opinion. According to the strength and sensitiveness of the censorship he finds himself compelled either merely to refrain from certain forms of attack, or to speak in allusions in place of direct references, or he must conceal his objectionable pronouncement beneath some apparently innocent disguise: for instance, he may describe a dispute between two Mandarins in the Middle Kingdom, when the people he really has in mind are officials in his own country. The stricter the

Studies 19 (December 1975): 181–209; Ernst Bloch, "A Philosophical View of the Detective Novel," in Bloch, *The Utopian Function of Art and Literature*, trans. Jack Zipes and Frank Mecklenburg (1987), pp. 244–64; and Donald P. Spence, "The Sherlock Holmes Tradition: The Narrative Metaphor," in Spence, *The Freudian Metaphor*, pp. 113–60. See also Muriel Gardiner, ed., *The Wolf-Man by the Wolf-Man* (1971), p. 146.

[3]On how Freud did just this, see Carl E. Schorske, "Politics and Parricide in Freud's *The Interpretation of Dreams*," in *Fin de Siècle Vienna*, pp. 181–207.

censorship, the more far-reaching will be the disguise and the more ingenious too may be the means employed for putting the reader on the scent of the true meaning. (142)

The dreamer functions here as both problem and solution, both divided kingdom under siege and political sage trying to heal the rift in the state. In dreams, the dreamer pits the "disagreeable truths" of desire against the injunctions of already internalized authorities. Dreams are "given their shape," Freud says, by the operation of these two opposing forces that occupy every mind—the forces of revelation and censorship, of "truth" and "disguise," of defense and attack. The unconscious of the dreamer is made up of these two contending "psychical agencies," and Freud claims that they find their most "complete analogy in political life" (144). In the language of Freud's analogy, the dreamer is at once criminal and police, the force of law and the force of lawlessness, a dynamic and "political" society unto him- or herself. In order to hold those opposing forces together, the dreamer functions like a writer of political fictions, armed with an ingenious capacity for simultaneously conveying and disguising the truth.

Paul Ricoeur calls the "repressing agency" of Freudian censorship "the psychological expression of a prior social fact, the phenomenon of authority, which includes a number of constituted historical figures: the family, the mores of a group, tradition, explicit or implicit education, political and ecclesiastical power, penal and, in general, social sanctions." He explains that in the psychoanalytic model of the human subject, "desire is no longer by itself; it has its 'other,' authority. What is more, it has always had its other in the repressing agent, an agent internal to desire itself."[4] The presence of the antagonistic other within the self is always a threat to the self's authority, just as the criminal is always a threat to the authority of a society. And each is always internal to the other. "Deprived of ordinary resources," Poe's Dupin says in a comparable description of the function of the detective, "the analyst throws himself into the spirit of his opponent."[5] The agency of the detective, that is, contains and is contained within the agency of the criminal. "The man may be taken as being quite on the same intellectual plane as myself," Holmes warns Watson of the arch-criminal Moriarty in the story aptly titled "The Final Problem." And when Holmes informs Watson that he can predict the master criminal's behavior by remembering the principle that "Moriarty will again do what I should do," Watson can only reflect, "One would think that we were the criminals" (1:475–76). Here, Watson has stated the basic assumption about the psychology of crime and detection, and about psychoanalysis itself. The "final problem" of both is that the agencies of

[4]Ricoeur, *Freud and Philosophy*, p. 178.
[5]Edgar Allan Poe, "The Murders in the Rue Morgue," *The Complete Tales and Poems of Edgar Allan Poe* (1965), p. 142.

"authority" and those of "disguise" are inextricably linked. They are engaged in a psychological conflict completely analogous to that of political life, a conflict to which there is no final solution. They both possess what Watson called in "The Red-Headed League" Holmes's "dual nature" (1:185). Authority is always already "an agent internal to desire itself." In the unconscious of every individual, the criminal and the authorities conspire.

In this chapter, I examine how certain nineteenth-century detective novels anticipated the psychoanalytic representation of the psyche as a political entity. We have seen how *Great Expectations* and *Jane Eyre* made use of an economic model of the unconscious to urge the dreamer to own and work through psychic material in order to produce and master a self. We have also seen how the gothic novel represented the mind as analogous to a body infected by disease and how its dreams demanded to be treated as symptoms and efforts to recover psychic health, rather than as psychic capital to be invested. These texts have much in common with the detective novel, and all of them make extensive use of medical and economic models for the psyche, as well as political ones. But as a matter of emphasis, these gothic and autobiographical fictions exhibit a difference from detective narratives in the way they represent the mind, a difference that explains why the former are more likely to assume plots of demonic possession or economic survival whereas the latter deal more specifically with crime and, in some cases, punishment. In the standard detective story, the concern is not so much with the production or recovery of a self as with the unmasking and disciplining of an aberrant member of the society. The self is an essentially social and political entity in these narratives. The individual is not merely living in a society; a society is living within him or her. Appropriately, then, the dream in the detective story is associated with a crime that not only upsets the course of the dreamer's life but threatens the order of the entire community as well. The dream constitutes a mystery that must be discovered and solved, therefore, not by the dreamer and not for the sake of the dreamer's health or productivity alone, but by and for the sake of the entire community. The real mystery of the detective novel is that its dreamers express "a prior social fact, the phenomenon of authority," and they seek to challenge that authority as well. The detective novel traces out a violation of social law in order to reassert that law through an explanation by the agencies of detection and, if possible, a confession by the criminal.

Explanation and confession are not only cooperative but synonymous acts of narrative completion in these texts. The crime that the community explains is a crime it is also guilty of; its collaboration to explain the crime is a kind of collective confession. The detective reconstructs the crime just as dream interpretation reconstructs the dream, not to cancel it and go on as if it hadn't happened but to assimilate its information into the narrative of the corporate psychic life of the community in the manner of a confession. The detective legally "censures" the act of criminal censorship by making public knowledge out of what had been the most private of secrets. This reading of the psychological significance of the detective novel opposes John G. Cawelti's claim that the analogies between psychoanalysis and detective fiction break down because of the detective story's failure to acknowledge collective guilt. Cawelti argues that whereas "Freud and other social and psychological critics such as Marx and his followers discovered everyone's guilts, Holmes and the other classical detectives absolved society by exposing the least-likely person or the master criminal."[6] I want to emphasize that while the detective plot normally fingers and exposes a single moral source of guilt, it also silently implicates (at least in psychological terms) the detective, the criminal, and the victim, by adumbrating a model of the psyche and of the dreams it produces as socially formed and politically organized.

The detective novel is, like psychoanalysis, centrally concerned with the acquisition of knowledge—with the gathering and interpretation of information about persons and the motives for their actions. But detective fiction and psychoanalysis are also both centrally concerned with power—with authority, with enforcement, with surveillance. That surveillance imposes limits on the conception of the self as independent, even as it seeks to preserve the "safety" of the individual within society. The goal of the detective story is not to produce a private memoir or a diary, therefore, but to provide a public explanation, an occasion when the community comprehends itself in the recitation of an accusation by the detective. Ideally, that public occasion includes a ritual of confession by the criminal as well as an accusation by the detective.[7] These are complementary social and political acts, expressed in the intolerance of the detective story for the secret life it seeks to expose. In this genre, knowledge is literally power, and to lack knowledge is to be a victim of the one who has it. But the campaign against secrecy in the detective novel is also the other side of a persistent fascination. *The Moonstone* is a classic case of this ambivalence for the one who steals the gem in the novel does not even know it himself. Ignorance of this information severely impairs Franklin Blake's life, precludes his marriage, and renders the crime—and his fiancée—incomprehensible. The discovery of this information not only requires the consultation of the entire community but also takes place in a kind of theatrical public performance in which the community is both actor and spectator. In that performance, Franklin Blake redreams his dream, and the society redreams it with him. The community repeats the crime in which

[6]Cawelti, *Adventure, Mystery, and Romance*, p. 96.

[7]See Robert Champigny on the detective as cultural storyteller in *What Will Have Happened: A Philosophical and Technical Essay on Mystery Stories* (1977), pp. 46, 103. See also Edmund Wilson, "Why Do People Read Detective Stories?" *New Yorker*, October 14, 1944, for an analysis of the dialectic between innocence and guilt in the detective story and the "cathartic effect" of the confession scene in these narratives (p. 76).

it has conspired and reinforces itself by exposing the secret self of one of its citizens. The agencies of detection, that is, perform the analogous acts of exposure and rehabilitation within the psyche of the individual subject and within the structure of the collective society as well.

The singular, independent authority of Sherlock Holmes and Chevalier Dupin might appear to be exceptions to this pattern of privileging social collaboration over individual achievement. They religiously keep their own counsel. But they may more properly be regarded as symptomatic denials of the very anxiety implicit in the genre. Their attempts to preserve their independence and isolation are strategic repressions of their own professional goal: the exposure and interpretation of the secret self. Holmes and Dupin have important differences from each other, but they are similar in that they are both reclusive iconoclasts. Both also work as part of two-man teams, however, and their work has a rather symbiotic—if ironic—relationship with that of the official police forces as well. In fact, Holmes is always careful to designate himself as a "consulting" detective whose work is dependent upon the failure of others. "I'm a consulting detective, if you can understand what that is," he tells Watson (*A Study in Scarlet* 1:24). "Here in London we have lots of government detectives and lots of private ones. When these fellows are at fault, they come to me, and I manage to put them on the right scent. They lay all the evidence before me, and I am generally able, by the help of my knowledge of the history of crime, to set them straight." As Holmes's self-description indicates, his explanations are based upon his ability to integrate the inconclusive work of others, who fail to accommodate all the findings. Holmes is a mediator between London's "public" and "private" detectives, setting them straight, bringing them together, putting them "on the right scent." He helps them penetrate what they have disguised from themselves. "The stricter the censorship," Freud had said, seeming to paraphrase this description of the detective's skills, "the more far-reaching will be the disguise and the more ingenious too may be the means employed for putting the reader on the scent of the true meaning" (*The Interpretation of Dreams*, 142).

Successful collaborating and consulting are what Holmes is uniquely capable of accomplishing in his adventures. He seems to be virtually called into existence when he is called into consultation. Outside of that activity, his private life merely occupies a dreamy, criminallike void in a lonely room on Baker Street. Dupin performs in much the same way. He relies on the inadequate reports of witnesses or newspaper accounts (in both "The Murders in the Rue Morgue" and "The Mystery of Marie Roget") to form his "synthesis" of the crime material. His analysis, though it repudiates each of their individual conclusions, is also the synthesis of all their observations. "The popular opinion," Dupin asserts in "Marie Roget," "is not to be disregarded. When arising of itself—when manifesting itself in a strictly spontaneous manner—we should look upon it as analogous with that *intui-*

tion which is the idiosyncrasy of the individual man of genius" (195). Both Holmes and Dupin, then, may be figures of individual authority, but the ingenious solutions they propose to crimes are also "analogous" to the "popular opinion," which they seem to know intuitively and which they alone are able to express.

The detective novel developed in nineteenth-century Paris and London along with professional police forces and modern criminology.[8] Many of the plots for the detective stories of Poe, Dickens, Collins, and others originated in the police reports of the London and Paris police departments. In his important essay "Dickens: The Two Scrooges," Edmund Wilson identified the detective story (as it was conceived by Dickens) as a social fable. He maintained that such stories expose society to the realization that despite its deep connections, it is made up of private individuals living in isolated ignorance of their connecting links. The detective story reveals an anxiety about the virtue of the very individualism it idealizes and a desire to curtail the privacy and independence it seeks to preserve.[9] The form found its home in these sprawling urban centers of London and Paris because, as Poe dramatized in a short story, "the man of the crowd," surrounded by millions of people, could live a life of complete anonymity and seclusion. The modern world was the world of the stranger on the train, the man with the unknown past, where anyone might live a double life, where anybody might be "Somebody Else," as Blake says of his own fiancée when he tries to explain her incomprehensible behavior.[10] And he might have said the same of himself.

Detective fiction also developed at the height of European imperialism, when Britain saw itself as the policeman of civilization bringing order to the primitive worlds of what it called "the Orient"—the code word for any culture that was unknown, mysterious, different from itself. It is no mere stroke of exotic effect that *The Moonstone* opens in India and that it opens with an account of a violent assault by the British colonial forces on an Indian town. The first crime of the novel is committed during that attack when the Moonstone is stolen by Colonel Herncastle. That crime brings its revenge on the Verinder household and on English society with the counterinvasion of the Indians who eventually reclaim the gem and murder the man who holds it. The exoticism of the colonies penetrates the ordinary world of England in another way as well: in the form of opium. The theft of the Moonstone is traced back to the influence of opium on the unsuspecting

---

[8]See Philip Collins, "The Police," in Collins, *Dickens and Crime* (1962), pp. 196–219; and Ernest Mandel, *Delightful Murder: A Social History of the Crime Story* (1984), pp. 12–14.

[9]As Mandel indicates, the majority of the middle classes and intelligentsia were hostile to the police in the beginning of the nineteenth century, regarding them largely as "a necessary evil, intent on encroaching upon individual rights and freedoms. The weaker it was, the better" (*Delightful Murder*, p. 12).

[10]Wilkie Collins, *The Moonstone*, ed. J. I. M. Stewart (Harmondsworth, Eng.: Penguin, 1966), p. 215, hereafter cited in the text.

Franklin Blake. And the solution to the crime came through the same agent. One goal of the detective novel may be to solve (possibly by repressing) the mystery of the Orient—the unknown territory outside the boundaries of civilization and the unknown territory within us all, which threatens to "subordinate your judgment and your will," as Ezra Jennings puts it in *The Moonstone* (442). The exotic drugs of exotic states of mind weave together dreams of empire with nightmares of violent crime in these texts, pointing to the danger that may lurk within the very power that seems to express the strength of European society. Sherlock Holmes is, after all, a drug addict as well as a detective.

The connection between the dangers and mysteries of the political empire and those of the empire of the mind is reinforced in this figure who is the most famous development of the detective story in nineteenth-century England. The first Holmes novella, *A Study in Scarlet*, opens with an account of Watson's recollections of the British expedition in Afghanistan where he was seriously wounded in battle. The ailing doctor's meeting and teaming up with the consulting detective Sherlock Holmes may be seen as a direct result of the wounds inflicted by colonialism and as a form of recovery from these wounds. Watson soon recognizes that Holmes's remarkable powers of interpretation are connected with the dreamy state produced by his addiction to another exotic drug: cocaine. "On these occasions I have noticed such a dreamy, vacant expression in his eyes," Watson says of Holmes, "that I might have suspected him of being addicted to the use of some narcotic, had not the temperance and cleanliness of his whole life forbidden such a notion" (20). But Watson's initial suspicions about Holmes's addiction are well founded. The first scene in the next Holmes novella, *The Sign of Four*, shows the detective injecting his customary 7 percent solution just before (and immediately after) he takes on another crime connected with the empire, this time the murders surrounding the theft of a treasure originally stolen by British colonial forces in India. Here, once more, the crime Holmes and Watson collaborate to solve is a complex blend of the essentially political and the essentially psychological. One set of hieroglyphs the detective form uncovers are those of the mixed motives behind European colonialism, expressing the danger of the culture's "dual nature" in the more manageable form of the individual criminal. Repeatedly, the empire returns to London with the curse of its own achievement—in the form of exotic drugs, deadly speckled snakes, corrupt colonialists, and the embittered victims and criminals of imperialism—to expose a kingdom at home divided against itself.

In the same cities from which European imperialists explored the mysteries of the Orient, and in other cities, Vienna most notably, the science of psychology was also being developed along new lines, exploring (by various names) the uncharted territory of the unconscious.[11] In this realm, it was

---

[11]See Ellenberger, *The Discovery of the Unconscious*.

theorized, one could be a stranger not only to others but to oneself as well. Long before Freud's work on dreams, James Sully would write in the *Fortnightly Review* that our dreams could reveal to us "the primal instinctive impulses" that reside in "the dim depths of our subconscious" and speak to us of a mysterious "side of ourselves which connects us with the great sentient world."[12] Freud cited Sully's book-length study on dreams and hallucinations favorably in *The Interpretation of Dreams* and acknowledged his debt to the English scientist. F. W. H. Myers would later discern in our dreams the suggestion that there is a "cleavage between parts of the self" and that we may live in a state of "double consciousness" or "dimorphism," in which "alternating personalities . . . present themselves at different times in different forms in the same person."[13] Concurrently, the discipline of criminal anthropology was being developed as a field of research combining techniques and theories from psychology, sociology, and criminology.[14] Central to this discipline was the claim that conscious and unconscious intentions could be differentiated and that psychological and moral responsibility needed to be separated as well. The predominance of this view of the mind as a field of contending factions in the psychological literature of the period corresponded to the predominance of plots of double identity in the detective literature that emerged at the same time.[15]

If the detective novel is a social fable, then, it is also a psychological fable, and a political fable as well. An effective reading of such novels should bring to light these three crucial aspects and should point out how they interpenetrate one another—how, that is, knowledge and power are inextricably linked in the novels, and how psychological and social self-construction are figured as continuous processes. Collins's *Moonstone*, Dickens's *Mystery of Edwin Drood*, and Robert Louis Stevenson's *Strange Case of Dr. Jekyll and Mr. Hyde* all trace those relations, each with somewhat different results. All these novels attempt to explain a crime connected with a mysterious and repressed dream, a divided personality, and a fragmented society. Meanwhile, through an often repressed and marginalized subplot dealing with a crisis in the British Empire, all these tales also inform us that the same competing efforts of division and containment are being exercised on an international scale. The repressed criminal dream of the individual dreamer appears, that is, as the reconfiguration of the repressed anxieties of a national polity. And in both realms, detective fiction engages the problems of balancing social and

---

[12]James Sully, "The Dream as Revelation," *Fortnightly Review* 59 (March 1893): 358.

[13]Myers, *Human Personality*, 1:xvi; see also chaps. 2 and 4 for documented cases of these conditions.

[14]See Nigel Walker and Sarah McCabe, *Crime and Insanity in England* (1967); Hearnshaw, *Short History of British Psychology*; and Ellenberger, *The Discovery of the Unconscious*.

[15]For more on the connection between doubles and detectives, see Day, *In the Circles of Fear and Desire*, pp. 54–55.

personal authority as profoundly as the other forms of Victorian fiction I have considered thus far.

The detective story is a literary form founded upon doubt and suspicion, conditions it seeks to control not by denying them or by establishing an absolute certainty in their place. Rather, by linking doubts together, the detective story provides a tentative but sustainable fiction of coherence to which the community can consent and with which it can cooperate in composing the shared dream that it interprets to itself. "Psychoanalysis," Freud said in *The Interpretation of Dreams*, "is justly suspicious" (517). The same should be said of the practice of "justice" in the literature of detection and of its representation of the "political" configuration of the human mind. Like Freud and like a good detective, we should read this literature and the dreams within it "attentively" but suspiciously, remembering Watson's observation that the master detective Holmes has a "dual nature"—just as the criminal does—a nature that is capable of censoring and repressing as much of the "disagreeable truth" as it reveals. In the tactics of that censorship, however, in the terms the detective novel produces to represent the Victorian subject, the unavoidable truth of this literature is contained. The mysterious, unconscious realm from which dreams spring exhibits not only a psyche's medical and economic health but its political condition as well.

The Missing Dream in *The Moonstone*

> Under the stimulating influence [of the opium], the latest and most vivid impressions left on your mind—namely, the impressions relating to the Diamond—would be likely, in your morbidly sensitive nervous condition, to become intensified in your brain, and would subordinate to themselves your judgment and your will—exactly as an ordinary dream subordinates to itself your judgment and your will.
>
> —Ezra Jennings

The mystery of *The Moonstone* begins and ends in the same dream. The secret of the diamond's disappearance is locked in the repressed dream of Franklin Blake on the night the theft takes place. During that dream, Blake actually steals the gem in a sleep-walking trance and then has it stolen from him while he is still unconscious. The object of each of the subsequent narratives that compose the story is to return to that dream, to discover it, and then to reenact it. The real goal of the novel is not the recovery of stolen property (which never happens) but the recovery of the thief's memory of his missing dream and the completion of the story of how the Moonstone disappears. When, through the collaboration of the entire community Blake manages to dream his dream again, he confronts a deeper mystery than the loss of the gem: he is not the person he thought himself to be (359). He learns that he is not only the chief detective in the case but the criminal and the victim as well. At the same time, the community realizes that Blake's dream is also their own, that they have collaborated in its formation as well as its exposure. Operating within Blake, they discover, are the forces of their own unconscious desires and the countervailing authority of a censoring and disguising agency. The exposure and articulation of these conflicting forces within every unconscious mind is the crucial psychological achievement of *The Moonstone.*

It is appropriate that the crime in this first full-length detective novel in English should take place while the thief is lost in a somnambulistic dream.[16] The crime has frequently been read as a symbolic seduction, an expression of Blake's repressed desire to enter his lover's bedroom and rob her of her most precious possession, hidden in her most private place—and then to deny responsibility for that action.[17] Albert Hutter and Charles Rycroft offer such psychoanalytic readings of the novel which interpret it as an experiment in the resolution of sexual conflict within individuals.[18] There is clearly an important erotic component to the dream: Blake is especially subject to the power of the dream-inducing opium because he is "nervous" about his lover and, the doctor theorizes, because he has recently given up the smoking of cigars. But more important to this crime than its expression of anxiety or sublimated erotic desire is the sublimation itself: the anxiety or desire repressed and censored even to the desiring subject. This crime could take place only because the thief was unconscious of having done it. The crime is then completed by another—a man who has lived a double life as a public

[16]T. S. Eliot called *The Moonstone* "the first and greatest of English detective novels" in his essay "Wilkie Collins and Dickens," *Selected Essays of T. S. Eliot* (1960), p. 413. Dorothy L. Sayers said it was "probably the very finest detective story ever written." See "The Omnibus of Crime," in *The Art of the Mystery Story: A Collection of Critical Essays,* ed. Howard Haycraft (1946), p. 89.

[17]For Freudian readings of *The Moonstone* which emphasize the erotic elements of Blake's dream, see Lewis A. Lawson, "Wilkie Collins and *The Moonstone,*" *American Imago* 20 (Spring 1963): 61–79; and Charles Rycroft, "A Detective Story: Psychoanalytic Observations," *Psychoanalytic Quarterly* 20 (1957): 229–45.

[18]Hutter, "Dreams, Transformations, and Literature," provides the most extensive application of psychoanalytic strategies of dream interpretation to *The Moonstone.* Hutter emphasizes the representation of individual conflict resolution, arguing that "the ultimate conflict" in the novel is "within the reader who must distrust the story's various narratives in order to create his own more authentic story" (p. 221). I agree with Hutter on almost every point but want to emphasize how subversive *The Moonstone* is of a rigid interpretation of individual authenticity which disregards the collaborative act in the novel. Jennings, whom Hutter calls the "ultimate detective of the novel," is a case in point. His suspicious deciphering of Candy's statements would be useless without the other narratives' discoveries; and while he is the critical detective figure in the novel, his insistent self-possession ultimately costs him his life. See also Rycroft, "A Detective Story."

benefactor and a secret womanizer. And since Godfrey Ablewhite is also a rival suitor for the affections of Blake's fiancée, he is a double for Blake as well. Just as Godfrey Ablewhite's criminal actions are unknown to the world, Franklin Blake's are unknown to himself. Blake does in his dreams what Ablewhite does in his waking life: he has a secret, hidden existence that is in conflict with his officially sanctioned public life. In his dream, Blake's unconscious erotic life is hidden even from himself. Its power depends upon its being unknown.

But if the exposure of these contending forces occupies the central place of the novel and usurps that of the missing legendary stone, it is because the stone is also a sign of repression of another kind. As a prize of imperial plunder, the gem comes to represent the psychological conflict of the characters in political terms. As much as the theft of the stone is an expression of personal sexual desire, it is also an expression of British colonial domination. The disappearance of the stone from the novel is a denial of this disagreeable political truth as well as a personal denial. The crime of *The Moonstone* links psychological and political repression in the dream of an unwitting criminal to sketch out a conception of the mind as an empire divided against itself. The criminal element here goes beyond the criminal actions of the bloodthirsty British troops who plunder the colonial village, the mysterious Indians who are originally suspected of the theft, the servant woman with the criminal past who is also suspected, and even Franklin Blake once he discovers that the gem was stolen from him, too, while he was still in his dream. The real criminal of *The Moonstone*, who victimizes them all, is the renowned and respected philanthropist, the image of English political exploitation disguised behind missionary zeal. This figure of divided intentions stalks the dreams of all the characters and provides the "social parallel" to "internal events in the mind" for the novel as clearly as the political writer did for Freud's description of the psychic agency of censorship (*Interpretation of Dreams*, 142).

Many critics have admired *The Moonstone* for its brilliantly patterned plotting, but Collins maintained in his preface to the first edition that his object was not simply to provide an elaborate plot but "to trace the influence of character on circumstances" (27).[19] The crime can be solved only if Blake can elude the censorship of his dream, and he is enabled to do so by a prototype of the psychoanalyst, who traces the influences that circumstances exert on characters. Ezra Jennings is a medical man and a "metaphysical theorist" who informs Blake that "an ordinary dream subordinates to itself your judgment and your will" (438, 442). Jennings's claim that the dream is

---

[19]See, for example, Winifred Hughes, *The Maniac in the Cellar: Sensation Novels of the 1860s* (1980), 155–62; and Ian Ousby, *Bloodhounds of Heaven: The Detective in English Fiction from Godwin to Doyle* (1976), pp. 112–28.

an independent agency with power to "subordinate" reason and will is based upon his claim for the continuity and permanence of an unconscious self that both preserves and selectively censors "every sensory impression that has been recognized by the perceptive unconscious" (440). The "unconscious" mind, in other words, is composed of more information than the selective memory of the conscious mind has retained, and in it are the "links" that connect the individual with the public world. Jennings's theory also claims that these unconscious "impressions" may be "reproduced," that they are accessible and repeatable under the proper conditions. "You shall steal the Diamond, unconsciously, for the second time," Jennings instructs Blake, "in the presence of witnesses whose testimony is beyond dispute" (439).

The doctor manages to reproduce the dream by getting information that eluded even the master detective Cuff. He is able to do so for one reason: he has access to this unconscious world of dreams, and he understands that those dreams are public property. In Jennings's realization that the key to the crime—and to Franklin Blake's secret life—is in the public repetition of a dream, he is the forerunner not only of the modern psychoanalyst but of the practice of medical science as a form of discipline and of police work as a form of therapy. These two disciplines will be explicitly joined again in the most popular incarnation of the detective form—the team of Doctor Watson and consulting detective Mr. Sherlock Holmes. But here, in the first English detective novel, detection and therapy are expressly combined to reveal that a social crime is the playing out of a psychological conflict expressed in a dream. It is a conclusion strikingly prophetic of the "repressing agency" of Freudian dream theory as Ricoeur described it: the "psychological expression of a prior social fact."[20]

But there is another reason why Jennings should prove to supply the vital information for this particular case, beyond his status as a medical doctor and a theoretician of the unconscious. Jennings also embodies the repression of the prior social fact with which the novel is most deeply concerned—the declining British Empire. The most conspicuous feature of Ezra Jennings is his secrecy about himself. "Nobody knows who he is," as Betteredge informs Blake in his explanation of Jennings's strange behavior and suspect reputation. Jennings makes it a point to guard his personal mystery vigilantly, and he insists on one condition before he commits himself to cooperating in the solution of the mystery: "I don't profess, sir, to tell my story (as the phrase is) to any man. My story will die with me" (427). Jennings does die with his story untold, insisting in his last words "that he would die as he had lived, forgotten and unknown" (515). Although his death is directly caused by an unspecified illness from which Jennings has long suffered, it is hastened by his own self-consumed and self-destructive way of life, which is a direct conse-

[20]Ricoeur, *Freud and Philosophy*, p. 178.

quence of this refusal to be known or to tell his story (as the phrase is). In fact, his illness is itself a symptom of his own character disorder, which Blake refers to as "unsought self-possession" (419). Jennings's death cannot be separated from the air of secrecy that surrounds him or from Candy's final comment about him: "The world never knew him" (516). His obsessive self-possession denies him access to the shared life of the community as much as it denies the community access to his private life. He simultaneously acts as doctor and patient in the novel, a secret and an explainer of secrets, a mystery and a solver of mysteries.

Appropriately, therefore, Jennings provides the key to solving the case even as he maintains the deadly secrets that connect him to the one responsible for the mystery itself—Colonel Herncastle. Whereas Herncastle is an agent of British colonialism, Jennings seems to have been its victim. He is an outcast, repeatedly described as a dark-skinned gypsy, and he alludes to but does not reveal some horrible and unjust accusation under which he suffers. At one moment Jennings lets down his guard and allows part of his secret past to escape when he tells Blake, "I was born, and partly brought up, in one of our colonies. My father was an Englishman; but my mother—We are straying away from our subject, Mr. Blake; and it is my fault" (420). Jennings is, it would seem, the bastard child of the British Empire. But to speak of the empire is to stray from the subject for him. That subject is the repressed crime of the novel. Herncastle and Jennings conspire in maintaining the same secret—the violence and cruelty of British imperialism which obscures its motives and hides its victims.[21] *The Moonstone* suggests the criminal intentions lurking beneath the official ideals that originally justified the British Empire, casting the sense of shame and guilt for the ethic of conquest back upon British society. The society experiences that guilt at least partly as fear: fear that the "Indian Plot" would reclaim and revenge the profits of empire. Like Blake, the Indians are also working under the influence of a dream in the novel, a dream in which Vishnu appears to three Brahmins and instructs them to maintain possession of the divine diamond at any cost until "the end of the generations of men" (34).[22] But the Indian plot is as unfathomable to everyone as Herncastle's motives. Nobody knows how the Indians know what they know. Nobody knows for sure what Herncastle intends in giving Rachel the gem of Indian legend. Nobody knows the content of Franklin Blake's dream. And nobody knows for sure who Ezra Jennings is. *The Moonstone* is an empire of secrets.

[21]For an extensive discussion of the "transvaluation of values" which enabled the British transition from the altruism of the antislavery movement to the cynicism of empire building, see Patrick Brantlinger, "Victorians and Africans: The Genealogy of the Myth of the Dark Continent," *Critical Inquiry* 12 (Autumn 1985): 166–203.

[22]For more on how the Indian Mutiny provoked a new repression to retain British influence in the East, see L. C. B. Seaman, *Victorian England: Aspects of English and Imperial History, 1837–1901* (1973).

Collins first became interested in the circumstances of the Indian colonies ten years before he published *The Moonstone*. After sharing a country excursion with his friend Charles Dickens in 1857, the two returned to London together to learn of the Indian Mutiny. Like many Londoners, Dickens was outraged by the incident and urged Collins to write a piece on the event for *Household Words*. Collins obliged. But he disappointed Dickens, for his article, titled "A Sermon for Sepoys," simply urged a less bloodthirsty policy on all sides, instead of condemning the Indians outright as Dickens had desired. The event nevertheless captured Collins's imagination and provoked him to do extensive research on the Indian colonies and to use them as the background and pretext for the domestic crime in his great detective novel some ten years later.[23]

The mutiny had profound meaning for Collins's readers and provided a controversial setting for the novel. A flood of material was published on the event in the years that followed—from eyewitness accounts to historical epics, novels, poems, plays, even sermons. "Of all the great events of this century, as they are reflected in fiction," Hilda Gregg claimed in an 1897 article in *Blackwood's Magazine*, "the Indian Mutiny has taken the firmest hold on the popular imagination."[24] The event had outraged and fascinated most English people, as it had Dickens, primarily because the official policy of the British Empire had been so squarely based upon the "burden" of improving the colonies that the idea of a revolt by the beneficiaries of the policy seemed absurd. But the uprising, which amounted to a protest by disaffected soldiers and civilians in India against the increasingly oppressive imposition of alien English culture, challenged the official rationale of the empire. As James Morris indicates, the mutiny was one of the decisive events of British imperial history because it so dramatically exposed the contradictions in British policy. The unrest had been developing for some time, according to Morris, "as British intentions in India became more radical, more earnest, and more ideological," and the violent military reaction seemed to reveal the hypocrisy of the "civilizing" and "modernizing" ideology behind British foreign policy: "Whole villages were burnt and all their inhabitants hanged. Passers-by who ventured to turn their backs upon a punitive column were often shot for insolence. Looting was indiscriminate and unchecked—'the men are wild with fury and lust of gold,' reported an eyewitness at Lucknow,'—literally drunk with plunder . . . faces black with powder; cross-belts specked with blood; coats stuffed out with all sorts of valuables.'" This description correlates perfectly with the vivid "eyewitness" account Collins gives in the beginning of *The Moonstone* of the murderous,

[23]Nuel Pharr Davis, *The Life of Wilkie Collins* (1956), pp. 207–8.
[24]Hilda Gregg, "The Indian Mutiny in Fiction," *Blackwood's Magazine* 161(February 1897): 218–31. See also Patrick Brantlinger's extensive and useful treatment of this literature in *Rule of Darkness: British Literature and Imperialism, 1830–1914* (1988).

plundering attack by the British troops during which Herncastle steals the diamond. The effects of these events, Morris claims, "found their echoes all over the British Empire, permanently affecting its attitudes, and leaving scars and superstitions that were never quite healed or exorcised."[25] As *The Moon-stone* demonstrates, those scars and superstitions were registered back home as well, in the dreams and the wakings of families like the Blakes and the Verinders.

The mystery and superstitions surrounding Jennings as the son of the empire make him resemble the other casuality of the novel—the secretive Godfrey Ablewhite upon whom the colonies take their vengeance directly. On the surface of things, Ablewhite's life is dedicated to a domestic version of the official imperial policies of benevolence, philanthropy, and respectability. But beneath that public persona, Ablewhite is a cheat, a thief, and a philanderer. Jennings, the figure most crucial to the solution, and Ablewhite, the figure who commits the crime, both die in this novel with their stories left untold. They collaborate in the conspiracy of secrecy. But as Ablewhite's secret makes him the ultimate criminal in the story, Jennings's makes him the ultimate victim. He is falsely accused and can never manage to acquit himself because the accusation itself cannot be spoken about. "The cloud of a horrible accusation has rested on me for years," he tells Blake, apparently alluding to some forbidden romantic attachment (428). The exact nature of the "horrible accusation" itself is never specified: it is censored by Jennings and left unspoken by his accusers. It remains a "cloud" of suspicion which obscures the truth about his sexual life and perhaps the larger moral scandal of British foreign policy as well. In addition to this association with the conscious criminal Ablewhite, then, Jennings is also associated with the unconscious criminal Blake: both suffer under an accusation, both are unable to acknowledge the exact nature of that accusation, and both can only assert their innocence. The two stand accused of an unspoken crime in which political intrigue and romantic desire are intermingled within their subconscious lives. But unlike Blake, Jennings cannot finally disprove the accusation leveled against him because he never reveals what it is. In his silence, he also stands doubly accused.

If national and individual failure to know and tell the true story of oneself lead to the crime in *The Moonstone*, the solution appropriately comes in the form of a series of testimonies—each of which has the same "unquestion-able value" that Blake accords to the narrative of the voluble Miss Clack's. It is "an instrument for the exhibition of . . . character" (236). But if these characters are not known or "exhibited" to one another here, a deeper problem is that they are not known or "exhibited" to themselves either. "Do what I might," Blake confesses to Jennings when he recounts his bewildering

[25]James Morris, *Heaven's Command: An Imperial Progress* (1973), pp. 222, 245, 246.

experience, "I did it without my own knowledge" (431). The theft of the gem is only incidental to the essential mystery in this novel—what Jennings calls the undiscovered "motive under the surface" of our own actions, un-discovered even to ourselves (450). "When the pursuit of our own interests causes us to become objects of inquiry to ourselves," Blake says to Rachel at the height of their mutual confusion over the disappearance of the diamond, "we are naturally suspicious of what we don't know" (410). Blake's remark suggests that the inquiry into the theft is really an inquiry into "ourselves," that "what we don't know" about the crime is bound up with "what we don't know" about ourselves. Blake, whose repressed dream covers the mystery of the theft, suspects that we must be most suspicious of ourselves, and the outcome of the inquiry confirms the suspicion.

The individual narratives of this novel are informed by their own set of intentions and suspicions, which compete with one another. The effect of combining them with the other narratives of suspicion, however, is to trans-form these competing claims into cooperative ones and to replace mutual suspicion with mutual trust. "In this matter of the Moonstone the plan is not to present reports," says Betteredge, "but to produce witnesses" (233). More important than the explanation itself, in other words, is the provision of a forum in which witnesses will be "produced." Persons are most important as witnesses here, participants in a social situation. Such participation is what at least in part produces them, what helps to bring them into being. Franklin Blake's suppressed dream must become a public spectacle for the crime to be solved and for the dreamer to cease being an object of suspicion to himself. Essential to the understanding of the individual in *The Moonstone* is the recognition that the self is a combination of selves, constituted by the discourse of the society.

Ezra Jennings's piecing together of Mr. Candy's delirious ramblings is crucial to unlocking the mystery of *The Moonstone* because that process forms the model of the cooperative hermeneutic drama that the novel posits as necessary to overcome the suspicion in which we must hold ourselves both individually and corporately. Candy has something important to say about the night of the crime, but because of some trauma associated with his illness, he cannot remember the events completely or give an account of them. While he is "painfully conscious of his own deficiency," he is not conscious of what he has repressed or why, and he desperately tries to "hide it from observation" (418–19). "If he could only have recovered in a com-plete state of oblivion as to the past," Jennings speculates, "he would have been a happier man. Perhaps we should all be happier . . . if we could but completely forget" (419). However ingenious our strategies of repression, however, we never *completely* forget, and the traces of Candy's memories haunt him as the traces of any trauma will. The doctor has repressed the professional "act of treachery" toward Blake with which he responded to

Blake's doubts of the power of medical science (436). Candy has slipped Blake the opium that brought on his dream to prove a point about the power of medicine.[26] But in his ensuing state of delirium, Candy has also proved a point about the power of repression and the dual agencies of desire and repression that compose the self.

Like Candy, Blake has something important to say about the night of the crime, but he cannot recall it. Also like Candy, the community cannot tell the story of itself because it is missing crucial information: no one knows who stole the diamond, why it was stolen, or how it was done. No one is even sure why the gem is in England. The mysteries of psychological, criminal, and political motives converge in the missing object of the Moonstone. Theorizing about Candy's case, Jennings questions whether "the loss of the faculty of speaking connectedly, implies of necessity the loss of the faculty of thinking connectedly" (423). Both Candy and the community of *The Moonstone* seem to have lost the faculty of thinking connectedly, of recognizing the contradictions within themselves or the reasons for the censorship operating in their own memories. They do not recognize that the authority of the other is always already present and powerful within the self. The novel demonstrates that the only remedy is to acknowledge and understand that one's own desire operates simultaneously with a "repressing agency" of social authority, to accept the mysterious possibility that every individual is the object of his or her own inquiry—is the criminal, the victim, and the police in any action. The results of Jennings's experiment demonstrate just this. Once the community is able to "speak connectedly" again, it is able to "think connectedly" as well.

Just as Candy's "broken phrases" about the events of the night in question provide Jennings with a kind of "puzzle," as he calls it, so do the narrators in this novel find themselves assembling their narratives like the pieces of a puzzle in order to understand the crime. When Jennings makes a transcript of Doctor Candy's broken phrases and puts it together with the text of his own broken phrases, he creates what he calls a complete "intelligible statement" (424). As Freud would do later in linking together the dream thoughts of Dora or the Wolf-Man, Jennings refers to his own half of the statement as "the links of my own discovering," which effectively fit into and connect with Candy's fragments because of Jennings's intimate knowledge of the doctor. "The product (as the arithmeticians would say) is an intelligible statement— first, of something actually done in the past; secondly of something which

---

[26]Significantly, Collins was working under the influence of opium himself when he wrote *The Moonstone*. "When it was finished," he claimed, "I was not only pleased and astonished at the finale, but did not recognize it as my own." It would seem that Collins experienced in the writing of his own text, the "displacement" of individual authority over the unconscious that is enacted and thematized in *The Moonstone*. See Kenneth Robinson, *Wilkie Collins: A Biography* (1952), p. 214.

Mr. Candy contemplated doing in the future, if his illness had not got in the way and stopped him" (424). Jennings's combination of his patient's text with his own constructs a "theoretical fiction" to fill the gaps in Candy's memory, and perhaps in a whole society. Through his construction, he is led to the scene of Blake's dream as the key to the crime and as a key to the deeper psychological mystery of the novel as well.

The Moonstone is aimed at this recovery and reconstruction of individual and collective memory with a cooperative "intelligible statement" that makes sense out of what "gets in the way" between the past and the future. The crime (like the dream) is a type of illness, a "self-possession" that impedes the progress of the society. In writing the text that parallels and complements Candy's, Jennings proposes a remedy that precisely anticipates the methods of psychoanalysis, and at the same time he exposes the duplicity of an imperial policy that presents itself as innocent. Freud would regard the patient's inability to give "the whole story of his life and illness" as essential to his analysis, since that inability "coincides with the history of [the patient's] illness." The gaps and missing connections in his patients' recollection of events Freud would call "anamnestic knowledge," which "disappears while they are actually telling their story."[27] His role, as analyst, is "divining" and "communicating constructions" by which he is able to put together the "fragments" of the patient's life story, a final product, which he calls a "synthesis."[28] This product strikingly resembles what Jennings (who is writing a book on the origins of delirium) produces out of his patient's "wanderings":

> I filled in each blank space on the paper, with what the words or phrases on either side of it suggested to me as the speaker's meaning; altering over and over again, until my additions followed naturally on the spoken words which came before them, and fitted naturally into the spoken words which came after them. The result was . . . a confirmation of the theory that I held. In plainer words, after putting the broken sentences together I found the superior faculty of thinking going on, more or less connectedly, in my patient's mind, while the inferior faculty of expression was in a state of almost complete incapacity and confusion." (424)

Jennings summarizes his achievement as having "penetrated through the obstacle of the disconnected expression to the thought which was underlying it connectedly all the time" (437).

This synthesized text is, in miniature, exactly what *The Moonstone* (and any detective novel) is all about: bringing together the witnesses' apparently disconnected expressions to discover the links between them. Jennings's

[27]Sigmund Freud, "Fragment of an Analysis of a Case of Hysteria," *SE* 7:16.
[28]Freud, "From the History of an Infantile Neurosis," in *SE* 17:19, 50–51, 72.

representative synthesis directly results in the repetition of Blake's dream before the "witnesses" of the community. This event succeeds in connecting Blake's unconscious intentions with his conscious ones, and in connecting the two parts of the double life of Godfrey Ablewhite at the same time. Freud, too, defined the science of dream interpretation as the production of a synthesized text. He compared the creation of that text to driving shafts into the dark underground of the unconscious, where they "make contact with the intermediate thoughts and the dream-thoughts now at one point and now at another," all in order to produce what he calls "interpretive chains" (*Interpretation of Dreams*, 532). This process brought him to the Wolf-Man's dream as the key to the puzzle of the patient's neurosis, for example, and it led to the collaborative account and interpretation of the dream which was so essential to the Wolf-Man's therapy. Jennings's statements relate to Dr. Candy's in much the same way as Freud's do to his patients'. Indeed, all the narratives of *The Moonstone* are related to Blake's dream according to this model. Together, they form the chain that interprets the mystery of which Blake and the entire community had been unconscious.

When Blake says that he "resolved—as a means of enriching the deficient resources of my own memory—to appeal to the memory of the rest of the guests," he embraces the truth that his unconscious life is not his own possession. It is a "resource," formed and shared by the "constituted historical figures" of his family and society (410). With this realization Blake takes over as the chief detective figure in the case, replacing the detective Sergeant Cuff and the police superintendent Mr. Seegrave. Although Sergeant Cuff is clearly a more competent detective than Mr. Seegrave, he fails to understand the case completely because he has not faced the psychological truth that Blake has faced: the inquiring subject is also an object of inquiry. Blake's taking responsibility for the inquiry represents the community's taking over from the outside agency of the official detective the responsibilities of detecting and knowing itself. Cuff's secret and authoritarian methods in supervising the investigation do not acknowledge that the agencies of authority are already within, that censorship and desire are involved in a dynamic struggle within the criminal and the investigator alike. This detective seeks to preserve his externality from the persons involved in the crime, and in so doing he dooms the investigation. "It's only in books that the officers of the detective force are superior to the weakness of making a mistake," Cuff confesses to Blake once the case has been broken. "How any man living was to have seen things in their true light, in such situation as mine was at the time, I don't profess to know" (491). Cuff cannot know, nor can any *one* person living know what must be known here. But in excusing his false accusations, Cuff has still not made himself an object of inquiry, nor has he focused his suspicions upon himself as Blake did. Since he has not allowed himself to be known by the community and has not accepted the repression that must be operating within his essentially plural personality, he cannot know the community—or himself either.

Despite his protestations, Cuff is the archetypal rationalist detective. He keeps his theories and methods secret, subjects everyone but himself to his scrutiny and suspicion, and frequently even rebukes Betteredge and Blake for meddling in his deep, undisclosed investigative strategies. Cuff's analysis is intelligent and thorough. But in the psychological terms of the novel, his investigation fails because of his studied remoteness from the objects of his inquiry, because his methods are *too* objective, because he is not the object of his own inquiry. D. A. Miller's brilliant essay on *The Moonstone* argues that "Cuff's failure and departure are precisely what the novelistic community *has wished for* because the detective is perceived as an alien, disruptive force in the community, just as the crime is."[29] Although certain elements of the community may have this wish, however, it is certainly not universal or uncomplicated. Cuff is reprehensible to the community—and fails to solve the crime—not so much because he is an alien force but because he does not subject himself to the same suspicion to which he subjects everyone else. Nor is he as forthcoming as he expects everyone else to be about what he knows and doesn't know. Since social knowledge is the principal resource in the novel, Cuff's refusal to be known by the community is more suspicious than his failure to know the members of it.

Unlike Cuff, Blake takes this knowledge quite seriously in his analysis of the puzzling situation in which he becomes the chief suspect of his own investigation. When Blake is bewildered by the strange behavior of Rachel, whom he had thought he knew well, he employs a method of thinking he learned on the Continent (where, coincidentally, the theory and practice of dynamic psychiatry were rapidly developing at this time): he alternates between an "Objective" and a "Subjective" view of the case. Betteredge dismisses this habit of Blake's as the inevitable confusion caused by the young man's exposure to the trivial and undesirable influence of French and German intellectualism. But Blake pursues the point and assures the skeptical Betteredge that "Rachel's conduct is perfectly intelligible if you will only do her the common justice to take the Objective view first, and the Subjective view next, and the Objective-Subjective view to wind up with" (215).

This comic treatment of Blake's European affectation is in fact deeply

---

[29]D. A. Miller also claims the community is "innocent" of being the "subject of detection" because "*The Moonstone* promotes a single perception of power." "Its paradoxical efficiency lies in the fact that an apparent lack of center at the level of *agency* secures a total mastery at the level of *effect*" (p. 170). Miller therefore dismisses the formal structure and apparent polyphony of the novel (figured in the collaborative narration) as a "ruse" for a strictly monological text (p. 167); he thus places himself in the position of associating the community with the secrets and deceptions of crime, rather than the "principle of detection" which he claims, "works through" and "transcends" the community's intentions (p. 160). D. A. Miller, "From *Roman Policier* to *Roman Police*: Wilkie Collins's *The Moonstone*," *Novel* 13 (Winter 1980): 153–70.

significant for the linked psychological and political claims of *The Moonstone*. According to Blake's theory, the objective consideration of the facts of the case must be combined with a subjective consideration of them: events must be viewed dialectically "from within outwards" as well as from Cuff's viewpoint of "outside-in" to decipher their true motivations. Rachel's situation must be seen from within Rachel's point of view as well as from outside if it is to be properly and "justly" understood. Then it must be seen from both perspectives at once. This erosion of the boundaries between inside and outside, between self and other, leads directly to the psychological hypothesis that Blake forms to explain Rachel's behavior: she is "not herself" when she behaves uncharacteristically. She is temporarily someone else. She has internalized another set of motives: "Rachel, properly speaking, is not Rachel, but Somebody Else" (215). What sounds like double-talk to Betteredge is, of course, a precise description of the criminal Godfrey Ablewhite, but it is also descriptive of Blake himself when he steals the gem in his dream without knowing it. He is, for the time being, somebody else; he is behaving under the intentions and judgments of a set of drives other than his own more familiar conscious ones. Like every unconscious mind, Blake's and Rachel's register the desires and the prohibitions of an entire society.

Blake's theory explains why Godfrey Ablewhite's is not the only double life in *The Moonstone*. The "innocent" thief, Franklin Blake, is himself deeply divided and profoundly unknown. The most forthcoming of all the characters and narrators, he is also a mystery to those who are presumed to know him best. According to Betteredge, Blake had become a stranger to him, no longer exhibiting any of his old familiar qualities since returning from the Continent, where, Betteredge "suspects," he has succumbed to foreign influences and engaged in an undisclosed "imprudence" (91). "He baffled me altogether," the steward says of this old friend. "He had come back with so many different sides to his character, all more or less jarring with each other, that he seemed to pass his life in a state of perpetual contradiction with himself" (60, 76–77). But this "state of perpetual contradiction" is the model of human personality in *The Moonstone*, not the exception. Rather than distinguish Franklin Blake from everyone else, it only makes him appear very much like them. The same analysis can be extended not only to each of the other characters in the novel but to the psychology of the larger political issues as well. Together, Blake and Jennings articulate a view of the world which acknowledges the possibility of hidden motives lurking beneath the obvious ones. Betteredge entirely scorns the theory as un-English. And indeed it is. When he delivers the gem to the Verinder household, Blake implicitly links his ignorance of Herncastle's motives in giving them the stone to a suspicion about the larger motivations behind the empire. He confesses that he does not know whether he is unwittingly "serving his [Colonel Herncastle's] vengeance blindfold" or "vindicating him in the character of a penitent and Christian man" (75). The British Empire may be vengeful or it may be vindicated. It may be violent or penitent. It may always be something other than it appears to be.

Blake has, in his confusion, stumbled upon what has become a psychological commonplace but was just being theorized in nineteenth-century criminology and psychiatry: we are all "somebody else" at different moments. As our dreams reveal to us, there are disguised strangers asleep within us whom we do not ourselves know. Just before his dream is staged, Blake is appropriately "pursued" by other dreams in which, as he says, "Objective-Subjective and Subjective-Objective" were "inextricably tangled together in my mind" (408). The subjective-objective alternation as described by Blake sets up the displacement of the individual as an independent authority capable of solving the mystery, and the strategy serves as a kind of program for both the composition and the reading of the novel, as well as an insight into the contending agencies at work in our dreams. "Dreams constitute a second and revived life," James Sully would say in 1893, "which interrupts our normal waking life." As early as 1876, however, he connected the "loss of volitional control of internal thought" with the apparent randomness of mental activity during dreams.[30] Claims such as these were deeply disturbing to the essentialist conception of the human subject as, at least ideally, a stable, unified, and rationally controlled "character." Along with novels like *The Moonstone*, propositions of this kind provoked the kind of radical redefinition of personality which would find its fullest statement in psychoanalytic theory.

The development of a theory of the mind as fundamentally divided against itself can be traced directly to the earlier influence of nineteenth-century psychiatry on the study of criminology. Foucault contends that the sudden extension of the profession of psychiatry into criminal legal defenses in the latter part of the century was produced in large part by the need to find a psychologically intelligible link between the criminal act and its author in cases where there seemed to be no motive for the crime. This necessity corresponded to the growing emphasis on gaining knowledge about the person who committed the crime, rather than about the crime itself—on achieving an understanding, possibly even a rehabilitation, of the criminal. But what began as an attempt to explain the extraordinary case of the unintelligible crime committed by the temporarily insane criminal increasingly became part of a general view of the nature of the human mind, a development that Foucault attributes directly to the rise of detective fiction:

> Corresponding to this, throughout the whole second half of the century there developed a "literature of criminality," and I use the word in its largest sense,

---

[30]Sully, "The Dream as Revelation," p. 361; Sully, "The Laws of Dream Fancy," *Cornhill* 34 (1876): 544–45.

including miscellaneous news items (and, even more, popular newspapers) as well as detective novels and all the romanticized writings which developed around crime—the transformation of the criminal into a hero, perhaps, but, equally, the affirmation that ever-present criminality is a constant menace to the social body as a whole. The collective fear of crime, the obsession with this danger which seems to be an inseparable part of society itself, are thus perpetually inscribed in each individual consciousness.[31]

The extensive use of dream experience in detective literature in general and in *The Moonstone* in particular is consistent with the anxiety Foucault notes about the hidden criminality inscribed within every individual consciousness. Freud's theory of the origin and meaning of dreams is a further development of this interest in finding an intelligible link between the unintelligible criminal act and its author. Freud seeks to discover connections between the indecipherable dream material and the waking thoughts of the dreamer, connections necessarily hidden from and by the dreamer. Ricoeur describes the basis of Freud's theory as the use of interpretation as a tactic of suspicion and as a battle against masks with which the self may have been disguised. Ricoeur explains that this disillusioning procedure "restores" a "fullness of meaning" to the subject by "shift[ing] the origin of meaning to another center which is no longer the immediate subject of reflection."[32] That other center is, in *The Moonstone*, the social body—the group of narrators whose united accounts strip away both literal and psychological masks and restore "a fullness of meaning" to the mystery they are confronted with. Suspicion of the individual becomes the ground of assurance in the community; mutual self-doubt becomes the basis of collective knowledge.

The Freudian conception of mind as "a scene of action where roles and masks enter into debate" and engage in both "ciphering and deciphering" also describes the plot of a standard detective story.[33] In "The Man with the Twisted Lip," for example, Sherlock Holmes manages to discover both the victim and the perpetrator of a kidnapping by becoming more a master of disguise than the kidnapper. After he disappears into the same opium den where the missing man was last seen, Holmes discovers that the kidnapper and the missing man are the same man, that the "victim" has been living a disguised, secret life. Holmes reveals this duplicity by washing away the man's disguise while he sleeps, and the man with the twisted lip awakens to confess his own "self-deception." This is what *The Moonstone* proposes as a

---

[31]Michel Foucault, "About the Concept of the 'Dangerous Individual' in 19th-Century Legal Psychiatry," trans. Alain Baudot and Jane Couchman, *International Journal of Law and Psychiatry* 1 (1978): 12. See also *Discipline and Punish* (1979) on the shift from interest in the criminal act to interest in knowledge of the criminal's "soul," and Havelock Ellis, *The Criminal* (1892), on the growth of criminal anthropology in the late nineteenth century.

[32]Ricoeur, *Freud and Philosophy*, p. 54.

[33]Ibid., p. 70.

solution to the problem of the unknown "second self" present in our dreams—"the dangerous individual," as Foucault calls it, inscribed in every human consciousness. Authority becomes invested in the collective capability of the community to recognize these activities and then to expose them. This resolution is, by definition, a provisional order; it exists only in the consensus of the community and in the authority they agree to confer upon the "text" they cooperatively compose. In this, the "solution" admits to its own limitation: it is only a temporary holding pattern against a general pattern of psychological and social disintegration. It will invariably require revision once another unintelligible crime is committed or another dream is dreamt.

Perhaps more important than understanding the specific meaning of the dream in *The Moonstone* is mastering its power by simply having knowledge of how it operates. The achievement of the novel is in displaying and sharing the tactics of censorship, rather than penetrating them. In *The Moonstone* the unconscious mind finds its most complete analogy in a blend of the erotic and the political in Blake's dream. The secret crimes of the personal and the political intersect and are expressed there, albeit in a deeply disguised, distorted way. Blake's unconscious theft of the diamond is poised between Herncastle's politically motivated plundering of the stone and Ablewhite's personally motivated theft of it. His unconscious shows Blake to be both a private, desiring man and an internalized, repressive empire. When Cuff presents his recapitulation of the case, he begins by relating the crucial piece of information which has not been spoken by the other narrators: "Mr. Godfrey Ablewhite's life had two sides to it" (506). This is the admission that Godfrey Ablewhite never makes himself; it is the story he dies leaving untold. But all the characters in this novel have two sides—one manifest and one hidden—which remain in conflict in their own unconscious lives. This is the story they tell themselves in narrating *The Moonstone*. When Ablewhite dies, he both literally and figuratively wears a mask. Blake earlier describes himself and Rachel as the "victims" of a "monstrous delusion which has worn the mask of truth" (394). The climax of the novel is to expose Ablewhite as the embodiment of that masked delusion of which they are all the victims and the psychological equivalents as well—both individually and collectively. That Ablewhite wears his mask to his final dreamless sleep when he is murdered by the Indians stands as a warning of the costs of such repression when it is unacknowledged. Even the disguise he chooses—that of a merchant seaman—identifies him with the political illusion in which they all participate. The disagreeable truth told by this novel is that such repression can be as costly for the perpetrators of a duplicitous national policy as it can for a duplicitous individual.

The Moonstone provides only a tentative solution to the linked nineteenth-century anxieties over a disintegrating sense of psychological coherence, a decaying social order, and a declining empire. Dickens's *Mystery of Edwin Drood* and Stevenson's *Strange Case of Dr. Jekyll and Mr. Hyde* also focus on the dream as the symptom of a disruption in the communal sense of order and the continuity of the dreamer's psyche with that disordered condition. Like *The Moonstone*, these texts also demonstrate the need to share the dream with the community. But they acknowledge and confront what is only suggested and repressed in *The Moonstone*: that a deeper skepticism underlies the detective genre and its dreams. These later works suspect the dream itself of springing from a source of power that is uncontrollable, the "syntax" of which spells out not the basis of a restoration of communal order but the most radical threat to it. The dreams of *Edwin Drood* and *Jekyll and Hyde* are dreams of perpetual repetition—dreams that never end. The dreamers in these works are not just divided into public and private selves as in *The Moonstone*. They are, rather, figures with no definable centers, whose "identity" is a mystery that eludes every solution.

The Unintelligible Dream in
The Mystery of Edwin Drood

> It is not much of a dream, considering the vast extent of the domains of dreamland, and their wonderful productions; it is only remarkable for being unusually restless, and unusually real.
> —Charles Dickens, *The Mystery of Edwin Drood*

The Mystery of Edwin Drood is best known for what it is not: complete. Dickens's untimely death provided scholars with the opportunity to speculate endlessly about how he might have ended the novel and why.[34] But despite the effort spent on completing *Drood*, the novel has, just as it stands, a strange symmetry and a certain wholeness. The book begins and ends with the repetition of different parts of the same dream, dreamed by the presumed murderer, John Jasper. That dream appears first in the opening chapter, titled "The Dawn." It recurs in what remains the final chapter, titled "The Dawn Again." Jasper claims to have dreamed it "millions and billions of times" between these two scenes in a London opium den, and in the last

[34]There have been a number of attempts to "complete" *The Mystery of Edwin Drood*, some seeking to confirm Jasper as the murderer, others seeking to exonerate him. For representative "solutions" of the mystery, see Montagu Saunders, *The Mystery in the Drood Family* (1914), and Charles Forsyte, *The Decoding of Edwin Drood* (1980). Philip Collins's chapter "The Mysteries in *Edwin Drood*" convincingly argues that Dickens left little doubt that Jasper was the murderer (pp. 290–319).

accounting of the dream he implies that it contains the secret of the mystery of Edwin Drood's murder.[35] But since Jasper's accounts of the dream are (like the novel) incomplete, we can only assume this is the case. Both times he dreams, Jasper struggles to keep the words he speaks in his opiated delirium "unintelligible" to anyone who might overhear them. "Unintelligible" is, in fact, the first word he speaks in the novel, and it is nearly the last. His last words—like his first—are spoken while he dreams. But in the final instance, Jasper ends his dream by saying, "It's over!" (271). And with that, he grows silent on the dream that haunts him and on the mystery that surrounds Edwin Drood.

The intelligibility of the crime in *Drood* apparently depends upon the intelligibility of a dream, just as it did in *The Moonstone*. Unlike *The Moonstone*, however, Jasper's success in suppressing the intelligibility of the dream has frozen the world of *Drood* into a state of incompleteness where the solution of the crime remains a mystery and the dream must therefore be compulsively dreamed "over and over again" (269). The "mystery" of *Edwin Drood* is not whether Edwin was really murdered or whether Jasper was the murderer. It is the making intelligible of this dream. The text itself, along with Dickens's notes for and direct statements about the novel, seems to make the murder question quite clear. Asked whether he had actually allowed Drood to be killed in the novel or whether the murder was only a snare like that of John Harmon in *Our Mutual Friend*, Dickens responded "I call my book the Mystery, not the History, of Edwin Drood."[36] Dickens even took pains to instruct the original illustrator of the novel to include a certain kind of double necktie in his representation of Jasper because, the artist claimed, Dickens informed him that this was to serve as Jasper's murder weapon.[37] Throughout the novel Jasper is prominently portrayed as a villain under the sway of murderous impulses. He explicitly acknowledges the violent passion that drives him and for which he would willingly sacrifice his supposed loyalty to his nephew Edwin. He not only makes self-incriminating statements to Rosa, he records them in his diary. He devotes himself to framing the clearly innocent Neville Landless for the murder and to using whatever means he can to extort Rosa's agreement to marry him. Finally, over and over again in his dreams, Jasper replays some unspoken bloody deed that he has already performed. As Rosa concludes after one of her harrowing

[35]Charles Dickens, *The Mystery of Edwin Drood*, ed. Arthur J. Cox (Harmondsworth, Eng.: Penguin, 1974), p. 269, hereafter cited in the text. A. E. Dyson argues (perhaps for this reason) that the entire novel "feels" more like "a shifting dream" than the more characteristic Dickensian social observation or criticism (*"Edwin Drood:* A Horrible Wonder Apart," *Critical Quarterly* 11 [Summer 1969]: 141).

[36]Kate Perugini, *"Edwin Drood* and the last days of Charles Dickens," *Pall Mall Magazine* 37 (1906): 643–44, quoted in Philip Collins, *Dickens and Crime*, p. 294.

[37]Letter from Luke Fildes in the *Times*, 3 November 1905, quoted by Collins, p. 294.

interviews with this man possessed of some hypnotic power over her, Jasper is undoubtedly "a terrible man, and must be fled from" (233).

Whether or not we regard all this evidence against Jasper as intentionally misleading, the real mystery of *Edwin Drood* is not "Who did it?" but "What is the nature of the person driven to this crime?" More than discovering or proving the guilt of the murderer, the novel is interested in acquiring knowledge of the forces that twist the criminal's personality, in learning, as the narrator says, to "read" the symptoms of "the criminal intellect, which its own professed students perpetually misread" (233). The novel is ultimately concerned, as is even Jasper himself, with making intelligible the real forces expressed in his unintelligible dream. And despite the narrator's claim that the criminal intellect as exemplified in Jasper is "a horrible wonder apart," fundamentally different from "the average intellect of average men," the same impulses that govern Jasper's dreams and his irrational behavior seem to be present in many of the more innocent characters in the novel too. Like *The Moonstone*, *The Mystery of Edwin Drood* proposes a model of the human psyche that can be most clearly seen in the figure of a criminal whose unconscious remains unintelligible to his conscious mind; but it is a model to which the "average intellect of average men" conforms as well. Also like *The Moonstone*, Dickens's detective novel suppresses beneath its murder plot the case study of a psyche in conflict, which is tied in an essential way to a repressed political plot. Once again the criminal mind is a symptomatic expression of a political situation originating in the Orient. Once again the linking of the criminal, the psychological, and the political anticipates Freud's description of the "political" activities of transgression, repression, and censorship as they are manifested in dreams. The "criminal intellect" in *Edwin Drood* is portrayed as a projection of the conflicted psyche of the community, just as the psyche of each member of the community is conceived in political terms. Here, as in *The Moonstone*, the mind is represented as a battlefield where psychic agencies enter into secret conflict with each other. But in contrast to Collins, Dickens indicates that even in its finished form, the *Drood* mystery would never be "solved"; if the criminal intellect continued to be regarded as "a horrible wonder apart," the mystery would only remain a more elaborately repressed political and psychological secret.

More important to any story of detection than answering the question of who committed the crime is discovering how the detective and the community decode and assemble fragmentary clues into a complete account of a crime—how the unintelligible dream is made into an intelligible story. The importance of telling the story of the crime in *Drood* figures prominently in the account Dickens gave to John Forster of how he planned to conclude the book. He insisted that the idea behind the novel was "not a communicable idea," but went on to say that he intended to end the book with a "review of the murderer's career by himself at the close, when its temptations were to be dwelt upon as if, not he the culprit, but some other man, were the tempted."[38] Dickens's withholding of the identity of "the culprit" in these remarks may simply be attributable to his desire to preserve the suspense of the plot. But it may also indicate that the culprit's name is not the mystery; his psychological makeup is. As Dickens's remarks to Forster indicate, the culprit's "identity" is a "mystery" even to the culprit himself. When he does speak of himself, he does so as if he were "some other man," as if (in the terms of *The Moonstone*) he were Somebody Else. Dickens explained that the final chapters of *Drood* "were to be written in the condemned cell" by the murderer, "elaborately elicited from him as if told of another."[39] These last chapters were to consist of a confession, in other words, but a confession of a very strange kind. It would elaborately disguise the self behind the mask of an alternative identity apparently unrecognizable to the "confessing" culprit. Beneath the confessional act of making the self intelligible in this novel, then, is the deeper unintelligibility of a self censored from itself, speaking with a voice not its own. Rather than a release from the hidden forces of compulsive, unconscious behavior (like the collective dream account of *The Moonstone*), this confession was to be an act of repression as well as revelation, a further sign of the opposing forces locked in contention within "the criminal intellect." It was also to be a sign of the individual's inability to know and understand the operation of his or her own psychic agencies without the aid of the external agencies of detection. The psyche is a field of knowledge, that is, which is composed by its cultural situation in some fundamental way and can be fully known only in a cultural context—in this case, a prison cell.

The Mystery of Edwin Drood is the culmination of a series of "mystery novels" written late in Dickens's career in which the discovery of a secret crime is connected with the discovery of a secret identity and the exposure of some political institution. In *Bleak House*, Esther Summerson's paternity and identity became inextricably bound up not only with the secrets, lawsuits, and sexual crimes of the past but with the nightmare bureaucracy of Chancery Court and the murder mystery of the lawyer Tulkinghorn as well. Her discovery of the identity of her mother and her assertion of her own will in the novel are also accompanied by dreams, as Esther recovers from an illness that alters her appearance. Like her illness, the dreams seem both to scar her and to separate her from the "crimes" of her past—crimes which she has to confront after becoming the unwilling but indispensable assistant to the detective Mr. Bucket, who pursues her disguised mother and finds her dead body at the grave of Esther's unknown father.[40] Pip's identity in *Great Expec-*

---

[38]Forster, *Life of Dickens*, p. 808.

[39]Ibid.

[40]Dianne Sadoff sees in the double narrative of *Bleak House* a specific repression: Dickens's "double attitude toward the project upon which all his novels embark: the attempt to come to terms with the father as his own metaphorically sinful diseased origin and the desire not to know what it all means" (*Monsters of Affection*, p. 17).

tations, Arthur Clennam's in *Little Dorrit*, and John Harmon's in *Our Mutual Friend* are all interwoven with criminal plots and with the uncovering of some mysterious secret scheme or legacy to which their own personal destinies had been subordinated.

In *The Mystery of Edwin Drood*, however, the interest of the mystery turns away from questions of the legal system, paternity, or even romance toward questions about the psychology of the criminal and the psychological effects of a policy of imperial repression. The dark, divided John Jasper dominates the manifest content of the novel in a way that none of the criminal characters of the preceding novels did. Unlike its predecessors, *Drood* presents the double life of its criminal not as a dramatic revelation late in the novel but as an evident fact from the very outset. Jasper's dark complexion, his association with opium and the orient, and his mysterious past may recall the detective figure Jennings from *The Moonstone*, but he in no way resembles either of the "criminals" Ablewhite or Blake. In *Drood* the criminal's double life does not serve as a source of surprise to explain the mystery; rather, it is a source of psychological interest, which explains the mystery before the fact, but which itself remains mysterious. This fascination with the operation of Jasper's mind corresponds with a deepening public consciousness about the problem of criminal insanity during the period, a problem brought into focus by the developing science of criminal anthropology. Later in the century, Havelock Ellis's pioneer work in the field, *The Criminal*, would claim that "out of 100 insane persons brought to the bar of justice only 26 to 28 are recognised as insane."[41] By 1889 the medical inspector of prisons in England would report that of the same number, "no less than 93 sentenced prisoners were found to be insane upon reception."[42] Detective novels like *The Moonstone* and *Drood* both fueled and responded to this interest in the psychology of crime, the difficulty of defining "insanity," and the implications for establishing appropriate methods for punishment and correction.

The very beginning of *Edwin Drood* focuses upon the importance of Jasper's state of mind, establishing his dream life as the central mystery of the novel. *Drood* opens with an unidentified voice engaged in a troubled dialogue with itself, asking a series of confused questions, offering uncertain speculations in response to those questions, and thereby dramatizing what Jasper himself later calls the "self-repressed" character of his mind (231):

> An ancient English Cathedral town? How can the ancient English Ca-
> thedral town be here! The well-known massive grey square tower of its
> old Cathedral? How can that be here! There is no spike of rusty iron in
> the air, between the eye and it, from any point in the real prospect. What
> IS the spike that intervenes, and who has set it up? Maybe, it is set up by

---

[41]Ellis, *The Criminal*, p. 3.
[42]Walker and McCabe, *Crime and Insanity in England*, p. 59.

the Sultan's orders for the impaling of a horde of Turkish robbers, one
by one. . . . Still, the Cathedral tower rises in the background, where it
cannot be, and still no writhing figure is on the grim spike. (37)

The novel begins here as if it were being told in the first person. But there is
no first-person pronoun in the passage to confirm that it is. The voice
interrogating itself cannot rest in any single point in "the real prospect"; it is
like the phantom "writhing figure," impaled on the spike that is imagined but
not present, torn between a fantastic Oriental world and the more familiar
prospect of an English cathedral town. The mind these words represent
expresses itself as a divided kingdom in conflict with itself—at once English
and Oriental, Christian and pagan. The mystery of who it is that speaks these
words extends into the next paragraph, when another narrative voice identifies the previous passage as the ramblings of a "scattered consciousness" that
has "fantastically pieced itself together" (37). The passage turns out not to
represent spoken words at all, in fact, but the last dream thoughts of a man
emerging out of unconsciousness—a man who is intent on *not* saying what is
on his mind. As soon as the dreamer rises from his sleep, he approaches the
other dreamers in the opium den and listens carefuly to the "incoherent
jargon" of their dreamy mutterings, "reassured" when there is "no sense or
sequence" to their words. "Wherefore 'unintelligible' is again the comment
of the watcher, made with some reassured nodding of his head, and a gloomy
smile" (39).

This scattered consciousness is later identified as belonging to the choirmaster John Jasper, and its "piecing together" is precisely what he apparently
wants to avoid here. His goal in this scene and throughout the novel is to
preserve the fragmentation of his consciousness, the split between how he is
perceived and how he perceives himself. Jasper's own double life as the
Cloisterham choirmaster in public and a London opium smoker in private
enacts his struggle to prevent in his own life the "sense or sequence" that are
the characteristics of a unified personality. Jasper is, therefore, placed at the
center of this world where narrative and psychological coherence are breaking down, where neither the fragments of the murder mystery nor the scattered pieces of human consciousness can be put together again—
fantastically or in any other way. He strives to keep his waking life, like his
unconscious dream life, deeply unintelligible to the world. In contrast to *The
Moonstone*, in which Franklin Blake's dream material at least seems to be
involuntarily repressed, *Drood* represents this dream from the start as involving a conscious version of what Freud would call the "deliberate . . . dis-
simulation" of censorship (*Interpretation of Dreams*, 141). "The dreamer
fighting against his own wishes," Freud said in explaining the operation of
the censorship in dreams, "is to be compared with the summation of two
separate, though in some way intimately connected, people. . . ."[43] The

studied duplicity of Jasper's waking life and the scattered consciousness of his dreams enact this description of two persons who are at once deeply separated and intimately connected, a psyche locked in contention with itself much as Franklin Blake was in his dream and as Henry Jekyll would more dramatically be in *Jekyll and Hyde*. In his dreams, Jasper is a citizen of two very different worlds.

The mystery of Edwin Drood goes unsolved not only because Dickens did not finish the novel but also because Jasper's dream remains unintelligible—because he does not allow its content to be directly related to his waking life. Even as it stands, the novel presents a comprehensive case study of what it calls "self-repression" in the "criminal intellect." "The echoes of my own voice among the arches seem to mock me with my daily drudging round," Jasper confesses to his nephew; he then immediately follows with a contradictory resolution: "I must subdue myself to my vocation" (48–49). This pattern of first revealing his self-alienation and then engaging in self-repression is consistent for Jasper. It is perhaps most evident in the book he is writing during the course of the novel—his diary. That book dramatizes the contending voices within Jasper, one urging him to disclose himself, the other to disguise himself. Like the culprit's words that were to conclude the novel, Jasper's words in his diary show his conflicting impulses. "My Diary is, in fact a Diary of Ned's life too," he says to Crisparkle when he presents the text to him to read (132), betraying in this description the duality of his impulses—to tell his own life and to tell it as another's, to speak for himself and to disguise himself as someone else—in this case, the victim of his crime. In his diary Jasper also attempts to preempt the community's act of detection by accounting for the crime before the fact. He tries to make the case against Neville Landless so compelling that Neville's guilt would be the obvious and irrefutable conclusion to the mystery of Edwin's disappearance even before it takes place.

Jasper has chosen an appropriate instrument for this purpose. A diary is presumably a place where the writer puts away disguises and confronts his own thoughts and feelings candidly. Jasper's diary pretends, at least, to be doing just this. In giving it to Crisparkle, Jasper claims to be representing "what my state of mind honestly was" on the night that Neville and Edwin quarreled (132). In fact, he is intending to generate suspicion about Neville's violent state of mind toward Edwin. Even Crisparkle is able to penetrate Jasper's designs once the murder takes place, speculating to Grewgious that the diary was written to "expose" Neville "to the torment of a perpetually reviving suspicion" rather than to "expose" anything about Jasper himself (213). But the goal of Jasper's diary is rightly perceived here as continually "reviving suspicion" rather than actually establishing guilt or providing a

---

[43]Freud, "Wish-Fulfilment," *Introductory Lectures on Psychoanalysis, SE* 15: 218–19.

complete and compelling explanation. It is in his interests to keep the mystery (and the meaning of his dream) in a state of suspension, to keep the novel unfinished as it were. Yet, in the very tactics of repression, the repressed material manages to make itself known. The deceptive words of Jasper's diary indict him perhaps more powerfully than they do Neville. Jasper describes the keeping of his diary to Crisparkle as "an antidote to my black humors," but it functions more as a symptom of those dark psychological influences than as a cure for them because he never understands where those dark humors originate or what they signify (132).

The unconscious, irresistible impulse on the part of the criminal to indict himself by a telltale clue or by a compulsive return to the scene of the crime has become a conventional feature of the detective story and a fundamental principle of criminal anthropology and psychology as well. Novels such as *The Mystery of Edwin Drood* and *The Moonstone* perform this function for England just as Jasper's diary does for him. They return us to a scene of political criminality as well to a story of psychological distress. "The criminal's improvidence is," according to Theodor Reik, "an unconscious piece of providence which aims at self-betrayal and is dictated by dark intentions unknown to himself. His secret is stronger than his will."[44] The self-incriminating language of Jasper's diary operates as a paradigm for this kind of providential improvidence, as Jasper seems to be unconsciously aware when he declares his intention to destroy the diary. "A man leading a monotonous life, and getting his nerves, or his stomach, out of order," Jasper tells Crisparkle, to defend himself against accusations of exaggeration, "dwells upon an idea until it loses its proportions. That was my case with the idea in question. So I shall burn the evidence of my case, when the book is full, and begin the next volume with a clearer vision" (181). Clearly more is out of order here than Jasper's stomach. In his threat to burn "the evidence of my case," Jasper implicitly identifies the still-undisclosed "case" of the crime with his own case history as he has recorded it, betraying his intention to suppress them both. He is seeking in this action to render his own words as unintelligible as his dream and to guard against any admissions he might have made under the influence of ideas that he acknowledges are both out of control and out of proportion. And just as Jasper is doomed to dream his dream over and over, he resolves here to start writing his diary over again once he has destroyed the first version of it. Jasper's secret self is clearly stronger than his own will. The more he seeks to repress it, the more forcefully it evidences itself.

Jasper's accusations about Neville in his diary invariably rebound on himself with greater force. But they also reverberate into a general accusation of

---

[44]Theodor Reik, *The Compulsion to Confess* (1945), p. 49.

the British Empire. "The demoniacal passion of this Neville Landless, his strength in his fury, and his savage rage for the destruction of its object, appal me," Jasper writes in the diary (132). What is really appalling for Jasper, however, is that he is himself driven by just such a "demoniacal passion," as he admits on more than one occasion. He has already confessed to Edwin that the agony of his wretched, dull life has driven him to "carving demons . . . out of my heart" (48). "I have made my confession that my love is mad," he says later to Rosa, and then lends to his mad passion a demonic element: "In the distasteful work of the day, in the wakeful misery of the night, girded by sordid realities, or wandering through Paradises and Hells of vision in which I rushed, carrying your image in my arms, I loved you madly" (228–29). In the same diary entry that refers to Neville's violently driven nature, Jasper admits, "I have a morbid dread upon me of some horrible consequences resulting to my dear boy, that I cannot reason with or in any way contend against" (132). Here and elsewhere, Jasper's diary resembles a gothic novel, as he refers over and over to his being driven by some irrational, "demoniacal" force that blends erotic and violent impulses. "So profound is the impression" upon Jasper of impending violence toward his nephew, he admits, in an apparent prophecy of his own murderous intentions, that he has twice "gone into my dear boy's room, to assure myself of his sleeping safely, and not lying dead in his blood." Jasper has even gone so far as to warn Edwin that his life is in danger and to record that warning in his diary, following it with another allusion to his own helpless entanglement with uncontrollable dark powers. "I am unable to shake off these dark intangible presentiments of evil," he says (132). Analogously, Jasper's own calculated words seem unable entirely to shake off his own guilt upon Neville Landless: his diary accuses when it pretends to confess and confesses when it seeks to accuse. As in his confused, unintelligible dreams and as in the confession that was to end the novel, Jasper speaks of himself in his diary as if he were "some other man."

But that "other man" is not just Neville. It is all that Neville signifies. While Jasper recognizes he is being governed by his passions, he never realizes the political content and character of this domination. His most violent passions are political, even on the most literal level, since they are directed against a young man who is about to take a professional position in the empire and one who has just returned from it as a victim. Jasper's violence is consistently expressed in dreams that are connected with the empire. They are induced by opium imported from the East, and they are always engaged in with exotic characters from the Orient. As we have seen, the content of those dreams is also political, and Jasper's experience of them manifests itself as a form of foreign occupation by forces he is unable to "shake off." Eve Sedgwick has pointed out that *Drood* and some related texts deploy the thematics of empire to alter the terms of gothic discourse about sexual matters.[45] But the very features that Sedgwick connects with this new "orientalized" gothic—exploitative sexual acting-out, mechanisms of psychic dividedness, opium addiction, "Oriental" technique—also specify key features of the detective genre in the nineteenth century. The linkage of domestic crime, psychic dividedness, and the politics of empire in the early detective novel brought to light the psychological repressions involved in British imperial policy as well as the empirelike repressions that characterize the operation of the "criminal intellect" in all of us.

Jasper's crime is political for more reasons than the analogy between "the criminal intellect," torn between two worlds, and a fragmented civil state in rebellion against itself. While Jasper has repeatedly alluded to the "dark humors" that cloud his deathly boring existence, and he has admitted to Rosa that the "madness" of his passion for her might have caused him to turn against "my dear lost boy" and "swept even him from your side when you favored him," he gives no indication of anxiety over any larger political issues (229). Ernest Mandel's study of the social history of the crime story criticizes its common suppression of political content from its analysis of the motives for a crime. He considers the frequent recourse to "blind passions, crazy plots, and references to magic, if not to clinical madness," to be a way of explaining why criminals commit crimes by not explaining them. These stories generally attribute violent crime to what Mandel calls an implicit irrationality that undergirds bourgeois rationalism, rather than to real social conditions. Mandel argues that "even if individual passion were the dominant motive for crime, there would still be the question of why a given social context produces more and more madness while another does not—a question the classical detective story never raises."[46]

But the foundational British novels of detection do raise this question by linking the tactics of political and psychological repression in their plots. As was true of *The Moonstone*, the clue to the political dimensions of the *Drood* crime is encoded in the culprit's dream and in the conditions surrounding it. First, like Franklin Blake's dreams, Jasper's are induced by opium, a drug associated in the novel with the exoticism of India and of the Orient in general and with the potentially threatening effects of the colonies upon the homeland in particular. The opium den in which Jasper indulges his habit and entertains his murderous dreams is a dangerous world unto itself, peopled by "Chinamen" and East Indian "Lascars," one of whom physically threatens Jasper in the opening scene. The content of Jasper's dream also combines visions of empire with those of violent crime: fantastic Oriental scenes (involving Asian hordes, thieves, sultans, and tortured executions)

[45]See Eve Kosofsky Sedgwick, "*Edwin Drood* and the Homophobia of Empire," in *Between Men: English Literature and Male Homosocial Desire* (1985), p. 182. For more on the relation between empire and gothic, see Brantlinger's chapter "Imperial Gothic," in *Rule of Darkness*.
[46]Mandel, *Delightful Murder*, p. 43.

always follow the enactment of the unspecified "miserable thing" that Jasper rehearses and replays in his dream—presumably the murder of Edwin in the ancient cathedral town. The juxtaposition of images of the "unintelligible" crime, confused visions of an imperial kingdom, and the familiar landscape of England suggests a repressed relationship among them all. That relationship is made manifest in the victim of Jasper's unspoken crime and in the victim of his accusations about who is responsible for the crime. In Edwin and Neville, the implicit political aspects of the dream and the crime in *The Mystery of Edwin Drood* are made explicit.

The manifest explanation for Jasper's murderous thoughts toward Edwin and Neville is that these young men rival Jasper for the love of Rosa Bud. They are obstacles between him and the object of his mad passion. But there are more subtle explanations for his antagonism as well. Edwin is already engaged to Rosa because of an arrangement made in the wills of their fathers. Both have misgivings about the foreordination of their romance, however, and they eventually break it off (though Jasper is unaware of this development). But Edwin has inherited something other than a fiancée from his father. Seeming to begin his story where Pip's left off, he has also inherited a profession in the colonies. When Edwin enters the novel, he is about to depart for Egypt, where he intends to work as an engineer. "My small patrimony was left a part of the capital of the Firm I am with, by my father, a former partner," he informs Neville proudly; "and I am a charge upon the firm until I come of age" (97). Earlier, Edwin complains to his uncle that his life is not something he has chosen but something he is obliged to carry on as part of an inheritance from his father. "*You* can take it easily," he tells Jasper. "*Your* life is not laid down to scale, and lined and dotted out for you, like a surveyor's plan. *You* have no uncomfortable suspicion that you are forced upon anybody, nor has anybody an uncomfortable suspicion that she is forced upon you, or that you are forced upon her. *You* can choose for yourself" (47). Edwin's complaint refers explicitly to his engagement here, but by describing his life in the engineer's language of surveying and drawing to scale, he suggests that he may have some misgivings about the other part of his inheritance—about being forced upon the unwilling colonies as well as upon the unwilling Rosa. Edwin harbors an "uncomfortable suspicion" about more than his romantic engagement, as becomes more evident in his painful confrontation with Neville Landless, who speaks out directly against English imperialism and expresses his feelings most strongly to Edwin himself.

If Edwin, the object of Jasper's violence, is connected to the colonies by his future, Neville Landless, the object of Jasper's accusations, is connected to the colonies by his past. Neville freely admits to his tutor Crisparkle that he has a violent character, which he entirely attributes to being raised in Ceylon by a cruel and miserly stepfather. Neville's account of his "tyrannical" upbringing portrays him as both an agent and a victim of British imperialism, and his words both indict the empire and testify to the pathology of his own temperament.

> I have had, sir, from my earliest remembrance, to suppress a deadly and bitter hatred. This has made me secret and revengeful. I have always been tyrannically held down by the strong hand. This has driven me, in my weakness, to the resource of being false and mean. I have been stinted of education, liberty, money, dress, the very necessaries of life, the commonest pleasures of childhood. This has caused me to be utterly wanting in I don't know what emotions, or remembrances, or good instincts—I have not even a name for the thing, you see! (90)

This candid revelation of his own suppressed and violent nature joins Neville with the angry and passionate Jasper. But Neville's candor and directness here also distinguish him from the self-repressed machinations of Edwin's uncle. More important, however, Neville's litany of physical and emotional deprivation and exploitation culminates in his admission that he cannot finally express the precise nature of his victimization: it is "the thing" that cannot be named, the "unintelligible" anxiety of the imperial project which cannot be uttered. And he is at least in part victimized as a participant in that project, for sharing a prejudice against the "inferior race" of the Ceylonese with whom he believes he has "contracted some affinity," from whom he has received a portion of their "tigerish blood" simply by being among them (90). The vengeful, dark-complected Neville represents a danger that is about to strike British society from within, and he in turn harbors a caged beast within his own psyche. He would have killed his own stepfather if he had the chance, he tells Crisparkle, an admission that "unspeakably shocks" and frightens the mild-mannered cleric who has been engaged to tutor the wild young man. "Nothing," Crisparkle says indignantly, "could justify those horrible expressions you just used" (88). Neville's words are as objectionable to Crisparkle as his proposed bloody deeds. Such an indictment of the empire should not be spoken, the cleric implies, and it cannot be justified.

The argument between Neville and Edwin is also presumably provoked by their competing desires for Rosa, just as Jasper's resentment of Edwin's had been. But Edwin's imperial arrogance and racial prejudice are what really infuriate Neville and finally bring the two to blows. Neville reprimands Edwin for the vanity and conceit expressed in his imperial plans. "In the part of the world where I come from, you would be called to account" for such conduct, he challenges Edwin. "How should you know?" Edwin responds to his accuser. "You may know a black common fellow, or a black common boaster, when you see him (and no doubt you have a large acquaintance that way); but you are no judge of white men" (102). At this moment the fight erupts which Jasper later exploits to inflame suspicion of Neville and to provide a motive for Neville's supposed murder of Edwin. But it should be noted that the fury and competition between the two young men are specifically formulated as a racist and imperial issue. Their fight is the effect of a collision between their two worlds. As Edwin's caustic racist remarks make plain, Neville's dark, vengeful character *is* a judgment against Edwin as one of the white men who conduct the unjust operations of British imperialism. Neither recognizes, however, that the criminal intellect inhabits the empire of their own minds.

The violently juxtaposed images of England and the Orient in Jasper's recurring dreams portray this political conflict from the beginning of the novel, and they portray it as a repressed issue. The "reality" behind the dream and the reality of Edwin's murder are continually linked in the narrative. The political implications of the murder and the dream are at least tacitly supported by the critics who have proposed along with Felix Aylmer that Jasper's attack on Edwin may be connected to the Indian cult of Thuggee, whose members strangled unsuspecting victims as a form of devotion to the goddess Kali. Regarded as emblematic of the pagan barbarism of India, the cult became a principal target of British reform in the 1820s and 30s.[47] There is scant textual evidence to associate **of** Jasper with the cult, but if we regard his criminal pathology as a projection of the anxieties of English culture, his probable murder of Edwin and his resolution to destroy Neville may be viewed in a more compelling and important way as manifesting a desire to repress the impending costs of an imperial economy. The murder of Edwin and the execution of Neville would silence both the heir and the accuser of a tyrannical empire. The phantom writhing figure impaled upon the grim Oriental spike that "intervened" on the prospect of the English cathedral town in Jasper's dream may aptly stand for the missing colonialist Edwin and the mixture of pride and guilt that accompanied the late nineteenth-century expansion of the British Empire.

As we have seen, that expansion in India was a direct consequence of the increasing unrest among the Indians about the degree to which British rule was destroying their own culture. As we have also seen, Dickens viewed the most dramatic manifestation of colonial unrest—the Indian Mutiny—as an outrageous attack on the mother country. He maintained that the only appropriate response would be to kill off as many Indians as possible.[48] Since the article he commissioned Wilkie Collins to write on the question did not

---

[47]See Morris, *Heaven's Command*, pp. 71–85, for a description of the cult and the elaborate British efforts to eliminate it. For a development of the theory of Jasper's connection to the cult see Howard Duffield, "John Jasper: Strangler," *Bookman* 70 (February 1930): 581–88; and Felix Aylmer, *The Drood Case* (1964).

[48]See *The Letters of Charles Dickens*, ed. Walter Dexter (Bloomsbury: Nonesuch Press, 1938), 2: 889.

satisfy his sense of justice, Dickens proposed that the two cowrite another piece "to shadow forth the bravery of our English ladies in India."[49] In the resultant story, "The Perils of Certain English Prisoners," Dickens managed to portray the rebelling natives as plundering imperialists in reverse— "villains who have despoiled our countrymen, barbarously murdered them, and worse than murdered their wives and daughters."[50] Patrick Brantlinger has demonstrated that this kind of reinterpretation of the political uprising as a purely "criminal" act on the part of the Indians was the rule in British literary representations during the decades following the mutiny.[51] But the years between 1857 and the publication of *Drood* in 1870 may have tempered and complicated Dickens's political views. The escalated aggression of the "doctrine of lapse" instituted by Governor General Lord Dalhousie had been exposed as a brutal, expansionist policy and was abandoned by 1860. Then, the even more brutal revenge taken by the British troops in the years after the mutiny radically undercut the claim that the British purpose in India was to benefit and civilize the barbaric colonies. Despite these changes in official policy, the economic and political effects of British rule grew more and more exploitative of the Indians. It became increasingly difficult for even patriotic Englishmen like Dickens to think of their colonial project as any kind of "burden" other than a burden of guilt. That burden may have found a displaced expression in the murder of the heir to empire in *Edwin Drood*, a violently repressed wish for the end of the violence of empire.

In *Drood*, Dickens's more complicated feelings about the psychology of empire and the empire of the psyche are played out in some detail. If Jasper seeks to project the guilt for his own crimes upon someone else, the novel may at least on the manifest level seek to cast guilt for the international "crime" of empire upon the "criminal intellect" that it maintains is a unique case, a pathological and "horrible wonder apart," distinct from the intellect of "average men." But the novel also demonstrates that such a projection can only be accomplished as an elaborate act of repression. Like Jasper's efforts at covering up his own crime, the duplicitous strategies of the novel also betray themselves. The "average" men and women of Cloisterham are not completely "apart" from Jasper at all. In fact, virtually everyone in Cloisterham has something to hide or cultivates a confusion about his or her identity. Mr. Sapsea, the voluble mayor and auctioneer of the town, prides himself in being mistaken for the dean of the cathedral, and encourages the confusion by "intoning" his voice to resemble the dean's. He goes so far as to "'dress at' the Dean; has been bowed to for the Dean, in mistake; has even been spoken to in the street as My Lord, under the impression that he was the Bishop come down unexpectedly, without his chaplain" (62). Sapsea's

[49]Davis, *Collins*, p. 207.
[50]Quoted ibid.
[51]Brantlinger, *Rule of Darkness*, pp. 203–4.

duplicity is accompanied by his patriarchal and imperial airs, which he expresses not only when he converts his wife's gravestone into a monument to himself but also when he describes his business. "If I have not gone to foreign countries," he tells Jasper, "foreign countries have come to me. They have come to me in the way of business" (64). For Sapsea, foreign countries are his business, and only that; they are the things he can buy and sell at a profit with the authority and dignity of a man of the cloth. In a number of respects, the mayor of Cloisterham seems to be characterized by the same "unclean spirit of imitation" that possesses Jasper, another man to whom foreign countries have come—in the psychological form of his habitual opium dreams and in the human form of his rival Neville Landless (39).

But Cloisterham contains other, even more innocent characters engaged in "fraudulence" or self-division.[52] Miss Twinkleton, the director of the town's "Seminary for Young Ladies," separates the phases of her life as rigidly as Jasper; she exists in "two states of consciousness which never clash, but each of which pursues its separate course as though it were continuous instead of broken" (53). Miss Twinkleton is stern and reserved with her pupils but romantic and ebullient in their absence. Her "two distinct and separate phases of being" are demonstrated in her insistent censorship of the very passionate passages that most interest her when she reads novels to Rosa: "She cut the love scenes, interpolated passages in praise of female celibacy, and was guilty of other glaring pious frauds" (263).[53] This censorship may well have produced rather deleterious effects in the demure Rosa Bud, who is herself a divided personality, displaying somewhat darker inclinations. She is vacillating and indecisive about her engagement to Edwin, but she also suffers from a "fascination of repulsion" toward the conniving Jasper (234). Although she is repelled by his advances, she is also irresistibly "compelled by him" (226). It is when Jasper "wanders away into a frightful sort of dream," she says, that he "threatens most," because "he himself is in the sounds" he whispers to her (95). That Jasper's erotic power, no matter how distastefully expressed, appeals to some suppressed, uncon-

---

[52]Charles Mitchell characterizes the novel as a conflict between the "inner" and "outer man," which produces in most of the characters either a brooding introspection (Jasper) or an artificial public self (Sapsea). These distinctions break down, I think, since the agencies of the outside are so thoroughly internalized in these characters, and the "inner" drives are so palpably expressed in their public personas. See "*The Mystery of Edwin Drood*: The Interior and Exterior of Self," *ELH* 33 (June 1966): 228–46.

[53]Roy Roussel argues that Rosa's story culminates in her "escape" into literary fantasy, which "represents a search for an alternative ground for a completed story not available in the cyclic structure of nature." See "The Completed Story in *The Mystery of Edwin Drood*," *Criticism* 20 (Fall 1978): 383–402. To regard this as "escape" is to underestimate the importance of the literary for Dickens, I think, and it is Miss Twinkleton's censorship, rather than the reading itself, which is the problem. *Drood*, like other detective novels, explores the "nature" of the human mind in ways that science was not yet prepared to do, expressing a need for a science that would.

scious desire of Rosa's seems evident when the narrator says of Jasper's attempted seduction that "it had pursued her into her insensibility, and she had not a moment's unconsciousness of it" (231). The indecisive and impressionable Edwin also innocently claims an ominous psychological connection with his uncle when he says that no one was ever so "wrapped up in another" as Jasper was in him (167). Even our first vision of Crisparkle depicts internal conflict: he is shown boxing with himself before a mirror, "feinting and dodging" his own reflected image (78). We also learn that the attorney Mr. Grewgious has feinted and dodged his way around his passionate self; he has suppressed a secret, unconsummated, and unconfessed love affair with Rosa's late mother, which drives him to reproving the reflection of himself in a "misty looking-glass" as if he were someone else (146).

Even though they are expressed in these apparently benign and sometimes comic forms, the "self-repressed" features of the intellect seem anything but "a horrible wonder apart" in Cloisterham. Jasper is unquestionably more deeply at odds with himself than the others are, and he obviously possesses a more pathological and dangerous repressive agency. But everyone seems to have some share in these psychic strategies, and in one way or another they all share in this novel's "mystery": the repression of violent deeds. Such complicity is perhaps most evident in another dream, that of the town stonemason Durdles, on the night he spends with Jasper in the cathedral tombs, when, according to Dickens's notes for the chapter, "the ground" is prepared "for the manner of the murder, to come out at last" (289). Durdles's self-repression recalls the planned ending of the murderer's proposed confession in his cell, for Durdles too "speaks of himself in the third person; perhaps being a little misty as to his own identity when he narrates" (68). In order to preserve the secrecy of his mysterious deeds in the tombs that night, Jasper drugs Durdles's liquor with a heavy dose of opium, inducing a dream that is "only remarkable for being unusually restless, and unusually real":

> He dreams of lying there, asleep, and yet counting his companion's footsteps as he walks to and fro. He dreams that the footsteps die away into distance of time and of space, and that something touches him, and that something falls from his hand. Then something clinks and gropes about, and he dreams that he is alone for so long a time, that the lanes of light take new directions as the moon advances in her course. From succeeding unconsciousness he passes into a dream of slow uneasiness from cold; and painfully awakes to a perception of the lanes of light—really changed, much as he had dreamed—and Jasper walking among them, beating his hands and feet. (157)

The dream is remarkable, the narrator claims, because, as in Jasper's own dream, reality and illusion are hopelessly confused within it, because Durdles's waking life is "much as he had dreamed" it. Upon this shifting ground between consciousness and unconsciousness the mystery of *Edwin Drood* rests. Its solution might well have come through Durdles's fuller recovery and the deciphering of this dream. But the most disturbing image of the dream is that of Jasper "walking among" the other images, merging his own criminal mind with Durdles's as he does with everyone in the novel. Like the bewildering figures in any dream, no one is quite sure who anyone else is in this novel or who stalks their dreams. Everyone seems to remain at least "a little misty" as to their own desires and identities when they tell—or refuse to tell—about them. Young "Deputy" may be the most explicit manifestation of this psychological mystery. His nickname indicates that his identity is only a substitute for someone else's; he is known only by his function as a deputy. He has, in fact, been "deputized" by the stonemason to enforce Durdles's own will when he is too drunk to do it himself. Deputy personifies Durdles's repressive agency, literally driving him home by stoning him when his instincts overcome his intentions. "I never means to plead to no name," Deputy tells Datchery. And when the legal authorities try to "put me down in the book," he says that he responds by simply defying them to "find out" who he might be (276).

The mystery of *Edwin Drood* might be how to "give a name" to anyone. We are not even certain about who the detective is in this detective novel, much less who the culprit is. Mr. Dick Datchery, the mysterious figure who enters the book in its final chapters, is commonly regarded as the detective, but the range of speculation about him is appropriate to the confusion about identities in the novel. Datchery is variously said to be a disguised version of Helena or Neville Landless, Tartar, Mr. Grewgious, or even the resurrected Edwin Drood himself.[54] The most compelling case can be made for Grewgious's clerk Mr. Bazzard, whose absence from the office Grewgious notes "with great mystery" after Datchery appears in Cloisterham, stating only that his clerk has some "secret" and that he is "off duty here, altogether, just at present" (238). More important than the detective's name in this novel, however, is the fact that his identity remains as shrouded in mystery as the culprit's and that this novel ends with the detective figure performing an act that strangely echoes the act with which the culprit began it. Datchery, who has spent a good deal of time asking questions and making notations around Cloisterham, is shown in the last scene at his lodging expressing his appreciation for "the old tavern way" of keeping track of accounts: "Illegible except to the scorer" (278). The last line of fiction that Dickens ever wrote describes Datchery making just such a mark as he prepares to eat his dinner: "Before sitting down to it, he opens his corner cupboard door takes a bit of chalk from its shelf; adds one thick line to the score, extending from the top of the cupboard door to the bottom; and then falls to with an appetite" (280).

[54]See Philip Collins's summary of these possibilities and his notation of their sources in *Dickens and Crime*, p. 295.

This novel of detection, which was based on the author's incommunicable idea and which opened with the criminal's account of an unintelligible dream, ends with the detective making an illegible mark.

The secret illegibility of the detective's interpretations matches the secret unintelligibility of the criminal dreams in *Edwin Drood*; and both remain unaccounted for, locked in the mysterious incompleteness of Dickens's final novel. In the dream and the crime it leaves uninterpreted, *The Mystery of Edwin Drood* expresses a desire for an explanatory scheme that would open the illegibly marked cupboard door and decipher the "political" agencies of the unconscious—distorted, censored, and illegible as they are to the conscious mind. If Bazzard is the disguised detective in the novel, then his writing of a play to which he has given the title "The Thorn of Anxiety" is a most appropriate complement to the thorny, anxiety-plagued diary written by the chief suspect of the novel. The criminal dream from which this anxious community suffers remains uninterpreted because its citizens have not recognized the politics of their own "self-repression" and have not acknowledged that their own minds resemble "criminal intellects," as deeply divided against themselves as aspects of the British Empire were. They have repressed their own repression, and this novel is both a distorted personal diary and a displaced public performance of the same divisions and anxieties. It is also a fitting final work for the novelist whose dreams prevented him from writing his own autobiography and whose last years were preoccupied with his obsessive public performances of the murder scene from *Oliver Twist*. In those performances, and in his last work, Dickens may well have been indirectly telling of his own anxieties and of his own criminal intellect, even if he presented them "as if told of another."

The dreams in *The Moonstone* and *Edwin Drood* point out the existence of forces within the self that are produced by the dreamer and yet are entirely outside the authority of his or her conscious will. Those forces can erupt without warning. As Jennings told Blake, an ordinary dream can "subordinate to itself your judgment and your will." In *Drood* John Jasper makes an analogous statement to Rosa. Because of our passions, he says, we "sometimes act in opposition to our wishes" (227). Psychological claims of this kind not only shaped the plots of detective fiction in the late nineteenth century but contributed to an overwhelming interest in the nature of the "criminal intellect" in criminal law and criminal anthropology as well.[55] In addition, they contributed to the development of a model of the psyche with, as Freud put it, a "complete analogy in political life" (*Interpretation of Dreams*, 144). For Collins, for Dickens, and for Doyle, that analogy was expressed in a growing anxiety over the costs of empire and the potentially destructive

[55]For more on the relationship between psychological theory and the development of criminal law at the end of the nineteenth century, see Foucault, *Discipline and Punish*, esp.19–22. See also Ellis, *The Criminal*. Of particular interest is Ellis's "Criminal Literature and Art" (pp. 176–92).

power of the repressed colonies in the East. Whereas the autobiographical novels I have considered represent dreams as opportunities for achieving unity and independent authority for the self, these detective novels present another, more disagreeable truth: dreams evidence a fundamental division within the self and an internalization of the "prior social fact" of an outside, public authority.

Carl Schorske, Terry Eagleton, and other commentators have shown how psychoanalysis suppresses history by reducing political realities to biographical details.[56] This suppression is consistent with a seemingly irresolvable nineteenth-century ambivalence about authority as it was expressed in the internalization and abstraction of social content chronicled in both *The Moonstone* and *Edwin Drood*. But psychoanalysis can also be deployed to reveal a dialectical relationship between the personal and the political, in which each sphere projects its influence back upon the other. Such a use of psychoanalysis is appropriate for a responsible reading of the repressed materials encoded in the dreams of these detective novels. Here the unconscious is an exotic place, an unassimilated foreign territory within the boundaries of the mind, censored and defended against by what Freud would later call "the repressive agency." The psychological manifestation of this political fact is not only the situation with which the psychoanalytic theory of repression begins; it is where Stevenson's quintessential fictional account of the idea, *The Strange Case of Dr. Jekyll and Mr. Hyde*, begins as well. But Stevenson's tale is more than a detective story about Victorian repression. It is technically not a story at all, in fact. As its title indicates, it is the history of a "strange case." In it the main character defines himself not as an individual but as an "empire," a "polity" of independent forces "that contended in the field of my consciousness" (82). But the book is also an elaborate transcription of a nightmare that terrified its author. In both the fictional case history and autobiographical dream account, however, the political plot is completely absorbed by the politics of psychological processes, and the British Empire is reconfigured as a besieged internal empire of desire and repression.

The Solution of Dreams in
The Strange Case of Dr. Jekyll and Mr. Hyde

I received Lanyon's condemnation partly in a dream; it was partly in a dream that I came home to my own house and got into bed. I slept after the prostration of the day, with a stringent and profound slumber which not even the nightmares that wrung me could avail to break. I awoke in

[56] See Schorske, *Fin de Siècle Vienna*; Terry Eagleton, *Literary Theory: An Introduction* (1984).

the morning shaken, weakened, but refreshed. I still hated and feared
the thought of the brute that slept within me.

—Dr. Jekyll

The Strange Case of Dr. Jekyll and Mr. Hyde ends as a detective story
customarily begins: with the discovery of a mysterious corpse, the unexplained disappearance of a character, and the appearance of an enigmatic
text. In this case, the one who has disappeared is also the author of the text,
Dr. Henry Jekyll. Left in his place are the disfigured body of the criminal
Mr. Hyde, wearing Jekyll's garments, and Jekyll's "Full Statement of the
Case." That document, along with the letter written by the dead Dr. Lanyon
is to be one of the "two narratives in which the mystery was now to be
explained."[57] But these two narratives confound rather than explain the
mystery, and Dr. Jekyll's statement, though "full," is by no means complete.
Instead of explaining Jekyll's disappearance, the statement confesses his
inability to do so. "Here, then, as I lay down the pen, and proceed to seal up
my confession," read the final words, "I bring the life of that unhappy Henry
Jekyll to an end" (97). In Jekyll's statement, we learn only that the "end" of
his life corresponds to the end of his writing, recalling an earlier remark in
the "confession" in which Jekyll seems to excuse himself from responsibility
for the crimes of Hyde because, as he claimed, in his Hyde incarnation "I
did not even exist" (86).

Right from the outset, Jekyll's confession sounds remarkably like the one
that was supposedly to end *The Mystery of Edwin Drood*. In both cases, the
culprit speaks of himself as someone else. "I cannot say, I," Jekyll maintains
as he insists on referring to the perpetrator of the increasingly violent and
destructive acts in the third person (94). But only a few pages earlier Jekyll
has identified himself with the criminal Hyde: "Of the two natures that
contended in the field of my consciousness," he remarks, "I was radically
both" (82). This contradiction in Jekyll's own testimony demonstrates how
the formal dualism typical of the detective story—in which an incoherent,
fragmentary narrative sequence is replaced by a coherent and complete
one—becomes a formal and psychological schizophrenia in *Dr. Jekyll and
Mr. Hyde*. Here, contradictory and incomplete narrative lines exist side by
side without reaching any resolution, much as the dual personalities of Jekyll
and Hyde oscillate back and forth without ever being reconciled with one
another. "This incoherency of my life," as Jekyll calls it, which "was daily
growing more unwelcome" (85), also finally overwhelms the mystery story in
Dr. Jekyll and Mr. Hyde and converts it into a case history. Utterson observes

[57]Robert Louis Stevenson, *The Strange Case of Dr. Jekyll and Mr. Hyde* (Harmondsworth,
Eng.: Penguin, 1979), p. 73, hereafter cited in the text.

that the events he is involved in investigating constitute a "very strange" and "rather a wild tale," and he is convinced that "things cannot continue as they are" (65, 42). In the confusion into which Jekyll's wild and strange life story dissolves, things don't continue or conclude. They don't weave themselves into a story. They just stop.

More explicitly than any other story of crime and detection, perhaps, *The Strange Case of Dr. Jekyll and Mr. Hyde* takes as its subject the composition and operation of the criminal mind and the symptomatic failure of that mind to construct a coherent life story. Although the novella assumes the form of a murder mystery, its interests are much more deeply rooted in the divided personality of the criminal who eventually becomes his own victim than in the crime itself or even in its detection. Here, the "criminal intellect" is anything but a horrible wonder apart. On the contrary, the criminal is the most respected and upright of citizens. In his own closing statement of the case, Dr. Jekyll acts as both the accusing detective and the confessing criminal when he recounts his schizophrenic existence: "A moment before I had been safe of all men's respect, wealthy, beloved—the cloth laying for me in the dining-room at home; and now I was the common quarry of mankind, hunted, houseless, a known murderer, thrall to the gallows" (93). This direct placement within the same mind of the agencies of order and criminality distinguishes *Jekyll and Hyde* from the more ambiguous *Edwin Drood* and *The Moonstone*. In fact, the attempt to separate the "criminal" aspects of the mind from its "virtuous" aspects constitutes Jekyll's crime and costs him his humanity. Like its predecessors in detective fiction, *Jekyll and Hyde* locates the expression of criminality in the common experience of dreaming. But the increasingly involuntary alternation between the personality of the criminal and that of the upright citizen is represented in this "case" as a deepening confusion between waking and sleeping "states." The murderous Mr. Hyde is finally described by the philanthropic Dr. Jekyll as "the brute that slept within," a force that comes upon him at least "partly in a dream" and becomes "awakened" in his nightmares (94). "If I slept," Jekyll says, "it was always as Hyde that I awakened" (95). These remarks seem to represent each of the two contending personalities as the dream of the other. And each of the dreams is also experienced as a political force—as a set of "powers," Jekyll says, that could be "dethroned from their supremacy" by the force of the opposing power (83).

Mr. Hyde is first seen by Stevenson, he tells us, as a grotesque and mysterious figure in a dream.[58] This is also how he first appears to the detective figure Utterson—in a troubling dream about his friend and client Dr. Jekyll. From the point of this dream onward, Utterson is preoccupied by his attempts to discover the identity of the faceless figure in his dream and to

[58]See, for example, Jenni Calder's biography *Robert Louis Stevenson: A Life Study* (1980).

provide an explanation for the strange behavior of his friend—to give an account of this troubling dream. The dream is provoked by the strange provision in Jekyll's will, which bequeaths his estate to an unknown Mr. Hyde in the event of Jekyll's "disappearance or unexplained absence" (35). Hyde is also the subject of a vague account of a crime, related to Utterson at the outset of the novella by his "distant kinsman" Mr. Richard Enfield, a story that suggests another mysterious and criminal connection between Hyde and Dr. Jekyll. The dream Utterson has after hearing this story calls attention to itself because it is about dreaming. But it is also about "power." In his dream, Utterson sees Jekyll dreaming, and Mr. Hyde appears as the embodiment of that dream:

> He would see a room in a rich house, where his friend lay asleep, dreaming and smiling at his dreams; and then the door of that room would be opened, the curtains of the bed plucked apart, the sleeper recalled, and lo! there would stand by his side a figure to whom power was given, and even at that dead hour he must rise and do its bidding. The figure in these two phases haunted the lawyer all night; and if at any time he dozed over, it was but to see it glide more stealthily through sleeping houses . . . through wider labyrinths of lamp-lighted city, and at every street corner crush a child and leave her screaming. And still the figure had no face by which he might know it; even in his dreams it had no face, or one that baffled him and melted before his eyes. (37–38)

The images and action of the dream are characterized by power, stealth, and self-censorship. The power is, in fact, rooted in the censoring agency of the dream: it is because Utterson could not "know" the figure by its face "that there sprang up and grew apace in the lawyer's mind a singularly strong, almost inordinate, curiousity to behold the features of the real Mr. Hyde" (38). Hyde is as much Uttersons's dream as Jekyll's here. His "power" is exercised over both of them. Utterson is "the law" to Jekyll's crime, and his response to the dream demonstrates that he is as subject to its bidding as Jekyll is. "If he be Mr. Hyde," Utterson resolves, "I shall be Mr. Seek" (38). Out of this dream the mystery of the story springs and the project of dispelling it begins.

The irresistible effect of the dream is to turn the lawyer into a detective, driven, like the criminal, by an "almost inordinate, singularly strong" compulsion. On his ensuing "nightly patrols" in pursuit of Hyde, Utterson feels as much like a criminal as a policeman, "conscious of the terror of the law and the law's officers which may at times assail the most honest men" (38, 48). Like the man he seeks, Utterson has internalized both forces, and he must therefore continually "combat the reinvasion of darkness" which seems to assault his mind (48). The further effect of his dream of Mr. Hyde is to confront Utterson as the embodiment of law with the "disagreeable truth" discovered by Jekyll as the embodiment of medicine: the psyche is best understood as a "polity" engaged in a power struggle analogous to political life. In *Jekyll and Hyde*, personal psychic health and official public policy contend for control of the dream.

The meaning of *Dr. Jekyll and Mr. Hyde* is rooted in how the meaning of this dream is understood. Stevenson reinforces the essential relationship between the tale and its dreams in his essay "A Chapter on Dreams," in which he describes his method of composition and the origin of this particular tale as well. He begins the essay by relating the story of a student he knew at Edinburgh College who had such an elaborate and powerful dream life that he began "to dream in sequence and thus to lead a double life—one of the day, one of the night—one that he had every reason to believe was the true one, another that he had no means of proving to be false."[59] The dreams consisted of two recurring scenes: first, a "surgical theatre," where the dreamer witnessed the most "monstrous malformations and the abhorred dexterity of surgeons"; and second, a long staircase, which he continually climbed and where he encountered a series of bizarre, solitary faces, "stair after stair in endless series." The student became plagued by the intensity and frequency of these dreams to the point that he could no longer distinguish between his dream and his waking experience. The merging of the two states so disrupted and disordered the student's life that he eventually was compelled to visit a doctor for treatment. The doctor prepared a potion for him, and "with a single draught he was restored to the common lot of man" (218). As was at least initially the case with Dr. Jekyll's mysterious draught, the drug taken by the student managed to release him from the power of his dreams, enabling him to keep his conscious life free of its troubling unconscious material.

Later in the essay, Stevenson explains the basis for his interest in the student's dreams. First he confesses that the dreamer referred to as a student acquaintance was really himself. Then he notes how intrigued he was that the dreams remained fragmentary; regardless of how often he dreamed them, they never reached a conclusion but repeated themselves endlessly. "My imperfect dreamer," Stevenson says, was "unable to carry the tale to a fit end" (219). These remarks take on considerable interest later in the same essay when Stevenson describes how his own tale *Dr. Jekyll and Mr. Hyde* originated in a dream. Like the student's, this dream was also divided into two distinct "scenes." The first was "the incident at the window," which in its incarnation in the story shows Jekyll "like some disconsolate prisoner" staring out the window of the chemical lab, which had been converted from a "surgical theatre" (60–64). The other scene was of Mr. Hyde, who, "pursued for some crime, took the powder and underwent the change in the presence of his pursuers" (224). These scenes, though different in certain

[59]Robert Louis Stevenson, *The Lantern Bearers and Other Essays*, ed. Jeremy Treglown (New York: Farrar, Straus, Giroux, 1988), p. 219, hereafter cited in the text.

details from those in the earlier dreams, also bear remarkable similarities to them. The surgical theater appears in both dreams as a setting for "monstrous malformations" of the self, and the pursuit of Hyde for his unnamed crimes in the later dream recalls the eerily obsessive climbing of the staircase in the younger Stevenson's dream (218). Finally, in both cases the dream and the waking life become uncontrollably intertwined, and the scene of medical therapy (the surgical theater) becomes the site of social discipline (the prison cell).

The importance of the parallels between the two sets of dreams is rooted in the reasons Stevenson gave for his interest in the student's dreams: the dreamer he spoke of as someone else was really himself, and the dreamer could not make the dream "fit" with his waking life: he could not take control over and relate the parts of the dream in any coherent way. He was unable, in Freud's terms, to recognize the dream as his own disguised wish and to complete the act of "dream synthesis" by providing the missing connections between the fragments of the dream which were erased in the course of the dream work. Stevenson's essay has sketched out a theory of the distortion of censorship, and he has also revealed his own failure to decipher it. This is the same bind in which Dr. Jekyll finds himself with his dream, Mr. Hyde. Jekyll continually refers to his Hyde "nightmares" as "the horror of my other self," and he finally dies in his frustrated effort to make a "Full Statement of the Case" of his increasingly incoherent life (94–95). The story of *Jekyll and Hyde* seems to demonstrate that Stevenson could only represent the "disagreeable truths" he discovered in the surgical theater of his own dreams by censoring and distorting them once more in the "innocent disguise" of this strange case history of a mad scientist and a curious lawyer, just as Jekyll could only speak of his own dark urges in terms of an alien personality living within him. *Dr. Jekyll and Mr. Hyde* finally acts as the "fit end" the younger Stevenson was unable to give to his dreams when he dreamed them. It is the gothic tale of a misguided scientist transformed into the detective story of an obsessed lawyer.

It may not be entirely proper to designate Jekyll's understanding of his dream a complete failure any more than it would be to so designate Stevenson's. Although Jekyll's criminal behavior in the person of Mr. Hyde represents a clear moral failure, his psychological discoveries in the person of the physician advance the nineteenth-century understanding of the complex operations of the "criminal" psyche. Jekyll's final statement acknowledges his moral guilt, but it also makes a truth claim about the political structure of the human mind—as morally scandalous and disagreeable as that truth might be. "From both sides of my intelligence, the moral and the intellectual," Jekyll says, "I thus drew steadily nearer to that truth by whose partial discovery I have been doomed to such a dreadful shipwreck: that man is not truly one, but truly two. I say two, because the state of my own knowledge does not pass beyond that point. Others will follow, others will outstrip me on the same lines; and I hazard the guess that man will be ultimately known for a mere polity of multifarious, incongruous and independent denizens" (82). Jekyll wants to make a clear distinction here between the "moral" and the "intellectual" aspects of his "discovery."[60] The very information that wrecked his own life and turned him into a criminal, he suggests, may contribute to an understanding of the self as a political entity composed of contending forces operating in apparent independence of each other. Despite the moral scandal this claim might entail, Dr. Jekyll's statement implies that this same information may help to accomplish the announced aim of his "scientific studies": "the furtherance of knowledge" and "the relief of sorrow and suffering" (81).

That the mind is best understood in *Jekyll and Hyde* as a "polity," modeled after a government whose constituents are in a state of "perennial war" is reaffirmed by Jekyll's self-descriptions throughout his confession (82). He speaks of himself as existing first "under the empire of generous or pious aspirations," an empire that is then put under siege by the "insurgent horror" of Hyde, who "usurp[ed] the offices" of his authority, sold him as a slave, and finally "deposed him out of life" (95–96). It would appear that the marginalized political plots of the other novels of detection I have considered are completely subsumed into the densely political discourse with which Jekyll describes the self. This language is also symptomatic of Jekyll's increasing withdrawal into the conflictual operations occupying his own mind, which not only blind him to any larger social or political reality but eventually deprive him of any society outside himself whatsoever. By the end, his only "links of community" are between himself and the "beloved daydream" that has become his most dreaded nightmare (95, 82). Jekyll may have achieved his first aim of a "furtherance of knowledge" about the workings of censorship in the unconscious, but he does not accompany that knowledge with any therapeutic discovery that might give "relief" from his own psychological "sorrow and suffering." In fact, since Jekyll continues to speak of Hyde as someone completely independent of himself, rather than as one aspect of his own complex personality, he fails to acknowledge the implications of his own discovery. Jekyll has discovered the forces at work within his dream, but he has failed to accept and master them. In him, the reign of one empire is simply replaced by that of another. His repression by the forces of social

60It is the moral dimension of *Jekyll and Hyde* which is (I think mistakenly) most commonly emphasized in readings of the tale. Jenni Calder's *Life* is typical in its description of the novella as an argument against hypocrisy (pp. 220–23). Hanna Wirth Nesher compares *Jekyll and Hyde* unfavorably to *The Turn of the Screw* and *Heart of Darkness* because of its relative moral simplicity. But to emphasize the moral is to divide moral aspirations from psychological realities. See Nesher, "The Stranger Case of *The Turn of the Screw* and *Heart of Darkness*," *Studies in Short Fiction* 16 (Fall 1979): 317–25.

respectability is merely usurped by the more powerful psychological repression of the brute that sleeps within him.

Stevenson's "Chapter on Dreams" makes an explicit connection between *Dr. Jekyll and Mr. Hyde* and the author's own confusion about his "identity" and personal "authority." The essay demands that the mystery of one be seen in terms of the mystery of the other. In both the essay and the novella, a "mystery" surrounds the identity of the dreamer and the means by which that identity is either disguised or confused. Stevenson's presentation of his own dreams as someone else's in the essay corresponds to the way Jekyll speaks about and deals with the crimes of his alter ego Hyde. In both cases, the unconscious is represented not as a sign of the psyche's coherence in a single personality but as a sign of an essential discontinuity and multiplicity within the self. Whereas Jane Eyre sees her dreams as representations of something fundamental and central about who she is, Stevenson's and Jekyll's dreams manifest independent, oppositional forces functioning within them. And whereas Jane's and Pip's narratives serve to unify the apparently disparate pieces of their lives under their "authority" as the composers of their own life stories, Stevenson's and Jekyll's texts testify to the presence of many voices speaking through the unconscious of their authors. "For myself—what I call I, my conscious ego," Stevenson says in "Dreams," "I am sometimes tempted to suppose he is no story-teller at all." Instead of the "teller," Stevenson suspects he may be more properly regarded as a dissembler, as the agent of "some unseen collaborator, whom I keep locked in a back garret" (224). The shift between first- and third-person pronouns in this statement echoes Jekyll's confusion, and it enacts the uncertainty of both about whether they are the subjects or the objects of their own subversive texts.

Stevenson's "Dreams" essay, like his novella, connects the author with the scientist of the mind. When Stevenson includes in the same essay an account of another dream in which he murders his own father and conspires with his stepmother to suppress the evidence of the crime and then to marry her, he connects the author with the criminal. Finally, Stevenson's description of himself as a writer echoes both Jekyll's self-characterization and his remorse over it. "I am at bottom a psychologist," he says elsewhere, "and am ashamed of it."[61] In fact, Stevenson had intently explored matters of psychological import in his extensive correspondence with one of the leading figures of the Society for Psychical Research, F. W. H. Myers, and in his membership in the London branch of that society. Fanny Stevenson even claimed that her

---

[61]Letter to H. B. Baildon, Spring 1891, quoted in Edwin M. Eigner, *Robert Louis Stevenson and Romantic Tradition* (1966), p. 37.

husband's development of the story of *Jekyll and Hyde* was directly based on his reading of a paper on "subconsciousness" in a French scientific journal.[62] Psychological theorist James Sully, Stevenson's friend and fellow club member attributed the basis of his essay "Dreams and Their Relation to Literature" to a conversation with Stevenson on the origins of *Jekyll and Hyde*.[63] Both in his story and in his "Dreams" essay, Stevenson specifically focuses on the "power" of the unconscious to dominate the conscious life, a power he relates to a repressive, censoring agency operating within the experience of dreams. The most complete analysis of this agency is in Jekyll's final statement, in which, as we have seen, he adumbrates a model of the mind as an "empire of aspirations" under siege from within. It is an apt description of the British Empire at the time Stevenson was writing *Jekyll and Hyde*, a subject about which he had strong feelings. "It is strange," Stevenson's stepson Lloyd Osbourne once remarked, "how many of Stevenson's strongest opinions failed to find any expression in his books."[64] But though Stevenson may have repressed any full statement of his political views in *Jekyll and Hyde*, those views find some distorted expression in the political language of the psychological allegory.

Stevenson's political ideas in the 1880s seem to have been as deeply characterized by double-mindedness and self-censorship as were his psychological theories. His views on the increasingly complicated political situation of the British Empire were an irreconcilable mixture of idealism and guilt. "I was not ashamed to be the countryman of Jingoes," he wrote in protest of the Transvaal War in 1881. "A man may have been a Jingo from a sense, perhaps mistaken, of the obligation, the greatness, and the danger of his native land, and not from any brutal greed of aggrandisement or cheap love of drums and regimental columns. . . . But I am beginning to grow ashamed of being the kin of those who are now fighting. . . . We are in the wrong, or all that we profess is false; blood has been shed, glory lost, and, I fear, honour also."[65] The sense of shame and lost honor which dominates Stevenson's political sentiments here repeats the shame expressed over his psychological views. And his pride follows the pattern of the very psychological aspirations—"perhaps mistaken" as they were—which led to Jekyll's acts of brutality, bloodshed, and shame. Brantlinger even calls *Jekyll and Hyde* an example of "imperial gothic" because it evidences a displaced engagement

---

[62]Eigner, *Stevenson*, p. 37. See also Myers's frequent references to his correspondence with Stevenson in *Human Personality* (1: 91, 126, 303).

[63]See Ed Block, Jr., "James Sully, Evolutionist Psychology, and Late Victorian Gothic," *Victorian Studies* 25 (Summer 1982): 443–67.

[64]Quoted in Malcolm Elwin, *The Strange Case of Robert Louis Stevenson* (1950), p. 178.

[65]John A. Steuart, *Robert Louis Stevenson: A Critical Biography* (1924), 2: 410.

with the social and political problems of a declining empire. He agrees with David Punter's assessment that Hyde's behavior may be seen as an urban version of "going native," behavior that is justified in Jekyll's mind by the same sense of moral superiority with which the British justified the brutality of empire.[66]

The correspondence between political and psychological ambivalence in the novella is reinforced in other expressions of Stevenson's political views. While he seems to voice William Gladstone's liberal line in urging retreat from a policy of aggressive empire building in his sentiments about the Transvaal War, he was in fact deeply critical of Gladstone and his policies. In the same year in which he wrote *Jekyll and Hyde*, he spoke out vehemently against the liberal prime minister. Stevenson had been commissioned to write a tribute to Wellington, but ostensibly because he was so enraged at Gladstone's abandonment of Gordon's besieged troops at Khartoum, Stevenson rejected his publisher's urging that he consult Gladstone for his personal reminiscences of Wellington. "I do not really see my way to any form of signature," Stevenson says in refusing to write a letter to propose such a consultation with Gladstone, "unless, 'your fellow criminal in the eyes of God.'"[67] Stevenson's dread of being a "collaborator" in what he perceived as "criminal" double-mindedness and his shame over the whole issue of the empire were clearly expressed in a letter he did write to his friend John Addington Symonds soon after, in which he condemned Gladstone's policies and accused himself as well: "But why should I blame Gladstone, when I too am a Bourgeois? when I have held my peace? Why did I hold my peace? Because I am a sceptic: *i.e.*, a Bourgeois. We believe in nothing, Symonds: you don't, and I don't; and these are two reasons, out of a handful of millions, why England stands before the world dripping with blood and daubed with dishonour."[68] Stevenson continued to hold his peace. He never published any of his political views despite the vehemence with which he held them. His silence may be partially attributable to his fear of hurting sales and losing royalties, but it also reflects the dilemma of a whole nation that had built its empire on the principle of being the savior of the world but found itself turning into the bully of the world instead. In political terms, Britain's Dr. Jekyll was turning into a Mr. Hyde. The empire was speaking in two voices at once.

James Morris's history of the empire characterizes the generally divided state of mind in Britain during the latter part of the century in much the

---

[66]Brantlinger, *Rule of Darkness*, 232; David Punter, *The Literature of Terror: A History of Gothic Fictions from 1765 to the Present Day* (1980), pp. 62, 241.
[67]Elwin, *The Strange Case*, p. 177.
[68]Letter to Symonds quoted ibid.

same way. As a result of the uprisings in various parts of the empire, the original impulse to liberate and illuminate the colonies was being replaced by the necessity to control and perhaps profit by them. "The British conviction of merit," Morris says of this period, "was growing into a conviction of command." In the 1830s and 1840s, Britain had seen the establishment of its empire as a generous and pious aspiration, as a moral imperative to extend and enforce the abolition of slavery in the colonies. Especially after the Indian Mutiny of 1857, however, that dream turned into an anxiety of control. It became apparent that the foreigners, and particularly the mysterious "Orientals," might not be converted to British ways; they might remain violent and uncivilized. By the 1870s and 1880s, the nation seemed to vacillate between faithfulness to its loftier ideals and admiration for its own power, between preserving its honor and retaining its influence—a kind of political schizophrenia that was personified in the policies of its two leading prime ministers, Disraeli and Gladstone: "the one man would always be identified with patriotic dash," Morris says, "the other with liberal humanity, but both were to find themselves in the end the agents of imperialism."[69]

In his dreams, and in his psychological allegory of the "profound duplicity of life," perhaps Stevenson did express the disagreeable truth of his and a whole generation's political views—divided, anxious, and self-contradictory as they were (*Jekyll and Hyde*, 81). And as the function of the empire increasingly became a policing function, the reading public at home became increasingly obsessed with the literature of crime and detection. When men like Doyle's Dr. Watson returned from Afghanistan, Collins's General Herncastle arrived from India, and Dickens's Neville Landless left Ceylon for England, the crimes of the empire came home, and the moral and political authority of the homeland were placed under attack. The detective novel that contained these figures also served an imperial function for the national psyche: it reassured the public that order could at least be preserved at home and that the wounds of the empire could be healed by native British intelligence and moral values.

Stevenson's political contradictions were perhaps most articulately expressed in the final years of his life when he retreated from the public world of Britain to the South Sea island of Samoa just two years after the publication of *Dr. Jekyll and Mr. Hyde*. There he identified himself with the interests of the natives and championed their grievances against a corrupt white rule. But he did so by becoming a great white father who was endowed with supernatural powers and worshiped as a god. He acquired such dominance over the islanders that he "wielded the authority of a patriarchal chieftain of a

[69]James Morris, *Heaven's Command*, pp. 381, 387.

Highland clan" according to Stevenson's biographer Malcolm Elwin. "His concern with their affairs awakened in him," he continues, "that instinct to legislate and govern which has rendered the British the greatest race of empire-builders since the Romans."[70] Stevenson's retreat into the idealized island dream world of Samoa and his instinctive establishment there of an "empire of pious or generous aspirations" repeats the psychological retreat of Dr. Jekyll into an ideal "empire" of his own. Stevenson's unresolvable political conflicts and Jekyll's irreconcilable psychological impulses become synonomous. Both disguise a will to power with a call for piety and end up replacing the sense of lost authority and honor with an urge for power and domination. Both seek to control "the brute that slept within."

I do not wish to press too hard for an interpretation of *Jekyll and Hyde* or of any other detective novel as a political allegory for the problems of the empire. Clearly, the appearance and immense popularity of the form in the latter part of the nineteenth century in England does correspond in compelling ways to the widespread public concern with the state of the empire and the shifting terms in which the imperial question was being contemplated and acted upon in England at the same historical moment. Moreover, the consistent references in detective stories to characters and events in the empire imply a profound connection. But I am more interested in the analogical significance of these political issues in a developing conception of the self—the ways in which psychological matters were being understood in political terms during this period. Specifically, such detective stories as the Holmes series, *The Moonstone, Edwin Drood,* and *Jekyll and Hyde* (in which divided personalities suffer from repression and censorship, dream of crime and detection, and find it difficult to recover and master these dreams on their own)—all contributed to a conception of the human psyche as a political entity. In each of these cases, the psyche is represented as composed of conflicting "agencies," as Freud would describe them, and the agents of individual pleasure and acquisition are "policed" by internalized agents of social control. Appropriately enough, Freud's explanation of the censoring agency compared it to the work of a writer who has a politically controversial message to communicate and can express that message only in disguised form. The political writer always seems to speak about something else. The detective story may be regarded as acting in this subversive way on matters of both political and psychological significance.

Jekyll and Hyde is a fully developed version of the same kind of project. Yet it defies the expectations that detective stories conventionally offer even as it raises those expectations. The psychological interests of this "strange case" finally overwhelm its detective characteristics. As I indicated earlier, *Jekyll*

[70]Elwin, *The Strange Case*, p. 238.

and Hyde begins very much in the tradition of the detective story. Along with the lawyer Utterson, we are presented with a series of enigmatic scenes, stories, and crimes. As in *Drood* and *The Moonstone*, the detective function is taken over from the police officials—in this case primarily by Utterson. The lawyer investigates the baffling mysteries involving his friend and client, offers a series of mistaken explanations, and is finally presented with the two documents that presumably will provide the necessary links between the conflicting pieces of evidence. The last event in the novella is Utterson's withdrawal into his office "to read the two narratives in which this mystery was now to be explained" after he has discovered those narratives along with the body of Hyde in the same laboratory into which Jekyll had disappeared (73). Thus far, the tale conforms to the pattern familiar to the reader of the detective story.

But the content of the narratives themselves cancels these expectations. Rather than provide an explanation, they relate a failure—or refusal—to explain the mystery or account for the dream. These narratives are accounts of the triumph of censorship over revelation. They ultimately represent a frustration of the detecting process, and they supply the evidence for psychological breakdown rather than recovery.[71] The first narrative, that of the deceased Dr. Lanyon, begins by referring to the assurance Jekyll had given him that if he obeyed the bizarre instructions contained in Jekyll's letter, the mystery would "roll away like a story that is told" (75). This is, of course, false assurance, for the story is never fully told to him. Within Lanyon's narrative is a prophetic account of his own disappointed reading of an enigmatic text—the confused notebook belonging to Dr. Jekyll, which he had instructed Lanyon to retrieve along with his powders. Lanyon recalls only two things in that book: the frequent recurrence of the word "double" and the emphatic exclamation "total failure!!!" (76). These words may have impressed him because they would eventually characterize his own double-minded and failed text. At the crucial point of his narrative, when he is about to reveal the connection between Jekyll and Hyde, Lanyon duplicates Jekyll's acts of censorship: "What he told me in the next hour I cannot bring my

[71]Irving S. Saposnick has argued that "in contrast to other multiple narratives whose several perspectives often raise questions of subjective truth and moral ambiguity, the individual narratives in *Jekyll and Hyde* provide a linear regularity of information, an incremental catalogue of attitudes toward Hyde's repulsiveness and Jekyll's decline" (p. 722). While it is true that these several narratives do not challenge one another's credibility, they do not exactly form a "linear regularity of information." Each seems, rather, to be independent, to stand on its own, and to censor itself at the critical moment. I read the first-person narratives in particular as raising a number of ambiguities about how to explain the mystery and how to bring the several "pieces" of the narrative together. See Saposnick, "The Anatomy of *Dr. Jekyll and Mr. Hyde*," *Studies in English Literature, 1500–1900* 11 (Autumn 1971): 715–31.

mind to set on paper. I saw what I saw, I heard what I heard" (80). In admitting that he cannot report what he witnessed, Lanyon acknowledges the power of his own self-repression, which not only manages to maintain the mystery but also costs him his life.

The second narrative, "Henry Jekyll's Full Statement of the Case," is just as self-censoring and just as costly. Jekyll's account of things is no more satisfactory in setting down on paper the explanation that binds the pieces of this story together than Lanyon's. By the third page of this "full" confession, Jekyll admits that it will not be full because even his own knowledge of what he has done remains "incomplete" (83). Furthermore, he says he "will not enter deeply into this scientific branch of my confession" because others might be tempted to repeat his attempts to "cast off" the "doom and burthen of our life." The result of such an effort, he claims, is that "it but returns upon us with more unfamiliar and more awful pressure" (83). These are obscure, puzzling claims for Jekyll to employ in excusing his censorship of information. Exactly what constitutes the "doom and burthen of our life" is intentionally obfuscated here. But Jekyll's words at least seem to indicate that the means by which he uncovered the censoring agency (the technique of "casting off" this burden) will remain censored in his account, for fear of what happens when that agency is evaded or repudiated. When cast off, he says, its "pressure" only returns with even more force. This admission, along with Lanyon's admitted failure to commit to paper the transformation he had witnessed, may cover another admission, which Stevenson is making in this tale—that he fears the laying down of the white man's "burden" and the transformation of British national identity entailed in it. Like Jekyll, he may prefer to repress this truth, however, and allow his dream self to become more and more "unfamiliar" until eventually he can declare with Jekyll, "I had lost my identity" (85).

So Jekyll vanishes from the text, virtually censoring his own identity from it. He is both murderer and victim in this mystery. In his place he leaves behind two objects: the text of the narrative itself, and the "body of a self-destroyer," as Jekyll calls "Hyde" (70). The two are, in important ways, the same thing—instruments of the censorship that hides the criminal within the mind of the respected citizen. Jekyll suggests this disagreeable truth in the final fear about Hyde which he expresses in his statement—that Hyde will suppress his text. It is only through "great prudence" and "great good luck," Jekyll claims, that "my narrative has hitherto escaped destruction," for "should the throes of change take me in the act of writing it, Hyde will tear it in pieces" (96–97). Jekyll's anxiety over Hyde's destruction or distortion of his written text is ironic since Hyde is from the outset the product of Jekyll's writing and since Jekyll's writing has always been severely self-censored and self-repressed anyway. Not only does Hyde begin his existence as the chemical formula Jekyll writes out in his notebook; he is sustained by the bank-notes and account books Jekyll writes for him to secure the secrecy of their connection. Hyde even has his future provided for by the will that names him heir—again, in Jekyll's own handwriting. Lanyon is first introduced to Hyde by way of a letter written (apparently) by Jekyll, and Utterson learns of Hyde's existence from the handwritten text of the controversial will. But although Hyde's existence depends on these texts, he also seems bent on altering, disfiguring, or destroying them.[72] Hyde has burned the account books in the fireplace of the rooms Jekyll rented for him, "scrawl[ed] blasphemies" on the pages of Jekyll's books, burned his letters, and destroyed his father's portrait (96). Hyde even writes in Jekyll's own hand, but he alters it once again to disguise his identity with Jekyll. As Jekyll's dream self, Hyde is both an expression of his identity, and a disguise for it—the object of Jekyll's self-censorship and its agent as well. Ultimately, Hyde is the sign of Jekyll's inability to make a coherent life story by binding the aspects of his psychological polity together. He is the text of Jekyll's own self-censorship.

As the principal detective in the story, Utterson eventually discovers an important clue: that Jekyll's writing is in the same hand as Hyde's. But Utterson comes even closer to the heart of the mystery when he observes a feature common to all the documents Jekyll writes about Hyde. In each of them, the author—Jekyll—alludes to his own "disappearance." Utterson becomes concerned that "the idea of a disappearance and the name of Henry Jekyll" are always "bracketed" together in these texts (59). Inscribed in each of Jekyll's written expressions of Hyde, in other words, is the admission that he represses a criminal within him. This admission is most clearly evidenced when Jekyll strives to counteract Hyde's "usurpation" of his authority at the end by appealing to the authority of his original text of himself—by trying to replicate the formula of powders that he had used to "blot out" Hyde. When Jekyll fails to duplicate the compound, he speculates that the original batch of chemicals must have been "impure" (96). But the point that Jekyll misses here is that he fails because all the texts he has written have been "impure"; all have exercised some censorship, some denial, some refusal to acknowledge his dream as his own and to reveal it to his community. The result is that he becomes more rather than less unfamiliar to himself and to his community. In his efforts to "blot out" Hyde, he blots out himself and his social identity. His internalized agency of disguise is so effective that even he is unable to penetrate its tactics any more.

---

[72]I argue this point more fully and connect *Jekyll and Hyde* with the shift in modern literature toward seeing the act of writing as equivalent to the "death of the author" in "In the Company of Strangers: Absent Voices in Stevenson's *Dr. Jekyll and Mr. Hyde* and Beckett's *Company*," *Modern Fiction Studies* 32 (Summer 1986): 157–73.

Jekyll and Hyde represents the fullest development of the psychological claims of the detective story. But it also establishes the limits of its therapeutic powers. As was true of the gothic and autobiographical novel, the treatment of dreams in the detective novel expresses a desire for a science of the self which can make sense of these shadowy and disagreeable truths. In developing models of the psyche that drew from the disciplines of pathology, economy, and politics, these novelistic forms of the nineteenth century helped both to develop and to challenge conventional notions of the bourgeois subject. These fictions of the unconscious helped the science of psychoanalysis to construct a model of the psyche which combined all of them, and they provided the vocabulary to suspect that model as well.

But *Jekyll and Hyde* also takes the process a step farther. In challenging the assumption of an essential, coherent, and unified subject, Stevenson's story repudiates the fundamental confidence in language that undergirds gothic, autobiographical, and detective fiction, and forms the basis of psychoanalytic interpretation as well. In so doing, *Jekyll and Hyde* anticipates the widespread resistance to the claims of psychoanalysis expressed by the high modernists and their skepticism about the coherence of the psyche and the dependability of any single interpretive strategy. We might also say that *Jekyll and Hyde* anticipates the Lacanian emphasis upon the problems of linguistics within the discipline of psychoanalysis. Other modernist fiction will also prefigure this development. When Marlow says to his audience in *Heart of Darkness*, "I am trying to tell you a dream," he tries to explain that his intention is not to interpret the dream but merely to "convey the dream sensation"—which attempt he is certain will fail, because "no relation of the dream can convey the dream sensation" or "that notion of being captured by the incredible which is of the very essence of dreams."[73] The power and truth of the dream, contained in its sensation, are fundamentally transformed by attempts to interpret or master them in language. Likewise, the mystery of the identity of Lord Jim is not to be solved through skilled detective work or psychological analysis, any more than the unspeakable truth of Kurtz is. Jim and Kurtz can be presented only as "one of us," as part of who we are, as immersed with us in "the destructive element" of the "dream" into which we are all born.[74] When Stephen Dedalus realizes that his life is "not a dream from which he would awake," he acknowledges that he too is continually immersed in a dream in which his language is not a means of mastery but was only another aspect of the dream sensation.[75]

[73]Conrad, *Heart of Darkness*, p. 39.

[74]Conrad, *Lord Jim* (Boston: Houghton Mifflin, 1958), p. 153.

[75]James Joyce, *A Portrait of the Artist as a Young Man*, ed. Chester G. Anderson (Harmondsworth, Eng.: Penguin, 1981), p. 146.

Lacan was to make an analogous claim in his reinterpretation of Freudian dream theory. Though he concedes that an unconscious discourse speaks through the conscious discourse of the dream account, he questions whether this factual description can ever be employed to provide an accurate metaphor about the nature of the unconscious itself. Indeed, in collaboration with the modern novelists I will consider in the final chapter, Lacan's return to Freud exposes the self-criticism already built into the psychoanalytic configuration of the psyche. Together, they level a critique of the radical individualism assumed by certain psychoanalytic and novelistic fictions of the unconscious, as they undermine the authority of the discourses in which those fictions were articulated.

René Magritte, *L'Art de la Conversation* (1950)

Surrealistic painting, like modernist and postmodernist fiction, both responded to and challenged the claims of psychoanalysis. Such artists as Max Ernst, Salvador Dali, and René Magritte sought to represent the world of their dreams through techniques that approached the precision and clarity of photography instead of the random, spontaneous images of earlier surrealists. They commonly mixed text with image—sometimes even applying scraps of novels directly to canvases—to obscure the boundaries between nature and culture, the conscious and the unconscious, language and reality. In *The Art of Conversation,* Magritte renders the natural landscape as language, spelling out the word "dream" (*rêve*). Like the work of Beckett and Lacan, the painting's images and title together suggest that language necessarily mediates all our experience, even the unconscious world of our dreams. (Reproduced courtesy of the New Orleans Museum of Art. Gift of William H. Alexander.)

CHAPTER FIVE

Against Interpretation: The
Dream of the Modernist Novel

The dream-thoughts to which we are led by interpretation cannot, from the nature of things, have any definite endings; they are bound to branch out in every direction into the intricate network of our world of thought.
—Sigmund Freud, *The Interpretation of Dreams*

Do you see the story? Do you see anything? It seems to me I am trying to tell you a dream—making a vain attempt because no relation of a dream can convey the dream sensation.
—Joseph Conrad, *Heart of Darkness*

I have put the language to sleep. In writing of the night, I really could not, I felt I could not, use words in their ordinary connections.
—James Joyce on *Finnegans Wake*

In the final chapter of *The Interpretation of Dreams*, Freud summarizes the claims of the book and responds to certain criticisms of his analytic method. He concedes that there are limits to the extent a dream can be interpreted, that interpretation can take us only so far in understanding what our dreams are about and how they relate to our waking life. Ultimately, Freud admits, "there is no possibility of *explaining* dreams as a psychical process, since to explain a thing means to trace it back to something already known" (511). Inasmuch as dreams emerge from what we cannot know about ourselves, we must be satisfied with setting up reasonable "hypotheses" about the structure of the mind that produces dreams, and about the forces that shape them. We can only "know" the unconscious through acts of reconstruction and analysis. But "as soon as we endeavour to penetrate more deeply into the mental process involved in dreaming," Freud warns, "every path will end in darkness" (511).

In an uncharacteristic moment, Freud concedes in his final chapter that his book must end "in suspense." Like an unresolved modernist novel, *The*

Interpretation of Dreams concludes inconclusively. Until the processes of dreaming "can be related to the findings of other enquiries which seek to approach the kernel of the same problem from another angle," Freud says, the nature of the relationship between waking life and dream life will remain a mystery (511). Here, at the conclusion of his greatest work, Freud marks the limits of his achievement after all the claims he has made for its limitlessness. He admits, in the end, to the ultimately obscure origin of dream experience, resorting to a description of the celebrated "tangle" at the center of a dream "which cannot be unravelled":

> There is often a passage in even the most thoroughly interpreted dream which has to be left obscure; this is because we become aware during the work of interpretation that at that point there is a tangle of dream-thoughts which cannot be unravelled and which moreover adds nothing to our knowledge of the content of the dream. This is the dream's navel, the spot where it reaches down into the unknown. . . . The dream-thoughts to which we are led by interpretation cannot, from the nature of things have any definite endings; they are bound to branch out in every direction into the intricate network of our world of thought. It is at some point where this meshwork is particularly close that the dream-wish grows up, like a mushroom out of its mycelium. (525)

That the source of the dream should finally be unknowable and even uninterpretable, that it should have a life of its own, mysteriously located "where it reaches down into the unknown," is an exceptional remark in a work that at least intends to be as systematic and comprehensive as this one does. Freud's gesture here may be seen as an act of resistance to his own "theoretical fictions," an acknowledgment of the figurative nature of his own explanations. He is possibly even anticipating the direction that some of his followers—most immediately Jung—would take in regarding the dream less as a sign or symptom of something else (specifically, a repressed wish) and more as a source of meaning in itself. Jung would maintain that a dream is obscure not because of the operation of such retrospective processes as distortion or censorship but because it functions symbolically and prospectively. Instead of having their meaning rooted in a thought or wish from the past which has been repressed and disguised, dreams, in Jung's view, are directed toward a future wholeness that our consciousness is not yet able to grasp. A dream is "something like a text" that we have not yet learned to read, and its significance "cannot be adequately expressed in the familiar words of our language."[1] For Jung, a dream produces the possibility of new meaning instead of concealing a prior one.

Jung both absorbed Freud's theory of dream interpretation and sought to

---

[1] Jung, "The Practical Use of Dream Analysis," *Collected Works* 16:149. The second quotation is from "Spirit and Life," *The Structure and Dynamics of the Psyche, Collected Works* 11:336.

move beyond what he regarded as his teacher's reductive tendencies. While he admired Freud for raising the status of the dream by considering it a meaningful psychic occurrence, Jung not only repudiated the principles of distortion and censorship in dream interpretation but also rejected such fundamental Freudian notions as the distinction between the manifest and the latent content of the dream. "The 'manifest' dream-picture is the dream itself," he said, "and contains the whole meaning of the dream. . . . What Freud calls the 'dream-façade' is the dream's obscurity, and this is really only a projection of our own lack of understanding." The dream, Jung would even maintain, is "its own interpretation."[2] As we shall see, Jung's critique of Freud here strangely both anticipates and sets up the critique Lacan will launch against the psychoanalytic establishment. For Lacan, while the dream resists any discourse that consciousness tries to impose on it, it cannot be regarded as its own interpretation. Rather, dreams manifest a kind of double discourse within an unconscious realm that is made up of two unconscious subjects—one, totally inaccessible to consciousness, trying to address the other.

As Freud had been a great reader of the nineteenth-century novel, Jung was a reader of the twentieth-century novel; indeed, he was commissioned to write an introduction for the German edition of *Ulysses*. In rather conspicuous ways, Jung's rejection of some of Freud's basic claims in psychoanalysis parallels the course taken by many of the most prominent modernist writers with respect to Freudianism. Although Joyce, Conrad, Lawrence, Woolf, Beckett, and others expressed profound interest in the representation of dreams and other unconscious mental processes in their work, they held psychoanalysis itself in suspicion. Like Jung, they preferred to view the dream as its own interpretation. Joyce claimed, for instance, that in his own novels he had "recorded, simultaneously, what a man says, sees, thinks, and what such seeing, thinking, saying does, to what you Freudians call the subconscious—but as for psychoanalysis," he added, "it's neither more nor less than blackmail."[3] Richard Ellmann would characterize Joyce's considerable interest in dreams as "pre-Freudian" because Joyce looked for revelation rather than scientific explanation in dreams. But we might more accurately regard Joyce's attitude as post-Freudian. Like Jung, Joyce learned from and reacted against what he perceived to be the exclusively scientific and mechanistic aspects of Freudian dream theory and sought to return some authenticity and authority to the manifest content of the dream.

Despite these parallels, however, it would be a mistake to equate Joyce or the other moderns with Jung, whom Joyce called "the Swiss Tweedledum" to

---

[2]Jung, "The Practical Use of Dream Analysis," 16:149; Jung, "Psychology and Religion," *Collected Works* 11:26.
[3]Richard Ellmann, *James Joyce* (1959), p. 538.

"the Viennese Tweedledee, Dr. Freud."[4] Coupled with the general modernist fascination with the unconscious was a general dismissal of the claims of psychoanalysis as reductive and formulaic. Virginia Woolf, for example, would concede the scientific and medical interest of psychoanalysis, but like Joyce, she maintained that compared to the novel, psychoanalysis "simplifies rather than complicates, detracts rather than enriches," because it denies persons their individuality by treating them as mere cases.[5] Likewise, D. H. Lawrence was convinced that he had essentially replaced psychoanalysis with his own theory of the unconscious, a "pseudo-philosophy" he had "deduced" from his novels and poems. "While the Freudian theory of the unconscious is valuable as a *description* of our psychological condition," Lawrence elsewhere maintained, "the moment you begin to apply it, and make it master of the living situation, you have begun to substitute one mechanistic or unconscious illusion for another."[6]

If the treatment of dream experience in the nineteenth-century novel expressed the need for, and contributed to producing, a scientific discourse to explain and interpret dreams, the dominant twentieth-century British novelists seemed to reject that language once it was formulated and expressed a wish to return to the chaotic material of the dream itself—to "put the language to sleep," as Joyce said of *Finnegans Wake*, when "writing of the night."[7] In many of the most influential modernist novels, the narrators express just such a suspicion about the value of interpretation and the efficacy of language to "explain" what is most important in dream experience. Joyce's Stephen Dedalus, Conrad's Marlow, and Beckett's chorus of skeptics exhibit a preference for impressionistic and dreamlike statements that at once invite and defy interpretation.[8] It might be said that the characteristic form of modernist novels resembles what Freud called the tactics of dream-work much more than the tactics of the dream interpretation. Instead of attempting to decode or make sense out of experience, they seek to preserve its apparently fragmented and random character. Rather than construct a coherent, connected narrative or compose a "life story," modernist texts attempt to capture moments of intense awareness which are laden with indefinite meaning. They do not interpret. They imitate what Conrad calls in *Heart of Darkness* (1902) "the terrific suggestiveness of words heard in

[4]Letter to Miss Weaver, 24 June 1921, quoted ibid., p. 525.
[5]Virginia Woolf, "Freudian Fiction," in *Contemporary Writers* (1965), p. 154.
[6]D. H. Lawrence, *Fantasia of the Unconscious* (Harmondsworth, Eng.: Penguin, 1979), pp. 10–11; Lawrence, Review of *The Social Basis of Consciousness* by Trigant Burrow, reprinted in *Phoenix: The Posthumous Papers of D. H. Lawrence*, ed. Edward D. McDonald (New York: Viking, 1968), p. 378.
[7]Joyce's statement was reported by Max Eastman in *The Literary Mind* (1931), and quoted in Ellmann, *James Joyce*, p. 559.
[8]Ian Watt has remarked, for example, that Conrad's "impressionistic" technique reminds us of "the precarious nature of the process of interpretation," which Watt regards as central to the impressionist and symbolist tendencies of the modern temperament. Watt, *Conrad in the Nineteenth Century* (1979), pp. 175–81.

dreams, of phrases spoken in nightmares."[9] In place of gaining control over the processes of the unconscious through a set of mastering discourses, then, the inclination of these post-Freudian novelists was to idealize the authenticity of a prelinguistic unconscious. They sought to gesture toward the "sensation" of the dream rather than to reveal its hidden syntax.

Ironically, the modernist movement into obscurity in narrative technique reflects a conception of the psyche that is itself indebted to the claims of psychoanalysis. Like psychoanalysis, modernist fiction undermines the idea that the self is an essentially rational being, a permanent and coherent "character." When Marlow says that no relation of a dream can convey the dream sensation, which he describes as "that commingling of absurdity, surprise, and bewilderment . . . which is the very essence of dreams," he implies that the dreamer is fundamentally a receiver and producer of sensations that are not necessarily controlled by any rational explanatory system. Works of fiction like *Heart of Darkness* show psychic life to be a "choice of nightmares," propelled by irrational, uncontrollable drives that persist in some unconscious level unavailable to the conscious mind (98). Rather than privilege consciousness over the unconscious, these modernist texts privilege unconscious drives over rational deliberation. "One's past," Marlow says, comes back "in the shape of an unrestful and noisy dream," and its "essentials" are not retrievable in language; they are "deep under the surface, beyond my reach" (48, 55). Conrad himself consistently responded to his friends' urging that he read Freud with a skepticism that echoed Marlow's suspicion of the deceptive and dangerous "ideas" with which we interpret our experience: "I do not want to reach the *depths*," he explained. "I want to treat reality like a raw and rough object which I touch with my fingers. That is all."[10]

Much modernist fiction is in harmony with this sentiment, looking to the rough structure of the dream itself, not to an interpretation of the dream, for a model with which to represent human experience. The "syntactic laws" as Freud called them, which characterize the dream work correspond to the features we have come to associate with the technical innovations of the modernist novel. If for the nineteenth century the dream is the "trouble" that must be contained and mastered through a series of professional discourses, that trouble breaks out in the modern period to dominate not just the conception of the subject but the linguistic texture of the work. Modernist experimentation, that is, can be thought of as a formal and thematic irruption into the fabric of the novel of the sort of dream material that the Victorian novel bracketed, mastered, and subordinated to the integrated self and the

---

[9]Conrad, *Heart of Darkness* (Harmondsworth, Eng.: Penguin, 1973), p. 95, hereafter cited in the text.
[10]Zdzislaw Najder, *Joseph Conrad: A Chronicle* (1983), p. 460.

linear plot. The very discourses of medicine, economics, and politics which represented a form of personal authority and control for the Victorians, appear to the modernists as molestations to individual authenticity and originality.

Instead of embedding and controlling dreams in a coherent narrative structure, then, high-modernist novels often resemble the confused structures of dreams themselves. It is a commonplace to note that Conrad, Woolf, Joyce, Faulkner, and Beckett may omit logical and narrative connections in their novels, for example, or that their representation of events involves distortions and displacements of value and emphasis, an extravagant or absurd concentration upon seemingly insignificant details, inversion of chronological sequence, uncritical blending of the fantastic with the commonplace, and a self-consciousness about and play with language. These are, of course, the same distortions that characterize the dream work as Freud described it in chapter 6 of *The Interpretation of Dreams*, distortions he sought to undo through the narrative procedures of dream interpretation. These tactics are not exclusively utilized by modern texts, of course; we have seen some of them employed in the gothic, autobiographical, and detective forms I have considered here. But like psychoanalysis, each of those forms also appropriated or helped to invent some discursive strategy to master and interpret the subversive forces expressed in dreams. Many modernist texts challenge the value of this mastery, maintaining that it removes us farther from the truth of our dreams, instead of bringing us closer to that truth. These novels reflect a declining confidence in science and a decomposition of capitalist and imperialist ideologies of the self. Dream interpretation when it is construed in such terms may simply, as Lawrence put it, substitute one illusion for another.

The conscious interpretation of dreams comes to be regarded in modernist fiction as a distortion and falsification of the dream work, just as Freud claimed the unconscious activity of the dream work distorted and falsified the dream thoughts. The distinction between dreaming and waking experience is, therefore, often blurred in many modern texts. Such a distinction seems arbitrary and problematical if the most intense experiences have the same affective psychological force whether they take place in a state of consciousness or unconsciousness. In Joyce's *Portrait of the Artist as a Young Man* (1914–1915), for example, each section of the novel contains a dream or dreamlike event that is subject to some interpretive or explanatory system that Stephen encounters, embraces, and then rejects. These systems of order—whether rooted in his family, the school, the church, or the nation— are invariably challenged and discredited by the more intense and compelling truth of certain of Stephen's isolated epiphanic moments which the interpretive schemes are not able to accommodate or explain. For Freud dream interpretation clearly replaced and undid the dream work, but Stephen's dreams so thoroughly blend into and out of his waking life that he often cannot discern where one begins and the other ends; he reflects at one point that his life is like a dream but "not a dream from which he would wake."[11] Stephen "moved among distorted images of the outer world," we are told, both "by day" and "by night" (99). This distortion affects the structure of Stephen's novel as well. There events are not presented sequentially but are arranged as in a dream, "radiating backwards and forwards," as Ellmann says, along a synchronic continuum of past, present, and future.[12]

The evidence of this identification of the "dream-sensation" with the sensation of waking life can be seen in the work of Lawrence and Woolf as well, but the implications are taken to an extreme in Samuel Beckett's novels, in which the narrators' monologues are tortured by the very thing that sustains them: the speakers' need to continue to try in vain to tell stories about themselves—to try and then to fail to interpret the dream of their lives. Each voice in these texts longs for the final dreamless sleep in which the terrible responsibility of self-authorship would end. "That is how it will be done," the narrative voice says in *The Unnamable* (1959), distressed because he cannot stop the voices that insistently spin off pieces of stories about himself whether he is asleep or awake. "Or quietly, stealthily, the story would begin, as if nothing had happened and I still the teller and the told. But I would be fast asleep, my mouth agape, as usual. . . . And from my sleeping mouth the lies would pour, about me."[13] Beckett's narrators wish to be done with their dreaming—to silence finally the voices that generate the fictions they tell about themselves. They give no privileged status either to the language of dreams or to the language of interpretation, for both merely lie about them. "Last everlasting questions," the narrator says longingly in *Stories and Texts for Nothing* (1955), looking toward the end of the dream, "infant languours in the end sheets, last images, end of dream, of being past, passing and to be, end of lie."[14]

At the same time that these twentieth-century fictions bring forward the dream in its uninterpreted state, they bring to the surface what I have been calling the hidden narrative plot of the novel. The quest for some individual or social authority and the attendant struggle to forge a discourse with which to master confusing experience which were implicit and submerged in earlier novels become explicit and central issues in many of these modernist texts. In *Heart of Darkness*, for example, Marlow explains that his obsession with Kurtz (whom Marlow calls "the nightmare of my choice") has to do with

[11]James Joyce, *A Portrait of the Artist as a Young Man*, ed. Chester G. Anderson (Harmondsworth, Eng.: Penguin, 1981), p. 146, hereafter cited in the text.

[12]Ellmann, *James Joyce*, p. 307.

[13]Samuel Beckett, *The Unnamable* (New York: Grove Press, 1978), p. 30, hereafter abbreviated *TU* and cited in the text. The first French edition appeared in 1953; the first English text in 1959.

[14]Beckett, *Stories and Texts for Nothing* (New York: Grove Press, 1967), p. 139.

Kurtz's "unbounded power of eloquence" and his existence for Marlow as "little more than a voice" (72, 69). Along with Marlow's frequent apologies for his inability adequately to express the meaning of his story, he repeatedly confesses his fascination with (and his desire to be in possession of) Kurtz's voice and the expressive power of his words. Similarly, Stephen Dedalus finally recognizes in *A Portrait* that there is a power in speaking the right words and that his freedom can be achieved only by mastering the discourses deployed by the figures of authority which have dominated his life. "He had heard about him the constant voice of his father and of his masters," the narrator says, "urging him to be a gentleman above all things and urging him to be a good catholic above all things. These voices had now come to be hollow-sounding in his ears" (83). It is only when Stephen "heard another voice," the voice of his own imagination, which combines all the others in a dreamlike palimpsest, that he is able to "forge" for himself what he calls the "uncreated conscience" of his race. At this juncture, the text becomes a diary spoken in the first person (253). Unlike Jane Eyre, for example, who converted all the voices from her past into aspects of her own voice, Stephen ends by allowing his voice to be blended with the voices of his past. He recognizes their fictionality, yet uses them to manage his own experience.

Joyce and Beckett also transform the terms with which the repressed narrative plot can be analyzed. The categories of narrative "recovery" or "possession" or "repression" with which I have analyzed the dreams in the previous chapters are based on a clear and confident distinction between the manifest and the latent dream material, as well as between the identity of the narrator and the discourses in the world he or she tells about. When these distinctions break down, as they do in *Jekyll and Hyde* and in even more radical ways in more modern texts, the differences between these narrative categories begin to disappear as well. It is meaningless to describe the achievement of narrative voice in terms of configurations of narrative power and control when there is no confidence at any given moment as to which "voice" or "voices" are speaking through the voice that seems to be doing the narrating. This is Marlow's dilemma as he struggles to retell the events leading up to his confrontation with Kurtz. Marlow's account of that time is infiltrated by a confusion of other voices that resonate in and around his (and Kurtz's) words: "I heard—him—it—this voice—other voices—all of them were so little more than voices—and the memory of that time itself lingers around me, impalpable, like a dying vibration of one immense jabber . . . without any kind of sense. Voices, voices—" (69). This "immense jabber" of voices bewilders the narrators of Beckett's trilogy as well, with more extreme consequences. These narrators challenge the modernist dream of a prelinguistic state. They see themselves as enslaved by the fraudulent power of their own voices, cursed with the illusion that they speak for themselves. *The Unnamable* begins with a disturbing recognition of this inescapable deception: "I seem to speak, it is not I, about me, it is not me" (3). "The voice that speaks . . . issues from me," the narrator adds later on, but "it is not mine. I have none, I have no voice and must speak. That is all I know" (26).

These narrators enact what Mikhail Bakhtin has defined as the central problem of the novel: the attempt "to find one's own voice and to orient it among other voices, to combine it with some of them and to counterpose it to others, or to separate one's voice from another voice, with which it is inseparably merged."[15] With increasing force the modernist and postmodernist novel acknowledges and works through the paradoxical nature of this enterprise. The voices that make up and speak through the self in these texts appear as inseparable from one another as "the tangle of dream-thoughts which cannot be unravelled" in a dream. In dreams, Freud had said, "all kinds of thoughts having a *contrary* sense" often "found voice" (*Interpretation of Dreams*, 208). The tactics of interpretation he prescribed sought to reconcile those contrary voices and discover the wish that gave rise to them. Joyce, Conrad, Beckett, and others take on a different project, directed toward the restoration and articulation of those contrary voices that find expression in both waking and dreaming states. "How tell what remains," the narrating voice asks in another of Beckett's stories. "But it's the end. Or have I been dreaming, am I dreaming? No, no, none of that, for dream is nothing, a joke, and significant what is worse."[16] Here Beckett's mysterious words extend Freud's claim that dream life is continuous with waking life and his warning that the pursuit of a dream "through the intricate network of the world of thought" to its unknown center would "end in darkness." In the heart of that darkness echo the voices of *A Portrait of the Artist as a Young Man* and Beckett's trilogy, *Molloy, Malone Dies*, and *The Unnamable*, along with the voices of Marlow and Kurtz.

Though dreams continue to figure in an important way in these texts, post-Freudian novelists treat them very differently from the nineteenth-century novelists I have considered here. The desire to free the dream from the power of a single linguistic explanation seems as deep as the desire of earlier texts to possess that power. The modernists' suspicion of what they regarded as the reductive and positivistic categories of psychoanalysis led them to forge another language, which imitated rather than translated the "work" of the unconscious. By so doing, they may have also contributed to the direction psychoanalysis would take with Jacques Lacan, who sought to return psychoanalysis to its linguistic concerns. As the author of what is generally recognized as the greatest modernist novel, Joyce spoke for many of his contemporaries when he said that he wrote "to suit the esthetic of the

[15]Bakhtin, *Problems of Dostoevsky's Poetics*, p. 201.
[16]Beckett, "The Calmative," *Stories and Texts for Nothing*, p. 43.

dream," where, he said, "the forms prolong and multiply themselves, where the visions pass from the trivial to the apocalyptic, where the brain uses the roots of vocables to make others from them which will be capable of naming its phantasms, its allegories, its allusions."[17] He may also have spoken for many other modernists—and for the new aesthetic of the novel—when he repudiated Jung's preface for *Ulysses* and insisted, "I have nothing to do with psychoanalysis."[18]

But a denial so often and absolutely stated also sounds to us like a symptom of resistance. The writers of the modernist novel have returned us to a revised Freud as surely as the writers of the nineteenth century novel anticipated and were revised by him. That they have done so may in part explain why Lacan—who also "returned" to Freud with a new discourse—said that he had been much "preoccupied" by the work of Joyce, even though that work manifested Joyce's refusal of psychoanalysis.[19] For Lacan and for Joyce alike, the fictions and theories of personal authority invented by the nineteenth century to replace divine and social systems of authority break down into more fluid, dynamic conceptions of the self and its relation to the world. In the modern novel and in Lacanian theory as well, the unconscious psychic material that the Victorians hoped to contain and to master turns into the evidence of what cannot be mastered.

Forging the Dream Work in
A Portrait of the Artist as a Young Man

25 March, morning: A troubled night of dreams. Want to get them off my chest.

—Stephen Dedalus

The first two sentences from Stephen Dedalus's diary entry for 25 March condense the entire story of his life as it is represented in *A Portrait*: a troubled night of dreams from which he wants to be released. Then, in the two final statements of the diary—and the last words of the novel—Stephen records the paradoxical outcome of that desire. First he declares the originality of his ambitions as a writer and his independence from his predecessors: "I go to encounter for the millionth time the reality of experience

---

[17]From a conversation with Edmond Jaloux, recorded in Ellmann, *James Joyce*, p. 559.

[18]Joyce's hostile response to Jung's preface came in a conversation with Daniel Brody, quoted in Ellmann, ibid., p. 642.

[19]Jacques Lacan, Preface to the English edition of *The Four Fundamental Concepts of Psychoanalysis*, trans. Alan Sheridan (1978), p. ix.

and to forge in the smithy of my soul the uncreated conscience of my race" (252–53). In his own soul, he claims, he will forge the as yet "uncreated" conscience of his race. But in his very next statement, Stephen implicitly confesses the opposing desire to be dependent upon his past and to be continuous with the ways of his predecessors. He invokes in a prayerlike petition the aid of his "old father" whose namesake he is: "Old father, old artificer, stand me now and ever in good stead" (253).

These two statements directly contradict each other, reflecting an important aspect of Stephen's final formulation of a theory of self-representation and, by implication, his ideas about dream interpretation as well. The contradictory impulses of resisting and submitting to the fathers and to a preordained pattern are present even in the first statement, when Stephen announces that he intends to "forge" the uncreated conscience of his race. He chooses in *forge* a word that indicates both invention and imitation, authorship and fraudulence, authenticity and counterfeit. To forge is to create something new and also to copy something already made. The "conscience" that Stephen announces he will go on to forge is like the dreams he wants to get off his chest. They both belong simultaneously to him and to his race. They both repeat and originate. Stephen has learned that any representation of himself, conscious or unconscious, will always also be a representation of the others who have gone before him. He has by this time also learned about the force of a pun and the power of language to shape experience, having discovered that it was through words that "he had glimpses of the real world about him" (62). He must have chosen the term *forge* very carefully, then, to name the process by which he would get his dreams off his chest, especially since he endorsed the choice in his very next statement with an appeal to the authority of the equally equivocal "artificer"—at once the inventor and the deceiver.

Stephen's attraction to the opposing forces in forging a conscience correlates with his desire to get his dreams off his chest rather than to interpret them. The content of Stephen's dreams repeats the movement between these two opposing impulses—between resistance and surrender to the forces around him, between rebellion and confession, between his invention of himself as entirely unique and his imitation of some sanctioned model. Like Freud's description of dreams as plagiarists, Stephen's dreams borrow from his waking life in order to reproduce that material in somewhat different form, ultimately enabling him to forge out of the official languages that have been prescribed for him a new, subversive language with which to represent himself. Much as a plagiarist might do, he eventually appropriates the very discourses—whether religious, economic, or political—that have mastered him, and turns them to his own purposes. But in getting his dreams off his chest, Stephen does not give them any final, authoritative interpretation. By reconfiguring the terms of the languages offered to him, he self-consciously "forges" himself into some new temporary artifice. Like many modernist texts, this novel actively resists interpretation rather than desires it. *A Portrait* seems to regress into the confusing pictographic script of dreams rather than to advance into the clarity of conscious analysis or interpretation.

The dream that most directly affects Stephen and most dramatically shapes his developing attitude toward dreams, occurs at the center of the book. Stephen's dream of hell during the retreat of Saint Francis Xavier is a direct response to the elaborate and powerful sermon delivered by the rector, whose voice, we are told, "blew death" into Stephen's soul (112). Consistent with the generally paradoxical work of language in the novel, the voice that claims to offer salvation here also imposes death. The goal of the sermon, which dominates the central chapter of *A Portrait*, is to persuade, to bring the listeners to the point of contrition and confession, to cause them to surrender the story of their life and subsequently to "amend" that story to conform to a sacramental pattern (135). "The surest sign that his confession had been good," Stephen realized, was "the amendment of his life" (153). The sermon's effectiveness is rooted partially in its vivid description of the eternal torments that await the person who fails to make the amendment but also in its detailed recounting of an entire cosmic narrative to which the individual's life is to conform. The rector's sermon charts the Christian account of history. It starts with the beginning of time in Genesis, proceeds through the redemption of time in the passion of Christ, and culminates in the final judgment—the "last things" that are to be the focus of the retreat. "He who remembers the last things," the rector declares, "will act and think with them always before his eyes" (111). Such a person will, in other words, amend his individual life story to be in accordance with the end of all stories, an end that is already written by the divine author and interpreter of history. When the sermon holds up "the story of the life of St. Francis" as a model of a life that has so revised itself, it stakes a narrative claim on Stephen and the others, demanding that they conform their lives to this universal history. The sermon serves as the central narrative act in the novel because of these ultimate claims that it makes, not only for religious language but for any language. It is the most extreme and persuasive example of the many linguistic strategies of interpretation by which Stephen is lured and in terms of which he is called upon to "amend" and interpret the dream of his life. The sermon interprets his dream even before he dreams it. As he typically does with these interpretive vocabularies, Stephen listens carefully to the claims that the sermon makes on him, believing that "every word of it was for him" (115).

The highly charged setting of these words shapes the content of Stephen's subsequent dream. The sermon deeply moves Stephen and nearly persuades him to make his confession, "to speak out in words what he had done and thought, sin after sin" (126). Stephen recognizes the enormity of this act, however, and shrinks from putting his life into certain "words" by speaking it to someone who represents that divine interpretation. To do so would be to reduce himself by redefining "what he had done and thought" as merely a series of "sins"—transgressions of the demands of this other story. "How could he utter in words to the priest what he had done?" the narrator agonizes over and over. "To say it in words! His soul, stifling and helpless would cease to be" (140, 142). *A Portrait* is largely concerned with the problem of putting experience into words, with the making of a narrative in which "the personality of the artist passes into the narration itself," as Stephen puts it in his aesthetic theory (215). But even here as a schoolboy at the retreat, Stephen seems to realize that the words he uses may both refine and extinguish him. If he agrees "to tell over his hidden sins" in the terms the church dictates, he knows that his soul would "cease to be" as it was before. Central to the sermon's appeal is its presentation of the soul's dilemma as a choice between sets of words, between conforming to the "voices" of sin on the one hand and to the "voices" of God on the other. That choice determines the individual's identity and his role in the divine narrative of history. The "foul demons who are made in hell the voices of conscience," according to the sermon, constantly remind the tormented sinner that God had previously spoken to him during his mortal life "by so many voices," in "language" that the sinner "would not hear" (123–25). "O my dear little brothers in Christ," the rector warns of these demonic voices, "may it never be our lot to hear that language" (124). The rector offers instead the "poor words" of the language of heaven, words that draw Stephen like a magnet, "every one for him" (125). In fact, Stephen will gradually recognize all the other "voices of conscience" which make these claims on him (not the least of which is the voice of the church) as demonic forces of control which he must exorcise with some other discursive strategy, some other redemptive language.

Despite its profound influence on Stephen, the sermon does not quite succeed in bringing him to pronounce the words that the rector urges his listeners to "repeat after" him (134). The other boys "answered" the priest's prayer of contrition "phrase by phrase"; but while Stephen joined them "with his heart," he could not speak the words, for "his tongue [was] cleaving to his palate" (135). Stephen intuitively resists the pressure to "speak out" his life in the words and phrases dictated by the priest here and tries in vain to "forget" his past and avoid the crisis instead. But the force of his past, especially as it is reconfigured by the language he has just heard, is insistent over his attempts to repress it. Stephen's memory now expresses itself in his dream of a field where "the leprous company of his sins closed about him, breathing upon him, bending over him from all sides":

> Creatures were in the field; one, three, six: creatures were moving in the field, hither and thither. Goatish creatures with human faces, horny-browed, lightly bearded and grey as india-rubber. The malice of evil glittered in their hard eyes,

as they moved hither and thither, trailing their long tails behind them. A rictus of cruel malignity lit up greyly their old bony faces. One was clasping about his ribs a torn flannel waistcoat, another complained monotonously as his beard stuck in the tufted weeds. Soft language issued from their spittleless lips as they swished in slow circles round and round the field, winding hither and thither through the weeds, dragging their long tails amid the rattling canisters. They moved in slow circles, circling closer and closer to enclose, to enclose, soft language issuing from their lips, their long swishing tails besmeared with stale shite, thrusting upwards their terrific faces. (137–38)

Stephen's response to the enclosure of this dream is dramatic. He flings himself from his bed, is seized with a convulsive fit of vomiting, and immediately decides that his previous attitude of reverence and humility is inadequate to save him from this, "his hell." He must agree after all to "tell over" his life in the words that would "amend" it, and he resolves to do so at his first opportunity. "Confess! Confess! It was not enough to lull the conscience with a tear and a prayer. He had to kneel before the minister of the Holy Ghost and tell over his hidden sins truly and repentantly" (139).

The dream, and not the sermon, finally brings Stephen to the point of verbal confession—of putting his life into words and freeing himself from the oppression of the dream. But the words into which he puts his life are not his own; they are the words of the sermon, the prescribed words of the Confiteor. And by telling over his life in those words, he gives over the authority of his life to the church. He becomes "the repentant," just as Helen Burns had been "the slattern" in *Jane Eyre* and Pip Pirrip "the gentleman" in *Great Expectations*. He does, in a sense, cease to be who he was before ("the sinner"); and later, arguing with Cranly about no longer believing church doctrine, he will claim in turn, "I was someone else then" to explain his days of belief. Stephen's life is a series of such self-amendments and erasures in which he is constantly becoming "someone else" in accordance with a succession of different discursive systems. The dream of hell is part of this process: it is provoked by a verbal performance Stephen listens to, and it then provokes another verbal performance by Stephen in which he redefines himself. Appropriately, then, this dream that moves him to utter his confession is itself concerned with the simultaneously seductive and repellent power of utterance.

Twice in the dream, Stephen sees the "goatish creatures with human faces" pressing on him with "soft language issuing from their lips." The characterization of the language as "soft" is surprising here and calls attention to itself, since every other image in the dream is severe and exaggerated, grotesque, repulsive. It is as if the beasts' "soft language" is the subtle source of their power over Stephen and the force that enables them to define "his hell" and enclose him in it. "They moved in slow circles, circling closer and closer to enclose, to enclose, soft language issuing from their lips." Stephen's feeling, just before the dream, that "the leprous company of his sins closed about him" is apparently the basis of this dream image of the enclosing "goatish creatures." But the creatures, with their human faces and human clothes, also represent the human authorities whose voices seek to enclose Stephen's life story within their own. What Stephen has not yet realized is that his dream indicates his hell is a tyranny of words, of soft language and subtle voices from which he cannot escape; they enclose him even in the unconscious scene of his dreams. On one of the many occasions in which Joyce spoke with hostility about psychoanalysis, he called it "the church to which I don't belong." "If we need it," he said on another occasion, "let us keep to confession."[20] For Joyce, both the superstition of the church and the science of psychoanalysis represent interchangeable master narratives that enclose rather than enhance the lives of their followers. As he did in his subsequent novels, Joyce sought in *A Portrait* to get the weight of those dreams off his chest—to escape the imprisonment of those confining languages not by avoiding them but by exploiting them.

Confession is a crucial element in defining the dreamers' relationship to their dreams in each of the novelistic forms I have examined here. Each makes use of the confession to signal a character's healing or liberation from controlling voices outside him- or herself. Stephen's dream, which raises similar issues of threatened subjection to alien voices, prompts an actual liturgical confession. Yet that confession compromises him. In the gothic, autobiographical, and detective novels I have considered, the conversion of the rite of confession—into a form of treatment, into an act of self-production and self-promotion, or into the reconstruction of a crime for the purposes of solving a mystery—has corresponded to the ways in which the characters convert dreams into words and achieve mastery over their own development. But though Stephen's confession in *A Portrait of the Artist as a Young Man* manages to get his dream off his chest, it also enslaves him to another system of symbols. Stephen's confession acknowledges the dangerous possibility that the self is nothing but a fiction—that Stephen himself is not just a teller of stories but also a story told by others. He is the dreamer and the dream, the narrator of and the listener to his own story. His response to his dreams demonstrates that no interpretation can clearly distinguish these two opposing states from each other. When one "tells over" one's dreams in any language, one linguistic illusion merely substitutes for another.

Over the course of *A Portrait*, Stephen becomes increasingly aware of the voices that seek to enclose him in their narrative and interpretive schemes. The first words of the novel are spoken by his father, telling the story of the

[20]Ellmann, *James Joyce*, pp. 641, 487.

"nicens little boy named baby tuckoo," with whom Stephen is identified (7). Stephen's earliest conscious thoughts about his own identity, then, are that "his father told him that story," and that "he was baby tuckoo" (7). Stephen was, in other words, a character in the story his father told him. In the retreat sermon, his spiritual father tells a more elaborate story, but in this one too Stephen is still only a character, this time the sinner who must confess his sins as "bestial," much as the infant Stephen was repeatedly told that he had to "apologise" (8). Later, when Stephen walks through Cork with his father, "listening to stories he had heard before," he begins to become aware that even his dreams and reveries are in some measure shaped by the "soft language" of the world outside him (91). "They too had sprung up before him," he realizes, "suddenly and furiously out of mere words" (90). When he speaks, Stephen begins to hear other voices—such as his father's—speaking through him until "he could scarcely recognize as his his own thoughts" (92). For all its oppression of him, Stephen's confession is essential in his coming to terms with these voices. The confession is Stephen's first formal acknowledgment that though he cannot entirely author himself or even own his own thoughts, he can "amend" his life and his thinking through a scrupulous forgery of the words and voices that enclose him and fabricate his dreams, whether or not he consents to it. Neither his personal voice nor the collective voices of his family, church, or society can be regarded as more authoritative than his own experience. Nor can his articulation of his experience entirely take authority over their languages. Rather, language and experience are engaged in a dynamic relationship in which each forms and reforms the other.[21]

In less formal but equally influential settings, Stephen learns early on that the teller of the story is in a position of power over the listener. The same chapter that begins with Stephen's father's putting him in a story ends with Stephen's triumphantly telling his own story to the rector of his school in protest over Father Dolan's unjust accusation and violent treatment of him. Once he gives an account of his broken glasses to the rector and accuses Father Dolan of injustice, Stephen's friends make him a hero, begging him to tell them what he had told the rector. Stephen proceeds to tell them the story of his triumph and revels in their admiration. But in the very next chapter, his father takes possession of that story and uses it to ridicule Stephen. "The rector . . . was telling me that story about you and Father Dolan," Simon Dedalus says to Stephen, and he then recounts the story,

---

[21]Hugh Kenner notes that in *Dubliners* Joyce's grammar suggests that many of the stories have a third-person narrator while the diction tells a different story. All the words "wear invisible quotation marks," he says, and may be thought of as being spoken in the first person. The same is true of *A Portrait*, but the further questions this book silently asks on almost every page are Who speaks? Who *is* the first person? What other persons are speaking through me? See *Joyce's Voices* (1978), pp. 16–21.

giving it a meaning entirely different from the one that Stephen had given it in his telling. In his father's version, Stephen appears as a small and foolish character, nothing more than an "impudent thief" (72). But Simon is the thief here, having stolen Stephen's story from him and made him a ridiculous character in it rather than its triumphant teller. This is the pattern the novel follows throughout: Stephen's appropriation of a linguistic strategy in one chapter is turned back on him in the next and used to enclose him once more. He must then appropriate another vocabulary or interpretive scheme to represent his experience. In this, Stephen alternates between being a Jane Eyre and a Pip Pirrip with respect to the threats to his authority. But as Stephen matures, he becomes more and more skilled at mediating between his roles as teller and listener, positioning himself within narratives that he can detect and amend, if not originate, forging himself in the new terms given to him. Telling over his life in the confession after his dream of hell becomes Stephen's model for making himself the narrator of one narrative as he becomes a character in another.

But this is a pattern Stephen is not always in control of. Each of Stephen's associates has a story for him to live out or an interpretation to impose upon his experience. He accepts the authority of their words until they begin to be "hollowsounding in his ears": "And it was the din of all these hollowsounding voices that made him halt irresolutely in the pursuit of phantoms. He gave them ear only for a time but he was happy only when he was far from them, beyond their call, alone or in the company of phantasmal comrades" (84). As the dream of the goatish creatures indicates, even Stephen's phantasmal comrades speak to him in voices that lose their power over him only after they have deeply influenced him. Such an influence is dramatized in Stephen's first dream in *A Portrait*: he is going home from Clongowes for Christmas and appears to be borne away by a tide of authority figures who determine the course of his life for him. After Stephen actually does return home and silently listens to his father and Dante argue about the politics of Parnell, Dante prophesies to Simon Dedalus that Stephen will "remember" the "language he heard against God and religion and priests in his own home" (33). Stephen's life story is, in fact, composed in this language of political authority and rebellion, just as it is also made up of his aunt's vocabulary of religious surrender to "the language of the Holy Ghost" (32).

Stephen's dream just prior to his return home has already registered the influence of these two "languages." In the dream, Stephen conflates an image of his own death with Parnell's and listens as the priest proclaims over the rebel's body "in a loud voice," "He is dead. We saw him lying upon the catafalque" (27). The rebel Parnell is subdued and silenced, pronounced dead and punningly accused of being a liar by the "loud voice" of the church ("We saw him lying . . . "). The importance for Stephen of this portrayal of a conflict between political and religious interpretive systems is underscored when he twice recalls the images of this dream: just before the sermon and during his visit to Cork with his father, when Stephen remembers "mass being said for him" by the rector and effectively replaces Parnell as the victor and victim in the dream. The substitution serves only to reinforce Stephen's sense of his subjection to the authorities that both threaten his life and insist on speaking "for him," surrounding him like a sea of voices (93). They provide him with the "words which he did not understand" but which he repeated "over and over again until he learned them by heart" (62). These words not only order his life; they make up his dreams and become the things by which he remembers himself.

It becomes increasingly difficult for Stephen to get his dreams off his chest in *A Portrait* because the "languages" of his dreams blend indiscernibly with the languages of his waking life. The images of Stephen's dream of hell are, at points, drawn directly from the words of the sermon on the same subject, and his experiences of the dream and of the sermon become more and more inseparable. The same is true of Stephen's erotic dreams, which in his memory become interwoven with his actual sexual experiences. When these dreams are described, they become confused with Stephen's nightly wanderings, since, as the text says, it was both "by day and by night" that Stephen "moved among distorted images" (99). "A figure that seemed to him by day demure and innocent came before him by night through the winding darkness of sleep, her face transfigured by a lecherous cunning, her eyes bright with brutish joy" (99). Stephen's visions are "transfigured" here as much by the words with which he recalls them as by the dream work itself: the images are "lecherous" and "brutish" because this is the "soft language" that the church has given him with which to interpret his sexual desire. The same words and images recur in Stephen's dream of the "leprous goatish fiends" (138). This "transfiguring" of images becomes a more and more important part of Stephen's waking life as he begins to live in a "languour of sleep" in which he is not quite sure where his dreams end and his waking life begins. "Was it an instant of enchantment," Stephen puzzles over his "dream or vision" of the seraphic life; or was it "long hours and days and years and ages?" (217).[22]

But even if Stephen's dreams and phantasies are largely determined by the language of his priests and his parents, he does not entirely surrender to their influence. Stephen is neither quite like Pip (who continually seeks out an authority for himself) nor like Jane Eyre (who consistently resists those

[22]Maud Ellmann's essay points out that an event will frequently be described as a repetition in *A Portrait* when it is in fact a first time. The supposed first occurrence may turn out to be a dream of a similar event, reinforcing the sense of the intermingling of dream with waking events in the constitution of Stephen's memory. "Disremembering Dedalus: *A Portrait of the Artist as a Young Man*," in *Untying the Text: A Post-Structuralist Reader*, ed. Robert Young (1981), pp. 189–96.

who would take that responsibility away from her). Rather, in surrendering to the language of certain authorities, he is able to repel certain others. His confession, for example, is a yielding to the voice of the church, but it is at the same time a means of mastering the "voices of the flesh," which had dominated him and his dreams in the previous chapter (152). In that chapter he is rendered "silent" by the fleshly voices, unable to respond to the words of the prostitute. He is seen at the end of the chapter "surrendering himself to her," and though "his lips parted" in an effort to respond to her, "they would not speak" (101). She speaks for him, much as the priest does when he makes his confession. While Stephen's confession to the priest is another surrender, then, it is also a taking command over the body by "telling over" his life in a language that silences the voices that had earlier silenced him.

Yet the "telling over" is not necessarily therapeutic. The pattern of Stephen's experience is endless paraphrase; he never completely gets his dreams off his chest through interpretation. The confession that follows the dream of the goatish creatures, for example, cannot properly be called a dream account or even an interpretation even though it is, technically, a verbalizing of the images of his dreams. Because Stephen does not know that he is papraphrasing a dream, his confession is more like the dream work itself. As Freud said of the dream work of secondary revision, it "does not think . . . at all"; rather, it unconsciously "restricts itself to giving things a new form" (*Interpretation of Dreams*, 507). The images of Stephen's dream are themselves unconscious importations from earlier dreams; the vile excrement and repulsively "lecherous" beasts in whose "hard eyes" the "malice of evil glittered" have replaced and borrowed from the "eyes bright with brutish joy" of Stephen's erotic dreams (137, 99). Then, his confession replaces those images with the official words of the church, which describe the pleasures of the body as "gluttony," "sloth," and "impurity" (144). By adopting the vocabulary of the church to describe how he "remembers" his experience (as the priest orders him to do)—effectively accounting for his dream—Stephen performs another of his many acts of secondary revision in which he both does and does not interpret his dreams. He replaces one "form" of representing his experience with another, not in order to understand it more clearly but in order to distort and destroy the previous form. Seemingly to emphasize the point, Stephen says that the "idea of surrender" to the voice of the church paradoxically "gave him an intense sense of power," because "by a single act of consent" he would repress "the insistent voices of the flesh which began to murmur to him again" and could "undo all that he had done" (152). Like his dreams, his confessions of them "undo" and replace his experience rather than explain it. This is dream work, not dream interpretation.

Other "confessions" by Stephen also resemble the veiled distortion of such dream work as secondary revision. Earlier during the retreat, for example, Stephen had recalled with horror his recent erotic dreams—those "monstrous dreams peopled by ape-like creatures and harlots with gleaming jeweled eyes" (115–16). The dreams, together with the actual sexual adventures into which the dreams merged, provide the basis for "the foul long letters he had written in the joy of guilty confession." The letters, which Stephen intended to be found and read by young women, were parodic confessions. They were written not to enable Stephen to give up his way of life but to allow him to celebrate and verify it by articulating it to someone, even if secretly. In the same way, Stephen achieves his own ends later on when he irreverently recites the Confiteor to Heron and Wallis when they accuse him of a romantic involvement to which they insist that he "admit" (78). Here again, Stephen uses the words and form of the confession ironically, deflecting the challenges and inquiries of his friends and hiding his true feelings behind the words of the Confiteor. By borrowing the tactics of their interpretive system, he evades their censorship and only appears to conform to their laws. He is forging his own "uncreated" story out of his forgery of a conventional one, echoing one of the sanctioned voices from his past to protect himself from domination by another. In Jean-François Lyotard's explication of Freud, the dream work is viewed as "the result of manhandling a text." "Desire does not speak" in a dream, Lyotard explains; "it does violence to the order of utterance."[23] These words precisely describe what takes place both in Stephen's dreams and in his articulation of them: he repeats and appropriates the sanctioned languages of his waking life in order to transgress them and break down their authority.

Joyce's career as a writer may itself be viewed as an enactment of this pattern of acquiring, dismissing, and setting discourses off against one another. Stephen's long nightmare, from which he cannot awake in *A Portrait*, is extended in *Ulysses*, where he wrestles with the memory of his mother, who repeatedly comes to him "in a dream, silently . . . her breath bent over him with mute secret words," urging him to confess and attend mass.[24] That dream merely seems to repeat the "soft language" of his dream of the goatish creatures in *A Portrait* and his dream of the priest saying mass over his dead body. The contending languages that make up Stephen's consciousness (and Bloom's) in *Ulysses* are even more elaborately built into the structure of the novel than they are in *A Portrait*, for in *Ulysses*, each chapter is actually written in another discursive form and voice. Finally, in *Finnegans Wake* Joyce writes a novel in the form of a linguistically fractured and experimental dream-fugue. *Finnegans Wake* is a text in which, he says, he attempts to put the language of waking life to sleep and to imitate "the esthetic of the dream."[25]

[23]Jean-François Lyotard, "The Dream-Work Does Not Think," *Oxford Literary Review* 6 (1983): 3.
[24]James Joyce, *Ulysses* (New York: Random House, 1961), p. 10.
[25]Ellmann, *James Joyce*, p. 559.

Stephen's description of himself in *A Portrait* as "a priest of eternal imagination, transmuting the daily bread of experience into the radiant body of everliving life" is the start of this process. It is at least a partial recognition that the words and voices of one aspect of his life can be artfully "transmuted" and "transfigured" into quite a different set of meanings when he combines them with other words and voices (221). The words that subject him can become sources of creative power. Stephen's consciousness of this power is perhaps most conspicuous when he is offered "the call" into the priesthood, a call that comes to him virtually as an offer of political power: "the power, the authority to make the great God of Heaven come down" (158). His submission to the discourse of the church, in other words, enables him to bring down the Father. "Through the words" of that call, Stephen "heard even more distinctly a voice bidding him approach, offering him secret knowledge and secret power" (159). It is to this voice and "through" its words that Stephen responds. The power he achieves thereby cannot rightly be called the power *of* the church or *of* the state or *of* the family. The power operates "through the words" and the "secret" of "transmuting" and reassembling all the voices within him by some other, always potential, "inaudible voice." Later, when Stephen refuses to respond to the call of the church, he is aware that he can refuse because he has already "assumed" "the voices and gestures which he had noted with various priests" (158). The secret knowledge of the power of their words frees him from their subjection, even as they define who he is. When Stephen conceives of himself, therefore, as being "apart in every order," he recognizes that he is both *in* a number of ordering systems and *apart* from them (162). Appropriately, then, when Stephen rejects the call to the priesthood, "the voice of the rector" who had urged it upon him so compellingly, now drained of the power it had wielded over him in the retreat sermon, "repeated itself idly in his memory" (162). "He knew now that it had already fallen into an idle formal tale," that the voice and the story to which he had once surrendered have become only one more of the many interpretive "orders" Stephen can be both "in" and "apart" from. Unlike Pip, who takes every word his authorities give him and abides by it, and equally unlike Jane, who "resisted all the way," Stephen begins "listening to the unspoken speech behind the words" and becomes more and more adept at discerning the power contained within them, even if he never fully masters them. He has seen through the "gothic" character of the religious images of his dream and recognized their political subtext.

Stephen's gradual realization of himself as both in and apart from the effects of the language of others in *A Portrait* may be measured by his increasing awareness of the secret power of the languages—sometimes soft and sometimes strident—that seek to subject him in explicitly political terms. "This race and this country and this life produced me," he says in defense of his choice to speak English rather than Irish to Davin. "My ancestors threw off their language and took another. . . . They allowed a handful of foreigners to subject them. Do you fancy I am going to pay in my own life and person debts they made? What for?" (203). Stephen acknowledges he is both "produced" and "subjected" by the languages he takes up and throws off, and he simultaneously declares his debt to and his independence from those languages. This alternating pattern of allowing himself to be remade by a discourse and then revising that discourse and replacing it with another constitutes the person Stephen becomes in *A Portrait of the Artist*. He refuses to be "subjected" by any language, and yet he also realizes there is a cost "to pay"—that "his language will always be . . . an acquired speech"—something he has borrowed from others, not something he has invented himself (189). "I have not made or accepted its words," he says of the language spoken by the English-born priest. "My voice holds them at bay. My soul frets in the shadow of his language" (189). Stephen has "acquired" and echoed many languages in *A Portrait*, shoring these linguistic fragments against the ruins of his inner life. Even in these remarks about his own self-expression he borrows (while he holds at bay) religious, political, and economic terms to represent how he is and is not "subjected." And even in his troubled dreams, Stephen is already interpreted to himself. He can never get those dreams entirely off his chest because they have produced him as much as he has produced them.

Stephen's last dream in *A Portrait* is the only one he relates in the first person, in a voice that at least implicitly seems to accept the conditions of the voices that subject him and the voice he has borrowed but not made. The dream occurs at the conclusion of the novel, where the text takes the form of a diary. Stephen's final dream is written into the center of this book of which he is author, and it brings to the surface the issues of authority and subjection that Stephen's other dreams have pointed toward. Just prior to this formal shift which reveals Stephen as the narrator as well as the main character of the text, he sets it up in his argument with Cranly about his "revolt" against the church and his refusal to "serve" it: "I will not serve that in which I no longer believe whether it calls itself my home, my fatherland or my church," Stephen says, "and I will try to express myself in some mode of life or art as freely as I can and as wholly as I can using for my defence the only arms I allow myself to use—silence, exile, and cunning" (246–47). These remarks are characteristically equivocal. Stephen will express himself most fully, he says, in an artful silence, most freely when banished into exile. Paradoxically, he says he will grow silent at the very moment when he is about to become the speaker of the text. Stephen's taking on of the first-person voice in the diary section of the novel may be read as his refusal to accept what he has already realized and what Cranly has told him again ("your mind is supersaturated with the religion in which you say you disbelieve"), or it may represent a cunning, silent acknowledgment of this exile in language, in what will always be "an acquired speech" (240, 189). The diary and the dream recorded within it form the scene of Stephen's dream work, where he takes both positions, alternately recognizing and resisting the "spell of arms and voices" which holds him in thrall (252).

Stephen's accession to the first person, his resort to the defense of silence, and the approaching end of his book are woven together in the dream he gets off his chest on the morning after he dreams it. The date of the dream is 25 March, nine months to the day before Christmas—the day, that is, of the annunciation. Even the time of the dream seems prescribed by another originary text and the dream itself appears to be saturated by the content of one of the most important dreams in the religion in which he says he disbelieves:

> *25 March, morning*: A troubled night of dreams. Want to get them off my chest.
>
> A long curving gallery. From the floor ascend pillars of dark vapours. It is peopled by the images of fabulous kings, set in stone. Their hands are folded upon their knees in token of weariness and their eyes are darkened for the errors of men go up before them ever as dark vapours.
>
> Strange figures advance from a cave. They are not as tall as men. One does not seem to stand quite apart from another. Their faces are phosphorescent, with darker streaks. They peer at me and their eyes seem to ask me something. They do not speak. (249–50)

Here, the images of authority that were speaking to and enclosing Stephen in his previous dreams have grown silent and still. The priests, prostitutes, and beasts of the earlier dreams all reveal themselves in this final dream as equivalent figures of kingly authority. But the kings are weary, blinded, and impotent. They have, in fact, become only "images of fabulous kings"; they are fictional representations of authority, not authorities that demonstrate any power at all. Then, even within the dream, they appear to be replaced by these other "strange figures," which are vague and indistinguishable from one another. And while "their eyes seem to ask" Stephen something, "they do not speak." This is the first time the figures of Stephen's dreams are silent, and yet they ask something of him, offering, it would seem, an invitation for him to speak. But in this dream, he does not speak either. These figures may represent the vague choir of voices that compose and saturate Stephen but no longer master him, because they do not impose a vocabulary upon him with which to interpret his life. Yet he does not master them either. In fact, not only do the figures not "stand quite apart" from one another, they do not stand entirely apart from Stephen either. Even in the silence of his dreams, Stephen is indistinguishable from these authorities that subject him.

Whenever Stephen believes that he can be separate from these authorities—that his voice or his mind can be independent of the voices with which it is saturated, he fails to accept the essential truth *A Portrait* has dramatized.

Stephen's voice is made up of the several voices that inform and shape his dreams and his vision; and although they do not have to subject him, he cannot subject them either. When they are silenced, Stephen is silenced as well, and the book of his life must end. But as Stephen's invocation to the "old father" and "artificer" in the very last diary entry attests, his adoption of the defense of silence is not absolute or final. He can amend again when he recognizes and acknowledges (as he does at one point in the diary) what the unspecified "voices" that call to him in his dreams are saying: "We are alone. Come. And the voices say with them: We are your kinsmen" (252). Stephen must accept that his eloquence lies not in any single mastering discourse but in the many voices he has echoed and acquired, in all the soft languages with which he has transfigured himself. His surrender to these discourses—if he also reforges them—is the source as well as the limit of his power. His eloquence does not come from his stubborn resistance or his illusions of freedom. Those illusions lead to a position of "defense" and "silence" which is the most perilous surrender. This condition is the "silence" that Stephen refers to in his diary as the life-threatening result of moving "from dreams to dreamless sleep"— to the dreamless sleep in which the self surrenders not only the obligation of self-authorship or self-interpretation but any possibility of becoming anything at all (251).

Stephen's "theory" of his own development here sheds some light on the relation between the modern novel—after Freud—and psychoanalysis. When Joyce responded to Jung's disparaging review of *Ulysses*, he objected to the psychoanalytic terms of Jung's critique rather than the critique itself. "Why is Jung so rude to me?" he asked. "People want to put me out of the church to which I don't belong. I have nothing to do with psychoanalysis."[26] But Joyce's equating of the functioning of psychoanalysis with that of the church in his denial here invites us to interpret his words as an echo of Stephen's. What Joyce may mean, in other words, is that psychoanalysis— like the Catholic church—is an "order" he is both inside and apart from, even if he does not "belong" to it. Psychoanalysis is also a discourse. Whatever importance it might have for him is not based in any authority contained in the specific discursive strategies it deploys or from which it borrows— medical, economic, or political, for example. It is based, rather, in the recognition in psychoanalysis that discourse has power. Especially as it took shape in the Lacanian interpretation of Freud, psychoanalysis is centrally concerned with the way the subject is constructed and inhabited by the language of "the Other." Lacan makes much the same point implied in Stephen's remarks about the words and voices that speak through him: "What I, Lacan,

---

[26]Joyce's remarks were made in an interview with Dr. Daniel Brody in 1954. Quoted by Ellmann, *James Joyce*, pp. 641–42.

following the traces of the Freudian excavation, am telling you is that the subject as such is uncertain because he is divided by the effects of language. Through the effects of speech, the subject always realizes himself more in the Other, but he is already pursuing there more than half of himself. He will simply find his desire ever more divided, pulverized, in the circumscribable metonymy of speech."27 The status of the subject is as "uncertain" an "effect of language" in the modern novel as it is in Lacanian theory. Stephen has already realized in his own life as it is portrayed in *A Portrait* what Lacan would theorize: "It is the world of words that creates the world of things."28

The Lacanian project of "returning to Freud" might even be read as repeating the corrective Joyce provided for the direction in which Jung and others had taken psychoanalysis. "Bringing the psychoanalytic experience back to the Word and Language as its grounding is of direct concern to its technique," Lacan claims. "Psychoanalysis may not actually be drifting off into the ineffable," he says, "but there has undoubtedly been a tendency in this direction." (53).29 The force of these correspondences between the conception of the subject as an effect of the language of "the Other" in Joyce and Lacan suggests that representations of the self in the modern novel may have revised psychoanalysis as much as psychoanalytic theory revised the modern conception of the self—not unlike the way in which the nineteenth-century novel provided material for the first wave of psychoanalytic theory.

In his dismissals of psychoanalysis, Joyce often joked that his name would be the same as Freud's if it were translated into German. It is a joke that may signify the novelist's unconscious awareness that Freud, whose name he shared, was also one of his "old fathers" and "old artificers," standing him in good stead when he forged the conscience of his own race. Like Stephen in his ambivalent relationship to Catholicism, Joyce and the other modernists may be saturated by the psychoanalysis in which they say they disbelieve. Lacan hints at the possibility of a transference and countertransference between the novels of Joyce and the development of psychoanalysis when in the same sentence in which he admits to being "preoccupied" by the Joyce who refused analysis and whose work exhibits that refusal, he also concedes that "art" was "an element in which Freud did not bathe without mishap."30 Lacan may have been contaminated by the same medium in his effort to bring psychoanalysis back to its grounding in the word and language, just as Joyce may have been influenced by the "esthetic of the dream" as it was defined by the Freud whose analysis he shunned.

27Lacan, "From Love to the Libido," in *Four Fundamental Concepts*, p. 188.
28Lacan, "The Function and Field of Speech and Language in Psychoanalysis," *Ecrits*, trans. Alan Sheridan (1977), p. 65.
29Lacan, *Speech and Language in Psychoanalysis*, p. 53.
30Lacan, Preface to the English Edition of *Four Fundamental Concepts*, p. ix.

Losing the Thread of the Dream
in Beckett's Trilogy

> Perhaps it's all a dream, all a dream, that would surprise me, I'll wake, in
> the silence, and never sleep again, it will be I, or dream, dream again
> dream of a silence.
>
> —Samuel Beckett, *The Unnamable*

In 1934, the year in which he began writing his first novel, his friends persuaded Samuel Beckett to enter psychoanalysis at the Tavistock Clinic in London. The writer's friends were concerned about the deep depression that had made him ill, had driven him to contemplate suicide on a number of occasions, and had even caused him to avoid sleeping because he was so afraid of his dreams. But it was Beckett's familiarity with the literary aspects of psychoanalysis which finally moved him to begin analysis.[31] From the start, Beckett's sessions with the analyst dealt more often than not with literary matters, and specifically with his struggles as a writer. *Murphy*, the novel he wrote during this same period, offered a direct literary response to Beckett's experience with psychoanalysis, or at least an artistic displacement of the depression that had threatened his life and haunted his dreams. The novel is set in a psychiatric hospital where the protagonist takes a job and becomes obsessed with one of the patients. It ends with Murphy's apparent suicide. But the trilogy of novels that was to follow *Murphy* expressed Beckett's response to psychoanalysis and its relation to literature in a more profound and complex way. These texts are Beckett's great contribution to the development of the novel and to the literature of subjectivity. They also indicate how deeply the postmodern novel redefined the dialogic relationship between the art of the novel and the science of psychoanalysis.

In *Molloy*, *Malone Dies*, and *The Unnamable*, Beckett performs a surgical dismemberment of traditional novelistic notions of the subject and an extended interrogation of the language with which we have distinguished the operation of the conscious mind from that of the unconscious. In the world of these texts, there is no purpose in attempting to construct a coherent self-representation, since what we call "the individual" is only a "succession of individuals" anyway. "At the best, all that is realised in Time," Beckett argues in his essay on Proust, "can only be possessed successively, by a series of partial annexations—and never integrally and at once."[32] Rather than make a series of self-amendments or acquire a number of "formal tales" about the self like those Stephen Dedalus acquired in *A Portrait*, the succes-

---

[31]Deirdre Bair, *Samuel Beckett: A Biography* (1978), pp. 174, 177–78.
[32]Beckett, *Proust* (New York: Grove Press, 1978), p. 7, hereafter cited in the text.

sion of narrators who speak through Beckett's trilogy involve themselves in a series of self-repudiations. Their quest is not for the dream that precedes someone else's interpretation but for the silence that precedes the dream of the self. Their persistent anxiety, however, is that such a prelinguistic state, free of desire and free of the tyranny of words, is itself a chimera produced in the inescapable laboratory of language.

"There is no great difference," Beckett says in his description of memory in Proust, "between the memory of a dream and the memory of reality. When the sleeper awakes, this emissary of his habit assures him that his 'personality' has not disappeared with his fatigue" (20). There is no great difference between the memory of a dream and the memory of reality in Beckett's own fiction either—in his case precisely because the speaker's "personality," whether in a dream or in reality, is constantly appearing and disappearing into another. Beckett's speakers spend their existence in what seems to be a dream state, but in which waking and sleeping are never clearly distinguished, and "the loss of consciousness," as Malone says, is "never any great loss."[33] What does seem to be lost to Malone and to the whole succession of evanescent narrators in Beckett's trilogy, however, is the ability (or the desire) to recollect and make sense of their dreams and thereby to maintain some trace of the "habit" of a continuous personality. The novels are composed, then, of a series of narrating voices, each of whose "waking was a kind of sleeping," as Molloy says, each of whom lives out the sentence of the figure Hugh Kenner claims is the basis of all Beckett's fiction—Dante's Belacqua, who spent eternity "dreaming over, at his ease, a whole life spent in dreaming."[34] "There were times when I forgot not only who I was," says Molloy, "but forgot that I was, forgot to be." "You have to be careful," he continues, "ask yourself questions, as for example whether you still are, and if no when it stopped, and if yes how long it will still go on, anything at all to keep you from losing the thread of the dream" (M, 65–66).

But these dreamers are constantly losing the thread of the dream, regardless of the questions they ask. Even the questions get away from them, and those who ask the questions cannot be sure whether they produce them or are produced by them. The Unnamable is puzzled by precisely this dilemma when he wonders, "If it's I who speak, and it may be assumed that it is, as it may be suspected it is not, how it happens, if it's I who speak, that I speak without ceasing, that I long to cease, that I can't cease" (143). For him, as for all Beckett's narrators, there is no possibility of constructing an account of

---

[33]Beckett, *Malone Dies* (New York: Grove Press, 1978), p. 6, hereafter abbreviated *MD* and cited in the text. The French editions of *Malone Dies* and *Malloy* were first published in 1951. The first English edition of *Malone Dies* appeared in 1958, and of *Molloy* in 1959.

[34]Beckett, *Molloy*, trans. Patrick Bowles (New York: Grove Press, 1978), p. 71, hereafter abbreviated *M* and cited in the text. The reference to Kenner is from Hugh Kenner, *Samuel Beckett: A Critical Study* (1961), p. 19.

the self from the dream or of providing an interpretation of the dream, not only because memory cannot be trusted and not only because there is never any certainty as to whether one is dreaming or not. More fundamentally, it is because one cannot even be certain whose voice speaks in the dream. "The desire of the dream is not assumed by the subject who says 'I' in his speech," Lacan says in an apparent echo of a Beckett narrator. "Articulated nevertheless in the locus of the Other, it is discourse— a discourse whose grammar Freud has begun to declare to be such."[35]

We might take Lacan's point here and argue that Beckett's novels, like Lacan's *Ecrits*, do not repudiate what Freud had said about the dream or the dreamer as much as they continue speaking in the discourse whose grammar he had begun to declare. Philip Rieff argues that many post-Freudian psychoanalysts distorted the primarily analytic orientation of Freud's theories of the unconscious in the effort to create a therapeutic culture—or, as in the case of Jung, a simulacrum of the old one—in which therapy took the place of faith.[36] Lacan's critique of the psychoanalytic establishment is launched against just such a therapeutic culture, which in his view has formalized technique and lost sight of the central dynamic character of Freudian theory. Current psychoanalytic technique, he says, "has in fact assumed the air of a formalism pushed to ceremonial lengths, and so much so that one might very well wonder whether it is not to be tagged with the same similarity to obsessional neurosis that Freud so convincingly defined in the observance, if not in the genesis, of religious rites." Lacan sought to correct this error by returning psychoanalysis to its analytic origins and emphasizing its linguistic aspects for practical as well as theoretical reasons: "Bringing the psychoanalytic experience back to the Word and to Language as its grounding is of direct concern to its technique."[37] Beckett sought to bring the novel back to the same ground, and to expose its complicity in the neurotic cultural obsession with the conception of a unified self.

If Lacan's task is to "keep on thinking the intolerable Freudian thought" by insisting that "repressed doctrine make its disruptive return to psychoanalysis," Beckett's fiction had already inserted the same disruptive force into the novelistic conception of character, denying the novel the kind of ceremonial, therapeutic formalism Lacan denied to psychoanalysis.[38] Beckett and Lacan both emphasize the necessarily subversive aspects of their respective disciplines by challenging the authority of any discourse that rigidifies or formalizes our conception of personality, whether it is therapeutic, economic, or political. In his essay on the *nouveau roman*, Alain Robbe-Grillet regards it as only "natural" that the novel, an art form that "claims to

[35]Lacan, "The Direction of the Treatment and the Principles of Its Power," in *Ecrits*, p. 264.
[36]See Philip Rieff, *The Triumph of the Therapeutic: Uses of Faith after Freud* (1966), pp. 29–34.
[37]Lacan, *Speech and Language in Psychoanalysis*, pp. 5, 53.
[38]See Bowie, *Freud, Proust and Lacan*, p. 103.

precede systems of thought and not to follow them, should already be in the process of melting down the terms" in which "character" has traditionally been formulated. He singles out the "hero-narrators" that have "occupied the sentences" in Beckett's novels as illustrating the point most dramatically: "Once these hero-narrators begin ever so little to resemble 'characters,' they are immediately liars, schizophrenics, or victims of hallucination."[39] For Beckett, and for other postmodern novelists, the nineteenth-century conception of the individual subject is itself the symptom of a cultural obsession, a "habit" that must be broken and seen for what it is if the truth is to be known about who we are.

As in many of the novels that precede his, Beckett's reformulation of the self takes place in the discourse in which his characters tell their dreams. But in Beckett's work, that discourse is questioned as soon as it is uttered. In the voice of Malone, Beckett makes two characteristically subversive points about what he calls "the long dream" of our individual subjectivity: "All my life long I have dreamt of the moment when, edified at last, in so far as one can be before all is lost, I might draw the line and make the tot" (*MD*, 4). Malone says, first, that he has dreamed "all his life long" and, second, that the desire of his dream is that he could master and interpret it—that he might awake from the dream and make something of it. The notion of the totalized, unified self, that is, is not a preexistent reality disrupted by the dream's distorted images. On the contrary, it is an illusory ideal, a wish, extrapolated from the fragmentation of the dream itself. The last page of *The Unnamable* makes essentially the same claim, tracing the illusion of the self that dreams ("I") to its obscure origin in language. "Perhaps it's a dream, all a dream," he says; "that would surprise me, I'll wake, in the silence, and never sleep again, it will be I, or dream, dream again, dream of a silence, a dream silence, full of murmurs, I don't know, that's all words, never wake, all words, there's nothing else, you must go on, that's all I know" (179). The distinction between dream and waking, between silence and speech, becomes unimportant when there is only language, when all we know is relayed through the words that murmur in our conscious and unconscious minds alike. By blurring the boundary between the illusory images of a prelinguistic unconscious and the linguistic structuration of the conscious mind, Beckett equates the problem of interpreting the dream—of adding it up and making the tot—with the confused, distorted work of the dream itself. He also turns the narrator's act of trying, and failing, to tell his own story into the only story that the novel can tell.

The hidden plot of retaining the privilege of narrative voice which I have described as repressed beneath the surface of the manifest plot in many first-person novels is thus made into the manifest plot of Beckett's trilogy. His

[39] Alain Robbe-Grillet, *For a New Novel: Essays on Fiction* (1989), pp. 160, 112, 162.

narrators are very much aware of the voices that conflict within their text and they constantly refer to that conflict. They know that the essential issue they confront is that they cannot be entirely sure whether or not they are the authors of the words they speak, or even if they speak those words. They tell their tales amidst a continuous drone of mysterious, competing voices, a "mixed choir," as Malone says, which is composed of their own thoughts, the words of the characters they have invented, and a host of other unrecognizable voices that speak to and through them. "It's entirely a matter of voices," the Unnamable says in summarizing the substance of the text he narrates; "it's a question of voices, of voices to keep going, in the right manner" (52, 66). "I have no voice and must speak," he says earlier on, "that is all I know" (26). There is very little that we can know in Beckett's work, very little we can hope for in the way of "cure" from the disease of which our dreams are symptoms. Rather than seek a speaking cure, in fact, his narrators long for a cure from the disease of language. Rather than desire to capitalize upon their dreams, they desire to end the confused sequence of dreaming, waking, and accounting for themselves. Instead of seeking to unify the fragmented state of their unconscious, they wish for release into a "dream silence" from which—unlike Stephen Dedalus—they would never have to wake (179).

Lacan's celebrated return to Freud resembles the reaction of Beckett and many other postmodernist writers to their high-modernist predecessors as it is described by Allen Thiher. The hostility to symbolism in the postmoderns, he says, "is part of a more general refusal, one that I take to be characteristic of postmodern writers in general, of the idea that language can be subject to any court of appeal other than its own self-contained surface. Latent contents, hidden depths, signs grounded in something other than signs—these are ideas that have failed to survive as part of the modernist legacy."[40] Beckett's treatment of dreams—like Lacan's—demonstrates this refusal. In Beckett's work the dream cannot be regarded as a series of hidden, symbolic meanings that can be deciphered by some interpretive language. Dreams are already produced by some mastering language, some alien voice that is not qualitatively different from the language of waking life. "Fortunately it's all a dream," the voice of the *Unnamable* concludes tentatively at one point, troubled that while he knows he is sometimes asleep and sometimes awake, he is incapable of detecting any appreciable difference between the confused voices that echo in each state. "I must doze off from time to time with open eyes," he says in bewilderment, "and yet nothing changes, ever. Gaps, there have always been gaps, it's the voice stopping, the voice failing to carry me" (114). Beckett's narrators know that their identities depend on language, on their ability to make accounts, on their voices "carrying" them and establish-

---

[40]Allen Thiher, *Words in Reflection: Modern Language Theory and Postmodern Fiction* (1984), p.100.

ing some continuity within the subject. But they find that the "gaps" and disorders of distortion characterize the language of the conscious and the unconscious alike. These subjects have no essential status apart from the words they speak, which carry them into being. And the words of consciousness have no more stability than those that murmur in their dreams. "Words and images run riot in my head," Malone admits, "pursuing, flying, clashing, merging, endlessly" (*MD*, 22).

The situation of these figures who seek to define themselves in the very words that seem to erase them resembles the situation of the subject as described by Lacan. "I identify myself in language," he says, "but only by losing myself in it like an object. What is realized in my history is not the past definite of what was, since it is no more, or even the present perfect of what has been in what I am, but the future anterior of what I shall have been for what I am in the process of becoming."[41] For all their efforts at telling the story of their past, even the unconscious of Beckett's narrators seems—like Lacan's—to be invented by the words they speak. Rather than tell the story of who the speaker is, those words act as the medium in which the speakers lose and objectify themselves. Beckett's narrators are, therefore, constantly becoming someone else in the process of trying to identify who they are in language. That is why the narrators' names keep changing, even though the substance of their stories alters very little. They may come to recognize that all they have to carry them is their voices, but they nevertheless continually get lost in the words their voices speak.

The development of Beckett's ideas about the nature of the unconscious is intricately interwoven with his encounter with psychoanalysis. During the time he was in analysis and writing *Murphy*, Beckett attended a lecture by Jung on the subject of dream analysis. The experience moved him deeply and gave impetus to his emerging conception of the unconscious as a field of contending discourses. Jung's lecture described the unconscious as consisting of "complexes" with fragmentary personalities of their own, which, when they appear in dreams and visions, "speak in voices which are like the voices of other people."[42] Jung seemed to Beckett to be perfectly describing his own sense of things, to be corroborating the validity of his characterization of Murphy's fragmented personality. The lecture also prompted him in his subsequent novels to take the idea a step farther, producing a succession of dreamers who assume the voice of some other person each time they awaken.

Even in its structure, *Molloy* tells this tale. When, in the second part of the novel, Moran is sent out to find the lost narrator of the first part (Molloy), Moran also takes over the narrating responsibility from Molloy, only to repeat the same story attempted by his lost predecessor. But Moran tells his

---

[41]Lacan, "The Function and Field of Speech and Language in Psychoanalysis," in *Ecrits*, p. 86.

[42]Bair, *Samuel Beckett*, p. 208.

version of the tale in what he calls "an ambiguous voice," which he claims is inexplicably "within me" but "is not mine" (*M*, 180). He even begins to question whether he might not be Molloy, since this object of his quest has come to preoccupy his thoughts and language so profoundly. Molloy had suffered under the same confusion, convinced that the words he spoke were not his own either but were being spoken through him by some ghostly predecessor:

> And every time I say, I said this, or I said that, or speak of a voice saying, far away inside me, Molloy, and then a fine phrase more or less clear and simple, or find myself compelled to attribute to others intelligible words, or hear my own voice uttering to others more or less articulate sounds, I am merely complying with the convention that demands you either lie or hold your peace. For what really happened was quite different. . . . In reality I said nothing at all, but I heard a murmur, something gone wrong with the silence. (*M*, 118–19)

The states of dream and waking are both contained within this linguistic maze for all the narrators of Beckett's trilogy. Both seem to be dictated by some alien voice within, to be the objects as well as the subjects of their discourse, and to be evidence for Lacan's claim that "the unconscious of the subject is the discourse of the other."[43] "About myself I need know nothing," concedes the Unnamable. "But the discourse must go on. So one invents obscurities" (7).

As the categories of the conscious and unconscious are exposed as the obscure and unstable contrivances of language in Beckett's trilogy, so are all the specific discourses of subjectivity by which the novel has formulated its conception of character. If the novel is the manner in which society speaks itself, Stephen Heath argues, the postmodern novel of writers like Beckett "is an essentially critical enterprise directed at a questioning of the assumptions of the Balzacian novel and, through that, of the habitual forms in which we define or write our lives."[44] Beckett's narrators begin that attack by challenging such notions as the medicalization of the self and exposing them as arbitrary discursive formulations. These figures invariably complain of some unnamed illness from which they cannot recover. But as Molloy admits, their psychic and bodily pain is merely part of an illusory habit of self-definition, nothing more than a "bad dream" they agree to indulge: "It is at the mercy of these sensations, which happily I know to be illusory, that I have to live and work. It is thanks to them I find myself a meaning. So he whom a pain suddenly awakes. He stiffens, ceases to breathe, waits, says, It's a bad dream, or, It's a touch of neuralgia, breathes again, sleeps again, still trembling" (151–52). "For I was already in the toils of earnestness," Malone

[43]Lacan, *Ecrits*, p. 55.
[44]Stephen Heath, *The Nouveau Roman: A Study in the Practice of Writing* (1972), p. 33.

adds. "That has been my disease" (18). Beckett's narrators consistently recognize that their descriptions of their physical and psychic illnesses are merely stories they tell themselves to find some meaning, "discourses" that do not heal them but which define their dreams and make up their disease.

In much the same way, the conception of the self as an economic entity struggling to gain possession of its psychic resources is exposed as an illusory device to contrive meaning and continuity for a fragmented personality. The economic "story" of the subject in the trilogy is summarized most cogently by Moran as the "growing recognition of being dispossessed of self" (*M*, 204). "Strictly speaking," Malone says to dramatize the point, "it is impossible for me to know, from one moment to the next, what is mine and what is not, according to my definition" (79). "I am lost," he concludes at last. "Not a word"—as if his loss of self is equivalent to his loss of the words to describe himself and give himself "definition" (92). Finally, the political psychology of the personality is both offered and taken away in the trilogy as well. Regardless of the elaborate mechanisms Beckett's characters contrive to govern their own behavior, their psyches are in a continual state of rebellion, alternately occupied and evacuated by "regiments of dragoons" or "delegates" who are intent upon "usurping" control of their minds and bodies alike (*TU*, 12, 20). The discourses of personal health, self-possession, and self-governance which dominated the nineteenth-century novel are repeatedly tested and then exposed in the trilogy as the agents of an absolute linguistic authority that seeks to contain the subject in a conception of itself as unified. "Even my sense of identity was wrapped in a namelessness often hard to penetrate," Molloy admits. "All I know is what the words know" (41).

That Beckett's narrators keep entertaining the theoretical possibility of an underlying namelessness that may exist beneath the wrapping of words seems to distinguish them from Lacan. They resist the final concession that there is no desire that is not produced by language, and they cling to the dream of a silence that precedes the words that envelop them. They cannot affirm that prospect as anything more than a wish, however. In the practice of their writing, Beckett and Lacan both reproduce the very "writerly" conception of the self initiated by Freud, in which the psyche translates and reinscribes itself indefinitely among a host of discursive conventions while it lends absolute authority to none. In the trilogy Beckett also performs this exercise by imitating and then emptying out the very formal conventions of the novel which have helped to construct the popular conception of personality. "The thing to avoid," says the Unnamable in defense of this principle of self-cancellation, "is the spirit of system" (4). *Molloy* avoids that spirit by presenting itself first as a novelistic quest for origins and an attempt by Molloy to explain in his writing of this autobiographical text how he came to occupy his mother's room. Then, midway through, Molloy disappears and the text turns into a parodic detective novel in which the investigating agent

Moran is deployed to find the missing narrator and protagonist. The next novel in the trilogy, *Malone Dies*, also imitates an autobiographical novel, and this one too has been turned inside out. The narrator begins by telling the story not of his life but of his death. His words recount not a gradual self-discovery or self-possession but a gradual loss of himself, his belongings, and any conception of what a "self" may be. *The Unnamable* extends the steady decomposition of narrative and psychic definition begun by its predecessors by retreating into a seemingly eviscerated, labyrinthine gothic text in which a host of "voluble shades" generate a "hell of stories" (122, 130). The terror experienced by all these narrative voices, however, is not of their loss of authority over themselves but of being unable to lose that authority, of never waking from the perpetual dream of those alien, disquieting words that, paradoxically, produce the unrealizable desire for silence.

To speak of dreams in Beckett's work, then, is to speak of the desire not to unify and reassure the self but to confront the self with its inescapable multiplicity and fictionality. Dreams may or may not be memories, as Freud claimed they were. But any effort to unify and master the disparate images of the dream through language and to transform them into a coherent expression of a single "individual" only corroborates the status of the individual as an illusory effect of one social discourse or another. The articulation of this problem in Beckett's fiction speaks to one of the central paradoxes of psychoanalytic theory: that the unconscious is at once structured like a language of its own and yet functions in opposition to the order and ordering of language. "The unconscious is that part of the concrete discourse," Lacan says in elaboration of this paradox, "in so far as it is transindividual, that is not at the disposal of the subject in re-establishing the continuity of his conscious discourse." The unconscious is a discourse that both produces and interrupts the conscious discourse of the individual. "The fact that desire was discovered by Freud in its place in the dream," he says later, "which has always been the stumbling-block of any attempt on the part of thought to situate itself in reality, should be sufficient lesson for us."[45] This stumbling block litters the territory that Beckett and other postmodern novelists painfully and tediously explore. Their narrators repeatedly present themselves as fitfully starting from the dreams they cannot even be sure were dreams at all, uncertain whether what they say about those dreams is invented or recollected. "Saying is inventing," says Molloy, who then immediately retracts the statement. "Wrong, very rightly wrong" (*M*, 41). Beckett's Molloy, like Conrad's Marlow, is suspicious that whatever he says is a distortion of the truth. At the same time he suspects, in a more radical way than Joyce's Stephen Dedalus, that he can distort nothing, that whatever he says is dictated by some voice within him which is not his own. "You invent noth-

[45]Lacan, *Ecrits*, pp. 49, 263.

ing," he continues; "you think you are inventing, you think you are escaping, and all you do is stammer out your lesson, the remnants of a pensum one day got by heart and long forgotten, life without tears, as it is wept" (41).

Lacan's description of the subject as an effect of language reads like a commentary on Molloy's words and those of all his successors. "Yes, the truth of his history is not all contained in his script," Lacan says, "and yet the place is marked there by the painful shocks he feels from knowing only his own lines, and not simply there, but also in pages whose disorder gives him little comfort."[46] Caught in the painful region between dream and waking, between invention and memory, between story and history, the voices that produce Beckett's disordered pages live their lives in a "perpetual dream" in which, according to the Unnamable, in order to dream "you merely have to sleep, not even that" (128). Since they don't even have to sleep to dream or to experience the gaps and shocks and confusion that riddle their perpetually troubled dreams, Beckett's narrators cannot awaken from or account for those dreams with any confidence about who speaks or even who dreams. In these texts, the dreamer is as imaginary a construct as his dream. "I nearly said, as in a dream," Molloy catches himself saying to give us the sense of his confusion, and then adds as if to acknowledge the impossibility of making the distinction between himself and his dream, "but no, no" (53).

Freud described the doubting of our ability to remember our dreams clearly and accurately as a form of resistance. Certainty, he claimed, was not important in dream interpretation. "In analysing a dream," Freud says, "I insist that the whole scale of estimates of certainty shall be abandoned and that the faintest possibility that something of this or that sort may have occurred in the dream shall be treated as complete certainty" (*Interpretation of Dreams*, 516–17). By thus suspending the scale of certainty, "it is always possible to go *some* distance: far enough, at all events, to convince ourselves that the dream is a structure with a meaning" (525). Beckett seems to take the opposite course. In suspending the scale of certainty, he holds everything in doubt, especially that our dreams—or our lives—can be construed as structures with a meaning. But in the effort to tell their stories, Beckett's narrators cannot dismiss the possibility either. "How tell what remains," the voice of "The Calmative" asks, echoing the perpetual dilemma of all Beckett's dreamers. "But it's the end. Or have I been dreaming, am I dreaming? No, no, none of that, for dream is nothing, a joke, and significant what is worse" (43). In his quest for "the end," Beckett cannot ignore the possibility that though our dreams may be nothing, they may also be significant. They may mean. His narrators continue the effort of the narrators of novels that came before them, therefore, attempting to tell their dreams as they tell their lives, to make something out of nothing.

[46]Ibid., p. 55.

Beckett's remark about the inescapable sense of a serious meaning lurking behind jokes and dreams seems to be a direct allusion to Freud, and his attempt to dismiss the importance of dreams slips into a reminder of their significance, or at least of our habitual desire to make them so. The remark reveals how writers after Freud, including Joyce and Beckett, have absorbed many of the impulses and problems that were brought into focus by the gothic, autobiographical, and detective fiction of the nineteenth century—as well as by the psychoanalytic discourse that fiction helped invent. Beckett's novels become at least in part exercises in analysis, just as they resist any systematic formal analysis. They are, perhaps, among the inquiries into dreams toward which Freud pointed in the last chapter of *The Interpretation of Dreams*—those inquiries that must approach the kernel of the same problem he approached from another angle (511). Along with other modernist and postmodernist novels, they are the fictions of the unconscious which allow the theory of psychoanalysis to be rethought. But they are also the novelists' collective assertion that the dream—like our conception of ourselves—is an act of imagination which ultimately eludes analysis. These novels stand as reminders that the dreams of our unconscious will always derive their authority as much from the disruptive energies of literature as from the explanatory systems of science.

Bibliography

Armstrong, Nancy. *Desire and Domestic Fiction: A Political History of the Novel.* New York: Oxford University Press, 1987.

Auerbach, Nina. *Woman and the Demon: The Life of a Victorian Myth.* Cambridge: Harvard University Press, 1982.

Aylmer, Felix. *The Drood Case.* London: R. Hart-Davis, 1964.

Bagehot, Walter. "Charles Dickens" (1858). In *Literary Studies.* London, 1898.

Bahti, Timothy. "Figures of Interpretation, the Interpretation of Figures: A Reading of Wordsworth's 'Arab Dream.'" *Studies in Romanticism* 18 (1979): 601–27.

Bair, Deirdre. *Samuel Beckett: A Biographer.* New York: Harcourt, Brace, Jovanovitch, 1978.

Bakhtin, Mikhail. *The Dialogic Imagination.* Edited by Michael Holquist. Translated by Caryl Emerson and Michael Holquist. Austin: University of Texas Press, 1981.

_____. *Problems of Dostoevsky's Poetics.* Translated by R. W. Rotsel. Ann Arbor: Ardis Press, 1973.

Barthes, Roland. *S/Z.* Translated by Richard Miller. New York: Hill and Wang, 1974.

Baumgarten, Murray. "'Calligraphy and Code': Writing in *Great Expectations.*" *Dickens Studies Annual* 11 (1983): 61–72.

Beaty, Jerome. "*Jane Eyre* and Genre." *Genre* 10 (Winter 1977): 619–54.

Beckett, Samuel. *Malone Dies.* 1958; rpt. New York: Grove Press, 1978.

_____. *Molloy.* Translated by Patrick Bowles. 1959; rpt. New York: Grove Press. 1978.

_____. *Proust.* New York: Grove Press, 1978.

_____. *Stories and Texts for Nothing.* New York: Grove Press, 1967.

_____. *The Unnamable.* 1959; rpt. New York: Grove Press, 1978.

Bernard, Catherine A. "Dickens and Victorian Dream Theory." In *Victorian Science and Victorian Values: Literary Perspectives.* Edited by James Paradis and Thomas Postlewait. New York: New York Academy of Sciences, 1981: 197–216.

291

Bersani, Leo. *A Future for Astyanax: Character and Desire in Literature.* Boston: Little, Brown, 1976.

Bivona, Daniel. "Alice the Child-Imperialist and the Games of Wonderland." *Nineteenth-Century Literature* 41 (September 1986): 143–71.

Bloch, Ernst. "A Philosophical View of the Detective Novel." In Bloch, *The Utopian Function of Art and Literature.* Translated by Jack Zipes and Frank Mecklenburg. Cambridge, Mass.: MIT Press, 1987: 244–64.

Block, Ed, Jr. "James Sully, Evolutionist Psychology, and Late Victorian Gothic." *Victorian Studies* 25 (Summer 1982): 443–67.

Bloom, Harold. *"Frankenstein, or the Modern Prometheus."* In Bloom, *Ringers in the Tower.* Chicago: University of Chicago Press, 1971: 119–29.

_____. *Poetry and Repression: Revision from Blake to Stevens.* New Haven: Yale University Press, 1976.

Bodenheimer, Rosemarie. "Jane Eyre in Search of Her Story." *Papers on Language and Literature* 16 (Fall 1980): 387–402.

Bowie, Malcolm. *Freud, Proust, and Lacan: Theory as Fiction.* Cambridge: Cambridge University Press, 1987.

Brantlinger, Patrick. *Rule of Darkness: British Literature and Imperialism, 1830–1914.* Ithaca: Cornell University Press, 1988.

_____. "Victorians and Africans: The Genealogy of the Myth of the Dark Continent." *Critical Inquiry* 12 (Autumn 1985): 166–203.

Brontë, Charlotte. *Jane Eyre.* Edited by Richard J. Dunn. New York: W. W. Norton, 1971.

Brontë, Emily. *Wuthering Heights.* Edited by Hilda Marsden and Ian Jack. Oxford: Oxford University Press, 1981.

Brooks, Peter. "Godlike Science/Unhallowed Arts: Language, Nature, and Monstrosity." In *The Endurance of "Frankenstein": Essays on Mary Shelley's Novel.* Edited by U. C. Knoepflmacher and George Levine. Berkeley: University of California Press, 1979: 205–20.

_____. *Reading for the Plot: Design and Intention in Narrative.* New York: Knopf, 1984.

_____. "Repetition, Repression, and Return: *Great Expectations* and the Study of Plot." *New Literary History* 11 (Spring 1980): 503–26.

Bruss, Elizabeth W. *Autobiographical Acts: The Changing Situation of a Literary Genre.* Baltimore: Johns Hopkins University Press, 1976.

Calder, Jenni. *Robert Louis Stevenson: A Life Study.* New York: Oxford University Press, 1980.

Carroll, Lewis. *The Annotated Alice.* Edited by Martin Gardner. New York: New American Library, 1960.

Cawelti, John G. *Adventure, Mystery, and Romance: Formula Stories as Art and Popular Culture.* Chicago: University of Chicago Press, 1976.

Certeau, Michel de. *Heterologies: Discourse on the Other.* Translated by Brian Massumi. Minneapolis: University of Minnesota Press, 1986.

Champigny, Robert. *What Will Have Happened: A Philosophical and Technical Essay on Mystery Stories.* Bloomington: Indiana University Press, 1977.

Chase, Cynthia. "Accidents of Disfiguration." *Studies in Romanticism* 18(1979): 547–66.

Coleridge, Samuel Taylor. *Poetical Works.* Edited by Ernest Hartley Coleridge. London: Oxford University Press, 1967.

Collins, Philip. *Dickens and Crime.* New York: St. Martin's Press, 1962.

Collins, Wilkie. *The Moonstone.* Edited by J. I. M. Stewart. Harmondsworth, Eng.: Penguin, 1966.

Conrad, Joseph. *Heart of Darkness.* Harmondsworth, Eng.: Penguin, 1973.

_____. *Lord Jim.* Boston: Houghton Mifflin, 1958.

Davis, Nuel Pharr. *The Life of Wilkie Collins.* Urbana: University of Illinois Press, 1956.

Davis, Robert Con, ed. *Lacan and Narration: The Psychoanalytic Difference in Narrative Theory.* Baltimore: Johns Hopkins University Press, 1983.

Day, William Patrick. *In the Circles of Fear and Desire: A Study of Gothic Fantasy.* Chicago: University of Chicago Press, 1985.

DeFoe, Daniel. *Robinson Crusoe.* Harmondsworth, Eng.: Penguin, 1965.

DeLuca, V. A. *Thomas DeQuincey: The Prose of Vision.* Toronto: University of Toronto Press, 1980.

DeQuincey, Thomas. *The Collected Writings of Thomas DeQuincey.* Edited by David Masson. 14 vols. Edinburgh: Adam and Charles Black, 1889–90.

_____. *Confessions of an English Opium-Eater.* Edited by Alethea Hayter. Harmondsworth, Eng.: Penguin, 1978.

_____. *Confessions of an English Opium-Eater, the English Mail Coach, and Suspiria.* London: Constable, 1927.

Derrida, Jacques. "Freud and the Scene of Writing." In Derrida, *Writing and Difference.* Chicago: University of Chicago Press, 1978: 196–231.

Dexter, Walter, ed. *The Letters of Charles Dickens.* 3 vols. Bloomsbury: Nonesuch Press, 1938.

Dickens, Charles. *A Christmas Carol.* In *The Christmas Books.* Vol. 1. Harmondsworth, Eng.: Penguin Books, 1971.

_____. *Great Expectations.* Edited by Angus Calder. Harmondsworth, Eng.: Penguin, 1978.

_____. *The Mystery of Edwin Drood.* Edited by Arthur J. Cox. Harmondsworth, Eng.: Penguin, 1974.

Doody, Margaret Anne. "Deserts, Ruins, and Troubled Waters: Female Dreams in Fiction and Development of the Gothic Novel." *Genre* 10 (Winter 1977): 529–72.

Doody, Terrence. *Confession and Community in the Novel.* Baton Rouge: Louisiana State University Press, 1980.

Doyle, Arthur Conan. *The Complete Sherlock Holmes.* 2 vols. Garden City, N.Y.: Doubleday, 1930.

Duffield, Howard. "John Jasper: Strangler." *Bookman* 70 (February 1930):581–88.

Dunn, Richard J. "Narrative Distance in *Frankenstein.*" *Studies in the Novel* 6 (Winter 1974): 408–17.

Dyson, A. E. *"Edwin Drood:* A Horrible Wonder Apart." *Critical Quarterly* 11 (Summer 1969): 138–57.

Eagleton, Terry. *Literary Theory: An Introduction.* Minneapolis: University of Minnesota Press, 1984.

_____. *Myths of Power: A Marxist Study of the Brontës.* London: Macmillan, 1975.

Eigner, Edwin M. *Robert Louis Stevenson and Romantic Tradition.* Princeton: Princeton University Press, 1966.

Eliot, T. S. "Dante." In *Selected Essays of T. S. Eliot.* New York: Harcourt, Brace, and World, 1960: 199–240.

——. "Wilkie Collins and Dickens." In *Selected Essays of T. S. Eliot.* New York: Harcourt, Brace, & World, 1960: 409–18.

Ellenberger, Henri F. *The Discovery of the Unconscious: The History and Evolution of Dynamic Psychiatry.* New York: Basic Books, 1970.

Ellis, Havelock. *The Criminal.* London: Walter Scott, 1892.

Ellmann, Maud. "Disremembering Dedalus: *A Portrait of the Artist as a Young Man.*" In *Untying the Text: A Post-Structuralist Reader.* Edited by Robert Young. Boston: Routledge and Kegan Paul, 1981: 189–206.

Ellmann, Richard. *James Joyce.* Oxford: Oxford University Press, 1959.

Elwin, Malcolm. *The Strange Case of Robert Louis Stevenson.* London: MacDonald, 1950.

Felman, Shoshana, ed. *Literature and Psychoanalysis.* Baltimore: Johns Hopkins University Press, 1977.

Forster, E. M. *Aspects of the Novel.* New York: Harcourt Brace Jovanovich, 1975.

Forster, John. *The Life of Charles Dickens.* Edited by J. W. T. Ley. New York: Doubleday, 1928.

Forsyte, Charles. *The Decoding of Edwin Drood.* New York: Scribner's 1980.

Foucault, Michel. "About the Concept of the 'Dangerous Individual' in 19th-Century Legal Psychiatry." Translated by Alain Baudot and Jane Couchman. *International Journal of Law and Psychiatry* 1 (1978): 1–18.

——. *Discipline and Punish.* Translated by Alan Sheridan. New York: Vintage, 1979.

——. *The History of Sexuality.* Vol. 1: *An Introduction.* Translated by Robert Hurley. New York: Vintage, 1980.

Freud, Sigmund. *Delusion and Dream in Jensen's "Gradiva."* Translated by New York: Beacon, 1956.

——. *Standard Edition of the Complete Psychological Works of Sigmund Freud.* Edited and translated by James Strachey. London: Hogarth Press and the Institute for Psychoanalysis, 1953–72.

——. *Three Case Histories.* Edited by Phillip Rieff. New York: Collier Books, 1963.

Frey-Rohn, Liliane. *From Jung to Freud: A Comparative Study of the Psychology of the Unconscious.* Translated by Fred E. Engreen and Evelyn K. Engreen. New York: Delta, 1976.

Gardiner, Muriel, ed. *The Wolf-Man by the Wolf-Man.* New York: Basic Books, 1971.

Gérin, Winifred. *Charlotte Brontë: The Evolution of Genius.* London: Oxford University Press, 1967.

——. *Emily Brontë: A Biography.* Oxford: Oxford University Press, 1978.

Gilbert, Elliot L. " 'In Primal Sympathy': *Great Expectations* and the Secret Life." *Dickens Studies Annual* 11 (1983): 89–113.

Gilbert, Sandra M., and Susan Gubar. *The Madwoman in the Attic: The Woman Writer and the Nineteenth-Century Literary Imagination.* New Haven: Yale University Press, 1979.

Gordon, Jan B. "The Alice Books and the Metaphors of Victorian Childhood." In *Aspects of Alice.* Edited by Robert Phillips. New York: Vintage Books, 1965. 93–113.

Gregg, Hilda. "The Indian Mutiny in Fiction." *Blackwood's Magazine* 161 (February 1897): 218–31.

Grinstein, Alexander. *On Sigmund Freud's Dreams.* Detroit: Wayne State University Press, 1968.

Grunebaum, G. E., and Roger Caillois, eds. *The Dream and Human Societies.* Berkeley: University of California Press, 1966.

Guiliano, Edward, ed. *Lewis Carroll Observed.* New York: Crown, 1976.

Hafley, James. "The Villain in *Wuthering Heights.*" *Nineteenth-Century Fiction* 13 (December 1958): 199–215.

Hardy, Barbara. "The Change of Heart in Dickens's Novels." *Victorian Studies* 5 (September 1961): 49–67.

____. *Tellers and Listeners: The Narrative Imagination.* London: Athlone Press, 1975.

Hartman, Geoffrey H. *Wordsworth's Poetry.* Cambridge: Harvard University Press, 1987 (1971).

Hayter, Alethea. *Opium and the Romantic Imagination.* Berkeley: University of California Press, 1970.

Hearnshaw, L. S. *A Short History of British Psychology, 1840–1940.* London: Methuen, 1964.

Heath, Stephen. *The Nouveau Roman: A Study in the Practice of Writing.* Philadelphia: Temple University Press, 1972.

Heilman, Robert. "Charlotte Brontë's 'New' Gothic." In *The Brontës.* Edited by Ian Gregor. Englewood Cliffs, N.J.: Prentice-Hall, 1970: 96–109.

Himmelfarb, Gertrude. *The Idea of Poverty: England in the Early Industrial Age.* New York: Random House, 1985.

Hogg, James. *The Private Memoirs and Confessions of a Justified Sinner.* Oxford: Oxford University Press, 1981.

Homans, Margaret. *Bearing the Word: Language and Female Experience in Nineteenth Century Women's Writing.* Chicago: University of Chicago Press, 1986.

House, Humphry. *The Dickens World.* 2d ed. London: Oxford University Press, 1942.

Hughes, Winifred. *The Maniac in the Cellar: Sensation Novels of the 1860s.* Princeton: Princeton University Press, 1980.

Hutter, Albert. "Dreams, Transformations, and Literature: The Implications of Detective Fiction." *Victorian Studies* 19 (December 1975): 181–209.

____. "The Novelist as Resurrectionist." *Dickens Studies Annual* 12 (1984): 1–40.

James, Henry. "The Future of the Novel." In *Theory of Fiction: Henry James.* Edited by James E. Miller, Jr. Lincoln: University of Nebraska Press, 1981: 335–44.

Jameson, Fredric. *The Political Unconscious: Narrative as a Socially Symbolic Act.* Ithaca: Cornell University Press, 1981.

Johnson, Barbara. "My Monster/My Self." *Diacritics* 12 (Summer 1982): 2–10.

Johnson, Edgar. *Charles Dickens: His Tragedy and Triumph.* Revised and abridged. New York: Viking Penguin, 1986.

Jones, Ernest. *The Life and Work of Sigmund Freud.* 2 vols. New York: Basic Books, 1953.

Jordan, John O. "The Medium of *Great Expectations.*" *Dickens Studies Annual* 11 (1983): 73–88.

Joyce, James. *A Portrait of the Artist as a Young Man.* Edited by Chester G. Anderson. Harmondsworth, Eng.: Penguin, 1981.

———. *Ulysses.* New York: Random House, 1961.

Jung, C. G. *The Collected Works of C. G. Jung.* 19 vols. Edited by Sir Robert Read, Michael Fordham, Gerhard Adler, William McGuire. Translated by R. F. C. Hull. Princeton: Princeton University Press, 1953.

Katz, Michael R. *Dreams and the Unconscious in Nineteenth-Century Russian Fiction.* Hanover, NH: University of New England, 1984.

Kavanaugh, James H. *Emily Brontë.* Oxford: Basil Blackwell, 1985.

Keats, John. *Poetical Works.* Edited by H. W. Garrod. London: Oxford University Press, 1970.

Kenner, Hugh. *Joyce's Voices.* Berkeley: University of California Press, 1978.

———. *Samuel Beckett: A Critical Study.* Berkeley: University of California Press, 1961.

Ketterer, David. *Frankenstein's Creation: The Book, the Monster, and Human Reality.* Victoria, B.C.: University of Victoria Press, 1979.

Kiely, Robert. *The Romantic Novel in England.* Cambridge: Harvard University Press, 1972.

Kinkead-Weekes, Mark. "The Place of Love in *Jane Eyre* and *Wuthering Heights.*" In *The Brontës.* Edited by Ian Gregor. Englewood Cliffs, N.J.: Prentice-Hall, 1970: 76–95.

Knoepflmacher, U. C. *Laughter and Despair: Readings in Ten Novels of the Victorian Era.* University of California Press, 1971.

Kofman, Sarah. *The Enigma of Woman: Woman in Freud's Writings.* Translated by Catherine Porter. Ithaca: Cornell University Press, 1985.

Krull, Marianne. *Freud and His Father.* Translated by Arnold J. Pomerans. New York: Norton, 1976.

Kucich, John. *Repression in Victorian Fiction: Charlotte Brontë, George Eliot, and Charles Dickens.* Berkeley: University of California Press, 1986.

Lacan, Jacques. *Ecrits.* Translated by Alan Sheridan. New York: Norton, 1977.

———. *The Four Fundamental Concepts of Psychoanalysis.* Translated by Alan Sheridan. New York: Norton, 1978.

———. *Speech and Language in Psychoanalysis.* Translated by Anthony G. Wilden. Baltimore: Johns Hopkins University Press, 1982.

Lawrence, D. H. *Fantasia of the Unconscious.* Harmondsworth, Eng.: Penguin, 1979.

———. *Phoenix: The Posthumous Papers of D. H. Lawrence.* Edited by Edward D. McDonald. New York: Viking Press, 1968.

Lawson, Lewis A. "Wilkie Collins and *The Moonstone.*" *American Imago* 20 (Spring 1963): 61–79.

Leavis, F. R., and Q. D. Leavis. *Dickens the Novelist.* New Brunswick, N.J.: Rutgers University Press, 1970.

Lefanu, J. S. *Best Ghost Stories.* New York: Dover, 1964.

Lever, Karen M. "DeQuincey as Gothic Hero: A Perspective on *Confessions of an English Opium-Eater* and *Suspiria de Profundis.*" *Texas Studies in Literature and Language* 21 (Fall 1979): 332–46.

Levine, George. "The Ambiguous Heritage of *Frankenstein.*" In *The Endurance of "Frankenstein": Essays in Mary Shelley's Novel.* Edited by U. C. Knoepflmacher and George Levine. Berkeley: University of California Press, 1979: 3–30.

———. *The Realistic Imagination: English Fiction from Frankenstein to Lady Chatterley.* Chicago: University of Chicago Press, 1983.

Lukacher, Ned. *Primal Scenes: Literature, Philosophy, Psychoanalysis.* Ithaca: Cornell University Press, 1986.

Lukács, Georg. *The Theory of the Novel: An Historico-Philosophical Essay on the Forms of Great Epic Literature.* Translated by Anna Bostock. Cambridge, Mass.: MIT Press, 1982.

Lyotard, Jean-François. "The Dream-Work Does Not Think." *Oxford Literary Review* 6 (1983): 3–34.

MacAndrew, Elizabeth. *The Gothic Tradition in Fiction.* New York: Columbia University Press, 1979.

Madden, William A. "*Wuthering Heights:* The Binding of Passion." *Nineteenth-Century Fiction* 27 (September 1972): 127–54.

Malcolm, Norman. *Dreaming.* London: Routledge and Kegan Paul, 1959.

Mandel, Ernest. *Delightful Murder: A Social History of the Crime Story.* Minneapolis: University of Minnesota Press, 1984.

Marcus, Steven. "Freud and Dora: Story, History, Case History." In Marcus, *Representations: Essays on Literature and Society.* New York: Random House, 1974: 247–310.

Marx, Karl. *Capital.* Translated by Ben Fowkes. 2 vols. New York: Random House, 1977.

Meltzer, Françoise, ed. *The Trial(s) of Psychoanalysis.* Chicago: University of Chicago Press, 1988.

Miller, D. A. "From *Roman Policier* to *Roman-Police:* Wilkie Collins's *The Moonstone.*" *Novel* 13 (Winter 1980): 153–70.

Miller, J. Hillis. *Charles Dickens: The World of His Novels.* Cambridge: Harvard University Press, 1958.

———. *The Disappearance of God: Five Nineteenth-Century Writers.* Cambridge, Mass.: Belknap Press, 1975.

———. *Fiction and Repetition: Seven English Novels.* Cambridge: Harvard University Press, 1982.

———. "The Stone and the Shell: The Problem of Poetic Form in Wordsworth's Dream of the Arab." In *Untying the Text: A Post-Structuralist Reader.* Edited by Robert Young. London: Routledge and Kegan Paul, 1981: 244–65.

Mitchell, Charles. "*The Mystery of Edwin Drood:* The Interior and Exterior of Self." *ELH* 33 (June 1966): 228–46.

Moglen, Helene. *Charlotte Brontë: The Self Conceived.* Madison: University of Wisconsin Press, 1984.

Morris, James. *Heaven's Command: An Imperial Progress.* New York: Harcourt Brace Jovanovich, 1973.

Moynihan, Julian. "The Hero's Guilt: The Case of *Great Expectations.*" In *Victorian Literature.* Edited by Robert O. Preyer. New York: Harper, 1966: 126–45.

Musselwhite, David E. *Partings Welded Together: Politics and Desire in the Nineteenth-Century English Novel.* London: Methuen, 1987.

Myers, Frederick W. H. *Human Personality and Its Survival of Bodily Death.* 2 vols. New York: Longmans and Green, 1904.

Najder, Zdzislaw. *Joseph Conrad: A Chronicle.* New Brunswick, N.J.: Rutgers University Press, 1983.

Nesher, Hanna Wirth. "The Stranger Case of *The Turn of the Screw* and *Heart of Darkness.*" *Studies in Short Fiction* 16 (Fall 1979): 317–25.

Onorato, Richard J. *The Character of the Poet: Wordsworth in "The Prelude."* Princeton: Princeton University Press, 1971.

Ousby, Ian. *Bloodhounds of Heaven: The Detective in English Fiction from Godwin to Doyle.* Cambridge: Harvard University Press, 1976.

Pascal, Roy. *Design and Truth in Autobiography.* Cambridge: Harvard University Press, 1960.

Phillips, Robert S., ed. *Aspects of Alice.* New York: Vintage Books, 1971.

Poe, Edgar Allan. *The Complete Tales and Poems of Edgar Allan Poe.* New York: Modern Library, 1965.

Poovey, Mary. *The Proper Lady and the Woman Writer: Ideology as Style in the Works of Mary Wollstonecraft, Mary Shelley, and Jane Austen.* Chicago: University of Chicago Press, 1984.

Praz, Mario. "Introduction Essay." In *Three Gothic Novels.* Edited by Mario Praz. Harmondsworth, Eng.: Penguin, 1968: 7–34.

Punter, David. *The Literature of Terror: A History of Gothic Fictions from 1765 to the Present Day.* London: Longmans, 1980.

Rackin, Donald. "Alice's Journey to the End of the Night." In *Aspects of Alice.* Edited by Robert Phillips. New York: Vintage Books, 1971: 391–418.

Rapaport, Herman. "*Jane Eyre* and the *Mot Tabou.*" *Modern Language Notes* 94 (December 1979): 1093–104.

Reik, Theodor. *The Compulsion to Confess.* New York: Farrar, Straus, and Cudahy, 1945.

Ricoeur, Paul. *Freud and Philosophy: An Essay on Interpretation.* Translated by Denis Savage. New Haven: Yale University Press, 1970.

Rieff, Philip. *Freud: The Mind of the Moralist.* New York: Viking Press, 1959.

———. Introduction to Sigmund Freud, *Dora: An Analysis of a Case of Hysteria.* New York: Collier, 1963: 7–20.

———. *The Triumph of the Therapeutic: Uses of Faith after Freud.* New York: Harper and Row, 1966.

Rigby, Elizabeth. Review of *Jane Eyre. Quarterly Review* 84 (December 1848): 153–85.

Robbe-Grillet, Alain. *For a New Novel: Essays on Fiction.* Evanston, Ill., Northwestern University Press, 1989.

Robert, Marthe. *From Oedipus to Moses: Freud's Jewish Identity.* Translated by Ralph Manheim. Garden City, N.Y.: Anchor Books, 1976.

Robinson, Kenneth. *Wilkie Collins: A Biography.* New York: Macmillan, 1952.

Roussel, Roy. "The Completed Story in *The Mystery of Edwin Drood.*" *Criticism* 20 (Fall 1978): 383–402.

Rubenstein, Marc A. "My Accursed Origin': The Search for the Mother in *Frankenstein.*" *Studies in Romanticism* 15 (Spring 1976): 165–94.

Rycroft, Charles. "A Detective Story: Psychoanalytic Observations." *Psychoanalytic Quarterly* 20 (1957): 229–45.

Sadoff, Dianne F. *Monsters of Affection: Dickens, Eliot, and Brontë on Fatherhood.* Baltimore: Johns Hopkins University Press, 1982.

Said, Edward W. *Beginnings: Intention and Method.* New York: Basic Books, 1975.

———. "On Repetition." In Said, *The World, the Text, and the Critic.* Cambridge: Harvard University Press, 1983: 111–25.

Saposnick, Irving S. "The Anatomy of *Dr. Jekyll and Mr. Hyde.*" *Studies in English Literature, 1500–1900* 11 (Autumn 1971): 715–31.

Saunders, Montagu. *The Mystery in the Drood Family.* Cambridge: Cambridge University Press, 1914.

Sayers, Dorothy L. "The Omnibus of Crime." In *The Art of the Mystery Story: A Collection of Critical Essays.* Edited by Howard Haycraft. New York: Simon and Schuster, 1946: 71–109.

Schopenhauer, Arthur. *The World as Will and Representation.* Translated by E. F. J. Pogue. 2 vols. New York: Dover, 1969.

Schorske, Carl E. *Fin de Siècle Vienna: Politics and Culture.* New York: Random House, 1981.

Seaman, L. C. B. *Victorian England: Aspects of English and Imperial History, 1837–1901.* London: Methuen, 1973.

Sedgwick, Eve Kosofsky. *Between Men: English Literature and Male Homosocial Desire.* New York: Columbia University Press, 1985.

———. *The Coherence of Gothic Conventions.* New York: Methuen, 1986.

Shannon, Edgar F., Jr. "Lockwood's Dreams and the Exegesis of *Wuthering Heights.*" *Nineteenth-Century Fiction* 14 (September 1959): 95–109.

Shelley, Mary. *Frankenstein, or the Modern Prometheus.* The 1818 Text. Edited by James Rieger. Chicago: University of Chicago Press, 1982.

Shelley, Percy Bysshe. *Poetical Works.* Edited by Thomas Hutchinson. London: Oxford University Press, 1990.

Shunami, Gideon. "The Unreliable Narrator in *Wuthering Heights.*" *Nineteenth-Century Fiction* 27 (March 1973): 449–68.

Skura, Meredith Anne. *The Literary Use of the Psychoanalytic Process.* New Haven: Yale University Press, 1981.

Smith, Joseph H., ed. *The Literary Freud: Mechanisms of Defense and the Poetic Will.* New Haven: Yale University Press, 1980.

Spacks, Patricia Meyer. "Logic and Thought in *Through the Looking-Glass.*" In *Aspects of Alice.* Edited by Robert Phillips. New York: Vintage Books, 1971: 267–75.

Spence, Donald P. *The Freudian Metaphor: Toward Paradigm Change in Psychoanalysis.* New York: Norton, 1987.

Spivak, Gayatri Chakravorty. "Three Women's Texts and A Critique of Imperialism." *Critical Inquiry* 12 (Autumn 1985): 243–61.

Stallybrass, Peter, and Allon White. *The Politics and Poetics of Transgression.* Ithaca: Cornell University Press, 1986.

Stange, G. Robert. "Expectations Well Lost: Dickens' Fable for His Time." *College English* 16 (1954–55): 9–17.

Steuart, John A. *Robert Louis Stevenson: A Critical Biography.* 2 vols. Boston: Little, Brown, 1924.

Stevenson, Robert Louis. *The Lantern Bearers and Other Essays.* Edited by Jeremy Treglown. New York: Farrar, Straus, Giroux, 1988.

———. *The Strange Case of Dr. Jekyll and Mr. Hyde.* Harmondsworth, Eng.: Penguin, 1979.

Stewart, Garrett. *Dickens and the Trials of Imagination.* Cambridge: Harvard University Press, 1974.

Stoehr, Taylor. *Dickens: The Dreamer's Stance.* Ithaca: Cornell University Press, 1965.

Sully, James. "The Dream as Revelation." *Fortnightly Review* 59 (March 1893): 354–65.

———. "The Laws of Dream Fancy." *Cornhill* 34 (1876): 544–45.

Sutherland, J. A. *Victorian Novelists and Publishers.* Chicago: University of Chicago Press, 1976.

Thiher, Allen. *Worlds in Reflection: Modern Language Theory and Postmodern Fiction.* Chicago: University of Chicago Press, 1984.

Thomas, Ronald R. "In the Company of Strangers: Absent Voices in Stevenson's *Dr. Jekyll and Mr. Hyde* and Beckett's *Company.*" *Modern Fiction Studies* 32 (Summer 1986): 157–73.

Timms, Edward, and Naomi Segal, eds. *Freud in Exile: Psychoanalysis and Its Vicissitudes.* New Haven: Yale University Press, 1988.

Tracy, Robert. "Reading Dickens' Writing." *Dickens Studies Annual* 11 (1983): 37–59.

Van Ghent, Dorothy. *The English Novel: Form and Function.* New York: Harper and Row, 1953.

Veeder, William. "'Carmilla': The Arts of Repression." *Texas Studies in Literature and Language* 22 (Summer 1980): 197–223.

———. *Mary Shelley and "Frankenstein": The Fate of Androgyny.* Chicago: University of Chicago Press, 1986.

Volosinov, V. N. [Mikhail Bakhtin]. *Freudianism: A Marxist Critique.* Translated by I. R. Titunik. New York: Academic Press, 1976.

Walker, Nigel, and Sarah McCabe. *Crime and Insanity in England.* 2 vols. Edinburgh: Edinburgh University Press, 1978.

Watt, Ian. *Conrad in the Nineteenth Century.* Berkeley: University of California Press, 1979.

———. *The Rise of the Novel.* Berkeley: University of California Press, 1974 (1957).

Welsh, Alexander. *From Copyright to Copperfield: The Identity of Dickens.* Cambridge: Harvard University Press, 1987.

Westburg, Barry. *The Confessional Fictions of Charles Dickens.* Dekalb: Northern Illinois University Press, 1977.

Wilson, Edmund. "Dickens: The Two Scrooges." In Wilson, *The Wound and the Bow: Seven Studies in Literature.* New York: Farrar, Straus, Giroux, 1978: 3–86.

———. "Why Do People Read Detective Stories?" *New Yorker,* October 14, 1944, 73–76.

Wilt, Judith. *Ghosts of the Gothic: Austen, Eliot, and Lawrence.* Princeton: Princeton University Press, 1980.

Wise, Thomas J., and J. Alexander Symington, eds. *The Brontës: Their Lives, Friendships, and Correspondence in Four Volumes.* New York: Oxford University Press, 1933.

Wolff, Werner. *The Dream—Mirror of Consciousness: The History of Dream Interpretation from 2000 B.C. and a New Theory of Dream Synthesis.* New York: Grune and Stratton, 1952.

Woods, Ralph L., ed. *The World of Dreams.* New York: Random House, 1947.

Woolf, Virginia. "Freudian Fiction." In *Contemporary Writers.* New York: Harcourt Brace Jovanovich, 1965: 152–54. Originally in *Times Literary Supplement,* 25 March 1920.

Wordsworth, William. *Wordsworth: Poetical Works.* Edited by Thomas Hutchinson. London: Oxford University Press, 1975.

Zola, Emile. "The Experimental Novel." In *Documents in Modern Literary Realism.*
Edited by George J. Becker. Princeton: Princeton University Press, 1963: 161–96.
_____. *L'Oeuvre (The Masterpiece).* Ann Arbor: University of Michigan Press, 1968.

Index

Library of Congress Cataloging-in-Publication Data

Thomas, Ronald R., 1949–
  Dreams of authority : Freud and the fictions of the unconscious / Ronald R. Thomas.
    p. cm.
  Includes bibliographical references (p.   ).
  ISBN 0-8014-2424-0 (alk. paper).
  1. English fiction—19th century—History and criticism. 2. English fiction—20th
century—History and criticism. 3. Freud, Sigmund, 1856–1939—Knowledge—Literature.
  4. Psychoanalysis and literature—Great Britain. 5. Subconsciousness in literature.
6. Authority in literature. 7. Dreams in literature. I. Title.
PR878.P74T48   1990
823'.08309—dc20   90-33550